FINANCIAL INTEGRATION AND DEVELOPMENT

As part of Structural Adjustment Programmes many governments in sub-Saharan Africa initiated a major restructuring of the financial system in the 1980s. Emphasis was placed on the need to adopt financial liberalization measures, and to enhance regulatory and supervisory functions. However, financial reform has at best had a limited developmental effect in the region so far, and widespread fragmentation of financial markets persists.

This volume examines the effects of financial liberalization on development, with a particular focus on sub-Saharan Africa. Looking at the relationship between formal and informal financial institutions, it focuses on structural features that separate formal and informal segments of the financial system. The findings are based on fieldwork conducted in Ghana, Malawi, Nigeria and Tanzania, and lead the way to a reassessment of the design of financial reform programmes and some proposals for effective institution-building policies. These include measures to deepen financial markets, to strengthen the financial infrastructure, to implement a new regulatory and incentive framework to advance market integration, to improve financial technology and to develop linkages amongst market segments.

One of the first systematic studies on this important area, the volume contributes to the literature on alternative theories of financial development and on the effects of financial liberalization. It will be of particular interest to students of development economics.

Machiko Nissanke is Senior Lecturer in Economics at the School of Oriental and African Studies, University of London. **Ernest Aryeetey** is Associate Professor at the Institute of Statistical, Social and Economic Research, University of Ghana.

ROUTLEDGE STUDIES IN DEVELOPMENT ECONOMICS

1 ECONOMIC DEVELOPMENT IN THE MIDDLE EAST
Rodney Wilson

2 MONETARY AND FINANCIAL POLICIES IN DEVELOPING COUNTRIES
Growth and Stabilization
Akhtar Hossain and Anis Chowdhury

3 NEW DIRECTIONS IN DEVELOPMENT ECONOMICS
Growth, environmental concerns and government in the 1990s
Edited by Mats Lundahl and Benno J. Ndulu

4 FINANCIAL LIBERALIZATION AND INVESTMENT
Kanhaya L. Gupta and Robert Lensink

5 LIBERALIZATION IN THE DEVELOPING WORLD
Institutional and economic changes in Latin America, Africa and Asia
Edited by Alex E. Fernández Jilberto and André Mommen

6 FINANCIAL DEVELOPMENT AND ECONOMIC GROWTH
Theory and experiences from developing countries
Edited by Niels Hermes and Robert Lensink

7 THE SOUTH AFRICAN ECONOMY
Macroeconomic prospects for the medium term
Finn Tarp and Peter Brixen

8 PUBLIC SECTOR PAY AND ADJUSTMENT
Lessons from five countries
Edited by Christopher Colclough

9 EUROPE AND ECONOMIC REFORM IN AFRICA
Structural adjustment and economic diplomacy
Obed O. Mailafia

10 POST-APARTHEID SOUTHERN AFRICA
Economic challenges and policies for the future
Edited by Lennart Petersson

11 FINANCIAL INTEGRATION AND DEVELOPMENT
Liberalization and reform in sub-Saharan Africa
Machiko Nissanke and Ernest Aryeetey

FINANCIAL INTEGRATION AND DEVELOPMENT

Liberalization and reform in
sub-Saharan Africa

Machiko Nissanke
and Ernest Aryeetey

London and New York

332.0967
N72f

First published 1998
by Routledge
11 New Fetter Lane, London EC4P 4EE

Simultaneously published in the USA and Canada
by Routledge
29 West 35th Street, New York, NY 10001

© 1998 Overseas Development Institute

Typeset in Garamond by Keystroke, Jacaranda Lodge, Wolverhampton
Printed and bound in Great Britain by Biddles Ltd, Guildford and King's Lynn

British Library Cataloguing in Publication Data
A catalogue record for this book is available from the British Library.

Library of Congress Cataloging in Publication Data
Financial integration and development : liberalization and reform
in Sub-Saharan Africa / Machiko Nissanke and Ernest Aryeetey.
p.   cm.
Includes bibliographical references and index.
1. Finance–Africa, Sub-Saharan–Case studies. I. Nissanke,
Machiko. II. Title.
HG187.5.A2A793 1998
332'.0967—dc21   97–37713

ISBN 0–415–18081–3

CONTENTS

List of tables   vii
List of illustrations   ix
Foreword   xi
Acknowledgements   xiii

1 Introduction   1
   1.1 Introduction 1
   1.2 Issues in finance and development: background of the study 5
   1.3 Problems of restructuring fragmented financial systems 10
   1.4 Research objectives, methodology and the structure of the book 12

2 Analytical framework on the sources of fragmentation,
  research hypotheses and overview of financial systems   18
   2.1 Introduction 18
   2.2 Explanations of market segmentation and dualism 19
   2.3 Roles of formal and informal finance in economic development 25
   2.4 Specialization, fragmentation and intermediation performance
        – research hypothesis 29
   2.5 Linkages, integration and financial policies 34
   2.6 Characteristics of household savings and the implications for financial
        sector development in sub-Saharan Africa 37
   2.7 Overview of financial systems 40
   2.8 Financial repression and policy reform 43

3 Characteristics and structure of financial systems   50
   3.1 Analysis of aggregate data: the savings–investment–growth nexus 50
   3.2 Financial structure in Ghana 64
   3.3 Financial structure in Malawi 68
   3.4 Financial structure in Nigeria 74
   3.5 Financial structure in Tanzania 79

v

CONTENTS

3.6 *Policy environment: financial repression and financial sector reform* 84
3.7 *Overview* 96

4 **Performance of formal financial systems and macroeconomic analysis of flow of funds**   101
4.1 *Savings mobilization and intermediation performance of the formal financial system under different policy regimes* 101
4.2 *Main features of the formal financial sector* 113
4.3 *Financial sector reforms and intersectoral financial flows* 131
4.4 *Synthesis* 160

5 **A micro-analysis of market specialization and fragmentation** 180
5.1 *The liabilities of formal and informal financial institutions* 181
5.2 *Assets of formal and informal financial institutions* 196
5.3 *Synthesis* 212

6 **Information, transaction costs and risk management among different institutions**   214
6.1 *Differences in risk assessments by lenders* 216
6.2 *Empirical approaches to uncertainty and risk management* 217
6.3 *Risk management and lending transaction costs* 233
6.4 *Synthesis* 245

7 **Linkages between segments of the financial market and gaps in financial services**   250
7.1 *Analysis of institutional linkages in deposit mobilization* 250
7.2 *Analysis of direct linkages in credit allocation* 254
7.3 *Indirect relationships between formal and informal finance* 259
7.4 *Market specialization and credit gaps for enterprise development* 263
7.5 *Conclusion* 272

8 **Conclusions and policy implications: towards greater financial integration**   277
8.1 *Summary of findings* 278
8.2 *Policy implications: towards greater financial integration* 283
8.3 *Synthesis* 306

References   308
Index   321

TABLES

1	Savings–investment–growth nexus, 1981–6 and 1987–91	2–3
2	Past and projected investment and savings required to achieve the growth target of 5 per cent a year by 2000	4
3	Savings–investment–growth performance indicators	51–2
4	Indicators on external balance	54–5
5	Fiscal position	57
6	Financial indicators	102
7	Government debt: Ghana, 1984–93	137
8	Government debt outstanding: Malawi, 1982–93	140
9	Government debt: Nigeria, 1977–90	143
10	Monetary indicators for case-study countries	149
11	Average number of depositors per branch/bank in Ghana, 1989–91	185
12	Branch-level deposit mobilization in Tanzania, 1990–2	187
13	Average number of depositors per branch/bank in Nigeria, 1990–2	188
14	Average amount mobilized by branch/bank in Nigeria, 1990–2	189
15	Composition of commercial bank assets, 1992	197
16	Private sector lending in total commercial bank lending, 1986–93	198
17	Sectoral allocation of credit, 1992	198
18	Loan screening cost as a proportion of loan administration costs	235
19	Loan monitoring cost as a proportion of loan administration costs	236
20	Contract enforcement cost as a proportion of loan administration costs	238
21	Loan administration costs as a percentage of loan amount, by type of bank	238
22	Default risk costs as a percentage of total loan amount, by type of bank and applicant in Ghana	239
23	Transaction cost of lending in Ghana as a percentage of total loan amount for sector, by type of bank	240
24	Mean loan administration cost, 1992	243
25	Determinants of lending and repayment	247

ILLUSTRATIONS

1 The flow of savings and credit   31
2 Aggregate savings rates (a) Ghana, (b) Malawi, (c) Nigeria,
(d) Tanzania   59–60
3 The savings–investment gap (a) Ghana, (b) Malawi,
(c) Nigeria, (d) Tanzania   61–2
4 Nominal interest rates, 1975–92 (a) Ghana, (b) Malawi,
(c) Nigeria, (d) Tanzania   85–6
5 Real interest rates, 1975–92 (a) Ghana, (b) Malawi,
(c) Nigeria, (d) Tanzania   87–8
6 Financial deepening indicators (a) Ghana, (b) Malawi,
(c) Nigeria, (d) Tanzania   104–5
7 Credit extended, by sector (a) Ghana, (b) Malawi, (c) Nigeria,
(d) Tanzania   107–8
8 Liquidity ratios (a) Ghana, (b) Malawi   120
9 Efficiency portfolio   123
10 The structure of interest rate terms, Ghana   128
11 Monthly liquidity ratios, Ghana   129
12 Financing the government deficit (a) Ghana, (b) Malawi,
(c) Nigeria, (d) Tanzania   134–5
13 The monetary base (a) Ghana, (b) Malawi, (c) Nigeria,
(d) Tanzania   147–8
14 Money multipliers (a) M_1, (b) M_2 151
15 Flow of funds: the consolidated public sector (a) Ghana 1987,
(b) Ghana 1992, (c) Malawi 1987, (d) Malawi 1992   162–3
16 Flow of funds: intermediation by the financial system
(a) Ghana 1987, (b) Ghana 1992, (c) Malawi 1987,
(d) Malawi 1992, (e) Nigeria 1987, (f) Nigeria 1991   164–6
17 Flow of funds: the private sector (a) Ghana 1987, (b) Ghana
1992, (c) Malawi 1987, (d) Malawi 1992   168–9
18 The composition of bank deposit liabilities before and after
the reforms   184
19 Interest rate spread in sample countries   201

20 Moneylenders' monthly interest rates, 1992   210
21 Market niches and credit gaps   274
22 Financial integration among segments   274

FOREWORD

This study emphasizes the importance of developing financial systems to integrate the full range of informal and formal financial institutions that inhabit the fragmented financial landscape typical of low-income countries. Its findings support the growing realization that financial sector strategies need to be more comprehensive and better integrated if they are to have a substantial impact on real sector growth and to reach lower-income populations, especially in African countries.

Well-functioning financial markets are important for growth in investment and real sector production, as well as for financial stability. Financial institutions facilitate economic growth by mobilizing savings and channeling them into productive uses. In most African countries, this developmental role has been limited by the very small proportion of the population with access to formal financial institutions and by inefficient intermediation of financial flows, especially under highly-controlled, state-dominated financial policies.

A number of African countries have undertaken substantial reforms over the last decade to liberalize financial markets and to improve the functioning of the banking sector. But this has not necessarily been translated into increased financial flows to private investors or, into deeper financial systems that serve the population as a whole. Financial systems have remained highly fragmented, with farmers, microentrepreneurs and the low-income population generally depending on a variety of informal mechanisms for savings and credit.

This study investigates the sources of fragmented financial systems in four African countries. It breaks ground in comparing the methods of formal and informal financial institutions and evaluating their relationship in order to suggest measures that can promote deeper, better-integrated financial systems. Using systematic survey data, it focuses on structural features that tend to separate market segments, high transaction costs and imperfect information in particular.

In this context, the study examines the impact of financial liberalization on the formal and informal financial sectors. The cross-country analysis yields some common characteristics and constraints. The expected positive effects on financial performance have been slow to emerge. Despite some improvements in supervision and competition, banks' balance sheets and liability/asset structures have not changed greatly, and banks have tended to contract in order to cut costs rather than seek new clients. Private investors have seen little expansion of available credit.

The study goes beyond the normal analysis of financial liberalization by examining the performance of informal financial markets. It finds evidence of substantial dynamism of informal institutions in responding to the increased demand for finance associated with economic recovery. This contrasts with the theory of parallel markets, which anticipates informal sector growth under increasing, rather than decreasing, government controls.

The authors find that the personalized methods of informal sector financial agents successfully address the cost and risk problems of small transactions, which banks prefer to avoid. Nevertheless, informal methods are difficult to replicate on a wide scale, and high effective lending rates mean that informal sector credit is not well-suited for long-term investment. Substantial gaps remain between demand for financial services and what existing institutions are able to provide.

The study concludes that better integration of formal and informal financial markets is essential if African countries are to improve the reach and efficiency of their financial systems and to achieve the intended benefits of financial liberalization. In light of the experiences of the countries studied, it suggests a range of measures to build institutions, adapt the regulatory and incentive framework to encourage innovation and integration, and develop linkages that enable formal and informal intermediaries to benefit from each other's comparative advantage.

The study was designed and implemented through collaboration between the World Bank, the Overseas Development Institute, the School of Oriental and African Studies and researchers associated with the African Economic Research Consortium. This approach has mobilized the detailed local knowledge of in-country experts, ensured analysis under a consistent conceptual framework, and made the findings available to analysts and policymakers. This book provides a comprehensive presentation of the methodology, findings and recommendations that will be useful to anyone researching the sources of financial fragmentation in low-income countries or designing a financial development strategy to facilitate faster, widespread real sector growth.

Tony Killick   William F. Steel
Senior Research Fellow   Lead Specialist, Private Sector Finance
Overseas Development Institute   Africa Region, World Bank

ACKNOWLEDGEMENTS

This study presents the synthesis of our research findings, including the main findings of the four country micro-level case studies as well as analysis of macroeconomic data and flows of funds. Field research was conducted by Ernest Aryeetey (Ghana), Mboya Bagachwa (Tanzania), C. Chipeta (Malawi), M.L.C. Mkandawire (Malawi), and Adedoyin Soyibo (Nigeria). The project was managed by Machiko Nissanke at the Overseas Development Institute, London and by William F. Steel and Hemamala Hettige of the World Bank, Washington and administered by the Overseas Development Institute. Analysis of macroeconomic data and flows of funds was carried out with assistance from Martin Wall at the School of Oriental and African Studies. The principal funding was provided by a grant from the World Bank Research Committee, the Swedish International Development Agency and the Leverhulme Trust. A grant from the Research Committee of the School of Oriental and African Studies helped to cover other expenses required to complete the study, including the cost of a workshop in London, in May 1995. We should like to express our sincere gratitude to all these organizations for their generous support.

The authors are most grateful to William F. Steel for his valuable overall guidance throughout the study and for his detailed comments and suggestions on drafts of substantial parts of the book. Tony Killick offered useful comments on the country case studies, which were previously published in eight ODI working papers. Our thanks to Deborah Johnston who, together with William F. Steel, undertook the editing of the manuscript for publication. We are also grateful for information and comments from Dough Addison, Zafar Ahmed, Ahmad Ahsan, Carlos Cuevas, Laurence Harris, Kazi Matin, Richard Meyer, Samuel Onwona, Ademola Oyejide, J. Hennie Van Greuning, and participants in workshops held in Accra, Dar es Salaam and London. All the participants in this collaborative project were able to build a strong sense of collegiality, thus facilitating friendly and productive academic exchange. Therefore, it was with great sorrow and regret that we received the news of the death of Mboya Bagachwa in the spring of 1996, on the eve of the completion of our first draft.

ACKNOWLEDGEMENTS

We are indebted to many of our friends and colleagues in Africa, London and Oxford for their endless support and encouragement over the years. While there are too many of them to mention here, we wish to express special thanks to Joan Maizels, Alfred Maizels, Laurence Harris, Ben Fine, John Sender, Terry Byres, Christopher Adam, William Cavendish, Valpy FitzGerald, John Norbury, Arthur Marsh, Julia Knight, Paul Collier, David Bevan, Frances Stewart, Jeffery Fine, Benno Ndulu and Francis Mwega. Robert Cassen and Percy Mistry helped in raising funds for an initial phase of the study at Queen Elizabeth House, Oxford University. We are also thankful to Patsy de Souza of ODI and Vivienne Geard of SOAS for efficient administration of the project and organization of the workshop in London, and Nalini Vittal for occasional research assistance. Finally, the warmest appreciation to our families: Machiko Nissanke to Nimal, Samaya, and Hikaru; and Ernest Aryeetey to Ellen and Nii Armah, for carrying much of the strain of this project for such a long time. They have been a vital source of support, love and encouragement.

M.N. and E.A.

1

INTRODUCTION

1.1 Introduction

In the 1980s in sub-Saharan Africa, many governments initiated major restructuring of their financial systems as part of structural adjustment programmes. In most programmes, the initial emphasis was on liberalization measures, such as the removal of controls on interest rates and credit allocation. Subsequent components of these reforms have included the restructuring of bank portfolios and the enhancement of financial sector competition. Using loans from donor agencies, several African countries have initiated special Financial Sector Adjustment Projects (FINSAPs) to support reform measures. Many FINSAPs have focused on improving the footing of distressed formal institutions through the restructuring and refinancing of balance sheets. These operations increasingly emphasize the necessity for enhanced financial supervision and an improved regulatory environment.

However, reform measures seem to have had limited *developmental* effect in the region so far. It is increasingly recognized that the adoption of a financial liberalization policy has not proved sufficient to generate greater savings mobilization, increased private investment or wider financial sector intermediation. Despite some improvements in economic growth during the period 1987–91, savings rates in most sub-Saharan countries remain at a depressed level (see Table 1). Many countries with improved macroeconomic indicators have failed to raise their savings rates sufficiently to finance domestic investment. Since the majority of these countries have increased public saving (or reduced public dissaving), this implies that private saving has not picked up significantly, despite policies which have been specifically targeted to vitalize the private sector. Countries which experienced deterioration in macroeconomic performance have invariably reduced the domestic savings rate further and, in most cases, public saving has also declined.

The low savings rates of these sub-Saharan countries suggest that investment and economic growth are still heavily dependent on foreign savings in the form of external finance. Indeed, the substantial interest rate payments on external debt in many of these countries implies that the

Table 1 Savings–investment–growth nexus, 1981–6 and 1987–91 (as percentage of GDP unless otherwise indicated)

Country	Gross domestic savings		Public savings		Gross domestic investment		Public investment		GDP growth rate	
	1981–1986	1987–1991	1981–1986	1987–1991	1981–1986	1987–1991	1981–1986	1987–1991	1981–1987	1988–1992
Large improvement in macroeconomic indicators										
Ghana	5.6	7.5	-1.7	2.6	6.3	15.1	1.7	3.2	2.7	4.1
Tanzania	9.7	-2.6	-4.2	-1.6	18.3	26.9	6.8	5.3	2.6	5.0
Gambia	6.2	8.2	-1.4	1.0	19.0	18.4	12.4	10.3	2.4	3.2
Burkina Faso	-4.9	1.5	-1.1	0.5	20.0	20.9	15.7	10.4	3.9	2.5
Nigeria	14.4	22.8	3.6	-1.2	16.5	15.4	9.5	5.6	-0.1	5.3
Zimbabwe	17.9	22.3	-3.7	-2.5	19.6	20.7	6.0	8.0	1.6	0.8
Small improvement in macroeconomic indicators										
Madagascar	1.9	5.9	0.2	1.5	9.1	12.4	6.6	7.5	1.0	-0.2
Malawi	13.3	9.0	-2.7	-0.3	17.6	18.7	8.7	6.7	3.2	2.6
Burundi	3.1	1.8	1.4	1.5	16.4	18.0	13.7	13.7	4.2	3.9
Kenya	20.7	18.8	-0.1	-1.1	23.1	23.7	7.1	6.0	3.6	2.4
Mali	-3.7	5.3	-2.3	0.8	17.2	21.6	10.5	11.1	2.6	3.0
Mauritania	4.3	8.1	-2.8	3.1	29.8	16.6	2.5	5.7	1.3	1.5
Senegal	-0.4	7.9	-3.3	-0.1	11.2	13.0	-3.8	2.8	3.1	2.2
Niger	5.1	4.6	-0.3	-2.7	12.9	10.9	8.7	8.2	-3.0	1.2
Uganda	–	–	-3.9	-0.7	7.8	11.1	2.3	5.0	-1.4	4.6

Table 1 (continued)

Deterioration in macroeconomic indicators

Benin	0.7	3.1	-2.6	-3.5	16.0	12.4	11.0	6.2	3.1	2.6
Central African Republic	-2.0	-0.7	-0.7	1.3	11.0	12.1	6.9	12.1	2.3	-0.3
Rwanda	6.0	4.8	1.1	-2.1	15.6	14.4	8.2	8.9	1.7	0.3
Sierra Leone	7.4	6.8	-8.9	-8.0	13.9	11.6	4.3	3.2	-0.5	2.4
Togo	18.8	13.4	3.7	0.9	25.3	22.7	10.7	7.4	1.5	-1.1
Zambia	14.1	13.4	-10.3	-7.4	17.2	12.8	4.9	5.4	1.6	-0.7
Mozambique	–	–	-2.5	-2.7	12.8	13.6	13.8	12.7	-3.4	2.4
Congo	35.7	23.1	11.1	-6.7	39.4	16.1	18.7	5.0	3.8	-0.6
Côte d'Ivoire	21.3	15.4	3.2	-9.8	17.9	11.5	10.0	3.5	0.0	-0.8
Cameroon	29.1	15.6	10.6	0.3	24.8	17.8	10.6	8.6	5.7	-5.0
Gabon	50.1	36.3	16.0	-1.0	37.2	29.0	16.7	6.0	-0.7	5.9
Unclassified										
Chad	-1.6	-15.7	–	–	5.9	8.9	–	–	7.0	3.6
Guinea	–	–	–	–	–	–	–	–	–	3.3
Guinea-Bissau	-4.7	-6.3	–	–	27.2	31.1	–	–	2.4	1.9
Sub-Saharan Africa	12.3	12.4	10.6	17.7	17.7	17.5	10.6	6.0	2.1	1.7

Note:
a Forty-six countries (excluding Nigeria); refers to sub-periods 1981–87 and 1988–92.
Sources: Data on savings and investment for 29 sub-Saharan countries are taken from World Bank (1994: tables A23–4). Country classifications are based on the performance of a number of macroeconomic indicators.

financing gap between national savings and domestic investment may be considerably higher than an analysis of Table 1 would initially suggest. For many countries of the region, dependence on concessional aid flows for economic development has been high and rising. In the early 1990s, aid flows to Africa increased at 6 per cent per annum in real terms and aid constitutes about 9 per cent of African GNP, as compared with 2 per cent in South Asia (Collier 1994). By 1994 aid had grown to 12.4 per cent of GDP. The aid–dependence ratio is much higher for some countries. For example, gross concessional aid flows accounted for 49 per cent and 27 per cent of GDP in 1991 for Mozambique and Tanzania, respectively.

Overall, Table 1 shows that the sub-Saharan countries, as a group, attained an average savings ratio of 12 per cent over the period.[1] This is substantially lower than the targeted regional savings rates of 16.6 per cent for 1995 and 20 per cent for 2000 that Calgagovski *et al.* (1991) estimate are necessary to achieve overall macroeconomic growth targets. Using the standard two-gap model, they calculated the minimum savings rate required to achieve economic growth of 5 per cent p. a. for the region by year 2000 (see Table 2). This growth target is, in turn, a minimum acceptable rate if the region is to attain a modest increase of 1.3 per cent in real *per capita* consumption by the turn of the century (World Bank 1989b).[2]

Actual savings rates have been substantially poorer than this target rate in many countries of sub-Saharan Africa. Their performance can be also compared unfavourably with that of Asian countries in recent years. For example, the gross domestic savings rates in China, India and Indonesia for the period 1988–92 are reported to have been 38.2 per cent, 22.2 per cent, and 36.9 per cent, respectively. Foreign savings financed about 6 per cent in India, compared with 25 per cent of investment in sub-Saharan Africa in 1992 (Global Coalition for Africa 1993).

The principal objective of this study is to explain the limited effects of financial sector reform so far undertaken in sub-Saharan Africa. As Hettige

Table 2 Past and projected investment and savings, sub-Saharan Africa, required to achieve the growth target of 5% a year by 2000

Indicators	1985–8	1995	2000
Real GDP (annual % change)	2.6	4.0	5.0
Real GNP (annual % change)	−1.8	4.2	5.4
Real consumption *per capita*	−0.7	0.1	1.3
Gross domestic investment (as % of GDP)	14.0	20.7	25.0
Gross domestic savings (as % of GDP)	11.4	16.6	20.0
Gross ODA required (as % GDP)	5.9	8.6	9.0

Sources: Calgagovski *et al.* (1991: table 2.4); calculation based on the two-gap model

(1992) notes for these countries, 'banking systems have remained uncompetitive and saddled with poorly performing portfolios. State-owned banks
have directed the bulk of their credit to public enterprises regardless of their
viability. Private banks prefer commercial credit and have little interest in
term lending or new, small clients.' The World Bank (1994a) acknowledges
that there have been few signs of sustainable progress arising from financial
sector and public enterprise reform and calls for a rethinking of strategy.

In the next section of this chapter, the key policy issues in finance and
development will be reviewed. This is followed by a description (in section
1.3) of the dominant features of financial systems in sub-Saharan countries. In
the final section (1.4), research objectives and methodology are presented.

1.2 Issues in finance and development: background of the study

With the recent shift in policy towards a market-based system of resource
allocation, increasing attention has been paid to the development of efficient
financial systems both in developing countries and in transitional socialist
economies (World Bank 1989a; Kessides *et al.* 1989; Caprio and Levine
1994).

Apart from the essential services of payment and medium of exchange,
the key function of financial systems in the saving–investment–growth nexus
is to act as an effective conduit for: (1) the mobilization and allocation
of loanable funds; and (2) the transformation and distribution of risks and
maturities. It is assumed that financial institutions channel funds from
surplus to deficit units by mobilizing investible resources and ensuring
efficient transformation of these funds into real productive capital. Through
the diversification of investment, these institutions have the potential to
efficiently transform maturity between savers and investors. Greater flows
of information also allow the intermediation of risk through techniques of
risk-reduction and risk-pooling.

Goldsmith's (1969) pioneering study demonstrated an empirical association between economic growth and the increasing size and complexity
of the financial system, i.e. the process of 'financial deepening'. Similarly,
Gertler and Rose (1994) argue that economic growth and financial sector
development are mutually dependent.[3] Other authors have emphasized that
financial sector policy can affect the pace of economic development. Following
Patrick's (1966) earlier work, Galbis (1977, p. 59), for example, suggests that
'it may well be that financial development is a prerequisite, if not a major
determinant, of the take-off into self-sustained economic growth'.

This dynamic link between financial innovation and economic development
is empirically investigated by King and Levine (1993). They argue that financial institutions lower the social cost of investing in intangible capital through
the evaluation, monitoring and provision of financing services. Montiel (1994)

also notes that economic growth can be spurred by 'innovations' in financial development that improve the efficiency of intermediation, increase the marginal product of capital and raise the savings rate.[4]

Whilst there is general agreement on the potentially vital contribution of the financial system, economists are divided on the appropriate policy to foster financial sector development. Contemporary financial economics offers two explanations for financial underdevelopment, yielding different policy prescriptions (see Chapter 2 for a more detailed discussion). The 'financial repression' school attributes underdeveloped and inefficient financial systems to excessive government control and intervention (McKinnon 1973; Shaw 1973; Fry 1982, 1988). It is argued that this *government failure* calls for a policy of financial liberalization. The 'imperfect information' paradigm locates the primary problem in *market failure* specific to the provision of credit (Stiglitz and Weiss 1981; Stiglitz 1989).[5] Imperfect and costly information resulting in voluntary credit rationing and may warrant state intervention, not only of the regulatory and supervisory kind but also directed credit and other interventionist policies. Indeed, Stiglitz (1994, p. 19) identifies 'circumstances in which some amount of financial repression may actually be beneficial'.

These paradigms can be assessed through an analysis of the financial policies implemented in many parts of the world. Government *intervention* was widely embraced as a means to correct market failure in the initial post-independence period in a large number of developing countries. In particular, following the Keynesian approach to investment demand, a low interest rate policy was viewed as one of the key instruments for promoting private investment. In practice, years of rigidly following a policy of fixed low interest rates combined with loose expansionary monetary policies led to the prevalence of negative interest rates and financial disintermediation. The policy adopted had often involved excessive restriction and control and proved counterproductive, resulting in financial 'repression'.[6] Even where credit was successfully delivered, the adoption of repressive policies appears to have retarded the development of financial systems in these economies.[7] However, there is also evidence that mild financial repression, in the form of controlled interest rates with directed credit, has been skilfully utilized to allocate resources in those East Asian countries with a record of rapid economic growth (World Bank 1993).

While the financial policy debate has often been polarized on the relative role of the state and the market, the actual outcome appears to depend upon the *manner* of government intervention, which can be either positive and welfare-enhancing or negative and deleterious for development. Cho and Khatkhate (1989) note that 'there is nothing basically wrong with government intervention *per se* when market failures are pervasive and pronounced'. The difficulty lies more with the manner in which intervention is implemented. Under an efficient administration, resources can be channelled to productive and commercially viable projects with high social returns. In this situation, financial and productive systems can be developed in a complementary way.

One of the principal causes of market failure in developing countries is incomplete markets and market-support infrastructure. Intervention which directly addresses this problem can be particularly valuable. Beneficial effects, rather than pervasive rent-seeking activities, can be expected when selective intervention is implemented within a disciplined and performance-based incentive system. However, when inefficiently used, intervention can inhibit dynamism and private initiative, and instead promulgate corruption and politicization of resource allocation.

An evaluation of the numerous *financial liberalization* policies initiated in developing countries also illustrates the extent to which outcomes are critically dependent on the context in which policy is pursued. The liberalization experiences in the Southern Cone countries of Argentina, Chile and Uruguay in the late 1970s and early 1980s provide arguments against sweeping measures of financial liberalization (Corbo and DeMelo 1985, 1987; World Bank 1989a). In general, completely and suddenly dismantling the framework of financial intervention does not work. In an environment of large macroeconomic imbalances, as observed in the Southern Cone countries, financial liberalization was often combined with policies aimed at stabilization. However, stabilization efforts were severely undermined by the complete deregulation of financial operations, resulting in financial instability and an increase in speculative transactions.

Furthermore, the combination of inadequate supervision and regulation and oligopolistic financial markets led to persistently high real interest rates and the proliferation of non-performing loans and distress borrowing.[8] Financial crisis led the public to anticipate an inflationary bail-out of insolvent financial institutions. This, together with the growing expectation of large-scale devaluation, spurred capital flight. By the early 1980s, all three countries landed in what Carlos Diaz-Alejandro (1985) referred to as 'financial crash'.

In contrast, three Asian countries, Korea, Malaysia and Sri Lanka, have taken more gradual approaches to liberalization (Cho and Khatkhate 1989). Tseng and Corker (1991) note that, in many Asian countries, interest rates typically remained under control but were frequently adjusted. Positive real interest rates were attained through monetary stabilization, which led to a reduction in inflation. This contrasts with the situation in Southern Cone countries, where there was a sharp rise in *nominal* rates in the aftermath of complete liberalization.

Two conclusions emerge from these experiences. First, abrupt and full-scale financial liberalization in the midst of pronounced macroeconomic instability and imperfect financial structures destabilizes the financial system. This magnifies macroeconomic instability, rather than promoting financial deepening as claimed by the McKinnon–Shaw school. It can also jeopardize the credibility of other reform policies.

Second, there is a crucial distinction between the wholesale liberalization of financial markets and properly monitored deregulation. In the absence of adequate regulation and supervision, implicit government deposit guarantees and interlocking ownership can intensify inherent failures in the credit market. Moral hazard, adverse selection and oligopolistic pricing can result in upward pressure on lending rates. In turn, high interest rates encourage excessive risk-taking and speculation, leading eventually to an increase in non-performing loans and widespread insolvency.

A consensus has emerged that macroeconomic stability and adequate financial supervision and regulation are necessary for successful liberalization (World Bank 1989a).[9] In addition, liberalization programmes need realistic *timetables*, within which financial reform can be designed. Recent literature points to the need for careful design of the sequence and timing of financial liberalization, and the importance of its coordination with macroeconomic conditions and other stabilization and adjustment policies.

However, even in the apparently successful Asian countries, the results of financial liberalization were disappointing. Cho and Khatkhate (1989) conclude that 'financial reform, whether comprehensive and sweeping or measured and gradual, does not seem to have made any significant difference to the saving and investment activities in the liberalized economies' (p. 106). Liberalization, in the form of increased competitiveness of the banking system, has not delivered any discernible benefits either in terms of the availability of long-term finance and credit or in terms of the reduction of intermediation costs. Furthermore, the quality of bank portfolios has uniformly deteriorated. The proportion of non-performing loans has risen, owing to high and volatile interest rates in relation to the real return on capital, which has exhausted sources of long-term credit for investment. Park (1994) also notes that 'deregulation shortens the economic horizons of savers and investors so much that banks are forced to match their assets and liabilities, thereby drying up long-term finance' (p. 19).

At a more general level, historical experience of both intervention and liberalization suggests that a successful strategy for financial sector development cannot emerge out of the stark choice between two opposing policy prescriptions. Instead, a position of pragmatic flexibility should be adopted, with policy that can surmount or at least mitigate both government *and* market failure. As noted by Collier and Mayer (1989), government failure in the form of incompetence, negligence and corruption does not necessarily justify exclusive reliance on markets and market signals. It should be explicitly recognized that there are no financial policies of general applicability to all conditions and circumstances. Rather, policies should be designed in the light of prevailing conditions in a specific historical context.

In this respect, it is intriguing to observe the high degree of *flexibility* and *adaptability* exercised by policy-makers in the more successful Asian countries. As Cole and Duesenburry (1994) document, many countries of East and South East Asia have professed to adopt significant reforms while in fact retaining or even reinstating substantial controls, as dictated by changing circumstances and conditions, in all the major areas of financial policy: allocation of bank credit, interest-rate setting, market competition, bank insolvency and foreign capital movement. Their experience confirms that the appropriateness of intervention depends critically on governmental capacity to implement policies. In this respect, measures to strengthen public administration, through increased transparency and accountability, should be one of the first priorities in any reform programme.

Indeed, it has become increasingly clear that financial liberalization on its own will not be sufficient to promote financial sector development and economic growth, as the financial repression school has postulated (Collier and Mayer 1989). Efficient markets and financial institutions are needed, and policies to strengthen institutions and markets must be an integral part of financial sector development. Moreover, much of the recent literature questions the 'wisdom' of liberalization itself. Thus Cottani and Cavallo (1993) maintain that 'no perfect empirical correlation exists between economic success and financial liberty in developing countries' (p. 39). They argue that deregulation of the financial system can be successful only in countries that have achieved a high degree of fiscal discipline, low inflation and macroeconomic stability. Similarly, Dornbusch and Reynoso (1993) debate that evidence on the beneficial effects of removing financial repression is episodic except when asset returns are significantly negative. They further argue, largely on the basis of the experience of Latin American countries, that financial liberalization in the face of a poor fiscal position, on the contrary, continues to be a major factor in accelerating inflation and instability.

There appears to be growing, if implicit, recognition that financial liberalization may not be the most critical step in financial reform programmes at the initial stage in countries susceptible to instability in macroeconomic conditions. A recent World Bank study echoes this general sentiment, stating that 'in general, liberalization will not necessarily lead to efficiency gains, and/or to the relaxation of financial constraints faced by firms in the presence of informational and enforcement problems' (Caprio et al. 1994). On the basis of a comprehensive review of financial sector reforms undertaken in six, mostly middle-income, countries, Caprio et al. (1994). conclude that financial reforms should begin with *prompt* moves on various aspects of *institution building* in finance, but it is best to be *gradual* with interest rate deregulation and the removal of portfolio restrictions.[10] This sequencing has even more relevance to low-income developing countries, where financial markets are thin and shallow, and the market-supporting infrastructure for financial institutions is grossly inadequate.

In designing a reform programme, it is also important to remember that financial sector development is closely linked with real sector development, and its evolution follows a certain sequence in response to demand for new kinds of financial services as the real sector develops (Gurley and Shaw 1967; Goldsmith 1969; see also the discussion in Chapter 2 below). The performance of the financial sector reflects prevailing conditions in the real economy. In this context, Gertler and Rose (1994) argue that financial liberalization should be supported by prudent 'real sector' policies to enhance the creditworthiness of borrowers.

In general, it is increasingly accepted that financial reforms in developing countries should encompass wide-ranging measures of institution-building in both the financial and the real sectors, before (or in parallel to) embarking upon a shift from a policy of restriction and repression to one of financial market liberalization. Furthermore, it is of the utmost importance to bear in mind that there is no single optimal financial system which is applicable to all countries at all levels of development. A simple replication of the systems that have worked rather well under specific historical conditions in one country or another may not create the best system in other countries. Each developing and reforming country has its own specific circumstances, experience, institutions and history, all of which should be taken into account in designing the architecture of its financial system, institutional arrangements and financial policies.

1.3 Problems of restructuring fragmented financial systems

In the introductory section (1.1) above, the poor savings–investment performance in sub-Saharan Africa was discussed. We will argue in this book that this poor performance revealed at the aggregate level is related, in a more critical way than hitherto recognized, to obstacles preventing financial market integration and improved intermediation. In most African countries, the indigenous private sector consists largely of households and small-scale enterprises that operate outside the formal financial system. Survey evidence indicates substantial demand for external finance by enterprises that want to expand beyond the limits imposed by self-finance (see Chapter 7). Informal savings activities (which involve little intermediation) indicate a *substantial demand for savings* that could be tapped to raise low rates of financial resource mobilization by the formal sector. Hence better integration among different segments of the financial system – formal, semi-formal and informal[11] – could facilitate economic development through more effective resource mobilization and by improving financial resource flows to enterprises with high potential, especially those that have historically lacked access to the banking system.

There are few systematic evaluations of the relationship between formal and informal financial institutions,[12] and little is known about the effect of financial liberalization on different segments of the financial system or on the relationship between segments. In order to investigate these issues, it is useful at the outset to make conceptual distinctions between the terms 'segmentation', 'fragmentation' and 'dualism' for the purposes of our analysis and discussion, although they are often used interchangeably in literature.

In this study, *segmentation* refers to the existence of multiple financial markets, where distinct institutions serve clients with different characteristics and needs. Segmentation *per se* is not necessarily undesirable and may indeed achieve high efficiency through specialization for different market niches (Von Pischke 1991). The key issue is the degree of integration between different segments. In an efficient market, prices and terms are comparable for similar transactions, so that the financial system as a whole can effectively perform its ascribed functions of resource mobilization and intermediation.

Fragmentation refers broadly to lack of interaction both across and within segments and is used pejoratively in this study to refer to a situation in which the negative effects of weak linkages among segments outweigh the benefits from specialization. *Dualism* refers to extreme fragmentation between formal and informal sectors that face different relative prices and barriers to flows between them. A lack of integration (i.e. 'fragmentation') is indicated by wide differences in interest rates, insignificant flows of funds between segments and limited access for clients to financial instruments and institutions. The lack of substitutability between segments means that fragmented and dualistic markets are unlikely to function efficiently in intermediating between savers and investors, in allocating financial resources or in transforming and distributing risks and maturities.

In contrast, in a well functioning system, formal and informal financial institutions are specialized for their market niches and are integrated through flows of funds or through choices at the margin. Well integrated financial markets would normally include direct flows between different segments and some degree of substitutability among institutions, in the form of over-lapping clienteles which can choose freely among them. Thus a distinction must be drawn between segmented markets, with specialization for niches, and fragmentation with impediments to efficient intermediation. Special-ization implies that differentiated risk and cost characteristics yield comparable risk-adjusted returns across segments. In fragmented markets, in contrast, differences in risk-adjusted returns are observed across segments and different prices are offered for similar products. In such situations, integrative mechanisms are needed to improve the efficiency of the financial system.

Different explanations of market segmentation and fragmentation will be discussed at length in Chapter 2, but are overviewed briefly here. The financial repression hypothesis explains fragmentation in terms of restrictive financial policies that have shifted the allocation of investible funds from the market to the government. This leads to the creation of parallel markets for those crowded out by government intervention. Many countries in sub-Saharan Africa instituted repressive financial policies in the past and have since attempted greater financial liberalization. While links between different market segments have begun to emerge, there is growing concern among policy-makers that liberalization has had little, or at best delayed, effect on access to finance by potentially dynamic small investors.

The imperfect information hypothesis focuses on inherent information problems as the source of segmentation and fragmentation. These informational problems may not be remedied simply by a switch from a repressive regime to a liberal one. For formal institutions, the high cost of obtaining information on and transacting business with small clients is likely to persist. In addition, weak legal systems, underdeveloped market-supporting infrastructure and the expatriate roots of banking in African countries offer institutional explanations for weak financial integration.

We will argue that a better integrated financial market is essential for more effective resource mobilization and intermediation. However, structural and institutional imperfections prevent a shift in policy environment from the repressed regime to the liberal one alone from achieving financial development. In particular, when intermediation between segments is weak, hasty deregulation of markets can give rise to unexpected side effects and destabilize the financial system. Attention should be paid to developing and integrating financial institutions, which will enhance the capacity for mobilization and intermediation of each segment and interactions among segments.

This study, therefore, focuses on structural features that tend to separate formal and informal segments of the financial system. Some of these features are country-specific, but others, particularly high transaction costs and imperfect information, are likely to characterize financial systems in low-income countries generally. The study also aims to contribute to the empirical literature on alternative theories of financial development and on the effects of financial liberalization. In particular, we will analyze impediments to financial deepening in Africa and the extent to which they can be removed through financial liberalization.

1.4 Research objectives, methodology and the structure of the book

The main objectives of the study are to:

1 evaluate the *nature* and *degree* of fragmentation and segmentation of financial markets and to investigate explanations of fragmentation;
2 examine the *comparative advantages* of formal and informal segments for resource mobilization and intermediation, and examine their ranges of specialization and respective operational constraints;
3 document *existing and potential relations* between and within segments, and the obstacles to such linkages;

12

4   identify *bottlenecks* in the financial system as a whole and *gaps* in financial services and credit for real sector development;

5   analyse the *extent* of financial liberalization and reforms, to evaluate their *effect* on financial systems and to identify the sources of financial market failure;

6   provide a policy framework for financial sector development and to evaluate which *policy and institutional measures* can most effectively overcome market imperfection and accelerate the financial system's ability to mobilize resources and intermediate between saving and investment.

To meet these research objectives, four African countries were selected for a comprehensive examination of the workings of financial systems. The countries examined were Ghana, Malawi, Nigeria and Tanzania. As these countries provide a range of experience of financial development and liberalization attempts, our cross-country analysis facilitates investigation of different explanations of fragmentation.[13]

Fieldwork was conducted using questionnaires addressed to formal, semi-formal and informal institutions and borrowers in both urban and rural areas.[14] Common questionnaires were used to collect information on behavioural characteristics and operational constraints (see Appendix 1.1). Data included: portfolio characteristics; trends and structure of interest rates; risk assessment and management; transaction and intermediation costs; delinquency and default rates; and linkages among different units and segments. Besides evaluating the direct linkages among these institutions, we examine the extent to which their clientele is distinct or overlapping, as an indirect measure of integration. The study estimates differentials in the costs and risks of financial transactions across different segments to address the factors that inhibit broader access to financial services. To facilitate a cross-country synthesis of micro-level research findings, analyses of macroeconomic data and flow of funds were also conducted.

This book presents the synthesis of our research findings, including the main findings of the country studies. The detailed results of fieldwork are found in eight country case-study working papers.[14] This book is structured as follows.

Chapter 2 presents a *literature review and discussion of market fragmentation/segmentation, the main research hypothesis and the key characteristics of savings, financial systems and financial sector reform programmes in sub-Saharan Africa.* This chapter provides the context for further investigation of the causes of and remedies for weak integration among financial market segments in the four case-study countries. The first section (2.2) presents theoretical explanations for the type of fragmentation that has been observed in Africa. In the light of this discussion, the roles of formal and informal finance in

13

economic development are re-evaluated (section 2.3). The following two sections (2.4 and 2.5) explore differences in the performance of segmented markets across countries, by focusing on the conceptual link between fragmentation and intermediation. Our main research hypothesis regarding the conditions typically prevailing in financial systems in sub-Saharan countries are elaborated here. The last three sections (2.6–8) summarize some general features of household savings, financial systems and financial sector programmes in sub-Saharan countries.

Chapter 3 outlines the *characteristics and structure of financial systems* in the sample countries. The chapter first presents macroeconomic indicators and describes the main features of financial systems. Then it discusses the evolution of financial policies and the scope of financial sector reforms undertaken in the sample countries.

Chapter 4 assesses the effect of *changes in the policy environment* on mobilization and intermediation by the *formal* financial system. After evaluating the effects in terms of conventional aggregate indicators, the main portfolio characteristics of formal banking institutions are analysed and discussed. The second section presents a *macroeconomic analysis of flow of funds* in order to examine financial intermediation among economic sectors/agents. This analysis also provides an overall picture of the fragmentation of financial systems.

Chapter 5 examines *market specialization and fragmentation* through an analysis of the assets/liability structure of different financial segments, using fieldwork data.

Chapter 6 presents an analysis of *transaction costs, risk and infrastructure*, in which the structural and institutional explanations of market fragmentation are evaluated. Applying the imperfect information paradigm and principal agent theory to the fieldwork data, the section discusses: (1) the effect of the risks and incentives for different lenders and borrowers; (2) the importance of information asymmetry in adjusting risks and incentives; and (3) efforts to reduce information asymmetry by different lenders. The relationship between cost of funds, transaction costs and risk premium in the financial system is examined. We attempt to identify the comparative advantage of each segment, its roles in deposit mobilization and in financial inter-mediation, and the scope for deepening specialization. The relationship between market-supporting infrastructure and the problem of imperfect information and contract enforcement is also investigated.

Chapter 7 makes an overall assessment of the *linkages between different segments and the gaps in financial services* in the sample countries. It begins with an evaluation of the existing and potential relationships among units and between/within segments. The second section discusses the spectrum of financial services and assesses critical gaps, particularly for private sector development.

Chapter 8 sums up *key research findings and draws policy conclusions*. The first section presents a comprehensive review of empirical findings from the study with respect to policy reform and institutional development. In particular, it tries to identify conditions leading to specialization, under which linkages between segments can take advantage of the comparative strengths and each segment can form a part of integrated financial systems. On the basis of these findings, the second section recommends integrative measures to improve information flows and lower transaction costs and risks for the financial system as a whole. Recent developments in new financial institutions and instruments in the region will be discussed in assessing the appropriate financial institutions and instruments for financial sector development.

Appendix 1.1

Selected Elements of Questionnaire

1 *General characteristics*

Size
Growth
Trends in savers/borrowers
Categories (SEEs, SSH, LSEs, private, public)
Types of depositors

1a *Deposit characteristics*

Size
Seasonality, saving cycles, maturities
Capital base, cost of funds, interest rate, opportunity rate

2 *Loan characteristics*

Borrowers
Loan maturity
Lenders' rate of return
Loan terms and conditions
Rejection rate
Default rate
Delinquency rate
Interest rate structure

3 *Transaction costs*

Screening and monitoring

Information
Methods
Costs

Contract enforcement costs

Cost of default risk
Collateral requirements, collateral substitutes

4   *Risk management methods*

5   *Characteristics in portfolio/liquidity management*

6   *Links between different segments*

Notes

1 However, the variation observed in savings rates across countries in the sub-Saharan region is substantial. Among forty-six countries studied by the Global Coalition for Africa (1993), fifteen countries had significantly negative savings, while nine had savings rates over 20 per cent.

2 For this to be realized, the investment rate needs to be increased to 20.7 per cent by 1995 and to 25 per cent by 2000. Eighty per cent of this investment must be financed by domestic resources, if gross external capital inflows, in the form of new financing or debt reductions, are to be kept to the level of US$28 billion to US$29 billion a year in 1991–2000. This external capital requirement includes gross official development assistance (ODA) flows equivalent to 8–9 per cent of GDP for the region. These calculations assume that half of these external resources would finance net imports of goods and services. The other half would be needed to finance debt service payments. It should be noted that this model incorporates some exceedingly optimistic estimates of the region's external trade conditions.

3 See Chapter 2 for their key arguments.

4 Nevertheless, it is pertinent to note that growth in financial assets is not a sufficient condition for economic growth, and improved financial intermediation *per se* may not necessarily lead to economic growth (Bhatia and Khatkate 1975). Dornbusch and Reynoso (1993) further argue that the role of financial factors remains largely speculative and financial factors are important only when financial instability becomes a dominant force in the economy. See also Hettige (1992) for a survey of literature on financial deepening and financial intermediation.

5 This is in addition to more general forms of market failure stemming from the wedge between social and private returns and the presence of externalities.

6 Cottani and Cavallo (1993) draw a useful conceptual distinction between regulation, restriction and repression of financial activities: They suggest that (1) owing to the nature of credit and financial transactions, prudential regulation is always necessary, while restriction can result from excessive regulation incurring high cost in terms of efficiency and welfare; (2) however, financial restriction becomes repression when regulations that limit competition are combined with high and growing inflation.

7 See Chapter 2 for the detailed experiences in sub-Saharan Africa.

8 High interest rates and distress borrowing had mutually destructive effects. Credit demand by distress borrowers put upward pressure on interest rates,

which in turn dragged other firms down. As non-performing assets rose, banks raised their deposit rates to attract funds to pay the interest on existing deposits. The supply of new funds was made available through deposit insurance and bad loans were continuously rolled over. This process continued in anticipation of an eventual government bail-out and the central bank became the only viable financial intermediary. High interest rates on commercial bank deposits required a continuous infusion of money from the central bank to keep banks' cash flow positive, which in turn made the money supply virtually impossible to control.

9 The World Bank adds two other requirements for success: fiscal discipline and a tax system that does not discriminate excessively against finance.

10 The countries surveyed were Turkey, New Zealand, Korea, Indonesia, Malaysia and Chile. The conclusion is based on the observation that the success of reforms depends on two factors: (1) initial conditions in finance, i.e. bank portfolios, their 'information capital' and their internal incentive systems; and (2) the performance of the real sector, in particular through the evolution of borrower net worth (Caprio *et al.* 1994, chapter 13).

11 The informal sector has been referred to by many different terms, such as unorganized, non-institutional and kerb markets. Conforming to the recent trend in literature, we adopt the term 'informal finance' to refer to all transactions, loans and deposits occurring outside the regulation of a central monetary or financial market authority (Adams and Fitchett 1992, p. 2). As will be discussed below, the semi-formal sector has characteristics of both the formal and the informal sectors and is usually only partially regulated.

12 A pioneering sociological work in this field was undertaken in the early years in five African countries: the People's Republic of Congo, Ivory Coast, Nigeria and Togo (see Seibel and Marx 1987).

13 Francophone countries were excluded from the current study because of the close integration of their financial and monetary policies with each other and with France. This has limited the scope for the type of financial policy reforms investigated here. The countries that were selected had good documentation of their financial systems and had experienced local researchers.

14 Sample sizes, sampling procedures and methodology guided in the fieldwork are presented and discussed in the four case studies (Aryeetey 1994, 1996; Bagachwa 1995, 1996; Chipeta and Mkandawire 1996a, b; Soyibo 1996a, b).

2

ANALYTICAL FRAMEWORK ON THE SOURCES OF FRAGMENTATION, RESEARCH HYPOTHESES AND OVERVIEW OF FINANCIAL SYSTEMS

2.1 Introduction

The conventional theory of 'financial dualism' suggests that the extent and degree of segmentation of financial markets reflect the inherent dualism of economic and social structures. Thus segmentation into formal and informal financial markets reflects a dichotomy between modern institutions and the population's traditional social values and practices. Since the informal sector itself has generally been considered to be primarily a transitory phenomenon which would disappear with economic growth, this view assumes that as development proceeds the informal financial sector will wither away and be integrated into the formal system.

Empirical evidence from developing countries indicates, however, that the actual interaction between the financial system and the real sector development is more intricate than this simple view suggests.[1] In some successful Asian countries, integration of the financial system has indeed taken place and the intermediation efficiency of the system as a whole has increased over time. However, a heterogeneous and dynamic informal financial sector continues to exist as a part of these well functioning financial systems, reflecting specialization in financial services by each sector (Biggs 1991; Ghate 1990).

In contrast, in less successful developing economies, financial dualism appears to have deepened over time, and the two sectors often form almost discrete financial enclaves. This type of market segmentation is detrimental to the efficient functioning of the financial system. The situation is a sharp deviation from the one observed in Asia,[2] which led Ghate (1988) to conclude, 'while theoretically there will always be scope for an informal credit market if it can improve on formal sector transaction costs and mediates funds that would not otherwise have been mediated, financial dualism is likely to become less pronounced as the formal sector itself is progressively liberalized, formal sector transactions costs decrease, and the capital markets become more perfect' (p. 66).

This chapter first investigates the factors which produce such diverse outcomes and sets out a framework within which to analyse the sources of market segmentation. Section 2.2 presents the analytical and conceptual tools needed to discuss segmentation and dualism. In the light of this theoretical discussion, the role of formal and informal finance in economic development is evaluated in section 2.3. Section 2.4 explores differences in the inter-mediation performance of segmented markets among developing countries. We present and elaborate here our main research hypothesis regarding the typical condition prevailing in many sub-Saharan countries. Section 2.5 discusses the nature of formal–informal sector linkages and the conditions for increased integration in the context of financial liberalization. The second half of this chapter (sections 2.6–8) introduces the main features of household savings, financial systems and evolution of financial policies in sub-Saharan Africa.

2.2 Explanations of market segmentation and dualism

The two leading theoretical paradigms in financial economics, referred to briefly in Chapter 1, provide an analytical framework for understanding financial market segmentation. In addition, segmentation has been linked with the stage of institutional development. These hypotheses are not neces-sarily competitive and can be thought of as complementary to each other. They may be grouped according to their main themes, as policy-based or structural explanations for segmentation.

2.2.1 Policy-based explanation: financial repression

The financial repression hypothesis attributes underdeveloped and inefficient financial systems mainly to excessive government control and intervention. Indiscriminate distortions of financial prices, control over credit allocation, interest rate ceilings and rigidly fixed exchange rates are seen as retarding economic growth by reducing the relative size of the financial system and emitting distorted signals. The main propositions of the McKinnon and Shaw school on the consequences of repressive policies are:

1   Economic growth in a financially repressed economy is constrained principally by the low level of saving, not by the absence of good invest-ment opportunities. Ceilings on *deposit* rates penalize financial saving and result in a lower rate of investment, which diminishes the potential for economic growth.[3]
2   Real interest rates should reflect capital scarcity, and thus interest rate

19

ceilings reduce the efficiency of capital allocation and with it the quality of investment. By reducing the scope for risk premia, loan rate ceilings discourage risk-taking by financial institutions. A large proportion of potentially high-yielding investments are thereby rationed out of the market.

The financial repression hypothesis argues that these repressive policies are also the prime cause of dualism and segmentation in financial markets.[4] Ceilings on deposit and loan rates tend to raise the demand for funds and depress the supply. Unsatisfied demand for investible funds then forces financial intermediaries to ration credit by means other than the interest rate, and this encourages the development of an informal market at uncontrolled rates. A segmented credit market emerges in which favoured borrowers obtain funds at subsidized, often highly negative, real interest rates, while others must seek credit in expensive and unreliable informal markets. It is argued that 'informal financial markets develop and thrive in circumstances where formal financial institutions are severely hindered by distorted policies and generally repressed' (Roe 1991, p. 22). According to this view, the liberalization of interest rates and removal of government control would ensure integration of the financial system over time.

2.2.2 Structural and institutional explanations

Structural explanations of segmentation emphasize differences in the costs and characteristics of different types of transactions that can lead to specialization within financial markets. For example, in low-income developing countries the financial savings of households tend to be small in size and high in frequency (Deaton 1989). For such savings to be mobilized, the cost of each transaction must be small to both the saver and the financial agent. Similarly, demand for credit usually involves relatively small amounts, making it important to keep transaction costs low for both parties. For these types of transactions, informal mechanisms could minimize risk and transaction cost. For instance, revolving saving and credit associations (ROSCAs) involve virtually no transaction costs and risk is minimized by forming groups among people well known to each other. At the other end of the market, large transactions can be handled by banks and other formal financial institutions that may take advantage of economies of scale.

Such a diversified structure of transaction costs and client demands may be reflected in market segmentation. As discussed in Chapter 1, this situation would not be classed as detrimental if there were sufficient flow of funds or overlap in clientele among segments to equalize risk-adjusted returns.

However, *imperfect information* can give rise to pervasive market failure and result in the persistent fragmentation of financial markets.

In the presence of imperfect information and costly contract enforcement, market failures are thought to result from *adverse selection* and *incentive effects* and *moral hazard*, all of which undermine the operation of financial markets. Adverse selection occurs when borrowers with investments, at reasonable rates of risk and return, are discouraged from seeking loans owing to rising interest rates. At higher rates, borrowers also have an incentive to adopt projects that promise higher returns but may involve greater risk. High interest rates may also lead some applicants to borrow simply to pay interest on previous loans or to avoid bankruptcy rather than to finance working capital or investment. As a result, the mix of applicants changes adversely and, beyond some optimum rate, the increased risk of default will offset the gains to the lender from a higher rate. Furthermore, there is a moral hazard problem, as the incentive to default on a loan grows with higher interest rates. The advantages of default increase as the costs of the loan rise and, at some point, will outweigh the detrimental effects of default on creditworthiness and reputation.

Thus the level of interest rates affects the risk composition of financial portfolios. In this context, lenders may choose not to raise interest rates to clear the market when faced with excess demand for credit, owing to concern about greater risk. Instead, they may opt to select borrowers through non-price rationing. As a result, market equilibrium may frequently be characterized by credit rationing even in the absence of interest rate ceilings and direct credit allocation. It is then argued that free markets do not ensure Pareto-efficient allocation, nor do policies that move the economy closer to market solutions.

It can be argued that not only does market segmentation result from structural differences in the cost and risk characteristics of different types of financial transactions; the extent and nature of market segmentation and fragmentation reflect also the scale of such market failures specific to credit transactions conducted in the environment of imperfect information. For example, Hoff and Stiglitz (1990) advance an explanation for extreme segmentation based on asymmetric access to information on creditworthiness and differences in the costs of screening, monitoring and contract enforcement across lenders.

Within this general framework, other authors have concentrated on a range of structural and institutional features of the financial markets of developing countries to explain segmentation, since the structure of financial markets, including the degree of market segmentation, closely mirrors the development and performance of the real sector.

Gertler and Rose (1994) analyse the symbiotic relation between finance and growth, based on two key concepts: a *premium for external finance* and *borrower's net worth*. These determine the relative efficiency of a financial system and its dynamic evolution. The former concept refers to an additional premium borrowers pay for uncollaterized loans and insurance, due to frictions introduced by informational and enforcement problems. The latter is defined as the sum of a borrower's net liquid assets and the collateral value of his illiquid assets. This consists not only of tangible physical assets but also of any prospective future earnings that the borrower can credibly offer as collateral. Thus the borrower's accumulated net worth depends both on past earnings and on anticipated future prospects. Development of the real sector, therefore, leads to increasing borrower net worth and 'tends to reduce the premium attached to external finance, which in turn serves to stimulate further development' (Gertler and Rose 1994, p. 32). The premium for external finance then is inversely related to borrower net worth, and they jointly determine the level of investment.

This two-way interactive relationship links the evolution of an economy's financial structure with a firm's changing financial needs over its life cycle. Thus as self-finance develops into external finance, intermediation by banking institutions increases and a securities market develops. Access to world capital markets increases and, finally, there is a narrowing of the spread between loan and deposit rates, along with a rise in the riskless rate. In this evolutionary process, the development of financial intermediation is critically dependent on improvements in monitoring, evaluation and enforcement technologies, which should reduce the premium on external finance and, hence, reduce the spread between the lending and deposit rates, which is an efficiency barometer of the financial system.

Segmentation and fragmentation may also result from weaknesses inherent in complementary institutions and market-supporting infrastructure, since the adequacy of institutions that support the financial system affects lenders' risk perception and the premium for external finance. For example, the legal environment influences the costs and risks associated with contract enforcement. On one hand, the ease with which contracts can be enforced influences the willingness of lenders to enter into financial agreements and the type of security they are willing to accept. On the other hand, where the legal system of contract enforcement is weak, formal lenders are more likely to insist on a clear title to landed property or other assets for collateral (e.g. buildings, livestock, consumer durables or jewellery). Further, the financial sector's ability to offset the risk of default will be limited by the absence of a well functioning insurance market and by the absence of markets for the sale of confiscated collateral (Binswanger and Rosenzweig 1986).

In developing countries that are characterized by grossly inadequate infrastructure and limited scope for legal enforcement, the need for collateral assets may exclude many otherwise creditworthy small-scale borrowers, especially where land tenure is not legally explicit. When strict collateral requirements restrict access to credit, various collateral substitutes, such as reputation and group responsibility, are likely to emerge in the informal sector.

Problems arising from imperfect information are also likely to be most pronounced in low-income countries. Economy-wide information flows may be extremely limited, and gathering information is costly. A problem of information asymmetries between would-be borrowers and potential lenders therefore becomes severe. Poor endowment of information capital in developing countries can encourage segmentation, by raising the cost of acquiring reliable information on both systemic and idiosyncratic risks for formal institutions, while informal agents exclusively rely on localized, personal information, which constrains their transformation into full-scale intermediaries.

Thus Teranishi (1994) attributes segmentation of financial markets in developing countries to a host of problems arising from imperfect information, where information disclosure is severely limited, mainly owing to family-owned production units. He argues that 'the efficiency of financial markets in such an economy hinges crucially on the degree of accumulation of information and establishment of information channels between lenders and customers as a device to cope with problems related to imperfect information' (p. 315). In this context, Caprio *et al.* (1994) draw a particular attention to the fact that years of financial repression in developing countries have led banks to underinvest in information capital. They emphasize, therefore, the importance of developing equity markets, accounting and auditing systems in order to build the economy's information capital base.

Historical weaknesses of the banking systems in developing countries may have also exacerbated structural tendencies towards segmentation. In many former colonies, banks were established primarily to serve import–export trade with the colonial centre. Many commercial banks of such an origin retain this particular feature. Their lack of interest and expertise in lending to indigenous, locally oriented firms has not been easily overcome. Furthermore, inadequate bank regulation and supervision over the years has propagated financial mismanagement and poor portfolio performance, which in turn have raised the perceived risk of term lending to small enterprises. In this situation, financial sector reforms may prompt banks to address management weakness and to diversify portfolios, but the response may be slow, as many parameters and exogenous conditions essentially remain the same.

All these factors in combination have given rise to structural bottlenecks in the efficient functioning of financial markets in many low-income countries. Thus inadequate market-support infrastructure has discouraged innovation and perpetuated the internal shortcomings of financial institutions. Even when there is no ceiling on interest rates and excess demand for loans exists, it may be unviable to lend to certain categories of borrowers, such as small and medium-sized enterprises (SMEs), if the costs and risks exceed those of known, lower-risk clients. In addition, in these economies, information about future prospects may be highly uncertain, especially if the economic structure is vulnerable to external shocks. In the absence of credible predictions, reliable information and appropriate financial instruments, perceived risk may be abnormally high for term lending, especially to small borrowers.

In developing countries characterized by these conditions, the growth of formal financial institutions is severely constrained. Formal institutions must retain their commercial viability and, in this environment of high risks and high transaction costs, banks are likely to be conservative and risk-averse in their portfolio management. They may prefer to hold government paper, with its lower risk, to extending loans to non-established borrowers, as discussed in Chapter 4. This explains *both* the failure to reach target groups of subsidized credit programmes administered through formal institutions *and* the high concentration of bank loans among the relatively well-off groups who have collateral or reputation at their disposal. Many credit guarantee schemes designed specifically to deal with the problems of high risk have not managed to alter this general tendency. Under such conditions, the dominance of self-finance and fragmented informal finance based on limited social relations can be expected.

2.2.3 *Synthesizing alternative explanations of segmentation*

It should be emphasized that the explanations of segmentation discussed above are not necessarily mutually exclusive. Ghate (1988) suggests that the informal sector consists of two parts; one part, represented by indigenous bankers, ROSCAs and pawnbrokers, is *autonomous* and historically antedates the formal sector. This component is adapted to the characteristics of informal market niches. The other part is *reactive*, developing in response to controls over, and deficiencies in, the formal sector. As observed in the Republic of Korea and the Philippines, this reactive component does not expand linearly over time, as it is affected by regulation and liberalization in the formal sector. This component of informal finance can be viewed as 'residual' finance, satisfying spill-over demand by those rationed out from the formal market (Bell 1990).

In a similar vein, a useful distinction is drawn by Roemer and Jones (1991) between a 'fragmented market' and a 'parallel market'. Parallel markets arise principally to evade government controls and regulations, but markets can fragment in the absence of government controls, owing to inherent operational characteristics. They suggest that 'credit markets in developing countries display characteristics of both parallelism and fragmentation'. Evaluated in this light, the financial repression hypothesis is concerned with parallelism, while fragmentation is more effectively explained by the imperfect information paradigm.

Now, if the informal financial sector is strictly a parallel market that evolved to avoid government controls and regulations, its activities will be reduced by liberalization measures. However, general evidence from the 1970s and 1980s seems to support the view that liberalization on its own cannot overcome the *fragmentation* of markets or promote financial integration.

Informal segments thrive even with considerably reduced government controls, as our fieldwork data confirm (see Chapters 3–5). Informal financial institutions may therefore have a lasting comparative advantage in serving certain segments of the financial market in developing countries, rather than being an institutional expression of the distortions caused by financial repression. To the extent that this is true, financial sector development should include measures to integrate formal and informal finance to take advantage of specialization, not simply to extend the formal sector's frontier (Seibel 1989). In the context of this discussion, the next section re-evaluates the respective roles of formal and informal finance in economic development.

2.3 Roles of formal and informal finance in economic development

This section evaluates the roles of the formal and informal sector in promoting economic development. For the purposes of this discussion we need to define what is meant by formal and informal institutions. The formal sector institutions are regulated and licensed as financial intermediaries, usually comprising the central bank, commercial and merchant banks, development or other specialized banks, non-bank financial institutions. We also observe greater diversity in the informal sector, which can be thought of as those units that operate without regulation. Adams (1992) suggests that there are three types of informal sector activity: (1) non-commercial transactions among friends and relatives; (2) group arrangements for savings, such as savings clubs, or arrangements combining savings and credit, such as ROSCAs;[5] and (3) informal finance organized on a commercial basis, conducted by money-lenders, pawnbrokers, landlords, traders and *susu* collectors. In addition, in many countries activities that seem to fall between the definitions of informal and formal have been observed, such as savings and credit co-operatives, credit unions and programmes managed by NGOs. These are often referred to as semi-formal, implying that they are legally registered and may be partially or cursorily regulated.

Informal markets are usually characterized by free entry and exit. However, this does not guarantee active competition because of the restricted information flows among participants. The ability of some commercial informal lenders to extract a monopoly rent is widely documented, and the share of monopoly rent in the interest rates is largely determined by the degree of competition prevailing in a particular market.[6] However, it is important to recognize that interest rates charged by such commercial informal lenders must also allow compensation for transaction costs, risk premiums and the opportunity costs of funds, as well as monopoly rents or profits (Bottomley 1975).[7] Monopoly rents or profits included are also related to the sunk cost of their operations and the contestability of markets. Montiel *et al.* (1993) further suggests that interest rates in informal credit markets in some cases may respond primarily to arbitrage opportunities between domestic lending and foreign lending (or the holding of foreign currency). It is also important to note the vast diversity of interest rates found in different segments of the informal financial market.

Commercial informal transactions can be money-based, land-based or commodity-based, such as those used by trader-moneylenders for interlinked market transactions (Germidis *et al.* 1991). Such tied credits may be ubiquitous, accounting for a large proportion of total informal credit in many countries. For example, Montiel *et al.* (1993) report a survey result from Malaysia, which suggest that the traders purchasing agricultural produce provided almost two-thirds of all rural credit.

Many group-based organizations operate on an agreed discipline and the principle of solidarity. They are often based on funds generated from members' savings and this indicates the importance of reciprocity. Linking credit with savings encourages the poorest to save and generally ensures high repayment rates. The assertion that informal finance consists primarily of consumption loans has been challenged by the concept of fungibility.[8] In addition, evidence is emerging from empirical studies to show that informal finance can be an important source of working capital for micro-enterprises and smallholders. For example, in India, the Republic of Korea and Thailand informal credit has become a significant source of funds for working capital and, in some cases, for the fixed investments of manufacturing firms operating in the formal sector (Ghate 1988).[9]

Informal financial activities are usually localized and confined to small and short-term transactions or seasonal requirements, e.g. cash flow and liquidity management. In contrast, formal institutions are largely located in urban areas, and their operations are characteristically urban-biased, involving larger transactions. Germidis *et al.* (1991) depict formal institutions by their *triple bias* in the mobilization and allocation of resources: a preference for (1) the public over the private sector; (2) large-scale enterprises and upper-income households over small-scale enterprises and low-income households; (3) for non-agricultural over agricultural loans.[10] The financial products and services offered by formal institutions do not easily correspond to those required by the majority of potential borrowers and savers – the provision of a small and short-term liquidity and savings facility.

Despite their potential advantage in exploiting economies of scale in portfolio management and diversification to allow risk pooling and maturity transformation, in many developing countries formal institutions suffer from a legacy of either conservatism or financial distress characterized by high transaction costs and severe loan recovery problems. Furthermore, a large number of formal institutions in developing countries are often chronically dependent on external donor funds rather than utilizing locally mobilized savings.

Operating in the same environment, informal financial activities develop a dynamism of their own, adapting to the needs of the communities in which they operate. The unsatisfied demand for credit of those excluded by the formal sector is met by heterogeneous informal lenders. Knowledge of borrowers, often based on close relationships, gives informal lenders a competitive edge in transaction costs, though at the same time it limits them to their local network. They insist less on the presentation of physical assets as collateral, relying instead on interlinked credit contracts with land, labour or product markets,[11] social pressure and personal knowledge of borrowers for risk management. Informal associations and agents also have a competitive edge in small and short-term deposit mobilization, which is untapped by formal institutions.

While increases in the provision of formal credit have been constrained by low income levels and the inadequacy of complementary institutions and market-supporting infrastructure in developing countries, these observations on the advantages of the informal sector have led to radical changes in our perception of informal finance and a reappraisal of its role in development (Adams 1992; U Tun Wai 1992). In the past, it was popular to view financial dualism as having an adverse impact on economic development, equity and the allocative efficiency of resources.[12] Hence it has been frequently argued that the informal sector should be regulated away. This negative view has been replaced by recognition of the existing and potential role of informal finance. Adams and Fitchett (1992) and Ghate (1988) emphasize the enhanced efficiency of resource allocation through informal finance.

Indeed, the share of the informal sector in financial transactions is estimated to be substantial, far exceeding that of the formal sector in many countries (Asian Development Bank 1990; Germidis *et al.* 1991; Montiel *et al.* 1993). Ghate (1988) reports that informal credit markets provide as much as half of rural credit and a significant part of urban credit in Asian developing countries. Montiel *et al.* (1993) reckon that the share of informal credit in total credit varies from about a third to about three-quarters in Asian developing countries. An OECD study estimates that the share of informal credit may range from 30 per cent to more than 80 per cent of total rural credit (Germidis *et al.* 1991). Our case studies in sub-Saharan Africa suggest that the share of the informal sector is larger than that of the formal sector in both credit provision and savings mobilization (Aryeetey 1994 and Chapter 3 below).[13]

However, the very factors which give the informal sector its comparative advantage can also constrain it from becoming an efficient financial intermediary. Christensen (1993) argues that financial intermediation by informal agents/associations is 'severely limited by lack of suitable collateral; the high transaction costs associated with small, short-term loans and deposits; and the difficulty of maintaining an adequate reserve'.[14] Instead, 'most informal financial agents tend to specialize in either lending or savings mobilization, according to their solutions to a subset of the underlying constraints. Each specialization reduces transaction costs by restricting operations to a limited clientele who are already well known, and by dispensing with formal loan procedures' (p. 728). Hence the needs of maintaining sufficient reserves for intermediation are avoided by lending mainly from equity (to a much less extent from borrowing too) in the case of specialized lenders, such as landowners, merchants and money collectors, and through well defined short-term contractual savings agreements by specialized savings associations, such as ROSCAs, fixed fund associations and savings and credit associations.

Generally, the advantages of informal agents/associations in solving informational and enforcement problems are confined to a limited geographical and/or social arena and small-scale operations. This acts as an obstacle to further diversification and full financial intermediation. Christensen (1993) argues that the characteristics of informal financial agents and institutions are such that the growth of operations within the informal sector is severely limited. Observing that *partial* intermediation is performed only by those informal agents who operate in both the formal and the informal sectors, he suggests that an expansion of the scope and scale of operations of informal agents/associations can be better realized by capitalizing on the links between the formal and informal sectors and the comparative advantages inherent in specialization.

Indeed, the presence of a dynamic informal sector predicates the potential in exploiting the comparative advantages of each sector – formal and informal. In low-income developing countries the capacity of financial systems could be enhanced in transitional periods if integrative mechanisms were developed that could reduce the operational constraints facing each sector, at the same time capitalizing on the comparative advantages conferred by each sector. A system of segmented financial markets may work more efficiently if the benefits of specialization can be fully exploited, while fragmentation can annul any such benefit, leaving the fundamental problems faced by formal and informal institutions/agents unresolved. However, the potential for integration is contingent on the nature and scope of the direct and indirect links between the two sectors.

Direct links can be conceptually subdivided into deposit and credit links. Deposit links, through the use of the deposit facilities of formal institutions, enable informal agents to minimize their holding of idle cash balances. At the same time, formal sector banks are provided with an enlarged liability base for credit expansion. Direct credit links, in the form of bank loans, enhance the capital basis of informal agents/groups and help to alleviate cash flow/liquidity constraints.

Indirect links operate through demand relations and can be complementary or competitive in nature. If the two sectors are substitutes, expansion of one results in contraction of the other, whereas, if they are complementary, growth can take place simultaneously.[15] The indirect links between formal and informal finance on the demand side can be diverse across countries and regions. They evolve dynamically, depending on the economic and policy environment.

For Asian economies where there is continuum of the integrated financial system, Ghate (1988) observes that 'the two sectors are substitutes over a range of credit needs that occupy the middle range of a spectrum of credit markets and purposes. Within this range they impinge on each other's share of the market, depending on lending and borrowing rates in each sector. At both ends of the spectrum, however, each occupies a number of markets which cannot be served by the other and which are therefore complementary' (p. 75).

It can be argued that the financial system as a whole can become more competitive if a range of demand, non-exclusive to one sector, expands. Further, in the presence of overlapping demand, there are spill-over effects from the formal to the informal segment. An example of such effects is analysed by Bell (1990). When informal lenders act as intermediaries for formal institutions, Bell shows, the resulting lower cost of funds to informal lenders will be passed on to borrowers, depending on the degree of competition in the informal market. Thus, where demand is non-exclusive, i.e. overlapping, direct credit links can have a positive effect on the efficiency of financial systems.

The next section examines the conditions in which a financial system is characterized by ineffective market fragmentation or efficient specialization. This will be followed by our main research hypothesis regarding the main characteristics of financial systems and market structure in sub-Saharan countries and the implications of policy reform.

2.4 Specialization, fragmentation and intermediation performance – research hypothesis

In examining the performance of segmented financial markets, it is interesting to note the argument forwarded by Biggs (1991), who suggests that decentralization of lending optimizes the screening and monitoring of loans and can reduce an economy's overall intermediation costs.[16] This can increase investment efficiency in LDCs with information-imperfect financial markets. In his analysis of Taiwan, Biggs found that the high opportunity cost of investible funds, determined by informal market rates, kept the efficiency of aggregate investment high. It deterred entrepreneurs from undertaking low-yield investments, even when they had access to cheap bank funds. He concludes that the development of a dual financial system – with the formal sector serving 'full information' borrowers and the informal lenders serving 'information-intensive' borrowers – 'helped credit intermediaries allocate funds to 'information-intensive' borrowers at a lower cost and more efficiently than would have been possible if all investible resources were channelled through formal sector banks' (p. 168).

29

Intermediation efficiency in the segmented financial markets of Taiwan appears to have been predicated on conditions that simulated the growth and expansion of each segment as well as the development of effective linkages between segments. First, the government adopted a deliberate policy to encourage an active informal sector as 'an efficient adjunct to regulated credit institutions' (Biggs 1991). Second, informal lenders have been active in developing new and innovative instruments for risky projects, enabling them to extend loans to borrowers without demanding real assets as collateral. Third, while financial market segments were clearly demarcated for borrowers, formal credits were indirectly available through an extensive subcontracting system. Larger firms acted as '*de facto* intermediaries' by offering on-lending facilities, such as trade credit, to their subcontractors and suppliers. The use of 'market interlinkage' and 'credit layering' has been instrumental in manufacturing success and hence supportive of economic growth.

In other Asian countries too, 'interlinking' of contracts across financial, trade and production transactions and 'credit layering' have been used by informal lenders for risk management in rural areas. These techniques improve information-gathering and contract enforcement. Yotopoulos and Floro (1991) report that informal lending operations with two-tier credit layering, involving trader-lender (commodity-based) and farmer-lender (land-based), are extensively used in the rural Philippines. Ghate (1988) reports numerous mechanisms by which funds flow between the formal and informal sectors in the Republic of Korea, Indonesia, India, the Philippines, Malaysia and Thailand. In particular, he notes that a great deal of trade credit originating in the formal sector is being on-lent informally. For example, 'in the Philippines and Thailand, financial "wholesalers" borrow from the formal sector and "retail" informally. Malaysia and the Philippines have experimented with schemes to use input and output dealers to onlend informally' (p. 74).

These experiences in Asia suggest that market segmentation is not necessarily a sign of market inefficiency, or a cause of inefficient intermediation. However, market segmentation becomes a problem when links between the different segments are weak, constraining severely the transmission of price and policy signals across the system. In such an environment, the weakness of each sector cannot be overcome, whilst the strength of each sector is not exploited in full for efficient specialization. Consequently, the system's potential capacity is circumscribed, as we observe in sub-Saharan countries.

Thus we postulate here our main research hypothesis, arguing that the cross-continental difference in intermediation performance can be explained partly by absent or underdeveloped links in low-income African economies (Nissanke *et al.* 1991; Nissanke 1993b).[17] We illustrate this hypothesis in Fig. 1 to elucidate the flow of funds (savings and credit) among different economic agents and sectors in these economies. Following the conventional classification adopted in the literature on 'dualism', economic activities (the

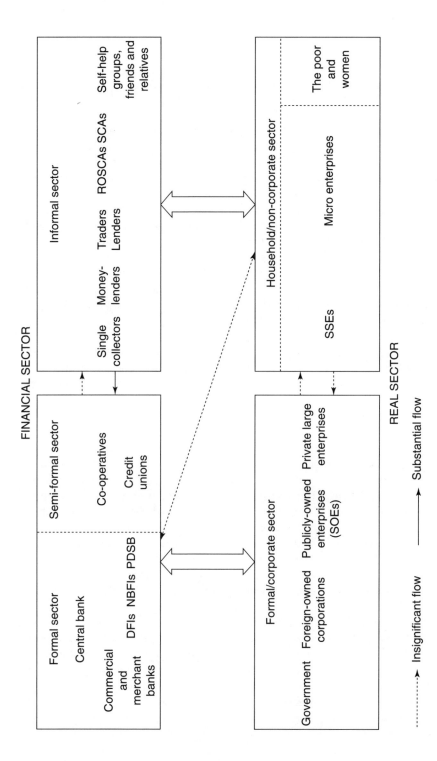

FINANCIAL SECTOR

Formal sector

Central bank

Commercial and merchant banks

DFIs NBFIs PDSB

Semi-formal sector

Co-operatives

Credit unions

Informal sector

Single collectors

Money-lenders

Traders Lenders

ROSCAs SCAs

Self-help groups, friends and relatives

REAL SECTOR

Formal/corporate sector

Government

Foreign-owned corporations

Publicly-owned enterprises (SOEs)

Private large enterprises

Household/non-corporate sector

SSEs

Micro enterprises

The poor and women

------> Insignificant flow   ——> Substantial flow

Figure 1 The flow of savings and credit

real sector) and financial services (the financial sector) are subgrouped into the formal (modern) and the informal (traditional) sectors. The basic stylized facts used to draw this diagram are:

1 Formal financial institutions in sub-Saharan Africa predominantly provide services to established large-scale 'formal' real sector activities. Many of these, particularly enterprises owned by the state, have shown very low returns and poor financial performance. Government has been the main beneficiary of central bank credit and government paper has been an important investment outlay for other formal institutions. However, government fiscal performance has been generally dismal, exposed to large external and internal shocks. The performance of many formal institutions has been correspondingly poor. Attempts to provide credit to small-scale firms, through developmental financial institutions and targeted credit schemes, have largely failed, because little attention was paid to the development of viable financial institutions (Meyer 1989, 1991). There have been few sustainable financial flows to the small-scale sector from formal financial institutions (diagonal flows from the upper left box to the lower right one).[18]

2 'Peripheral' activities, such as micro-enterprises, SMEs and small-scale farmers, obtain what finance they can from informal units. Diverse informal financial activities have developed, demonstrating flexibility and adaptability to the needs of local communities. However, informal financial arrangements are usually organized in a confined local vicinity; hence their intermediation function is often constrained by their limited scale of contacts and is often subject to highly seasonal funds and highly covariant risks affecting the whole local community.

3 Consequently, markets and financial flows are largely fragmented, as horizontal linkages are weak in both financial and real activities. Direct linkages between the formal and informal financial sectors (between the two upper boxes) are insignificant or lopsided, being largely confined to the use of formal sector deposit facilities by informal institutions (Aryeetey 1992b, 1994; Chipeta 1994; Chipeta and Mkandawire 1992b, 1996b; Bagachwa 1995; Steel and Aryeetey 1995).[19] Given passive liability management by formal banking institutions, deposits mobilized by informal agents/institutions are rarely intermediated for lending. No significant direct credit links exist between the two sectors. Since backward and forward linkages of economic activities also tend to be weak (between the lower boxes), formal credit fails to reach smaller borrowers through indirect routes such as 'credit layering' or subcontracting systems. Thus there are few effective linkages for the flow of information and funds between segments, and instead the flow of funds is largely vertical, confined to formal and informal enclaves.

Market fragmentation of this kind has resulted in weak mobilization of household savings by the formal financial system and inefficient financial intermediation.

High volatility and seasonality in income, especially in rural areas, leads not only to synchronized demand for credit and savings facilities within the community, but also to a preference for short-term, flexible forms of saving. Formal institutions are disadvantaged in providing such facilities, owing to the high transaction costs involved. Evidence suggests that domestic savings mobilization by the informal financial sector exceeds that of formal financial institutions in many African countries. Informal savings activities (which involve little intermediation) indicate a substantial demand for savings that could be tapped to raise low rates of financial resource mobilization by the formal sector.

Yet the lack of access to credit facilities has hindered African households from using the savings facilities of formal institutions, while many targeted credit programmes unrelated to savings have often failed to achieve sustainable recovery rates for small borrowers (Adams et al. 1984; Meyer 1989; Seibel 1989). At the same time, there is evidence that 'lack of access to finance represents the binding constraint on expansion for small- and medium-scale enterprises' (SMEs), at least for those which could expand beyond the limits of self-finance (Levy 1993; Frischtak 1990; Steel and Webster 1991; World Bank 1989a; Aryeetey et al. 1994).

As Von Pischke (1991) emphasizes, the propensity of entrepreneurs to cite finance as a constraint does not necessarily imply that they are all good candidates for credit or would use it productively. Lack of finance may reflect poor cash flow or economic distress. Nevertheless, studies have identified a particularly dynamic subset of SMEs, often catering to niche markets, which would benefit from better access to credit. Greater finance for these enterprises would also benefit the economy. At a minimum, there appears to be significant potential for financial 'widening' to serve both household savers and small borrowers who presently depend largely on the informal sector with its limited intermediation and lending capacity.

The coexistence of deficit and surplus units without active intermediation and the mismatch of financial assets and liabilities indicate extreme market fragmentation in many African countries. As discussed in subsequent chapters, the weakness of the financial system in Africa is often manifested in prevailing conditions such as:

1 excess liquidity and extreme risk aversion in the banking system, resulting in a low-level lending trap and de facto crowding out of the private sector;
2 a high rate of non-performing loans in banks' portfolio. This problem is particularly prevalent with development-financial institutions (DFIs)

that have been largely dependent on foreign assistance to on-lend to high-risk areas, with little capacity for risk assessment and loan management, and with highly vulnerable, insufficiently diversified loan portfolios;

3 little interaction among financial institutions for portfolio realignment through the money and capital markets;

4 weak intermediation and interaction *within* the informal financial sector, despite its important role in meeting the financial needs of a large part of the population.

In many countries of sub-Saharan Africa savings mobilization is currently fragmented into a large number of operations by diverse informal activities. In the absence of adequate information and market signals, funds mobilized through the informal sector are used by the savers mainly for consumption and trading ventures and are rarely channelled into investment and other economic activities. The limited capital base, the short-run nature of the saving/lending cycle and the localized nature of informal activities act as constraints on financial intermediation, though they may have a lasting comparative advantage in serving certain segments of the financial markets. Few informal financial institutions provide term finance (either directly or through linkages with the formal system). The potential use of savings mobilized through the informal sector for economy-wide diversification remains unrealized.

2.5 Linkages, integration and financial policies

Where functional specialization by each sector has not materialized as part of an integrated system, such as in the fragmented financial markets of sub-Saharan countries, the required policy would be not to deregulate markets in haste, but to work first on closer *integration* of the informal and formal markets (Roemer and Jones 1991). It is increasingly recognized that integration may not proceed automatically and that an attempt to achieve integration through the institutionalization of informal activities is not appropriate (Adams and Fitchett 1992; Ghate 1990; Seibel 1989; Seibel and Marx 1987). As suggested by Yotopoulos and Floro (1991), there may be several other ways to achieve integration: (1) infusing formal institutions with some of the flexibility of informal operations; (2) strengthening the structure and performance of informal market operations; and (3) developing linkages between the formal and informal financial sectors.

While these three measures can be successfully adopted in parallel, the first and second policy options are most effective, when the two sectors can *potentially* compete in providing finance, but this potential is not realized, as the formal sector lacks the financial technology to deal with small-scale borrowers and savers, while informal agents/institutions are not subject to competitive pressure to improve their performance.

The third option, i.e. the development of linkages, is attractive where risk factors and cost considerations, not liquidity, are the primary constraints in the formal sector, while the limited capital base and excessive cost of funds act as a check on the expansion of informal agents. In such circumstances, the informal sector can be used as a conduit for formal sector funds to reach borrowers otherwise rationed out. Such schemes can lead to improved repayment rates, owing to the screening and monitoring advantages of informal lenders. Thus the formal and informal markets could specialize but function in a mutually reinforcing, complementary manner.

Other recent studies have echoed this line of thinking. For example, Germidis *et al.* (1991) recommend policies of *integration* of the informal sector into the formal sector to reduce financial dualism, and also interlinkage between the informal and formal sectors on a more systematic scale, by maximizing the advantages and minimizing the disadvantages of each. The informal sector is seen as 'a means of retailing formal financial services to areas, sectors or population groups that are difficult to reach'. Germidis *et al.* propose that integration and interlinkage should be undertaken sequentially, arguing that linkage in the short term would bring integration in the long term. Linkage development is viewed as a strategy of 'soft integration', a step towards achieving the goal of an integrated and competitive financial system.

The preceding discussion suggests that policy towards financial development in sub-Saharan Africa should contain measures of market integration. At the same time, as Aryeetey and Hyuha (1991) argue for sub-Saharan Africa, the effectiveness of financial and monetary policies also depends critically on the scope and nature of the links between formal and informal segments of the financial market.

Yet designing appropriate integration measures requires in-depth knowledge of the operational capacity of each segment and of the *scope and scale* of existing and potential relationships among units on the supply side of financial services. The *nature of the symbiotic relationship* between the formal and informal sectors, i.e. indirect demand links, could also significantly affect the outcome of financial policies.

In this respect, it is pertinent to note that the debate on financial liberalization between the McKinnon–Shaw school and the neo-structuralists also centred on the flow of funds between the informal and formal sectors (Taylor 1983; Van Wijnbergen 1983). Instead of the higher supply predicted by the McKinnon–Shaw school, Van Wijnbergen (1983) argued that financial liberalization could reduce the total credit supply as a result of increased interest rates. Given that portfolios of the household sector include gold, currency, bank deposits and kerb market loans, he argues that an increase in time deposit rates would lead households to substitute time deposits for kerb market lending. In his model, based on the Korean economy, the kerb markets are seen as competitive and relatively efficient and act as an alternative to holding money balances.[20] There is perfect substitution between claims in informal credits and other forms of financial savings. In such cases a shift of funds to the banking sector would reduce the total supply of loanable funds available to business, because the reserve requirements imposed on the banking system are seen as a leakage in the intermediation process. This shift would also raise the kerb market rate, which would increase the cost of working capital. This could lead to a further reduction of output, thus deterring investment.

Thus the effects of interest rate liberalization in the formal sector on total loan supply depend critically on the degree of substitution between different forms of assets in household portfolios in general. In particular, if linkages between the formal and informal financial sectors are strong and kerb market loans are a close substitute for formal sector deposits, as in the case of Korea, interest rate liberalization can result in a substantial and abrupt shift of funds towards the formal sector, attracting funds away from the informal market. This can reduce the access of SMEs, smallholders and the poor to their only source of credit, i.e. informal credit, and so detrimentally affect their future income stream.

For sub-Saharan African countries, apart from the weak direct links discussed above, we may postulate the following hypotheses with regard to the indirect links:

1   The actual range of overlapping demand for credit may be limited by various barriers between segments. As a result, there is little substitution or competitive effect consequent upon price changes in one sector.
2   The complementary use of informal and formal finance for productive activities does not appear to be widespread, in contrast to the situation in Asia, where the informal sector acts as a vigorous provider of residual finance for enterprise development.[21]

To the extent that the hypotheses are valid in sub-Saharan countries, the changes in financial policies, including financial liberalization, are likely to have a negligible effect on the financial system as a whole.

These issues are taken up for empirical investigation in the subsequent chapters, where the structure of financial markets, flow of funds and the effect of financial liberalization in four case study countries are examined. We shall also investigate the extent to which the theoretical explanations, presented in section 2.2, identify underlying causes for market segmentation and fragmentation in the sample countries. Before proceeding to the next chapter, where the detailed characteristics and structure of the financial systems in the sample countries are presented, the remaining sections of this chapter (sections 2.6–8) introduce the main features of: (1) households savings with critical implication for financial sector development; (2) financial systems; and (3) changes in the financial policy environment in sub-Saharan Africa.

2.6 Characteristics of household savings and the implications for financial sector development in sub-Saharan Africa

The asset composition of household savings is influenced by the nature of the economic activities that a particular household is engaged in as well as a number of other factors such as the degree of liquidity, risk, return on different assets, and storage and transport costs. In particular, it is affected by households' liquidity preference, hence their *perceptions* of liquidity constraints and the ease with which they can switch between different types of asset: (1) non-financial assets (commodities and real assets); (2) financial assets in domestic currencies; (3) financial assets in foreign currencies.[22] From a purely economic point of view, the use of non-financial forms of asset-holding as a store of value suggests a large 'efficiency loss' to the economy. Instead financial savings could have been intermediated by the financial system for productive investment. In addition, unproductive commodity holdings can entail substantial storage and transaction costs, while they can act as a hedge against loss from inflation.

At early stages of economic development, *financial* savings are expected to have only a modest share in total household savings. In remote areas with less monetized economies, households tend to save in agricultural produce (e.g. grains, cereals and livestock). Where there is greater cash-crop production, more household savings are held in financial assets, land, jewellery, gold and ornaments. In urban areas, financial assets may constitute an even larger proportion of total savings. While household savings are affected by the institutional and economic environment, saving behaviour affecting the asset composition is also determined by a combination of cultural, demographic and other socio-economic factors reflecting the characteristics of the society in general. This includes factors such as the prevalence of inter-generational transfers, the demonstration effect, attitudes to risk and the rate of time preference.[23] The small share of financial assets in total savings is undoubtedly also a reflection of the insufficient degree of monetization of these economies.

Notwithstanding this general condition, it is important to note that in sub-Saharan Africa the unstable and high-risk political and economic environment, in particular the level and expected trajectory of the inflation rate, and expectations with regard to exchange rate depreciation, has had a significant effect on the asset composition of savings portfolio held by private agents. In many countries, the trend away from the domestic currency has increasingly taken the form of flight into other financial and non-financial assets, such as *demonetization, currency substitution* (or *dollarization*),[24] or *capital flight*, all of which also occurred in Latin America on a large scale in the 1980s.

In a number of African countries demonetization has taken place as more rural households have retreated back into the subsistence during the crisis periods. A clear example of this is Zambia, which once registered the highest coefficient of monetization in sub-Saharan Africa, at 93 per cent in 1975. A similar process of demonetization is reported to have occurred in Tanzania, Uganda and Ghana in the early 1980s. There was a drastic reduction in the real demand for money relative to income and output in all these countries, where the domestic currency almost ceased to function as a store of value.

Foreign currencies are used as a hedge and a refuge against losses in real wealth under high and persistent domestic inflation combined with financial repression. A substantial difference in the real expected rates of return on domestic- and foreign-denominated assets has emerged owing to the recent tendency in many African countries towards frequent and large devaluations necessitated by unviable positions on the balance of payments. Foreign exchange is also held for acquiring restricted imports. Thus these household portfolio adjustments between domestic and foreign assets have often been influenced by the existence of sizeable parallel markets for foreign exchange and tradable goods, which have emerged in response to extensive controls on foreign trade and capital transactions.[25]

In the case of currency substitution, cash balances in foreign currencies, originated in under-invoicing and smuggling of exports, over-invoicing of imports, foreign tourism, and the diversion of remittances through non-official channels, are held by private agents within national borders, in order to make transactions in the parallel foreign exchange market or for 'illegal underground' transactions in goods and foreign exchange. In the presence of a large and increasing demand for foreign currency, several countries have allowed domestic residents to open and operate foreign currency deposits within the domestic financial system.

However, residents, particularly wealthy elites, may still prefer to hold assets abroad in foreign currency deposit accounts, or in other forms of financial and real assets. This tendency is referred to as *capital flight*. Owing to its nature, it is difficult to estimate the size of such flows, but several methods have been proposed. On the basis of the estimate by Claessens and Naude (1993), Adam and O'Connell (1997) speculate that capital flight from sub-Saharan Africa by the beginning of the 1990s may have reached a scale which is equivalent to 90–100 per cent of GDP. Collier and Gunning (1997) reckon that African wealth owners have chosen to locate 37 per cent of their portfolio outside Africa. This share is compared with 29 per cent for the Middle East, 17 per cent for Latin America, 4 per cent for South Asia and 3 per cent for East Asia. Chang and Cumby (1991) estimate that thirty-six sub-Saharan countries experienced capital flight, amounting to US$32 billion to US$40 billion, from 1976 to 1987. The lower estimate is arrived at by calculating the increase in the private sector's stock of foreign assets unreported to the domestic authorities, while the upper estimate is based on an evaluation of the total net foreign assets held by the private sector. Nigeria and Sudan alone accounted for more than half of total capital flight.[26] Chang and Cumby suggest that several African countries have exhibited capital flight on a par with countries such as Argentina or Mexico in the 1980s, and that 'as is the case with the large Latin American debtors, there are often two-way capital flows, with the private sector increasing its external assets at the same time that the public sector is increasing its external liabilities' (1991, p. 162).

Both demonetization and capital flight are the direct result of private agents' response to an unstable political and economic environment as part of their asset portfolio management, which affects the composition of total household savings. They have a significant influence on the conduct of monetary and fiscal policies by reducing government revenues through a loss of seigniorage and inflation tax on the holdings of domestic cash balances.[27] They also constitute a large proportion of the substantial *leakage* of domestic savings that could have been intermediated for productive investment.

Notwithstanding these leakage characteristics, it is important to note that savings capacity and the potential for growth in the private sector are by no means negligible, even in the low-income economies of the region (Nissanke *et al*. 1991; Nissanke 1993b).[28] Household savings in these countries exhibit characteristics which should be considered when designing policies to improve saving–investment performance. First of all, it can be noted that voluntary savings capacity in rural areas may be substantial, with far more liquidity than is usually assumed. Whilst the liquidity generated does not necessarily constitute an economic surplus as such,[29] the agricultural production cycle creates an absolute need for savings. As a result, the savings patterns are distinctly 'short-run', governed by the seasonality of agricultural activity and the liquidity of rural household income.[30]

In general, household savings can be characterized as small in transaction size and short-term in frequency. As Deaton (1989) notes, saving by the household sector in developing countries is of a 'high-frequency' nature, as opposed to 'low-frequency' life-cycle saving in developed economies. In essence, savings protect livelihoods in high-risk environments by providing a buffer between uncertain and unpredictable income and an already low level of consumption. Under these conditions, households display a strong preference for more liquid assets and maximum flexibility. Even contractual saving within the informal sector, e.g. saving for insurance purposes, is undertaken within a very short-term time horizon and on a limited scale (see Chapter 5 below). The small scale and high frequency of saving imply high transaction costs for formal financial intermediaries that wish to operate in the household/non-corporate sector.

On the other hand, the operations of many informal associations, such as ROSCAs and *susu* collectors, have been based on small but regular savings by numerous householders/traders. This is one of the main reasons for the fact that, despite the rapid expansion of bank branches and the greater availability of institutional credit, most of the financial savings of the household sector continue to be mobilized through informal financial agents. In many countries, as will be discussed below, the volume of savings and credit handled by the informal sector has exceeded that of formal institutions. These informal sector savings are used for social and private consumption, as well as being put to productive use in farming or small-scale investment in retail and commercial activity.

Thus characteristics intrinsic to the household/non-corporate sector have an important bearing upon the way financial systems function in these economies, explaining both the relative size and the vibrancy of the informal financial sector. Continued fragmentation and limited progress in financial 'widening' can be understood in this context.[31] These factors will be discussed in greater detail in subsequent chapters. In the next section we shall continue with our overview of the main features of financial systems in sub-Saharan Africa, before proceeding to the more detailed discussion of each case-study country's system (Chapter 3), and of the operational characteristics of financial institutions (Chapters 5 and 6).

2.7 Overview of financial systems

In shaping the post-independence *formal financial sector* many governments attempted to diversify the institutional structure of the financial system and extend banks' branch networks. With the central bank at the apex, formal systems are now usually comprised of commercial banks, merchant banks, development financial institutions (DFIs) and several specialized financial institutions, such as insurance companies and provident funds. Governments have often nationalized commercial banks set up in the pre-independence years by expatriate banks primarily for financing external trade. Those commercial banks established in the post-independence era are typically publicly owned.[32] Branch networks have expanded rapidly since independence, and several specialized banking institutions have been established to provide financial services in rural areas, where other formal institutions find it difficult to operate.

Many commercial banks have continued to specialize in short-term banking services, although many publicly owned banks were asked to take on a more developmental role by extending loans to priority sectors. Recognition of the inadequacies of conventional banking practice and the dearth of longer-term credit to priority sectors has led to the establishment of DFIs in many countries. These are typically founded and financed either directly by external finance or indirectly via governments, often through refinancing schemes evolved by central banks. Owing to their specialization in high-risk sectors, the problem of non-performing loans is often most severe among the DFIs.

Non-banking financial institutions (NBFIs) have begun to play an increasingly important role in savings mobilization. NBFIs include institutions that mobilize contractual and compulsory savings from the household sector, such as insurance companies, pension schemes, provident funds and social security funds. These institutions can be a vital source of medium- to long-term investment because of the long-term maturity structure of the savings they mobilize. However, owing to the limited range of financial instruments and investment opportunities, their assets have typically been concentrated in government securities or deposited at banking institutions, where they have not been mediated for productive investment owing to banks' limited lending operations and portfolio management (see Chapter 4).

While financial systems in sub-Saharan Africa remain bank-dominated, the creation and development of active money and capital markets could considerably broaden the opportunities for diversification for both savers and investors. The money market, dealing in short-term financial instruments, can be used for active liquidity management by financial institutions and monetary control by the central bank. Fundamentally, the shift in monetary policy from direct credit control to indirect control requires operative money markets. However, money markets are currently dominated by treasury bills, central bank bills and other government securities. Few private commercial bills are traded and money markets have not yet been used for active interbank portfolio realignment.

Government tax policy often tends to discriminate against financial transactions and is widely seen as impeding the development of the money market. For example, Germidis et al. (1991) suggest that the practice of taxing all financial transactions renders very short-term overnight borrowing and lending uneconomic. They argue that so long as banks have access to in-expensive and unlimited loans through central bank discount facilities, interbank borrowing and lending are seldom practised.

The capital market can be potentially used as a channel for direct finance, providing long-term debt and equity instruments. The stock markets are typically in a rudimentary stage, constrained by limited demand and supply. In particular, underdeveloped secondary markets provide little opportunity for liquidity and risk management by prospective investors, and this acts as a disincentive to holding the financial instruments of the private sector.

Overall, despite efforts to create new institutions and instruments, the formal financial systems are still dominated by commercial banks. Further, formal institutions' responses to reform measures have been slower than expected, although it is the formal sector that has been the recipient of a great deal of restructuring effort and resources. This has often been because the operational constraints of formal institutions have not been addressed adequately in the reform efforts, as will be discussed in Chapter 4.

In the sample countries, informal sector transactions can also be grouped into those that are non-commercial, such as transactions between relatives and friends or small-scale group arrangements, and those that are commercially based, conducted by single collectors, estate owners, landlords, traders or moneylenders. Most informal financial agents/institutions tend to specialize in either lending or savings mobilization, while institutions engaging in both activities provide their services to members only. An example of the former are the 'mobile bankers' (Miracle *et al*. 1980) or savings collectors (*susu* collectors in Ghana), who mobilize savings through the daily collection of small amounts of savings at markets or other workplace. Savings mobilization is their main function, but they occasionally extend credit to their clients on flexible terms, mainly to finance the working capital needs of traders. The latter include rotating savings and credit associations (ROSCAs, known as *susu* groups in Ghana, *esusu* in Nigeria, *upatu* in Tanzania and *tontines* in francophone countries), which collect a given amount from members at regular intervals and give the total collection to each member in turn. They most commonly exist among traders with a specific market or among groups of workers in an office or a narrowly defined activity.

Professional moneylenders usually operate at high interest rates. They are considered 'lenders of last resort', which limits their significance in the provision of finance for investment or working capital. They lend from profits generated by other economic activities, such as agriculture and real estate development, and reinvest the returns from lending in these activities. Traders operate among producers in rural areas and among consumers in the urban centres. They will typically offer either supplier's credit or an advance payment from a 'middleman' against future purchases. Middlemen, who operate interlinked credit lines, do not ask for collateral but instead enter into agreements with the farmers, for example, to purchase all their produce over an agreed period. Imputed interest on these types of arrangement can be as high as 50 per cent of the principal for the farming season.

Informal financial units have been developed in response to the demand of a distinct clientele and each unit tends to serve a particular market niche (Aryeetey and Udry 1994). Thus the relative importance of different categories of the informal sector varies widely among the sample countries. Further, all four country studies suggest that the informal financial sector may far exceed the formal sector in coverage, influence and even value transacted. Rather than a contraction in response to reform, as predicted by the financial repression hypothesis, there has been a rapid increase in demand for informal savings and credit facilities in the more liberal environment of recent years. This growth in demand can be explained by an increase in unsatisfied demand for formal sector credit, which has been restrained as part of stabilization efforts. It may also result from the greater trading and commercial opportunities that have emerged in the adjustment period. While formal institutions have continued to find it hard to overcome their inherent constraints during the reform process, the informal financial sector, demand-driven by its nature, has responded first to the growing demand for financial services.

2.8 Financial repression and policy reform

The financial policies pursued in the sample countries in the pre-adjustment period are characteristic of 'repressive' regimes. As discussed briefly in Chapter 1, in such regimes, governments play a major role in determining credit flows through a system of subsidies, interest rate ceilings, credit allocation and direct intervention. Repressive policies typically encompass a set of measures, such as: (1) restrictions on entry into banking coupled with public ownership of major banks; (2) high reserve requirements on deposits; (3) ceilings on lending and deposit rates; (4) quantitative restrictions on the allocation of credit; and (5) restrictions on capital transactions with foreigners (Johnston and Brekk 1991; Montiel 1994). In combination, these measures are thought to have shifted the allocation of investible funds from the market to the government.

Most of the measures listed have been extensively applied in the case-study countries, although the degree and breadth of the measures have varied. Naturally, the degree of government control over banking institutions has reflected the overall economic development strategy.[33] So it was markedly higher in Tanzania and Ghana, compared with Malawi and Nigeria. The economic policy regime in Ghana and Tanzania was characterized by pervasive and severe controls and rationing before the reform programmes were put in place in the mid-1980s, whilst the activities of indigenous private agents were relatively more encouraged in Malawi and Nigeria in post-independence years. In Tanzania, at the extreme end of the spectrum, banking institutions became mere instruments for financing the budget deficit or covering operating losses incurred by parastatals (Collier and Gunning 1991).

Given the weak tax base in sub-Saharan Africa, the domestic financial system has been an indispensable source of government revenue, and finance has been readily available to the government through the instruments of financial repression. Thus government-imposed controls on domestic financial markets are often regarded as a form of implicit taxation. In particular, repression of interest rates is viewed as an instrument enabling government to finance deficits at low cost.

In the highly inflationary environment, infrequently adjusted ceilings on interest rates have led to significantly negative deposit and lending rates in many countries of sub-Saharan Africa, including the case-study countries. As will be discussed in Chapter 4, governments have often imposed high reserve requirements, in the range of 20 per cent to 25 per cent of assets but sometimes exceeding 40 per cent. In the pre-adjustment period, the share of government and public enterprise in domestic credit was over 80 per cent and 95 per cent in Ghana and Tanzania respectively, while the public sector accounted for well over half of domestic credit in Malawi and Nigeria.[34]

Several studies provide estimates of the size of government revenue resulting from 'financial repression'. Giovannini and De Melo (1990) measured the revenue from repression as the difference between the foreign and domestic costs of government borrowing. The unweighted average of 'financial repression tax revenue' thus calculated for twenty-four countries across the different continents amounted to 2 per cent of GDP for the period 1974–87. Chamley and Honohan (1990) included currency tax (seigniorage[35]), reserve requirements and the quasi-tax effects of interest rate ceilings in their measurement of the scale of implicit taxation of financial intermediation in five African countries. Between 1978 and 1988, explicit and implicit 'financial repression tax' jointly accounted for an average 4 per cent to 7 per cent of GDP in Ghana, Nigeria and Zambia, while in Kenya and Côte d'Ivoire it was estimated to be close to 2 per cent. Thus many emphasize that financial repression in sub-Saharan Africa has as deep fiscal roots as in Latin America.

If government expenditure were to be used effectively for productive investment and contribute to buoyant and broad-based economic growth, this pattern of highly skewed resource allocation might find some justification, since the private sector is often inherently weak in the initial stages of economic development. However, a case of public expenditure-led growth on a sustained basis is hard to find in sub-Saharan Africa.

Critically, the manner in which repressive policy has been implemented in sub-Saharan Africa has hindered development of the institutional capacity of financial institutions. The rationale of commercial viability has been largely subsumed to the dictates of government's other policy objectives as well as political goals. Many banks failed to develop the capacity to assess risk and monitor loan portfolios. In several countries, credit and interest rate restrictions reportedly discouraged savings mobilization. Once banks had enough deposits to meet their credit targets, further savings mobilization was deemed unnecessary and indeed discouraged (see Chapter 4). There was neither active liquidity and liability management, nor was there sufficient incentive to cut the costs of intermediation by increasing efficiency (Chapter 5 discusses this in more detail). Financial repression has also discouraged banks from investing in information capital, crucial to the development of financial systems. Institutions are typically burdened with severe agency problems in dealing with idiosyncratic risks, i.e. the problems caused by costly and imperfect information – adverse selection, moral hazard and contract enforcement.

Financial sector reforms have been implemented to address the problems arising from repression, guided largely by policy prescriptions advanced by the financial repression school. Under the two fundamental premises of liberalization and balance sheet restructuring, interest rates and credit allocation have been decontrolled and efforts have been made to strengthen the regulatory framework. The nature of these reforms is influenced by the portfolio position and the asset quality of financial institutions, as well as by government financing requirements and the general fiscal profile. With this in mind, extensive restructuring and recapitalizing operations have been mounted for distressed banks.[36] Although the number of banks privatized has been limited, the overall share of public ownership in banking institutions has fallen.

It is also envisaged that the method of monetary control should be changed.[37] In general, policy instruments used to control money supply include: credit ceilings, interest-rate controls, reserve requirements, re-discount and special deposit facilities, open market operations in government or central bank paper, and foreign exchange intervention. The degree of central bank intervention could vary for each policy instrument.

In the debate on the efficacy of monetary control in sub-Saharan Africa, administratively imposed ceilings on aggregate credit, frequently applied for stabilization objectives in the past, are seen as part of the 'repressive' control regime that undermines the risk–return configuration of bank lending (Roe and Sowa 1994). Aggregate credit ceilings have often been enforced with negative side effects, such as rent-seeking, corruption and leakages leading to an uncontrollable expansion of NBFI. In contrast, indirect control through open market operations affects monetary aggregates by fine-tuning those variables which are directly under central bank control, such as the reserve money stock, the money market liquidity level and interest rates. In recent years, indirect monetary control has increasingly been seen as preferable to direct methods for: (1) liquidity management, e.g. absorbing liquidity from the banking system, through policy that influences commercial bank reserves at the central bank; (2) providing non-inflationary finance for short-term government financial requirements; and (3) providing the central bank with a market-based mechanism for determining its rediscount rate.

However, effective indirect monetary control requires not only a detailed and up-to-date information base for financial planning but, above all, well functioning money markets, where government and commercial paper can be traded actively. If fluctuations in interest rates are not to be too large, deeper markets with a large number of participants and traded instruments are a prerequisite for successful open market operations. These conditions are conspicuously absent in the economies of sub-Saharan Africa.

Moreover, besides underdeveloped money markets, the efficacy of indirect methods in controlling the monetary base and money supply in sub-Saharan economies can be far from certain, for two reasons: (1) the large variability of net foreign assets and domestic credit to the public sector in the central banks' balance sheets, which is strictly not under their control; and (2) sizeable excess liquidity holdings (see Chapter 4 below). The use of fine-tuning of reserve requirements and rediscount rates is not typically effectual for short-term liquidity management when there are significant 'surplus' reserve holdings.

Nevertheless, many countries in sub-Saharan Africa, including our case-study countries, have recently abandoned direct credit ceilings and moved to the adoption of indirect monetary control as part of financial sector reforms. Open market operations have been initiated through primary sales of treasury bills or other securities, since this move is anyway necessary to foster the development of money and interbank markets. It is also hoped that open market operations will bring about institutional reform and a change in attitude towards interest rate determination, credit control and competition in the financial system (Johnston and Brekk 1991). However, control of the money supply can become more difficult immediately after liberalization, especially when reform measures are poorly sequenced or at too fast a pace, as discussed in Chapter 3.

Notes

1 U Tun Wai (1992) notes that the *relative* importance of informal finance in rural areas of Asia and Latin America has declined, despite its growth in size and complexity, because the formal sector has expanded faster. However, informal financial operations are still substantial and often exceed those of the formal sector, as reported in studies by the Asian Development Bank and the OECD (see below).

2 Naturally, countries in Asia are by no means homogeneous. In the Philippines, for example, we have observed a resurgence of informal finance after the collapse of the formal sector (Nagarajan *et al.* (1992).

3 The financial repression school challenged the conventional Keynesian proposition that low interest rates lead to increased investment and a high rate of output/income growth and savings. It argued a reverse flow of causality: a higher market-determined interest would induce higher savings, leading to the increased quality and quantity of investment and to faster growth of output and a consequently greater supply of financial savings and eventually a lower equilibrium interest rate.

4 The financial repression hypothesis also argues that the resultant distortion of relative prices leads to the inappropriate choice of technology. The expansion of capital-intensive industries is encouraged by low interest rates, which exacerbates unemployment and has negative implications for income distribution.

5 For descriptions of the working mechanisms of a number of ROSCAs see Ardener (1964), Besley *et al.* (1993), Bouman (1995), Germidis *et al.* (1991, pp. 100–1), Ghate (1988), Thomas (1993) and Von Pischke (1991).

6 Or in interlinked markets, where credit agreements are linked with transactions in other markets. These will be discussed below.

7 Thomas (1993) presents empirical studies to show that the share of monopoly rents in interest is relatively small if alternative returns and risk premiums are taken into account.

8 Consumption loans cannot be regarded as 'unproductive' *per se*. Ghate (1988) notes that there are four categories of consumption loans: (1) essential loans for emergencies and subsistence; (2) productive loans for housing, education, migration, etc.; (3) loans for the purchase of consumer durables which may be used for productive purposes, such as sewing machines and typewriters; and (4) loans for conspicuous consumption.

9 Montiel *et al.* (1993) report one of the survey results, indicating that lending among firms to ease each others' short-term cash-flow problems in India is estimated to be the equivalent to 13–25 per cent of total bank credit to industry.

10 Except when loans are to large-scale commercial farming estates.

11 Product-related loans can be output-tied loans, input-tied loans or loans from market agents (Germidis *et al.* 1991).

12 Chandavakar (1985) discusses the efficacy of monetary control in the presence of a large informal financial sector, while Montiel *et al.* (1993) examine the macro-economic implications of the presence of informal markets, including how it affects the transmission mechanisms of monetary and fiscal policies.

13 By its nature, it is difficult to arrive at a reliable estimate of the relative size of informal finance. However, the prevalence of informal finance in sub-Saharan countries which are not in our case-study sample is supported by numerous estimates. For example, in Cameroon 70 per cent of the population participates in the informal financial sector and informal sector saving is estimated to be more than 50 per cent of the total. It is estimated that over 80 per cent of Zimbabwean smallholders have access to informal credit, while in Zambia over 80 per cent of the urban population are estimated to participate in the informal financial sector (African Development Bank 1994).

14 Christensen (1993) defines informal financial intermediation as 'the mobilization of capital from savers and its simultaneous transformation and allocation to meet the needs of borrowers, as performed by informal financial agents' (pp. 721–2).

15 A detailed presentation of the relationship between formal and informal finance can be found in Aryeetey (1992b).

16 Biggs uses the terms 'fragmentation' and 'segmentation' interchangeably. However, we shall use the terms in accordance with the definitions presented in Chapter 1, as this differentiation is critical in crystallizing our discussion.

17 The lack of interaction between formal and informal institutions in Africa is also discussed in Seibel and Marx (1987) and Adams and Fitchett (1992).

18 There have been some changes in this condition in recent years with the proliferation of NGO and other experimental programmes oriented towards micro-finance. However, it is worth noting that these micro-finance programmes are usually administered outside normal banking operations (see Chapter 8 for the effects of such programmes on financial systems in sub-Saharan Africa).

19 See also Chapter 7 below.

20 Teranishi (1994) emphasizes that the informal kerb market in Korea in the 1960s and 1970s presents a special case, where the kerb market in the form of a private bond market played a highly efficient role in the allocation of funds both in the informal and in the modern sectors, and it complemented the role of the strictly regulated formal financial sectors.

21 See Aryeetey (1992b, 1994) and Chipeta (1994) for detailed analysis of the demand side for Ghana and Malawi, respectively. Also Chapter 7 for more discussion for existing linkages.

22 An example of such an all-encompassing portfolio balance model for households is to be found in Montiel *et al.* (1993), where households' portfolios consist of five assets: domestic currency, foreign exchange, bank deposits and credit, and kerb-market loans.

23 For more detailed discussion see Ghate (1992).

24 Hussain (1993) defines currency substitution as the demand for foreign fiat money by residents of a developing country, in excess of that required for international trade transactions.

25 For detailed discussion of the nature of parallel markets for foreign exchange and traded goods, and for a comprehensive literature survey of parallel market models, see Montiel *et al*. (1993).

26 Nigeria accounts for nearly half the sub-Saharan region's total capital flight, while Sudan accounting for another 20 per cent. Other countries that experienced capital flight of over US$1 billion were Gabon, Zambia, Zaire, Congo, Liberia, Ghana and Uganda (Chang and Cumby 1991).

27 See Montiel *et al*. (1993) for detailed discussion of the macroeconomic effects of currency substitution and parallel markets on foreign exchanges as well as informal credit markets.

28 Admittedly, in the absence of comprehensive household survey data it is difficult to estimate the value of savings and investment for the household/non-corporate sector. There are considerable conceptual and technical problems in defining and measuring, even approximately, the value of household income and total savings, as well as in breaking the latter down into financial and non-financial savings. Deaton (1989) discusses the difficulty of measuring saving in developing countries.

29 The relationship between economic surplus and financial liquidity is not linear. As Von Pischke notes, low levels of economic surplus do not necessarily accompany low levels of financial liquidity (1991 p. 81).

30 Uneven flows of income arise not only from the highly seasonal nature of agricultural production but also from inadequate post-harvest facilities and poor marketing infrastructure.

31 The process of financial widening can be viewed as extending the frontier of formal financial activities to include a larger share of households and businesses (Von Pischke 1991).

32 Public ownership dominates in the banking sector. The World Bank (1994a) reports that in sub-Saharan Africa, of a total of 213 commercial banks in 1982, governments were a majority shareholder in 106 banks and a minority shareholder in forty-seven. After restructuring, privatization and the relaxation of entry barriers to increase competition, the number of banks rose to 245 in 1992. Of these, seventy-six banks are government majority-owned, while in fifty-four banks the government is a minority shareholder.

33 However, Harvey (1996) notes the relative absence of government intervention in the financial sector in Zimbabwe since independence in 1980, despite the government's socialist objectives. Few changes in the ownership of banks were made, and there was no sectoral direction of credit, while interest rates were strictly controlled and the government put pressure on the commercial banks to provide mobile bank services to rural areas.

34 The public sector accounted for over 70 per cent of domestic credit in other sub-Saharan countries such as Sierra Leone, Uganda, Zambia and Zimbabwe. For indicators of the degree of financial repression in selected African countries see Seck and El Nil (1993) and African Development Bank (1994, chapter 8).

35 As Cottani and Cavallo (1993) note, seigniorage is defined as the amount of resources the government obtains from issuing fiat money. Thus if m is the ratio

of money to GNP and μ is the rate at which money is printed, the seigniorage (s) 'collected' as a proportion of national income is the product of the two , i.e. $s=\mu m$. Alternatively, seigniorage can be defined, in the long run, as the sum of the inflation tax (t) and the increase in money supply needed to meet the requirements associated with economic growth, i.e. $s=(g+\pi)m$, where g is GNP growth and π the rate of inflation, whereas the inflation tax is given by $t=\pi m$.

36 Popiel (1994) estimates that, between 1984 and 1993 the cost of bank restructuring operations in about twenty countries in sub-Saharan Africa was often equivalent to between 7 per cent and 15 per cent of their GDP.

37 Monetary control is concerned with policy objectives such as inflation, real income/output growth and the external balance. It is hoped that changes in these indicators will be achieved by targeting intermediate monetary variables, such as M_2, which are in turn controlled by particular policy instruments or operational variables.

3

CHARACTERISTICS AND STRUCTURE OF FINANCIAL SYSTEMS

This chapter outlines the *characteristics and structure* of the financial system in each of our sample countries. In order to provide the context for our later discussion of financial efficiency, the opening section presents a general overview of macroeconomic performance, focusing on the savings–investment–growth nexus (section 3.1). Although sharing the common features described in section 2.7, the financial system of each sample country displays several distinct features. Sections 3.2–5 present the structure and operation of the formal and informal financial sectors in our case-study countries. Section 3.6 evaluates the evolution of financial policies and the nature of financial sector reforms undertaken in the sample countries, and section 3.7 summarizes the main conclusions.

3.1 Analysis of aggregate data: the savings–investment–growth nexus

All four of the sample countries have undertaken Structural Adjustment Programmes in response to severe economic crisis in the early 1980s. The extent and scope of reform efforts have varied greatly among these countries, as have the outcomes. We shall evaluate the sample countries, Ghana, Malawi, Nigeria and Tanzania, in terms of policy aims and relative economic performance. Of the twenty-nine African countries examined in the recent World Bank study (World Bank 1994a), Ghana, Tanzania and Nigeria are classified among those countries that have experienced a substantial improvement in macroeconomic policies and have achieved better GDP *per capita* growth. Malawi is classified among nine countries that show a small improvement in macroeconomic policies.

Tables 3–5 summarize official statistics on economic performance and the fiscal and external environment for the pre-adjustment and adjustment periods. These are taken as 1981–6 and 1987–91 respectively.[1] Some broad indicators of domestic economic performance are shown in Table 3. A comparison of *per capita* income clearly shows that Ghana, which is viewed as a

Table 3 Savings–investment–growth performance indicators

GNP per capita

	1980	*1985*	*1991*
Ghana	410	370	400
Malawi	180	170	230
Nigeria	1,100	1,020	340
Tanzania	280	280	100

Real GDP growth rates[a] (period average) % p.a.

	1981–6	*1987–91*
Ghana	0.68	4.64
Malawi	1.79	2.27
Nigeria	−1.29	6.83
Tanzania	1.14	4.10

Gross domestic investment as % of GDP

	1981–6	*1987–91*
Ghana	6.3	15.10
Malawi	17.60	18.70
Nigeria	16.50	15.40
Tanzania	18.30	26.90
Sub-Sahara	17.20	16.30

Government investment[b]

	1981–6	*1987–91*
Ghana	1.70	3.20 *
Malawi	8.70	6.70
Nigeria	9.50	5.60
Tanzania	6.80	8.00

Gross domestic savings as a % of GDP (GDS)

	1981–6	*1987–91*
Ghana	5.60	7.50
Malawi	13.30	9.00
Nigeria	14.40	22.80
Tanzania	9.70	−2.60

Government savings[c] (GS)

	1981–6	*1987–92*
Ghana	−1.70	2.60

51

Table 3 (continued)

Malawi	−2.70	−0.30
Nigeria	3.60	−1.20
Tanzania	−4.20	−1.60

Private savings (GDS–GS)

	1981–6	1987–92
Ghana	7.30	4.90
Malawi	16.00	9.30
Nigeria	10.80	24.00
Tanzania	13.90	−1.00

Gross concession-aid flows as % of GDP

	1980	1985	1991
Ghana	4.60	5.20	8.30
Malawi	14.00	13.70	10.20
Nigeria	0.10	0.00	2.50
Tanzania	5.90	3.40	26.70
Sub-Sahara	3.00	3.80	8.30

Notes:
a Calculated as geometric means.
b Capital expenditure and net lendings.
c Government current revenues (excluding grants) minus current expenditure.

'front-runner in adjustment' in sub-Saharan Africa (World Bank 1994a), has barely managed to attain the income level it possessed a decade earlier. In early 1991 *per capita* GNP in both Nigeria and Tanzania was significantly lower than previous levels, partly owing to massive exchange rate devaluation (see discussion below). Only Malawi has improved its income level over the decade.

Despite the rather poor performance in GNP *per capita*, Table 3 shows that there has been a discernible improvement in economic growth in the adjustment period in all four countries. However, the foundation for *self-sustaining* long-run growth appears to be fragile.[2] For example, Nigeria's growth record is characteristically erratic from year to year, owing to pro-cyclical macroeconomic management and heavy dependence on world oil prices. Table 3 shows that in Tanzania, Ghana and Malawi dependence on concessional aid flows is alarmingly high, with the ratio of aid flows to GDP increasing sharply over the decade to 26.7 per cent, 8.2 per cent and 10.3 per cent respectively.

3.1.1 *External balance*

The *external balance* of these countries remains precarious, and the conditions that led to past balance of payments crises remain largely unchanged. The severe import constriction that characterized the pre-adjustment period in all countries has apparently eased, but substantial deficits continue to be recorded, with few signs of long-run structural change (Table 4). The sample countries have continued to depend on a few primary export commodities,[3] whose prices have followed a declining long-run trend around which there have been large short-run fluctuations (Maizels 1992; Grilli and Yang 1988). This has led to an unstable and narrow base for foreign exchange earnings and fiscal revenues. None of these countries has achieved a balance of payments position sustainable without large concessional capital inflows, mostly as official aid. Only Nigeria has been a recipient of foreign direct investment on a significant scale, one of a few exceptional cases in sub-Saharan Africa in recent years.

International reserves were lower in Ghana, Malawi and Tanzania than the three-month threshold level, while Nigeria's reserves fluctuate widely, depending on the oil price. Indeed, despite a substantial depreciation of its real exchange rate, Nigeria's balance of payments profile remains largely determined by prevailing conditions in world oil markets. The current account balance swings widely, as even in the early 1990s oil accounts for more than 95 per cent of export revenues recorded in official statistics.[4] Unlike the other three countries, Nigeria's external debt has been contracted on non-concessional terms and arrears have often accumulated with short-term trade credit. In the adjustment period, therefore, Nigeria has had to use on average about a third of export earnings for debt servicing. Yet arrears have accumulated, culminating in a cut-off of commercial lending in 1994, despite repeated debt rescheduling with both the Paris and the London Clubs.

In Ghana a 470 per cent devaluation of the real effective exchange rate has not improved the current account deficit, which remains at 5 per cent to 6 per cent of GDP despite impressive growth in export volume and apparent restraint in imports. A sharp decline in the price of cocoa has led to a substantial deterioration in Ghana's terms of trade, which is the largest decline among the case-study countries in the period concerned. On average, over a quarter of Ghana's export earnings was used for servicing external debt, and a steady flow of foreign aid has been vital to support its import needs. Similarly, Malawi has continued to record a substantial current account deficit, equivalent to 10 per cent of GDP, in the adjustment period. This deficit can be explained more by changes in volumes than in prices. Starting from a situation of import squeeze, the adjustment period saw a rapid growth in import volumes, far outpacing real export growth, while the terms of trade remained largely unchanged. Of all the sample countries, Malawi's real effective exchange rate has adjusted the least over the decade, and external

Table 4 Indicators on external balance

Current account balance as % of GDP

	1980–6	*1987–92*
Ghana	−5.21	−5.98
Malawi	−13.84	−10.25
Nigeria	−4.18	−1.87
Tanzania	−10.11	−27.75

Terms of trade (1980=100)

	1985	*1991*
Ghana	59	40
Malawi	104	108
Nigeria	93	57
Tanzania	89	66
Sub-Sahara	92	65

International reserves as months of imports

	1980	*1987*	*1990*
Ghana	2.10	2.80	2.30
Malawi	2.40	1.80	2.60
Nigeria	12.90	3.70	8.90
Tanzania	0.20	0.40	2.10
Sub-Sahara	4.70	2.80	4.00

Changes in the real effective exchange rate (%)[a]

	1980–90/1
Ghana	471.00
Malawi	6.80
Nigeria	355.50
Tanzania	182.20

Real export growth (% p.a.)[b]

	1980–6	*1987–91*
Ghana	4.20	16.09
Malawi	−1.56	6.87
Nigeria	−11.50	9.00
Tanzania	−5.10	0.31
Sub-Sahara	−4.06	5.29

Table 4 (continued)

Real import growth (% p.a.)

	1980–6	1987–91
Ghana	0.49	2.09
Malawi	−7.66	19.81
Nigeria	−19.12	8.78
Tanzania	−3.45	3.18
Sub-Sahara	−5.55	2.08

External debt service as % of export earnings

	1980	1986	1992
Ghana	13.10	28.40	26.70
Malawi	27.70	52.70	24.30
Nigeria	4.20	32.70	30.60
Tanzania	19.60	29.20	32.50
Sub-Sahara	10.90	19.60	16.90

Long-term debt stock as % of GNP

	1980	1986	1992
Ghana	31.80	48.80	63.10
Malawi	72.10	103.60	96.30
Nigeria	10.10	60.50	110.70
Tanzania	48.30	89.80	268.40
Sub-Sahara	30.10	63.50	69.70

Notes:
a An increase in REER constitutes a depreciation; a decrease, an appreciation.
b Calculated as geometric means.

debt service continues to command a quarter of its export earnings, despite a substantial reduction due to debt rescheduling.

Tanzania has registered a significant deterioration in its current account position, and its terms of trade have continuously declined. The large depreciation in its real effective exchange rate has not yet led to anticipated changes in relative growth in exports and imports. Debt service obligations have grown despite repeated debt rescheduling and relief, and the debt stock has continued to rise, reaching unsustainable levels. Thus the external position of Tanzania – the poorest of our case-study countries – remains the most precarious, and is heavily dependent on foreign aid.[5]

3.1.2 Fiscal balance

On the fiscal front, there has been a mixed performance, with Ghana in particular improving its fiscal situation, increasing its revenue-raising capacity from only 8 per cent of GDP in the pre-adjustment period to 13 per cent in the early 1990s. Nevertheless, this ratio is one of the lowest among the four countries and lower than the ratio of 20 per cent which Ghana achieved in 1970. The government deficit has been reduced substantially, and this fall remains significant even with the exclusion of external grants (7 per cent of government revenue). However, fiscal discipline deteriorated considerably in 1992 in connection with the election campaign.

Budget deficits in Malawi and Tanzania have proved difficult to control, despite serious efforts to cut expenditure throughout the period. The fiscal position has been worsened by a series of external shocks, including drought, war in neighbouring countries and high debt obligations. Thus fiscal balance in these two countries has become more dependent upon grants.[6] In both countries, current consumption accounts for a large part of government expenditure, as the deficit has been contained by cutting capital expenditure. In addition, as data on primary fiscal balance indicate, interest payments on externally and internally contracted debt account for a sizeable proportion of government expenditure, as in the other sample countries.

In Nigeria, while capital expenditure was scaled down, fiscal management is known to have been inconsistent, lacking transparency and discipline, with repeated recourse to extra-budgetary spending (Faruqee 1994). Rather than reflecting a strategic stance over the revenue cycle, spending decisions have been heavily influenced by the use of unstable oil revenues for achieving goals dictated by the political imperatives of the regime. The increasing burden of debt service on fiscal management is also evident; Nigeria's primary fiscal balance in the adjustment period shows a surplus of 6 per cent in relation to GDP, whereas the overall balance for financing remains in deficit of 6 per cent of GDP.

3.1.3 Saving and investment rates

An examination of the *savings–investment* nexus can shed some light upon the sustainability of growth in these economies. In this respect, the picture that emerges is not encouraging. National account statistics show that the savings–investment gap has been widening in Ghana, Malawi and Tanzania (see Table 3). The large increases in domestic investment rates recorded in Tanzania and Ghana have been supported by a significant rise in foreign savings (i.e. foreign capital inflows). In Malawi, too, the investment rate has been maintained above the average for sub-Saharan Africa, owing to an increased flow of foreign savings. In these three countries the savings ratios remain depressingly low, far below the average of the countries in sub-Saharan

Table 5 Fiscal position

	1981–6	1987–91	1990–1
Total revenue (excluding grants)			
Ghana	8.10	13.36	13.80
Malawi	20.00	18.99	19.00
Nigeria	13.10	16.80	19.70
Tanzania	18.40	20.68	22.10
Overall fiscal balance for financing as % of GDP (including grants)			
Ghana	−3.10	0.39	0.80
Malawi	−8.40	−3.73	−2.50
Nigeria	−5.80	−5.79	−4.50
Tanzania	−8.50	−10.47	−0.90
Fiscal balance, excluding grants as % of GDP			
Ghana	−3.40	−0.57	−0.70
Malawi	−11.40	−5.80	−5.80
Nigeria	−5.80	−5.79	−4.50
Tanzania	−11.00	n.a.	−5.10
Primary fiscal balance, including grants			
Ghana	−1.50	1.77	2.40
Malawi	−3.10	1.03	0.50
Nigeria	−2.70	5.65	5.80
Tanzania	−6.10	−5.82	2.60
Share of grants in total government revenue			
Ghana	2.72	7.34	
Malawi	11.60	9.81	
Nigeria	–	–	
Tanzania	14.89	–	
Capital expenditure as % of GDP			
Ghana	1.70	2.60	3.20
Malawi	8.70	5.88	6.10
Nigeria	9.50	6.45	4.80
Tanzania	6.80	3.45	3.90
Total expenditure as % of GDP			
Ghana	11.50	13.93	14.40
Malawi	31.40	24.83	24.80
Nigeria	18.90	22.59	24.20
Tanzania	29.40	31.15	27.10

Africa (13 per cent).[7] Only in Nigeria was there an increase in the domestic savings rate. This pattern in the savings–investment nexus also is evident for a longer time period than that considered in Table 3, and Figs 2–3 plot time series data on aggregate savings and investment for 1975–92.[8]

In *Ghana*, both gross domestic and national savings rates have been on a declining trend since the mid-1970s (Fig. 2(a)). The aggregate savings rates bottomed out in 1983, when the economy was hit by the severe drought and the forced repatriation of workers from Nigeria. After adoption of the Economic Recovery Programme, savings rates had recovered by 1988 to the level attained in the second half of the 1970s. However, in the most recent period, 1989–92, savings rates again began to follow a sharply declining trend, despite continuing commitment to liberalization and reform measures. As gross domestic investment continued to rise, the savings–investment gap has widened in recent years (Fig. 3(a)). Since 1983 the Ghanaian government has reduced the current budget deficit, and in 1985 it began to generate a surplus. This increase in government savings implies that the private sector savings rate, calculated as a residual, has been on a declining trend since the mid-1980s.[9]

In *Malawi* the overall trend of gross savings rates has also been negative, but not as dramatically as in the case of Ghana (Fig. 2(b)). However, the Malawian aggregate savings pattern is characterized by far greater yearly fluctuations. After experiencing a sharp decline between 1979 and 1983, there was some recovery in 1984. Since then savings rates have remained low, and adjustment efforts have failed to establish a definite upward trend. The government continues to have negative savings, though the extent of its dissaving was reduced significantly in the adjustment period. In addition, the parastatal sector, consisting of 130 public enterprises, has improved its financial position in recent years. Thus in Malawi as elsewhere, it is savings by private agents that have failed to respond to economy-wide liberalization and reform measures. Malawi's savings–investment gap has not shown any sign of decline in the recent period, 1987–93, although the level of investment has fallen sharply since the late 1970s (Fig. 3(b)).

The trend in aggregate savings ratios in *Tanzania* is negative, particularly in the second sub-period (Fig. 2(d)). Despite 'resolute action' in adjustment (World Bank 1994), savings rates turned negative and the gap between national and domestic savings ratios widened as net factor payments abroad rose. The government continues to dissave, although this dissaving has fallen in recent years, and it appears that the huge losses made by public enterprises have been a substantial drain on the economy's financial resources. Large inflows of external finance have allowed domestic investment to increase significantly, achieving a rate far above those attained in the other sample countries (Fig. 3(d)). In the context of restrained public expenditure, this high level of aggregate investment implies a significant increase in private investment activity.

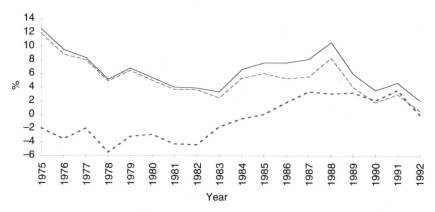

Figure 2(a) Aggregate savings rates Ghana

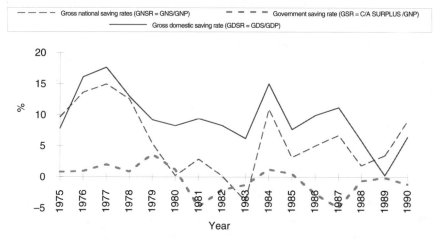

Figure 2(b) Aggregate savings rates Malawi

Trends in aggregate savings in *Nigeria* present an entirely different story. After a general decline during 1979–86, savings rates displayed a clear upward trend, although increasing debt service payments have widened the gap between national and domestic savings. The domestic savings ratio reached more than 30 per cent in 1990, high by international standards (Fig. 2(c)). The increase is largely accounted for by private savings, and government savings have fallen from the high of 10–14 per cent of GDP in the 1970s. However, the investment rate remains subdued in the adjustment period (Fig. 3(c)), partly owing to the decline of government investment. In the Nigerian case, the extremely low rates of return to investment during the oil boom years imply that an increase in the efficiency of investment may have higher

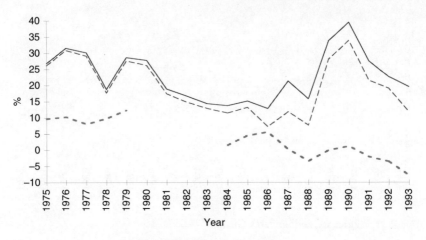

Figure 2(c) Aggregate savings rates Nigeria

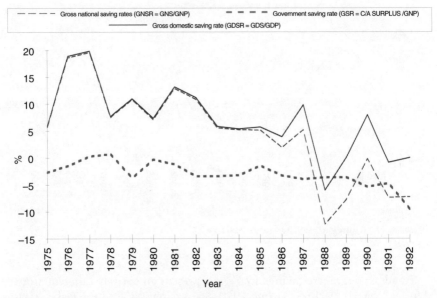

Figure 2(d) Aggregate savings rates Tanzania

priority than a simple increase in its level. There is no evidence that investment undertaken during the adjustment period has been more efficient than earlier. Instead, it appears that the higher rates of private saving have facilitated external debt service payments rather than being channelled into new productive capital.

Overall, the effect of adjustment on savings–investment performance in these countries was not encouraging. The savings ratio fell considerably in

Figure 3(a) The savings–investment gap Ghana. *Source:* IMF, IFS, GFS

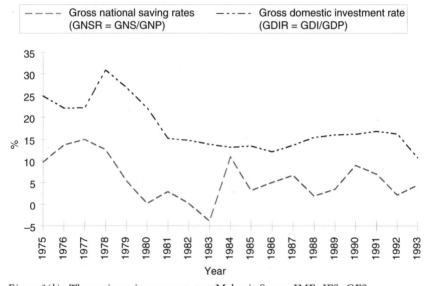

Figure 3(b) The savings–investment gap Malawi. *Source:* IMF, IFS, GFS

Malawi and Tanzania, with the latter recording negative savings in the adjustment period. As governments have improved their savings position in both countries, the large decline in aggregate savings was apparently caused by a reduction in private saving. Only in Nigeria was there an increase in the domestic savings rate. However, this significant increase, particularly in private savings, has not translated into increases in the rate of domestic investment.

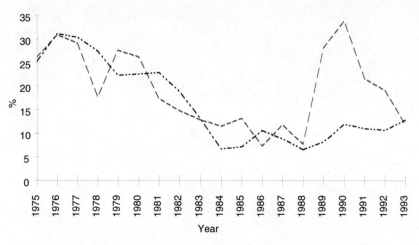

Figure 3(c) The savings–investment gap Nigeria. *Source:* IMF, GFS, IFS

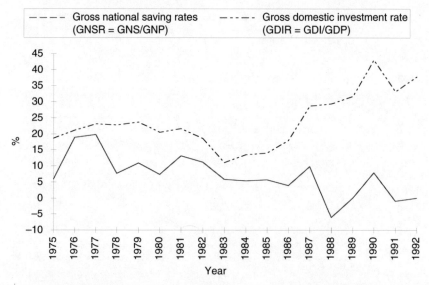

Figure 3(d) The savings–investment gap Tanzania. *Source:* IMF, GFS, IFS

To the extent that income levels remain extremely low and economic performance has been unstable and depressed in these economies during the prolonged period, as in the rest of the region, it may not be surprising that the savings–investment performance just discussed is so poor. Many statistical studies have explained aggregate savings performance in terms of income, economic growth, the return on savings, and other exogenous variables, such as the terms of trade, exports and foreign capital flows.[10] All these studies confirm that income and growth are the main determinants of overall savings. Hence it is possible to argue that recovery in the adjustment period is too recent and fragile to have been translated into a virtuous circle of high growth–savings–investment. Noting that in other countries high savings were preceded by fast growth, the World Bank study (1994a) concludes that 'Africa is still trapped in a vicious circle of low growth and low savings' (p. 186).

3.1.4 Problems of measurement

Nevertheless, caution must be exercised when interpreting trends derived from national accounts statistics. First, it should be noted that aggregate domestic and national savings are calculated as residuals from other components of national income. Therefore they could contain errors from the estimation of other variables. Secondly, it is recognized that a substantial part of domestic savings, capital formation and other economic transactions has not been captured in the official statistics. This is due both to non-monetized activities and to informal transactions that do not pass through official institutions and channels. For example, in Malawi, where almost 90 per cent of the population live in the rural area, 69 per cent of the total income of rural households was accounted for by non-monetized components in 1980/1, showing hardly any change from 1968/9, when an estimate of 70 per cent was reported (Nissanke et al. 1991).

Further, the high degree of uncertainty and instability characterizing the political and economic environments is known to have kept economic activities of a significant proportion of private agents away from the 'official' economy (Nissanke 1997). The so-called 'second' economy is indeed firmly anchored in African traditional values and social structures, which are characterized by the dominance of relatively autonomous networks bound by kinship, tribe, religion or community ties. These networks span rural/urban boundaries (Aron et al. 1997). The size of this second economy in Africa is estimated to be substantial.

For example, Bagachwa and Naho (1994) show that, because of incomplete coverage, official statistics for Tanzania grossly underestimate GDP and its components. They estimate that the 'second' economy in Tanzania has grown from 20 per cent of official GDP in the late 1960s to a sizeable 40 per cent of GDP since the mid-1980s.[11] Over time the 'second economy' has become an important source of livelihood, employment and income for most households. These estimates cast doubt on the reliability of macroeconomic aggregates and the gloomy picture painted by official statistics. Mans (1994) reports, for example, that Tanzania's domestic savings could have been as high as 13 per cent of GDP in 1986–91, if an estimate of unofficial exports (private transfers from abroad which help finance 'own funds' imports) is included. As part of unrecorded transactions, the problem of *demonetization* and *capital flight*, discussed in Chapter 2.6 should also be noted, as these conditions constitute a large proportion of the substantial leakage of domestic savings.

3.2 Financial structure in Ghana[12]

3.2.1 *Formal finance*

Ghana's formal banking system comprises the Bank of Ghana (the central bank), eight commercial banks, three development banks (DFIs), three merchant banks and 123 small unit rural banks. In addition, there are several types of formal non-banking financial institutions (NBFIs), including a stock exchange, numerous insurance companies, the Social Security and National Insurance Trust (SSNIT), building societies, a leasing company, two discount houses and leasing companies. However, by the end of 1992 the banks still accounted for 77 per cent of the total assets of the financial system.

With 25 per cent growth in the number of primary commercial bank branches in 1976–88 and the establishment of 120 rural banks since 1976, bank density in Ghana increased from 1.9 branches per 100,000 inhabitants in 1976 to over 3.2 branches in 1988, then it fell to 2.9 in 1992 with the rationalization of banking operations carried out as part of financial sector reform measures. As of 1993, there were 466 bank branches spread unevenly over the country. Despite the relatively high rate of banking diffusion in the region, Ghana ranks second only to Zaire in terms of financial depth, as shown below.

The Ghana Commercial Bank (GCB), Barclays Bank of Ghana (BBG), Standard Chartered Bank of Ghana (SBG) and the Social Security Bank (SSB) dominate the commercial banking sector.[13] GCB is government-owned, while BBG and SBG are foreign-controlled with 40 per cent of shares owned by the government. SSB, established in 1977, is wholly owned by the Social Security and National Insurance Trust. The four larger banks control over 90 per cent of the assets of the commercial banking sector. With the largest branch network, the GCB accounts for about 50 per cent of the deposits mobilized by the banking sector.

The merchant banks provide services, including trade and export finance, supplier credits and bill discounting. Besides the government-owned merchant bank, which holds 7 per cent of the deposit base, two private foreign-owned merchant banks, Ecobank and Continental Acceptance, were established in 1990. The former has so far been targeted at large corporations, while the latter specializes in the purchase and placement of commercial paper and securities. These new banks are reported to have exerted some much needed competitive pressure in the commercial banking sector.

The three DFIs, established by the central bank, are the National Investment Bank (NIB, 1963), the Agricultural Development Bank (ADB, 1965) and the Bank for Housing and Construction (BHC, 1973).[14] Despite the provision of finance from external sources and refinancing schemes evolved by the Bank of Ghana, the initial success of these institutions was soon replaced by acute insolvency problems due to high default rates and non-performing loans in high-risk sectors. Poor performance was reflected in several ways: large negative profits; meagre paid-up capital and reserve funds; and increasing reliance of their operations on loans from the central bank and external sources (25 per cent from the central bank and 75 per cent from foreign bilateral and multilateral donors). These DFIs were technically insolvent before restructuring.

After substantial recapitalization through the FINSAP programme, DFIs began to mobilize savings and improved their operational performance indicators. Faced with chronic insolvency problems from specialized lending to high-risk areas, they shifted from term lending to 'universal' banking, away from small borrowers towards short-term, self-liquidating loans to ensure their operational survival. For example, the share of smallholder credit in ADB's total lending declined to 15 per cent in 1992, while the share of lending to agriculture fell to 30 per cent. Short-term loans now constitute over 80 per cent of ADB's lending.

In Ghana a system of unit banks, called rural banks, was established in rural areas from 1976 to serve small-scale transactors in the mobilization of saving and the extension of credit. They are owned and managed by members of the local community and it was hoped they could assist in agricultural development and rural-based industrialization through loans to cottage industries. The Bank of Ghana holds preference shares, equivalent to one-third of the initial share capital, but the capital base is weak and paid-up capital, income surplus and reserves constitute only 7.5 per cent of total resources.[15] The major sources of funds are deposit liabilities, which made up 70 per cent of total resources in 1988.

The rural banks have been moderately successful at savings mobilization in the rural areas. In 1993 their share of total deposits mobilized and credit extended to the agriculture sector by both banks and credit unions stood at 27 per cent and 18 per cent respectively. However, this share has to be evaluated in terms of a general decline in the volume of credit available to the agricultural sector. Rural banks have followed this general trend, and increasingly extend credit to trading rather than agricultural activities. Moreover, like the commercial banks, Ghana's rural banks have accumulated excess liquidity (Chapter 4). It is reported that managers of the financially sounder rural banks have had to resort to low-risk investment in government securities to avoid many of the cases of bad debt. Many rural banks have become financially distressed and were closed down or restructured as part of the Rural Finance Project of FINSAP.

Among several NBFIs, the Social Security and National Insurance Trust dominates, accounting for about half of assets held by this sector. The SSNIT, which is also the sole shareholder of the Social Security Bank, runs mandatory pension and social insurance schemes for government employees. In the early years it used to invest its mobilized funds in low-yielding government stocks and paper far above the 50 per cent statutory level, reaching a peak of 62 per cent in 1983. After being freed from this statutory requirement in 1986, it began to branch out into real estate development as an inflation hedge, reducing the share of treasury bills to 30 per cent of its portfolio in 1987. In 1992 investment in short-term treasury bills and the Bank of Ghana bills and real estate accounted for over 80 per cent of total investments. So far it has failed to become a source of long-term finance for the economy, although it has developed a dominant position in stock markets.

There are about twenty registered insurance companies, four of which are foreign-owned. The State Insurance Corporation, government-owned, has long accounted for 80 per cent of insurance business. In the early years, government securities, cash holding and deposits with the banks accounted for most of their investment portfolio. Though these assets still dominate, the insurance companies have lately begun to diversify into consumer credit, mortgage loans, credit guarantee schemes for the import trade, and the holding of shares in the Consolidated Discount House and the Ghana Export Finance Company.

The Consolidated Discount House (CDH), jointly owned by eight banks and six insurance companies, was formally institutionalized in 1987 as an interbank intermediary for short-term assets in the money market. A second discount house, SDH, was set up in 1991, with assistance from the IFC, to provide a secondary market for commercial paper. Their principal portfolios are in Bank of Ghana bills, treasury bills, cocoa bills, grain bills, bankers' acceptances, negotiable certificates of deposit and government stocks. However, commercial paper has not featured significantly, and Bank of Ghana bills and government paper account for about 90 per cent of their assets, related to the attempt by the Bank of Ghana to increase open market operations and switch to indirect monetary control in 1990.

The capital (equity) market has not played an active role in the financial system yet, although the Ghana Stock Exchange was inaugurated in 1990. The number of listed companies has remained constant at seventeen since the late 1970s, and market capitalization has been low. Only in 1993–4 did capitalization increase substantially, with levels reaching those prevailing in Kenya and Zimbabwe. This increase was entirely triggered by the government's decision to sell its minority shares in several listed companies, including the Ashanti Goldfield Company, which has attracted foreign investors and large domestic investors such as SSNIT. There have been several new initiatives by merchant banks to set up venture capital funds and other instruments for large investors.

3.2.2 Informal and semi-formal finance

Non-commercial arrangements have traditionally included *susu* groups (ROSCAs, see Chapter 2.6) and loans from family, friends and neighbours for credit needs. Credit unions are popular among low-income civil servants in urban areas and in the rural Upper West Region, where the influence of the Catholic Church is strong. After a decline in numbers due to financial difficulties, the 250 surviving credit unions have recently reorganized with donor assistance.[16]

The commercial section of informal finance is dominated by *susu* collectors, moneylenders and traders in both rural and urban areas. *Susu* collectors are predominantly traders but also teachers and public employees who operate on a part-time basis. About 500 collectors, who operate among market women, have been registered with Greater Accra *Susu* Collectors Co-operative Society.

Based on similar principles to those of the *susu* collectors, *susu* companies emerged in the larger centres of Ghana. However, unlike *susu* collectors, they provided savers with guaranteed credit. Deposits were not returned to the saver monthly, as in the case of the *susu* collectors, but were held by the company for at least six months, after which the depositor could withdraw the savings and/or obtain a loan. These companies expanded rapidly in the 1980s, filling one of the critical gaps in financial services. However, imprudent management of funds by many companies led to frequent collapse and prompted the Bank of Ghana to regulate their activities. Under the new regulations governing savings and loan companies, only two institutions were registered by 1995, although others had applied.

The case study highlights several general characteristics of informal finance in Ghana. In the early years of the interventionist regime, rapid growth of the informal financial sector occurred at the same time that the formal financial sector appeared to be suffering from a process of financial 'shallowing'. This is indicated by a steady decline in the ratio of deposit money to M_2 from 63 per cent in 1975 to 44 per cent in 1984. The ratio of claims of domestic credit on the private sector to GDP fell from 14 per cent in 1977 to 6 per cent in 1984 (see Chapter 4). However, despite the extensive liberalization measures implemented in recent years, informal savings and credit facilities have continued to expand significantly. Today, informal financial operations remain distinctly vibrant and robust in comparison with formal institutions, which by comparison are either financially distressed or extremely risk-averse in their asset and portfolio management. Savings mobilization and lending operations by the informal sector are estimated to have increased by 50 per cent in 1990–1 alone.

Thus informal units are not strictly parallel markets, flourishing only in response to repressive policies (Aryeetey 1994). Instead, they appear to thrive on increased economic activity, which has particularly generated demand for short-term credit and saving among traders and consumers. Their flexibility and advantages in transaction costs and risk management imply the presence of sustained comparative advantages.

In particular, informal units in Ghana are extremely significant in mobilizing savings. As most 'informal savings mobilizers' (including *susu* collectors) use bank facilities for deposits, a substantial part of rural and urban financial savings end up in banks. It is estimated that informal sector activities (excluding non-commercial personal transactions among friends and family members) are responsible for the initial mobilization of at least 55 per cent of total financial savings.[17] In contrast to their dynamism as savings mobilizers, informal units are much less significant as independent financial intermediaries. Their main intermediary role could be performed through links with banks, as is the case with *susu* collectors. However, this potential has not been exploited, owing to conservative asset liability management by formal institutions and the absence of appropriate financial instruments to utilize these savings, which exhibit a highly synchronized monthly cycle (Aryeetey 1992b, 1994; Steel and Aryeetey 1995). While various informal units have increasingly used deposit facilities offered by formal institutions to safeguard their funds, in general, links between the two sectors through credit provision are not observed on any significant scale.

On the demand side, the complementary use of informal and formal finance is not widely observed, and competitive relations have not developed between the two sectors in any significant scale, owing to market segmentation. Given these general characteristics, and the fragmented and short-term nature of their operations, informal financial agents are unable to respond to SMEs, which require a larger loan with longer maturity. Thus informal finance is rarely used by SMEs in Ghana.

3.3 Financial structure in Malawi

3.3.1 *Formal finance*

Malawi's formal financial system is dominated by the central bank, the Reserve Bank of Malawi (RBM), and two large commercial banks, the National Bank of Malawi (NBM) and the Commercial Bank of Malawi (CBM). Other financial institutions include a newly established commercial/merchant bank (INDEBANK Financial Services); development finance institutions (the Malawi Development Corporation, MDC; the Agricultural Development and Marketing corporation, ADMARC; INDEBANK's off-shoot, the Investment and Development Fund (INDEFUND), and the Small Enterprise Development Organization of Malawi, SEDOM, 1983); a corporate bank (Finance Corporation of Malawi), the New Building Society and a few finance houses; the Post Office Savings Bank (POSB) and a number of insurance agencies. In addition, the Malawi Union of Savings and Credit

Co-operatives (MUSCCO) acts as an umbrella organization for 115 savings and credit co-operatives (SACCOs). At the end of 1992 commercial banks accounted for 68 per cent of the total assets of the financial system (excluding the RBM), INDEBANK (a new commercial and merchant bank) for 7 per cent, financing houses for 6 per cent, the building society for 11 per cent and the POSB for 8 per cent.

The number of branches and agencies of commercial banks and the POSB together rose from 185 in 1967 to 331 in 1988. However, owing to faster population growth, the ratio of banks to people actually fell, from 22,300 in 1967 to 25,000 in 1988.[18] Bank density is much higher in urban centres than in rural areas, as the two large commercial banks have branches only in urban areas. However, they operate mobile units to 100 rural points fortnightly, which handle deposits only.

The National Bank of Malawi holds 76 per cent of commercial bank deposits and over 60 per cent of assets, with the Commercial Bank of Malawi holding the rest. The third commercial bank, INDEBANK Financial Services, largely serves the corporate sector. Although on paper the two largest banks, the NBM and CBM, appear to be under mixed ownership, in practice there is significant government control, with a web of extensive interlocking shareholding, involving Press Holdings Corporation, ADMARC and Malawi Development Corporation (MDC). Press Holdings is a major shareholder in NBM and CBM. ADMARC is a shareholder in the first bank, and MDC in the second bank. Indeed, all three have diverse interests in various sectors of the Malawian economy. These interlocking ownerships have long impeded competition.[19]

In addition to their dominance in terms of asset size, these two banks accounted for around 80 per cent of the total deposit liabilities of financial institutions throughout the post-independence years. Their share of total domestic credit, excluding the central bank, still exceeds 50 per cent. Though increasingly mutually competitive, CBM and NMB still operate a number of bilateral agreements, for example in the division of mobile bank services and the location of sub-branches.

Relying heavily on foreign resources for their operations, Malawi's DFIs have not mobilized domestic savings, and their financial performance has generally been unsatisfactory. MDC was established in 1964 with equity participation by international financial institutions and acts as a holding company with investments in major Malawian firms. Adam *et al.* (1992) identify poor project selection, weak management and high gearing as the key factors in MDC's feeble portfolio. ADMARC was instituted in 1971 primarily to develop a marketing and distribution network for smallholder agriculture,[20] but also to promote the agricultural and industrial sectors as an investment holding company. While its crop marketing and distribution have proved profitable, ADMARC has experienced poor financial performance in its investment and development operations.

INDEBANK was initially established as a DFI in 1972 to provide equity capital, as well as medium- and long-term loans for new and existing industries and agricultural ventures. As its shareholders include four foreign organizations in addition to ADMARC, it has had considerable access to external finance. It encouraged joint ventures with foreign partners, as well as promoting joint ventures with Press Holdings, ADMARC and MDC, which together form about 60 per cent of its loan portfolio. It appeared to have enjoyed better performance, reporting higher pre-tax returns than MDC. In more recent years, as a newly established commercial/merchant bank, INDEBANK has been given licence to accept deposits, to float a local currency bond, to issue letters of credit and bankers' acceptances, and other merchant activities.

The portfolio of these DFIs was restructured through a fairly comprehensive asset swap programme involving Press, ADMARC and MDC, implemented in 1984–6. A series of divestitures was also carried out by MDC and ADMARC in 1984–9. However, Adam et al. (1992) conclude that the primary object of the asset swaps was to stem the losses of Press Holdings, and the main benefits of the process accrued to Press at the expense of MDC, and to a lesser extent ADMARC. Although the short-run effect of the asset swap was positive, it appears that the effect on the long-run health of portfolios is less certain.

While these larger DFIs have at least managed to generate positive, though minimal, pre-tax returns, the other two institutions (INDEFUND and SEDOM) specializing in providing services to SMEs have frequently shown an operational loss. INDEFUND, established in 1981, was targeted at medium-scale Malawian-owned businesses to provide advisory and training services, as well as medium- and long-term loans for start-up and working capital. With financial assistance from the European Union, SEDOM (established in 1983) specializes in the provision of term loans, technical assistance and advisory services to small-scale enterprises owned by indigenous Malawians. However, inadequate resources and staff shortages have made operational efficiency difficult for both institutions. In particular, in-house capacity to appraise, evaluate and monitor projects seems grossly inadequate. In the early years of its operations, it is reported, INDEFUND had arrears as high as 40 per cent and cumulative losses amounting to K0.9 million at the end of 1986, compared with an annual income of K0.6 million and K4.8 million of capital employed. Its financial position has been improving in the 1990s. SEDOM has also faced a rising level of arrears in its overall portfolio. The transaction costs of INDEFUND and SEDOM are also known to be extremely high: in 1988 INDEFUND and SEDOM incurred costs of K0.67 and K0.44, respectively, for every K1.00 lent.

Malawi's NBFIs include a few finance houses, the New Building Society, the Post Office Savings Bank and a number of insurance companies. Altogether they account for under 20 per cent of total assets held by the formal financial system. The majority of NBFIs are deposit-taking institutions, which are in direct competition with the commercial banks. The finance houses provide various financial services, such as leasing finance for the acquisition of capital equipment for agricultural, industrial and commercial enterprises; hire-purchase; block discounts of commercial debt; and import–export factoring. They accept fixed deposits of varying maturities at high interest rates. The New Building Society has started offering several deposit instruments of varying maturities with a low minimum deposit balance requirement.[21]

The Post Office Savings Bank has the most extensive coverage of all the formal institutions in the rural areas, where nearly 90 per cent of the country's population live. POSB has 286 deposit-collecting points and has mobilized over 12 per cent of total savings by formal financial institutions. Interest earned by depositors at POSB is tax-exempt, and this competitive edge in mobilizing resources over other financial institutions helps to explain the recent growth of its deposits. While a significant portion of the POSB's deposits appear to be corporate funds placed there because of the tax exemption, deposit liabilities in the POSB are noticeably affected by changes in rural cash income and by remittances of 'deferred payments' by Malawian migrant workers. As was historically required by statute, the POSB used to lend exclusively to the government through the purchase of government securities, providing an assured supply of credit. However, since 1989 it has been allowed to broaden its investments, and has done so primarily by placing funds with the New Building Society.

Given the lack of alternative instruments for investment, many NBFIs often resort to holding government stocks or deposits at commercial banks. Only small proportions of these deposits are for transaction requirements and the rest are treated as investment, illustrating the perceived scarcity of other investment avenues. No formal money markets exist, and the limited range and small volume of commercial paper are partly a result of the narrow base of the monocultural economy. Despite efforts in recent years, securities markets are almost non-existent in Malawi, and the range of non-government short-term paper is very limited. The primary commodity sector (tobacco and tea) has long established its own payment arrangements, which do not call for a significant volume of commercial paper. From time to time, small numbers of bills of exchange have been discounted by commercial banks, including those drawn by exporters of agro-based manufactured products, and some local bills by large manufacturers of agro-based products on large wholesalers. However, the volume of such bills has been declining in the 1980s. Treasury bills and other government stocks remain the major debt paper in the economy. By far the largest proportion of treasury bills has been held by commercial banks, and their shares of treasury bills remain in the range of 80 per cent to 90 per cent in recent decades.

Apart from the interbank credit arrangements existing among the commercial banks, inter-financial institutional claims are mainly in the form of deposits of NBFIs at commercial banks and at the central bank. The POSB and INDEBANK place their deposits at the Reserve Bank of Malawi, while other NBFIs, such as insurance companies and the New Building Society, hold their deposits at commercial banks, which exacerbates the problem of 'excess liquidity' at the commercial banks.

3.3.2 *Informal and semi-formal finance*

While non-commercial lending and social welfare schemes run by employers, friends and relatives account for a large part of informal credit extension in Malawi, commercial lenders such as landlords,[22] traders, grain millers, smallholder farmers and moneylenders (*katapila*) are also actively involved in credit provision. Further, many households participate in group associations, such as credit and savings associations (CSAs), which owe their origin to indigenous co-operative behaviour, based on solidarity and friendship. There was a boom in the formation of these associations, in the 1980s, when 94 per cent of the CSAs and 78 per cent of the SCAs are reported to have been formed.

Chipeta and Mkandawire (1991) report that the total credit extended by the informal financial sector (including employers, estate owners and personal loans among friends/families) was estimated at K281.5 million in 1988, amounting to 6.5 per cent of GDP. This compares with total credit extended to the private sector by the formal sector of K77.5 million. Thus informal sector lending to the private sector is at least three times larger than that of the formal sector. It is also estimated that the informal sector mobilized savings amounting to K265.6 million in 1989, while the formal sector mobilized savings of only K72.9 million that year.

The country case study (Chipeta and Mkandawire 1996a) suggests that the informal sector has grown significantly in the early 1990s despite liberalization of the formal financial sector. Informal finance continues to provide small and short-term savings and loans, the demand for which exhibits extremely high seasonal variations. Interlinked loans[23] provided by estate owners and traders dominate rural finance and are commonly used for production purposes, such as the purchase of fertilizer. However, as Bolnick (1992) notes, informal financial transactions occur only between close associates, except the expensive *katapila* loans, and informal financial services are not readily available to SMEs.

There are three types of semi-informal institution which operate in rural Malawi. A government-sponsored group lending scheme to smallholders, the Smallholder Agricultural Credit administration (SACA), began its operations in 1968 and is currently being replaced by the Malawi Rural Finance Company. Also operating are MUSCCO and a Grameen-type bank known as the Malawi Mudzi Fund.[24]

Administered by the Ministry of Agriculture, SACA's credit provision and repayments are often conducted in kind, as fertilizers, seed and insecticides, through farmers' clubs (the group lending scheme) or selling maize through ADMARC. In 1991 25 per cent of smallholder farmers are estimated to have been covered by the SACA-administered credit scheme. Although the SACA is known to have operated in favour of larger smallholders, the repayment rate has historically exceeded 90 per cent, with strict monitoring and enforcement rules in place.

MUSCCO, established in 1980, is an umbrella organization which aims to promote credit unions – SACCOs. It provides management assistance, training and loans to SACCOs to a maximum 50 per cent of their shares, while the SACCOs themselves provide loans to individual members. Short-term loans from the MUSCCO are used by the SACCOs for liquidity and to on-lend to members. The SACCOs now have 75 per cent of their assets in loans and 15 per cent in investments. SACCOs' business loans have been targeted at crop and livestock production (52 per cent), trade (28 per cent), manufacturing (15 per cent) and service activities (3 per cent). SACCO members interested in developing or expanding their businesses are referred to the Development of Malawian Traders Trust (DEMATT) for further technical and financial assistance. MUSCCO has experienced rapid growth, and at the end of 1992 represented 115 SACCOs with 18,000 members. However, both MUSSCO and SACCOs have an historical recovery rate of only 60 per cent.

The final semi-formal institution covered in the survey is the Mudzi Fund. Initiated in 1990, it is an experimental scheme to provide financial services to the poorest of rural households. The aim is to generate off-farm self-employment, mostly for women, based on income-generating micro-enterprise activities. Not surprisingly, the Mudzi Fund has demonstrated that the poor have an important potential for savings mobilization, but its loan recovery rate has not been high and operational costs have been more than three times the value of loans disbursed.

Since the heavy reliance of all three institutions on uncertain foreign aid flows makes it hard for them to operate on a sustainable basis, some reorganizations have been attempted in recent years, and now all the three institutions accept deposits. In addition, some of the thirty registered NGOs in Malawi have begun to operate savings and credit schemes, adopting group lending approaches.

The country study confirms earlier results suggesting that indirect and direct credit links between the formal and informal sectors are largely insignificant in Malawi. Only direct deposit links between formal and informal agents are of any observed importance. This implies that there is a high degree of market segmentation in Malawi, as was also the case in Ghana. Chipeta (1994) notes that in SME finance there is insignificant spill-over, in the form of credit demand rationed out by the formal sector, into the informal sector, nor can a complementary relationship between formal and informal credit be discerned. The lack of complementarity and competition between the two sectors, resulting from negligible overlapping demand, severely constrains the potential of informal finance to be exploited.

3.4 Financial structure in Nigeria

3.4.1 Formal finance

Along with Kenya and Zimbabwe, the formal financial system in Nigeria is one of the most diversified in sub-Saharan Africa. It is comprised of a large number of heterogeneous institutions under mixed ownership. At the end of 1992 there were sixty-six commercial banks, fifty-four merchant banks and 401 community banks licensed by the Central Bank of Nigeria. There are also a large number of banking institutions which are not licensed by the Central Bank of Nigeria, including several DFIs, 145 mortgage finance institutions, 228 people's banks and the Nigerian Export–Import Bank (NEXIM). In addition, there are at least ninety-two insurance companies and several reinsurance companies, over 700 finance houses,[25] several pension funds and the National Economic Reconstruction Fund (NERFUND). Capital market institutions include three licensed discount houses, and there are 132 foreign exchange bureaus.

Indeed, the most vivid response to financial deregulation has been a very rapid expansion in the total number of institutions since 1986. For example, between 1985 and 1992 the number of commercial banks increased from twenty-eight to sixty-six and merchant banks increased from twelve to fifty-four. Rapid expansion in banking institutions has resulted in a significant improvement in bank density: the number of people per bank branch fell from 57,000 in 1986 to 29,000 in 1992. Commercial banks alone increased their branches from 1,297 to 2,269 between 1985 and 1992, one-third of them in rural areas. Over the same period merchant bank branches rose from twenty-six to 116.

This proliferation of banking institutions, facilitated by a very liberal licensing policy, has created major regulatory problems. In particular, it appears that the primary interest of many of the new banks was not in banking operations but in the possibility of capturing considerable 'arbitrage rents' in the foreign exchange markets, where banks had secure access to allocations of foreign exchange in a weekly auction. Banks could make huge short-term returns on rents from this auction system (Stein and Lewis 1996). However, their deposit base and operations were unstable and the commercial viability of their banking operations was in question.[26] Though, in response to this emerging condition, a system of regulation and supervision was hastily instituted, it has been operationally ineffectual, as discussed below. Thus, despite this belated attempt, the number of banks under distress and classified as technically insolvent has increased in recent years, as will be discussed in Chapter 4.

With the entry of new private banks, the share of private ownership in paid-up equity capital increased to 70 per cent. The share of the federal government, which held a controlling share before deregulation, declined with the commencement of the privatization programme when fourteen federally owned banks were denationalized in late 1992. Foreign ownership accounts for only 8 per cent of commercial banking, with a limit of 40 per cent on foreign shareholdings in any single bank. In contrast to the other three sample countries, public ownership does not appear to be a prominent feature of the Nigeria's banking system today. However, the larger banks, which together account for the majority of commercial banking assets, have been government-owned, reflecting the indigenization programme pursued in the 1970s, as in the other sample countries.

Despite increased competition between commercial and merchant banks, with the latter moving into universal banking operation, commercial banks still account for about 80 per cent of savings and time deposits mobilized by all banking and non-banking institutions. The top five banks, including First Bank, United Bank for Africa and the Union Bank of Nigeria, with assets exceeding N5.0 billion each, account for 47 per cent of all deposits. The scale of their assets can be compared with the less than N1 billion of assets of smaller commercial banks. Thus the commercial banking sector is characterized by the skewed structure of market power in favour of the larger banks. Commercial banks also account for over three-quarters of total outstanding credit. The share of merchant banks in deposits is about 12 per cent, and, except the largest, the merchant banks are privately owned.

There are three federally licensed institutions which operate as DFIs, under an umbrella society, the Association of Nigerian Development Finance Institutions.[27] These three DFIs together account for only 3 per cent of the assets of Nigeria's entire financial system. They do not mobilize deposits but depend for their lending operations on Central Bank credit lines, penalty funds from other financial institutions[28] and grants from government, bilateral and multilateral sources. Having persistently distributed 'political' loans over the years, the non-performing loans of DFIs are known to reach 80 per cent to 90 per cent of their portfolio (see Chapter 4).

In addition, the federal government, the Central Bank and the African Development Bank established the National Economic Reconstruction Fund (NERFUND) in 1988 to provide local and foreign funds (with medium to long-term maturities of between five and ten years) to small and medium-scale wholly Nigerian enterprises. Drawing on capital grants and subsidised loans, the NERFUND channels its loans through commercial and merchant banks for on-lending to the targeted borrowers. At the request of the participating banks, which are responsible for risk assessment and the administration of the NERFUND loans, a preliminary long-term insurance scheme has been instituted to address the high risks of SME lending.

There are several other new officially supported institutions established in recent years, including community banks, people's banks and the Nigerian Export–Import Bank. Community banks, introduced in 1990, are unit banks similar to the rural banks in Ghana. They operate with a very low capital base in rural areas under a community development association (Alashi 1995). The minimum paid-up capital is N250,000 (0.5 per cent of the requirements of a commercial bank) with matching capital from the federal government to a maximum of N500,000. These banks are supervised by the National Board for Community Banks and regulated with respect to capital adequacy, liquidity ratios and provisions for non-performing loans, etc. Their deposits are insured by the Nigerian Deposit Insurance Corporation (NDIC), which also provides technical assistance. Community banks are not allowed to engage in foreign exchange transactions, corporate banking or non-banking functions. The number of community banks continues to grow, with over 1,000 operating in 1994, and 60 per cent of them operate in rural areas. However, Alashi (1995) points out that they generate an operating loss, and have difficulty covering overhead costs. In 1994, 151 community banks were classified as distressed and fifty were considered insolvent. Furthermore, the number *actually* distressed may exceed this estimate, particularly in urban areas. As with similar institutions, their credits are skewed heavily towards commerce and trading activities.

The people's banks, similar to the Grameen Bank of Bangladesh, are designed to serve low-income earners and to use collateral substitutes, such as peer pressure, within a group lending scheme. However, their operations are heavily dependent on government donations, with a negligible contribution from mobilized savings. Although they have recorded repayment rates of 85 per cent, they are known to incur very high operational costs, as will be discussed further in Chapter 6.

An array of non-banking financial institutions operate in Nigeria, many of which are closely linked with banks through a web of interlocking ownership.[29] Finance houses are the newest addition to the system, most of them having been established since the liberalization of the financial sector. Registered under the Companies Act, they are privately owned investment companies engaged in the provision of loans, hire-purchase, equipment leasing, factoring, project and export financing, debt administration and fund management. Finance houses are not allowed to operate cheque accounts, trade in foreign exchange or participate in clearing house activities. Many finance houses grew out of semi-formal financial institutions and have no banking licence, although they are now regulated by the Bank and other Financial Institutions Decree (BOFID) of 1991. They operate on average with N5 million to N6 million of paid-up capital, one-tenth that of average commercial banks (Soyibo 1996a). While banks collect over-the-counter deposits, finance houses are required by law to create liabilities by collecting lumpier 'wholesale loans' of not less than N100,000 from customers, and they offer extremely high returns, which are often paid up front. This has led to a large-scale shift of deposits from banks to the less regulated finance houses. Liabilities usually mature within a year, and over half have a maturity of up to three months. The investible funds they mobilize are not protected by deposit insurance.

Mainly offering short-term funds to small and medium-scale entrepreneurs with limited capital and collateral, finance houses have increased their share of credit operations, fluctuating between 15 per cent and 25 per cent of formal credit allocation in recent years. Less rigorous credit assessment procedures are applied, and there is less emphasis on collateral. Hence, the risk exposure of finance house investments is higher than that of banks. Yet they are not subject to such regulations as capital adequacy ratios and reserve requirements. It is not surprising that financial houses have registered high failure rates, with over 50 per cent of their borrowing (i.e. deposits) failing to meet matured obligations in 1993 (Soyibo 1996a). Indeed, as in NBFIs in Kenya, financial houses have been used by banks to circumvent central bank regulations. Many banks have set up subsidiary finance houses, and those of the larger banks tend to control a substantial share of the market. Finance houses and banks are also linked because 60 per cent of the liquid assets of finance houses have been kept as deposits in the banking system, despite unfavourable differentials in rates of return. The remaining finance house assets are invested in treasury bills and other money market instruments.

Looking at other categories of NBFI, despite the fact that over 100 companies operate in the insurance market, insurance premiums constitute an insignificant proportion, 3 per cent to 4 per cent, of financial savings. Funds mobilized in the insurance market tend to be short-term, while mobilized life insurance premiums have experienced negative real growth. Nearly 60 per cent of mobilized funds have been invested by insurance companies in government securities, far exceeding the stipulated share. Thus as in many other sub-Saharan countries, insurance funds constitute a readily available source of finance for budget deficits.

The National Provident Fund runs a state-administered pension scheme, while over 800 privately administered pension schemes operate as either insured or uninsured agents. While the state fund is required to invest in federal government stocks only, privately run pension funds must invest equally in the stocks and shares of private companies and in government stocks. In reality, they invest mainly in government securities and short-term bank deposits. As with insurance funds, savings mobilized by these pension and provident schemes have experienced negative growth in Nigeria's highly inflationary and unstable macroeconomic environment. On the other hand, primary mortgage finance institutions have been expanding rapidly, attracting funding from contractual savings schemes.[30] The Federal Mortgage Bank (FMBN) acts as the regulatory agency for all 145 mortgage institutions.

Finally, the Nigerian Stock Exchange operates four trading floors in Lagos, Ibadan, Port Harcourt and Kano. The floors are regulated by the Securities and Exchange Commission (SEC). Trading volume has been small, with a sharp decline in real terms during the 1980s. By the early 1990s, total market capitalization amounted to 6 per cent of GDP. Only a limited number of private equities have been listed, most of them the result of indigenization programmes of the early years or the more recent privatization programme.[31] There have not been active secondary markets, as most institutional investors such as pension funds and insurance companies acquire equities under government directives. Prices of new issues are set low by the SEC, while transaction costs are very high.

3.4.2 *Informal and semi-formal finance*

The heterogeneous composition of the informal and semi-formal financial sector in Nigeria is comparable to that found in Ghana. Informal finance, particularly in rural areas, is conducted both in cash and in kind. As in Ghana, cash finance is commonly carried out by *esusu* collectors or *esusu* groups. *Usufruct* loans pledged on trees, rubber, farmland or labour, or other interlinked credit transactions, are commonly extended by money-lenders and traders, particularly in the non-Islamic southern regions (Soyibo 1996b).

Although the overall size of the informal sector is hard to measure, estimates available for *esusu* groups suggest the high popularity of these arrangements as means of mobilizing savings. In 1989, for example, nearly 20,000 *esusu* clubs operated in the old Oyo State alone, and, with a membership of 1 million, covered 32 per cent of the rural population of the state. The estimated savings mobilized through these *esusu* groups was N69 million per month in 1989. Our fieldwork data confirm that savings mobilized by informal groups are substantial and there has been a steady growth in savings mobilized by informal units and in demand for informal credit. The FAO estimates that about 90 per cent of rural credit needs have been met from informal sources. Udry (1990) also reports that in northern Nigeria the share of formal loans is only 7.5 per cent of total credit provision.

Traders constitute the dominant group of clients for informal finance in both rural areas and urban centres. Besides consumption purposes, informal financial loans and savings are utilized by traders mainly to smooth working capital requirements for their commercial activities. In contrast, informal finance is not used as productive working capital or for investment by small and micro-enterprises on any significant scale, although urban moneylenders do grant loans to small business, and traders operate interlinked credit transactions among farmers. However, as in many countries of sub-Saharan Africa, personal savings or savings mobilized through *esusu* groups constitute the main source of start-up capital for small entrepreneurs. As expected, rural informal savings and credit transactions among farmers exhibit a high seasonality and volatility.

Distinct comparative advantages in transaction costs and risk management have led to the emergence of identifiable market niches, whilst there has not been any discernible convergence of interest rates charged by the different segments of informal finance. Liberalization of formal finance so far has had very little impact either on the market structure of informal finance or on the operations of individual segments. However, liberalization of the formal financial sector has led to a reduction in the savings mobilized by semi-formal institutions, such as the savings and loan companies in the urban areas.

While the deposit facilities (demand and savings accounts) of banking institutions are widely used by informal agents/associations, only a small proportion of moneylenders and *esusu* collectors have so far utilized bank loans and overdraft facilities for on-lending, despite the fact that their limited capital base is known to be a constraint on the expansion of their lending business. The performance of the semi-formal sector has not been encouraging. An exception is the Bauchi State Co-operative Finance Agency (the BSCFA) with strong links with primary co-operatives. It has a good record in loan recovery rates, exceeding 95 per cent over fifteen years. However, these co-operative agencies, including the BSCFA, have acted as a conduit for credit delivery of government subventions and external donor funds, hardly engaging in savings mobilization and hence in financial inter-mediation of locally generated resources.

3.5 Financial structure in Tanzania

3.5.1 *Formal finance*

Tanzania's formal system is much narrower in terms of institutional diversity than the three other case-study countries. It is also the most dominated by direct government ownership. As of 1993, the formal financial sector included the central bank, the Bank of Tanzania, three commercial banks, two thrift (savings) institutions, three development finance institutions, two insurance companies, two contractual savings institutions and one hire-purchase company. The formal financial system was highly regulated, with designated specialization, until 1991, following the nationalization of all financial institutions in 1967. The government owns most institutions, including all three commercial banks, all thrift institutions, the two insurance companies, the single social security institution and the develop-ment banks. Most of the formal financial institutions were concentrated in urban areas. With the exception of the National Bank of Commerce, which has 144 rural branches, none has branches at the rural (district) level.

The three commercial banks are the National Bank of Commerce (NBC); the People's Bank of Zanzibar (PBZ) and the Co-operative and Rural Development Bank (CRDB). The NBC, established in 1967 following the nationalization of nine foreign private banks, is 100 per cent owned by the government. It was the only commercial bank operating on the mainland until the CRDB embarked on commercial banking operations in 1984. The NBC, with its twenty regional offices, 203 branches and 295 mobile agencies spread throughout the country, accounted for 90 per cent of total deposits by deposit-taking institutions in 1970–92. Hence the NBC virtually monopolizes commercial banking in Tanzania, with its total assets thirteen times larger than those of the CRDB. At the same time, it has long been used by government as an agency to channel funds to parastatals, such as the agricultural marketing boards and co-operative unions, in order to cover their working capital requirements and operating losses (see Chapter 4). The NBC continued, until 1991, to extend loans to these parastatals, without matching increases in deposits, drawing heavily on the central bank's discount facilities.

The CRDB is owned by the government (67 per cent), the Bank of Tanzania (25 per cent) and the Co-operative Union of Tanzania (8 per cent), and operates with fifteen regional offices, seventeen branches and nine agencies. It provides short-term credit and overdraft facilities primarily to co-operative unions and primary societies. The CRDM also operates the Rural Savings and Credit Scheme, based on deposit mobilization by individual savings and credit societies (SCSs).[32] It also acts as a development bank on the basis of funds from the central bank and others. The People's Bank of Zanzibar operates only in Zanzibar, where it serves as the sole commercial bank and as a quasi-central banker to the Zanzibar government. All three commercial banks have long been known to be illiquid and insolvent, largely drawing on the discount facilities of the Bank of Tanzania. The lending to deposit ratio of commercial banks rose from 50 per cent in 1984 to 84 per cent in 1986 and then shot up to over 130 per cent in 1989–91 (see below).

In 1993 two new commercial banks, the Meridien BIAO Bank and the Standard Chartered Bank, began operations, while the private Bergolaise Bank was allowed to open a representative office. A new NBFI, the Tanzanian Venture Capital Fund, was launched in 1993, and a leasing company was in the process of being created in 1995.

The development finance institutions are the Tanzania Investment Bank (TIB), the Tanzania Housing Bank (THB) and the Tanganyika Development Finance Company (TDFL). The TIB was set up as a statutory corporation in 1970 with a 60 per cent share owned by the government, 30 per cent by the National Bank of Commerce and 10 per cent by the National Insurance Corporation. Based on loanable funds channelled by the multilateral agencies, it has provided medium and long-term foreign exchange loans mainly to industrial state enterprises, as an on-lending agency for the government.

With the worsening recovery rates and the exhaustion of external sources over time, the financial condition of the TIB deteriorated considerably in the 1980s. The proportion of *de facto* non-performing loans had increased to over 90 per cent by 1990, compared with the situation in 1980, when the delinquency rate was a mere 17 per cent (Kimei 1994).

In contrast, the TDFL, established in 1962 as a joint venture with 24 per cent of shares owned by government and the rest held by foreign financial institutions, has financed mainly medium-scale private enterprises. It has also provided equity funds to the private sector. Although its operation was scaled down in the 1980s in the generally difficult investment climate, it has been less exposed to political interference than the TIB and its financial condition has been better, with just over 50 per cent of its portfolio as non-performing loans.

The THB, established in 1972, and now with twenty-one branches country-wide, has a monopoly of the provision of loans for residential and commercial housing construction. It mobilizes fixed deposits, but can borrow from the Workers and Farmers Housing Development Fund. Government owns 47 per cent of the bank's shares, while the two government-owned NBFIs, National Insurance Corporation and National Provident Fund, own 30 per cent and 23 per cent of the shares, respectively. About 20 per cent of loans were extended to the government-owned National Housing Corporation. Like all the other institutions, it has a large proportion of non-performing loans, estimated to be equivalent to 60 per cent of its outstanding loans.

The two thrift institutions are the Tanzania Postal Bank and the Diamond Jubilee Investment Trust. Both mobilize savings and fixed deposits, and invest in government securities. The former, established in 1992 as a successor to the Tanganyika Post Office Savings Bank, is owned by public corporations[33] and intends to become a commercial bank with current account operations in the near future. It has 119 branches in urban areas and 281 in rural areas. In contrast, the Diamond Jubilee Investment Trust is a small financial institution (with about 600 accounts, mostly savings deposits) catering to the Ismaili-Asian community in Tanzania. There is also a hire-purchase company, which provides loans for the purchase of trucks, tractors and other equipment.

Two public insurance companies, the National Insurance Corporation and the Zanzibar Insurance Corporation, enjoy a monopoly on the mainland and in Zanzibar respectively. The government-owned National Provident Fund and the Parastatal Pension Fund mobilize contractual savings. These institutions are known to have suffered from numerous problems resulting in operational inefficiency and heavy financial losses. Coupled with high inflation rates, this has led to a sharp decline in the assets held in contractual savings, from over 5 per cent of GDP in 1985 to less than 1 per cent of GDP in 1987 (Kimei 1994).

As there are no functional capital or money markets, treasury bills and longer-term government bonds are held by the insurance and pension funds

81

and other savings institutions to maturity. Up to 1993, most of the banking and non-banking financial institutions were prevented by law from operating in primary and secondary financial markets.

Thus, as Bagachwa (1995) notes, Tanzania's financial system has developed several distinctive features. Most of the financial institutions are entirely or substantially owned by the government, and its interference in the day-to-day operation of formal financial institutions has been pervasive. Indeed, many institutions have long operated virtually as 'convenient agents of fiscal policy' in a highly monopolistic or oligopolistic environment. In this regard, Collier and Gunning (1991) argue that the banking system in Tanzania has not performed any intra-private agent financial intermediation and that there is little clear separation between fiscal and financial activities. Hence the balance sheets of the commercial banks should be consolidated with that of the government to reveal a close correspondence between the public sector deficit, increases in the money supply and the rate of inflation. With government guarantees to hand and the limitless and cheap refinancing facility made available by the central bank, these institutions have extended credit to clients, mostly parastatals, with little or no repayment prospects. This has curtailed any proper assessment of the degree of risk and return. In addition, banks' loan portfolios have been overly concentrated on agricultural finance through credit extended to marketing boards and co-operative unions (see Chapter 4 below).

The financial system has been functionally organized, with one institution generally having a virtual monopoly in its functional area and with very little competitive pressure. Government restrictions on entry and requirements for specialization, e.g. in retail banking, rural banking, etc., have further reduced this competitive pressure. Each institution is governed by its own statute, and the Bank of Tanzania's supervisory role over the totality of the financial system has been limited (Presidential Banking Commission, 1990). Non-performing loans of the major financial institutions have been so high that they have long been technically insolvent (see Chapter 4).

3.5.2 Informal and semi-formal finance

Four types of informal finance are dominant in Tanzania: financial arrangements on a non-commercial basis among relatives, neighbours and friends; commercial moneylenders (e.g. landlords, farmer lenders and traders); savings and credit societies; and ROSCAs. Although they all operate on a small scale, their financial services are increasingly utilized for expanding productive capacity, rather than solely spent on consumption. For example, credit from friends and relatives constitutes an important source of start-up capital for many micro-enterprises in urban areas and for farmers in rural areas. In some cases, non-commercial informal finance constitutes up to 55 per cent of total start-up investment funds.[34]

While previous studies suggest that informal commercial lending in Tanzania is not as extensive as in West Africa, our case study reports that the number of commercial lenders and their role in the provision of informal credit have been underestimated. Recent trade liberalization has allowed existing informal lenders to operate more openly and has also stimulated the emergence of new lenders. While landlords and farmer lenders lend mostly to farmers, traders tend to lend to other traders and, to a lesser extent, to micro-enterprises and farmers. Commercial lenders typically operate on a part-time basis, owing to the high seasonality in demand for their services and the high risk associated with their economic and lending activities. Indeed, it is the reduction in risks that explains the high frequency of interlinked credit transactions in rural Tanzania (over 70 per cent to 90 per cent of commercial lending were linked transactions).[35]

Savings and credit societies, consisting primarily of individuals with a common ethnic bond, exist in both rural and urban areas. Participants in these groups contribute payments periodically (monthly or fortnightly). They often originate from the co-operative movement and are the most significant informal deposit mobilizer in rural areas. There are 485 urban-based SCSs or credit unions and 438 rural-based co-operatives. Together, they mobilized savings amounting to 4 per cent of total commercial bank deposits in 1990. Traditionally SCS loans have been used to purchase consumer goods, but growing economic difficulties have prompted these societies to offer productive loans for income-generating activities, as well as provident and emergency loans for school fees, medical fees and other unforeseen requirements.

ROSCAs, known as *upatu* or *mchezo* in Tanzania, are spread widely throughout urban and rural areas. *Upatu* gained momentum in the late 1970s and early 1980s, when the erosion of real incomes forced many wage-earners to seek income-generating opportunities in the real informal sector. Thus *upatu* no longer solely served consumption needs; money was increasingly being used to finance productive investment in micro-enterprises.

As in the other three countries, Tanzania has seen a rapid increase in the volume of informal credit and savings mobilization, which has been concurrent with expansion of the real informal sector. For example, the total volume of deposits mobilized by SCSs increased by 57 per cent in real terms in 1990–2. Differentiated interest rates are charged to borrowers within the informal financial sector, confirming the high degree of market fragmentation. Information is extremely localized and does not flow across segmented markets. Furthermore, interactions between the informal and formal financial sectors are not two-way, and links are largely limited to the use of banks' demand and savings deposit facilities by informal groups.[36] Only a small number of bank loans are being used to enhance the lending base in the informal sector, despite growing demand for informal credit.

3.6 Policy environment: financial repression and financial sector reform

Having analysed the character and operations of the financial system in each of the sample countries, in this section we review the evolution of financial policies. Each country has gone through a radical shift in terms of policy environment in recent years, and the evolution of financial policies provides the background for analysis in later chapters of market responses to the on-going reform process. The general direction of reforms undertaken was similar in all the case-study countries as reviewed in Chapter 2.8, but the sequence and pace differed, as did the initial financial conditions, such as banks' and borrowers' net worth and the scale of fiscal imbalances in the pre-adjustment period. These variations have had a critical bearing on the effects of reforms.

3.6.1 Ghana

Before reform, Ghana's financial system was highly controlled and in deep distress. Banks were subject to interest rate controls, mandatory credit allocation and overall credit ceilings. Over 86 per cent of domestic credit was directed to the government and public enterprises (Table 6 and Fig. 7(a)), and a large proportion of loans were known to be non-performing. Implicit taxation of the financial system between 1978 and 1988 was estimated at 4.7 per cent of GDP and 61 per cent of government revenue (Chamley and Honohan 1990). Financial shallowing and financial disintermediation had occurred in 1976–83 (Fig. 6(a)) and several *ad hoc* measures affecting the banking system had severely undermined public confidence in formal institutions.[37]

The Economic Reform Programme initiated in 1983 adopted wide-ranging measures of macroeconomic stabilization and reform. They included public enterprise reform, rehabilitation of the infrastructure, fiscal restraint, and price and trade liberalization, with a weekly foreign exchange auction. Only in 1987, after several years of these real sector reforms and a comprehensive study of the financial sector, has major financial sector reform been undertaken. Two features of Ghana's reforms should be noted. First, the reforms were implemented in a relatively systematic and gradual manner under World Bank FINSAP management. Second, the high cost of reform was largely underwritten by external financial assistance.

Interest rate decontrol was phased in a series of discrete steps over a period of two years. The decline in inflation has enabled real interest rates to improve substantially since 1985 (Fig. 5(a)). With liberalization, the scale of actual interest rate adjustments has been small and neither lending nor borrowing rates have experienced large fluctuations (Fig. 4(a)). Controls on sectoral credit allocation by banks were removed in 1988 and abolished altogether in 1990.[38]

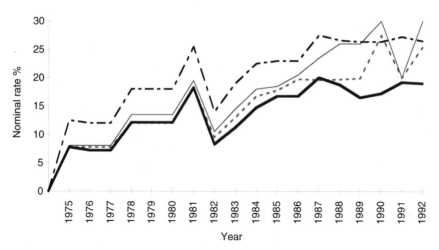

Figure 4(a) Nominal interest rates Ghana, 1975–92

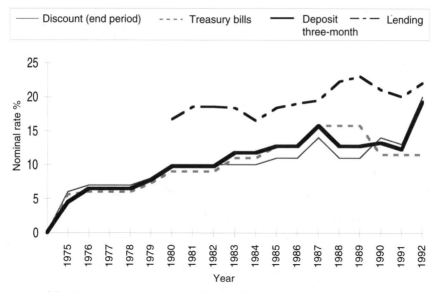

Figure 4(b) Nominal interest rates Malawi, 1975–92

Under the restructuring programme, the Bank of Ghana removed non-performing loans from the portfolio of banks. In 1990 the non-performing assets of public enterprises at commercial banks were replaced with 'risk-free' Bank of Ghana bonds, with a nominal interest rate of 8 per cent. In 1991 private sector non-performing loans were also swapped with Bank of Ghana bonds. In these two years, the total number of non-performing loans removed represented about 41 per cent of the total outstanding credit extended to

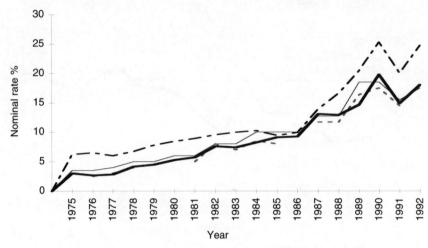

Figure 4(c) Nominal interest rates Nigeria, 1975–92

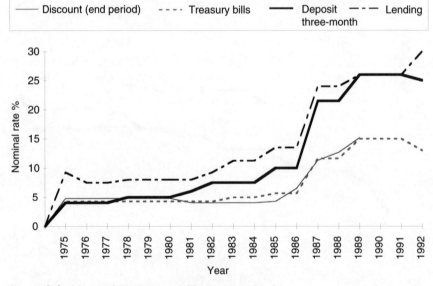

Figure 4(d) Nominal interest rates Tanzania, 1975–92

state-owned enterprises and the private sector since 1988. In most instances the bonds have since been rolled over for bonds with interest rates of about 15 per cent, significantly improving banks' operating income.[39] The Non-performing Recovery Trust and Tribunal were set up to expedite the recovery of non-performing loans.

Restructuring and recapitalization were undertaken in parallel with efforts to strengthen the supervisory and regulatory environment. A series of

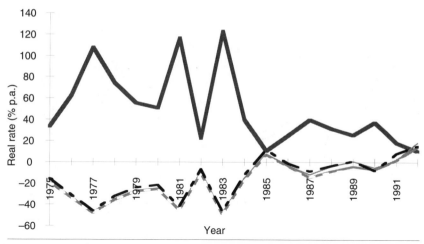

Figure 5(a) Real interest rates Ghana, 1975–92

Inflation year on year	Discount (end period)	Treasury bills	Deposit-three month	Lending

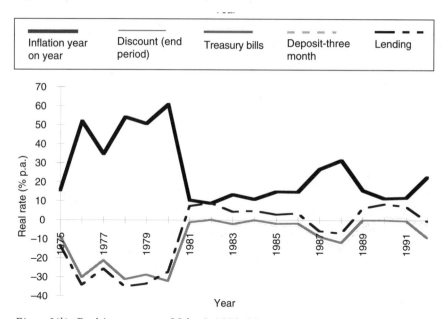

Figure 5(b) Real interest rates Malawi, 1975–92

measures were taken to build new institutions and create new instruments. Branch expansion has been stopped since 1985, and some branches closed in the process of consolidation. In 1989, the Banking Law was revised and upgraded to establish clear banking and accounting standards, defining capital adequacy, minimum capital requirements and prudential guidelines for banks. A bank supervisory division and training programme was also instituted at the Bank of Ghana. To improve the legal and regulatory

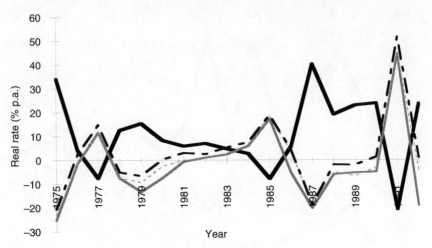

Figure 5(c) Real interest rates Nigeria, 1975–92

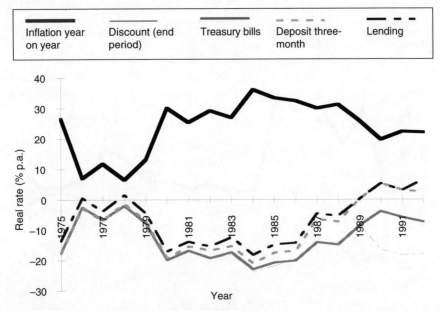

Figure 5(d) Real interest rates Tanzania, 1975–92

framework applicable to NBFIs, a Non-banking Financial Institution Law was enacted in 1993.

As part of the institutional reform programme, the Consolidated Discount House was established in 1987. In 1991 a second discount house was established to facilitate the development of the money market, especially interbank transactions. The Ghana Stock Exchange has operated since 1990, and two private banks have also been established. Divestiture of public sector shareholdings is also intended to increase competition in the banking system. Having introduced money market institutions, and with weekly treasury bill auctions in place, monetary management shifted from direct to indirect control in January 1992, with the intention to use open market operations (OMO) to regulate liquidity in line with developments in the rate of inflation and the underlying monetary and economic conditions.

3.6.2 Malawi

Malawi's financial system was also subject to several control measures prior to the reform process, which started in 1985. The instruments used included controls on bank deposit rates and credit allocation, with preferential rates for agriculture and other priority activities. However, the degree of control was generally not so extensive as in the other sample countries. For example, banks were allowed to set lending rates within prescribed limits. As inflation rates were brought down in 1981, real deposit rates were only mildly negative and real lending rates were positive. However, in 1986–7 the economy was again hit by external shocks and experienced macroeconomic instability (Figs 4(b) and 5(b)).

As part of the structural adjustment efforts begun as early as in 1981, Malawi implemented a series of major public enterprise and fiscal reforms in the first half of the 1980s. These included the financial restructuring of several key parastatal institutions, such as ADMARC and MDC, as well as the most prominent quasi-public conglomerate, Press Corporation. For example, non-performing loans to Press Corporation were replaced by government securities. Apart from the fact that they were major borrowers, the inter-locking ownership structure (discussed in section 3.3) meant that this recapitalization made a substantial difference to the balance sheets of Malawi's major financial institutions.

When financial reforms were launched in 1987 the financial institutions were in far less distress and the scale of the required changes was limited. Their early experience with rapidly increasing non-performing loans, arising from excessive exposure to the estate tobacco sector in the late 1970s, had also made the two large commercial banks cautious in lending operations in the 1980s. At the onset of reform, their operational profit positions had recovered and they were in a relatively stable condition. Thus the costs associated with recapitalization under the reform programme were far lower than in the other three sample countries.

Nevertheless, reform proceeded gradually. In 1987 credit ceilings were abolished and interest rates on deposits were adjusted upwards by three percentage points. However, this was immediately followed by a reduction in both lending and deposit rates. Rates have been largely stabilized since then, despite full interest rate deregulation in May 1990. The practice of setting preferential rates for lending to agriculture was discontinued in August 1989. Interest rate spreads increased, however, from 6 per cent to 7 per cent in the immediate pre-liberalization years to 8 per cent to 10 per cent in 1988–91 (Fig. 5(b)).

Efforts to improve regulation and supervision were initiated, and the legal framework of the financial system was revised in 1989. The new Banking Act facilitated the development of institutions and instruments, and the Capital Market Act of 1990 provided the framework for capital market development. The new Central Banking Act devised in 1989 prepared a move to indirect monetary control through open market operations, by allowing the issue of treasury bills with maturities of thirty, sixty-one, ninety-one and 182 days. The rate on these bills has been 'market-determined' since September, allowing denominations as low as MK1,000, to encourage small savers. The treasury bill rates and the reserve bank rate, which have become a benchmark rate for liberalized bank deposit and lending rates, rose sharply in 1993–4.

Meanwhile, several institution-building measures were intensified. Attempts have been made to increase competition for the two dominant commercial banks through diversification into commercial banking by existing financial institutions, such as INDEBANK and Malawi Finance Corporation. At the same time, the two commercial banks also diversified their activities into the leasing market, which effectively provides medium-term finance. While there has been a large-scale rehabilitation of the POSB, the Malawi Rural Finance Corporation is being formed to take over the provision of rural finance and extension services from the Ministry of Agriculture.

3.6.3 Nigeria

Nigeria's financial policies before 1986 were dominated by detailed annual guidelines regarding aggregate credit ceilings, sectoral credit targets,[40] interest rate controls and control over the structure and maturity of commercial and merchant bank assets. Implicit taxation of the financial system between 1978 and 1988 was estimated to be 4.0 per cent of GDP and 31 per cent of government revenue (Chamley and Honohan 1990). In Nigeria, however, these controls were typically ineffective in achieving their stated objectives. They provided banks with a fertile environment for political clientalism within which non-performing loans rose through the propagation of 'political' loans, and which thwarted the development of sound banking institutions that could manage banking operations on commercial principles. Further, the trend in real interest rates was dominated by the inflation rate, as the nominal rates were adjusted only marginally before 1986 (Figs 4(c) and 5(c)).

With these initial conditions, the government began financial reforms with deregulation of the foreign exchange market. An auction-based second-tier foreign exchange market was established in September 1986. As early as

August 1987, interest rates and the entry of new banks were fully liberalized. An interbank foreign exchange market, with market clearing interbank lending rates, was established following the unification of the first-tier and second-tier foreign exchange markets. These measures in combination had led to the proliferation of banking institutions with very little experience of or interest in providing core banking services. Section 3.4 discussed the rapid rise in the number of both commercial and merchant banks to take advantage of arbitrage opportunities existing in exchange rate dealings.

Controls over credit allocation were substantially eased. More than 70 per cent of the total loans of commercial and merchant banks had previously been targeted at priority sectors, but after 1986 commercial banks and merchant banks alike have been obliged to allocate 50 per cent of their credit to agriculture and industry.[41] It had also been a requirement that banks should allocate at least 15 per cent of loans to small-scale enterprises owned wholly by Nigerians. At present, banks remain subject to regulations on the maturity structure of their assets for the purpose of encouraging term-lending. For example, under the credit policy enacted in 1991, merchant banks are required to observe that at least 20 per cent of their loans carry maturities over three years and no more than 20 per cent of the loans carry maturities below one year. As a result, the maturity of loans by Nigeria's banks is tilted towards term lending, compared with the other sample countries (see Chapter 5). In the early 1990s over 50 per cent of merchant bank loans and 20 per cent of commercial bank loans carried a maturity of more than one year.

Despite substantial upward adjustments of nominal interest rates, it has proved difficult to maintain consistently positive real rates, owing to the highly unstable macroeconomic environment and large fluctuations in infla-tion rates. Meanwhile, the risk composition of loans began to deteriorate, owing to moral hazard problems and adverse selection and incentive effects. Many banks, particularly those owned by state governments, became distressed and undercapitalized. Already in 1989, for example, five out of fourteen banks owned by state governments were undercapitalized, while seven of them were distressed (see also Chapter 4).

Unstable conditions developed similar to those observed in Southern Cone countries following deregulation in the late 1970s and early 1980s. They were undoubtedly caused at least partly by the incorrect sequencing, timing and pace of implementing reform measures. Nigeria's macroeconomic conditions were never stable, while the asset quality of many banks was known to be sub-standard before deregulation. At the same time, no adequate system of regulation and supervision was in place to cope with the growing number of institutions. Indeed, as Stein and Lewis (1996) lucidly document, the licens-ing of new banks was a highly politicized process, with extensive involvement of military elites and retired officers who sought substantial gains from currency trading and financing arbitrage. The financial sector had quickly become a prime field for rampant rent-seeking. Round-tripping fund management for speculative gains, even pyramid schemes[42] and embezzlement, have been widely practised, taking advantage of interlocking ownership across regulated banking segments and unregulated NBFI segments.

In order to deal with the emerging crisis following imprudent deregulation, a number of *ad hoc* measures were subsequently taken. To restore public confidence in the banking system in the face of deteriorating portfolios, the Nigerian Deposit Insurance Corporation (NDIC) was established in 1988. To reduce excess liquidity in the system and thereby restrain banks' bids for foreign exchange, the Central Bank took several measures in 1989: (1) raising the reserve requirements of banks; (2) prohibiting banks from granting loans with the proceeds of foreign exchange-denominated accounts as security; and (3) ordering all federal and state governments and parastatals to transfer their deposits from commercial and merchant banks to the Central Bank. The last measure is known to have reduced banks' liquidity sharply.

In 1990 a set of measures to improve prudential regulation was again adopted. The capital adequacy ratio was revised upwards to 1:10 between adjusted funds and total loans and advances as against the previous ratio of 1:12, with at least 50 per cent of a bank's capital to be kept in the form of primary capital (paid-up plus reserves). The required paid-up capital of commercial banks was raised to N50 million from N20 million, while that of merchant banks was increased to N40 million from N12 million. A new uniform accounting standard for banks was introduced. The Banks and other Financial Institutions Decree and the CBN Decree of 1991 were enacted to strengthen the regulatory and supervisory system governing the operations of financial institutions. However, all these measures to improve supervision and regulatory enforcement proved nominal and ineffectual in the Nigerian context, where the Central Bank and the regulatory bodies such as the NDIC are 'badly overextended, significantly compromised and eclipsed by presidential intervention' (Stein and Lewis 1996).

Thus the financial crisis continued and deepened, with a growing number of distressed banks. In view of continuously disintegrating conditions, a series of short-term measures were adopted. Interest rate controls were reimposed in early 1991. Ceilings were imposed, with the maximum lending rate fixed at 21 per cent and minimum deposit rates at 13.5 per cent, and with a maximum spread of 4 per cent prescribed between deposit and lending rates. Then, in January 1992, interest rates were again deregulated, focusing on maintaining a spread at five percentage points. The nominal lending rates rose to an all-time high of 37 per cent in the second quarter of 1993 (Fig. 4(c)). The government finally set an embargo on the licensing of new banks. Eight distressed banks were suspended from granting credit, while the National Bank of Nigeria was taken over by the CBN/NDIC. The government had obviously lost overall direction in financial policy, and this undermined the credibility of any policy measures announced.

Against this background, efforts have been made to shift the instruments of monetary policy from direct to indirect controls. Weekly auctions of treasury bills were instituted in late 1989, with a commitment by the Central Bank to purchase unsold bills to support the predetermined reserve prices of treasury bills. This had the effect of increasing the monetary base (see Chapter 4). Financial institutions were the main buyers of treasury bills, with no active secondary market in government securities. Furthermore, treasury bills were acquired by banking institutions under the imperative of a 30 per cent reserve requirement. Insurance companies and pension funds are required to hold 25 per cent and 50 per cent of their portfolio respectively in government stocks. Other parastatals are also instructed to hold certain amounts of treasury bills and certificates. In 1990 stabilization securities – non-negotiable and non-transferable debt instruments of the Central Bank – were introduced primarily to control banks' excess reserves, and banks are mandated to purchase them at intervals. The yields on these securities are slightly higher than the treasury bill rate.

However, money markets have yet to be developed to facilitate indirect monetary control. Yet, in 1992, except for banks classified as unhealthy/distressed, all credit ceilings were dismantled to signal the shift in instruments. The use of indirect instruments of monetary control through open market operations was introduced in June 1993. All controls on the capital market were removed in December 1992 and the privatization programme of government-owned banks was initiated. With a deteriorating political climate since 1993, the problem of policy credibility has become serious. In 1994 a complete reversal of all deregulation measures was undertaken with government fixing the exchange rate and prescribing interest rate ceilings of 21 per cent.

Certainly, Nigeria's difficulty in sustaining a consistent policy stance and its poorer record by comparison with the three other countries are partly attributable to unstable general economic and political conditions. Stein and Lewis (1996) attribute the failure of financial liberalization in Nigeria primarily to the political and institutional setting of reforms. In particular, they argue that the abrupt financial liberalization propagated ample opportunities for speculative rent seeking in place of traditional forms of rent-seeking based on political patronage. The faulty design of the reform programme, with regard to timing, pace and sequencing, has also exacerbated instability.

3.6.4 Tanzania

Tanzania's financial policies in the pre-reform years were firmly engrained with the socialist convictions embodied in the Arusha Declaration. Monetary policy was implemented on the basis of the Finance and Credit Planning Act until the early 1990s.[43] Thus the responsibility for credit management was placed under the planning system. Within the ceiling set annually on aggregate credit formation, targets were established on the supply of credit to central government, parastatals and co-operatives. Under this system, credit to the private sector was clearly residual and monetary policy was subservient to fiscal policy. The central bank, the Bank of Tanzania, was given the responsibility of monitoring targets but had no power of enforcement over credit ceilings and deficit financing of the public sector. The credit targets were set using the previous year's lending as a basis, and, as targets were not linked with performance criteria, fresh credit was extended for the new season despite loans outstanding from the previous year. Consequently, over 95 per cent of total credit was allocated to the public sector, predominantly to agricultural parastatals.

Interest rates were hardly adjusted in the 1970s. Despite upward adjustments of the nominal rates in the 1980s, real interest rates became significantly negative as inflation accelerated (Figs 4(d) and 5(d)). Although a series of adjustment efforts began in 1983, amid the severe economic crisis, Tanzania's major macroeconomic adjustment programme – the Economic Recovery Programme (ERP) – was initiated in 1986 with the agreement and signing of the stand-by arrangements with the International Monetary Fund. Bank deposit and lending rates were raised between 1986 and 1989, with spreads widening to 12–14 per cent. Real interest rates turned positive by 1989.

It was clear that real sector reforms had to be advanced before the core problems facing the financial system could be addressed. In particular, parastatal activities had to be radically re-examined if the problem of non-performing loans was to be addressed. Therefore, while a major study of the financial sector was initiated in 1988, several market-building measures were undertaken from 1986. These included fiscal and public sector reforms, as well as the creation of indirect monetary instruments, such as open market sales of certificates of deposit, auctions of treasury bills and the institution of reserve requirements at 3 per cent.

Thus Tanzania's financial sector reforms are characterized by gradualism, rather than by the hasty deregulation accompanied by *ad hoc* corrective measures seen in Nigeria. However, the required scale of restructuring of the real sector, parastatals in particular, was far more extensive. Mans (1994) quotes a 1991 survey showing that only forty-three out of 220 commercial parastatals were able to generate adequate revenue to service their debts fully and that more than 50 per cent of parastatals required subsidies to continue operating. These problems have long been recognized, but little action has been taken to effect changes. Instead, direct treasury subsidies to the parastatals were largely withdrawn.

Meanwhile, financial institutions were left and expected to provide financial services as before. The continued extension of credit to financially non-viable parastatals naturally resulted in a drastic increase in the number of non-performing loans in banks' asset portfolios. This pattern persisted until 1991, when real efforts at financial sector reform began, with large-scale restructuring of banks' balance sheets. By then, most financial institutions were insolvent. They had negative net worth and needed to be recapitalized.

The new Banking and Financial Institutions Act in 1991 set the restructuring operation in motion by creating the Loans and Advances Realization Trust (LART), similar to the Non-performing Recovery Trust and Tribunal in Ghana. Interim financing was provided through a 'special account'. The non-performing portfolios of banks could be transferred or sold to the LART, whose liabilities were only to the Bank of Tanzania and are fully guaranteed by government. Its major functions were to clean banks' balance sheets and to collect the bad debt on their behalf. Once this operation was completed for commercial banks in October 1993, LART moved to address the problem facing the DFIs.

Measures were taken simultaneously to streamline branch networks and to strengthen internal controls. A system of supervision and prudential regulation was to be strengthened. Previously, there were no capital–asset ratio requirements, and the broadly defined liquidity ratios were not rigorously enforced. Loan classification standards were inadequate or non-existent, as were interest accrual rules and limits on lending concentration. Few on-site or off-site inspections were made, as clearly defined internal and external audit procedures were absent and there was no legal protection for either debtors or creditors. The new system was envisaged to address all these fundamental weaknesses.

In 1991 the Bank of Tanzania stopped prescribing a detailed interest rate structure. First, it established a maximum lending rate and a target deposit rate, defined as a one-year savings deposit rate that has to be positive in real terms. This was immediately followed by the complete deregulation of both lending and deposit rates. The new Banking and Financial Institutions Act provided a legal framework for banks to act on the basis of commercial principles. It also removed barriers to competition by encouraging the entry of new institutions.

At the same time, the Bank of Tanzania shifted to indirect monetary controls with the commencement of open market operations of thirty-five-day and ninety-one-day treasury bills. It was envisaged that open market operations would be conducted in a reserve money programming framework. The Bank of Tanzania's overdraft facility had been the major source of banks' liquidity for credit expansion to parastatals, and this unsustainable situation was finally attended to. Since July 1992 access to the Bank of Tanzania's discount facility by commercial banks has become more restricted. At the same time, public enterprise reform was eventually initiated, with the establishment of the Presidential Parastatal Sector Reform Commission in 1992. Marketing boards became agents of co-operative unions, and double financing was finally eliminated.

3.7 Overview

This country-wide review suggests that there are some discernible differences in the process of financial sector reform. With the Southern Cone experience as an example to be avoided, the necessary conditions for liberalization, i.e. macroeconomic stability and prudential supervision and regulation, were taken into account in Ghana, Malawi and Tanzania. In Ghana, along with other real sector reforms, macroeconomic stability was addressed before interest rate decontrol proceeded. Decontrol of rates and credit allocation was phased in over a two-year period. Simultaneously, the balance sheets of banking institutions were extensively restructured, with generous financial support from donors. Institution-building measures, such as strengthening the regulatory and supervisory environment and developing money and capital markets, quickly received attention. In Malawi, too, major fiscal and public enterprise reforms were attempted before financial liberalization. This substantially reduced the cost of bank restructuring. Decontrol of interest rates was attempted gradually, and institution-building measures were introduced.

In Tanzania the problem did not lie so much with the 'abruptness' of implementation or the incorrect sequencing of financial sector reform measures. Rather, banks' net worth had deteriorated significantly as their major borrowers, parastatals, experienced deeper financial crisis in the adjustment period. Since the financial and organizational restructuring of parastatals was delayed considerably, banks continued extending credit to those institutions while relying almost exclusively on a continued line of credit from the central bank. This ended in the large-scale accumulation of non-performing loans, which magnified the scale of balance sheet restructuring required when financial sector reforms finally began.

In contrast to the other three countries, the financial crisis in Nigeria can be attributed largely to the reform measures themselves. In particular, the wholesale deregulation of interest rates and entry requirements in the early years aggravated the instability of the financial system as well as the macroeconomic conditions. A series of *ad hoc* corrective measures was adopted to attend to problems as they arose, and this raised the question of policy credibility. Credibility was further undermined by political uncertainty.

These cross-country differences could partly account for the variable outcomes of the reforms, in terms of the volatility of interest rates, the quality of banks' portfolios and overall macroeconomic policy followed. We shall return to these issues after assessing the effects of financial reforms in more detail in the next chapter.

Notes

1 The precise timing of the beginning of adjustment is different for each of these countries. We have followed the demarcation of the periods in the World Bank study (1994).

2 Like many other countries in sub-Saharan Africa, political conditions remain fragile and unstable in the sample countries. In particular, political conditions in Nigeria increasingly militate against the pursuit of adjustment and growth policies. Our analysis, however, focuses only on economic conditions.

3 The main primary export commodities are as follows: cocoa, gold and timber in Ghana; tobacco, tea and sugar in Malawi; petroleum and cocoa in Nigeria; coffee, cotton and tea in Tanzania.

4 However, cross-border transactions which are not recorded in official statistics may be considerable in these countries, as in other areas of sub-Saharan Africa. In the case of Nigeria, Faruqee (1994) quotes a study which estimates that 'Nigerian textiles now supply as much as 30 per cent of the needs of the low-income group in the West African subregion' and 'about one-half of Nigerian cloth consumption in the early 1980s was coming from neighbouring countries, particularly Côte d'Ivoire and Cameroon' (p. 269).

5 Mans (1994) reports that Tanzania received US$6 billion of net foreign assistance in support of its adjustment programme and another US$1 billion in debt relief during the economic recovery programme.

6 Data on government finance are incomplete and difficult to interpret for Nigeria and Tanzania. No adequate record of grants is available, but it is estimated that in the 1991–2 budget of the Tanzanian government, for example, 39 per cent of total recurrent expenditures and more than 90 per cent of the development budget were provided by counterpart funds. Other foreign assistance, such as technical assistance and direct project financing, were not captured in the budget at all (Mans 1994).

7 However, as we noted in Chapter 1, the variation observed in savings rates across countries in the sub-Saharan region is substantial.

8 Since data on government finance cover only the operations of central government, private savings, calculated here as a residual, in fact include net savings of the public enterprise sector. (For discussion of disaggregation see Chapter 4 below.)

9 As mentioned earlier, the data for the private sector will encompass changes in the saving behaviour of the parastatal sector. However, even after allowing for the poor financial performance of over 300 state enterprises in Ghana, it is clear that these pessimistic figures do reflect the savings pattern of private agents over recent years.

10 For one of more recent comprehensive attempts to investigate the determinants of private saving in sub-Saharan Africa see Mwega (1996). His regression results based on panel data show that private saving rates in sub-Saharan Africa are largely explained by the dependency ratio, *per capita* income, economic growth, changes in the terms of trade and the public saving rate.

11 Their estimates can be compared with the size of the underground economy, estimated to be 20–30 per cent of officially measured GDP for some developing countries (Montiel *et al.* 1993). Montiel *et al.* (1993) also cite the findings of

studies which claim that in virtually all countries – both industrial and developing – a parallel or an informal economy operates alongside the more visible and better recorded official economy.

12 Since financial systems in the four case-study countries have been subject to continual radical changes in the 1990s, it should be remembered that our discussion reflects the conditions prevailing in these economies in 1994–5.

13 In addition, there are smaller publicly owned banks, the Ghana Co-operative Bank and the National Savings and Credit Bank (NSCB). The former is currently under the management of the Bank of Ghana, while the latter was merged with the SSB recently. Meridien Biao Bank, the newest commercial bank, commenced operations in 1993.

14 Thus in Ghana, the government owns eight banking institutions: four commercial banks (GCB, NSBC, Co-operative Bank, SSB), all three DFIs and one merchant bank.

15 Total capital assets of the 120 rural banks were estimated to be C424 million in 1993, compared with that of the ADB at C1.4 billion.

16 In 1993 the total stock of savings in credit unions was estimated at C3.2 billion.

17 The IPC study (1988) estimates that the value of informal credit in rural Ghana may be as high as five times that of formal credit, and particularly important is credit from friends/relatives. Aryeetey (1994) also reports an estimate based on the Ghana Living Standard Survey for 1988/9, which suggests that 80 per cent of household financial saving was done informally, while 90 per cent of loans came from friend/relations.

18 The comparable ratio for Ghana in 1988 was 29,200.

19 NBM was established in 1971 following the amalgamation of Standard Bank and Barclays Bank with the participation of Press Holdings and ADMARC. After several reorganizations, NBM is now owned by the Press Corporation (38 per cent), ADMARC (31 per cent), Standard Chartered Bank Africa (20 per cent) and South African Mutual Life Assurance Society (10 per cent). The Commercial Bank of Malawi was established in 1970, with initial shareholders divided between Banco Pinta and Sotto Mayor of Mozambique (60 per cent), Press Holdings (20 per cent) and MDC (20 per cent). CBM is now owned by Press Corporation 40 per cent, MDC 21 per cent, National Insurance Company 10 per cent and Malawi government 30 per cent. Thus the Malawi government together with its parastatal MDC has a majority shareholding and, through it, the ability to appoint the bank chairman.

20 To fulfil this role, ADMARC was granted monopsony control over all small-holder crop production, including maize, groundnuts, cotton and non-estate tobacco.

21 The New Building Society is owned by the Malawi government, Lonrho (Malawi) and Protea Assurance Company.

22 Of an estimated 1.8 million households in Malawi, 1.5 million are rural house-holds. Of these, 1.3 million are smallholder farmers, while 0.2 million are estate operators. The former cultivate customary land for food crops to generate subsistence income, while the latter, who manage leasehold or freehold land, employ labourers and tenants for tobacco plantation.

23 See Chapter 2.3 for a definition of interlinked loans.

24 The country report includes two small development finance companies

(INDEFUND and SEDOM) in the category of semi-formal institutions. These two organizations specialize in lending to small-scale and medium-scale enterprises as DFIs. Hence, in this main report, their performance was discussed together with that of other DFIs.

25 Of which 310 were licensed by the Central Bank.

26 Many of the newly established merchant banks were reported to be single-office operations, mainly facilitating foreign exchange transactions (Stein and Lewis 1996).

27 They are: the Nigerian Industrial Development Bank (NIDB); the Nigerian Bank for Commerce and Industry (NBCI); and the Nigerian Agricultural and Co-operative Bank (NACB). The NIDB, jointly owned by the federal government and the CBN, was established for promoting development projects through the provision of medium and long-term finance to public and private enterprises, with a minimum loan size of N50,000. The NBCI, established with the prime objective of aiding the indigenization of the Nigerian economy, provides medium and long-term finance for the acquisition, expansion and establishment of viable businesses by Nigerian individuals and corporate bodies. The NACB was established in 1972, jointly owned by the federal government (60 per cent) and the Central Bank (40 per cent), to promote agricultural production and enhance storage and marketing facilities. In 1981 it abandoned its early farmer-lending programme, which was channelled through co-operatives and state lending agencies. Since then, over 80 per cent of its lending has been allocated to state agencies, corporate businesses and large-scale commercial farmers.

28 'Penalty' funds are imposed on banks when they do not meet the required credit allocation, calculated as the difference between actual and required lending. They are collected by the Central Bank and then passed to the DFIs.

29 Stein and Lewis (1996) report more than 310 interlocking directorates among banks, insurance companies and other NBFIs.

30 Many mortgage houses were created following the announcement by the government of its intention to create a National Housing Fund (NHF) with funds mobilized from banks, employee contributions and federal matching funds.

31 Since the Structural Adjustment Programme was adopted in 1986, about sixty enterprises have been privatised through public offers and 'deferred' offers on the Nigerian Stock Exchange.

32 Apart from the Mobile Agency Scheme and the Rural Savings and Credit Scheme, these banks operate the Estate Agency Scheme, the Cumulative Deposit Scheme, the Money Box Scheme, the Deposit-linked Life Assurance Scheme and other bank retailing schemes to encourage savings and help reduce the transaction costs of mobilizing small savings (Kimei 1990).

33 The ownership shares are as follows: government of Tanzania 41 per cent, Tanzania Posts 30 per cent, Zanzibar government 10 per cent, with the remaining 19 per cent reserved to the private sector.

34 A survey result (Hyuha et al. 1993) shows that informal finance is used for food consumption (20 per cent), crop production (25 per cent), the purchase of farm machinery (13 per cent), the purchase of livestock (4 per cent), business/trade finance (17 per cent) as opposed to house building (5 per cent), children's education (9 per cent) and weddings (6 per cent).

35 While there were no stereotypical moneylenders in their survey area of Kilimanjaro, Temi and Hill (1994) also suggest that commercial lenders, engaging in interlinked transactions, provide rural dwellers with credit for a wide range of purposes.

36 For example, the SCC usually retains a third of the total deposits of its members and deposits the rest with a branch of the Co-operative and Rural Bank, as discussed above.

37 In 1979 the government undertook a currency conversion. In 1982 it demonetized the C50 note, froze bank deposits in excess of C50,000 pending investigation for tax liability and recalled bank loans for financing trade inventories.

38 Commercial banks were earlier required to allocate at least 20 per cent of their total credit to the agricultural sector. Global credit ceilings were retained for each bank until 1992, when aggregate and institution-specific ceilings were abolished in a switch to full-fledged open market operations.

39 These swapped Bank of Ghana assets, amounting to C47.5 billion, qualify as secondary reserves.

40 There have been strict guidelines on the proportion of credit allocated to indigenous borrowers as well as to the agricultural sector.

41 Commercial banks are required to allocate 10 per cent and 40 per cent of their total loans to agriculture and industry respectively, while the stipulated shares for merchant banks are 15 per cent and 35 per cent.

42 Stein and Lewis (1996) reckon that many financial houses were indeed established for pyramid schemes to start with, and the presence of the interbank market sustained the speculative practices of financial institutions.

43 Naturally, details of the implementation of the Finance and Credit Plan and monitoring of its performance changed radically from 1986 with the adoption of Structural Adjustment Programmes (see below).

4

PERFORMANCE OF FORMAL FINANCIAL SYSTEMS AND MACROECONOMIC ANALYSIS OF FLOW OF FUNDS

This chapter investigates the performance of the formal financial sector in our sample countries. The first section uses aggregate measures to assess the overall performance of formal financial institutions under different policy regimes. Section 4.2 discusses banking portfolios, highlighting those features that have persisted despite changes in the policy environment. This persistence provides some critical explanations for the constraints banks face in responding to reform measures. Section 4.3 summarizes findings from an economy-wide analysis of the flow of funds (see Appendix 4.1 for details). Changes in intersectoral financial flows over the period 1987 to 1992 should highlight the differences, if any, brought about by liberalization attempts.

4.1 Savings mobilization and intermediation performance of the formal financial system under different policy regimes

As discussed in Chapter 3, despite some critical differences in the scope, speed and sequencing of reform measures, financial systems in all four countries have recently experienced some radical changes in the policy environment. There has been a general shift in policy from 'repressed' regimes to 'liberalized' ones. The effects of these policy changes on savings mobilization and financial intermediation in the formal sector are assessed below by conventionally used aggregates. Table 6 presents period averages of three indicators of financial deepening proposed by King and Levine (1993): the M_2/GDP ratio; the ratio of private sector credit to GDP; and the share of credit to the public sector (government and public enterprise) in total domestic credit. The results are discussed below.

Further, Fig. 6 shows the time series data for each of the sample countries on financial deepening. These figures graph the ratio of currency in circulation, M_1 and M_2, to GDP,[1] to show the performance of the banking system in savings mobilization. The ratio of the difference (M_2-M_1) to GDP

Table 6 Financial indicators

Real interest rate (deposit + rates)

	1981–6	1987–92	1990–1
Ghana	–16.4	–6.0	2.8
Malawi	–3.7	–4.4	–0.3
Nigeria	–5.9	–5.1	1.7
Tanzania	–20.9	–7.5	5.0

Inflation rates (% change in CPI)

	1981–6	1987–92	1990–1
Ghana	56.0	27.0	27.6
Malawi	13.3	20.0	12.2
Nigeria	17.4	30.2	10.2
Tanzania	30.6	25.2	21.0

M_2/GDP ratio

	1981–6	1987–92
Ghana	14.6	15.0
Malawi	21.1	21.4
Nigeria	31.7	20.2
Tanzania	37.6	30.5

Ratio of private sector credit to GDP

	1981–6	1987–92
Ghana	2.37	4.14
Malawi	14.62	9.05
Nigeria	17.39	11.27[a]
Tanzania	2.25	2.15[b]

Share of credit to the public sector (CG and SOEs) in total credit

	1981–6	1987–92
Ghana	86.32	74.53
Malawi	63.33	53.55
Nigeria	55.29	50.26
Tanzania	94.82	61.63

Notes:
a   1987–91 only.
b   1987–8 only.

102

indicates non-transaction demand for money, with a higher ratio indicating a shift in the composition of financial asset holdings in favour of interest-bearing assets with longer maturities.

Figure 7 shows the pattern of domestic credit allocation by each part of the formal financial sector, which has been subdivided to illustrate differences in credit extension by three categories of lenders: the monetary authorities (MA); deposit money banks (DMB); and, where relevant, other banking institutions (OBI). These credits are in turn distributed into: central government (CG); non-financial public enterprises (NFPE); financial institutions (DMBs and OFIs) and the private sector (PR).

4.1.1 Ghana

Data in Table 6 suggest that Ghana's financial depth remains the lowest among the case-study countries. Despite being the most advanced of the four countries in adjustment of both the financial and the real sectors, formal sector credit to the private sector accounts for just over 4 per cent of GDP in the adjustment period. The public sector still accounts for three-quarters of total domestic credit.

Other studies support this conclusion. According to a World Bank study (Neal 1988), in 1985 Ghana had the lowest ratio of M_2/GDP (13.5 per cent) in the world, second only to Zaire. Between 1977 and 1984 most other indicators declined (measured as a percentage of GDP); demand deposits fell from 11.6 per cent to 4.6 per cent; savings and time deposits from 7.1 per cent to 2.6 per cent and domestic credit from 38.8 per cent to 15.6 per cent. Thus Ghana changed its position from one of the more deeply financialized countries of Africa to one of the least financialized during this period of economic decline.

Such a historical trend is also evident in various financial deepening indicators, shown by in Fig. 6(a): the ratios reached a peak in 1976 (M_2 at 30 per cent and M_1 at 22 per cent), after which they declined sharply and reached the bottom in 1983 (11 per cent and 9 per cent respectively). Having gradually improved since then, the M_2/GDP ratio reached 17.5 per cent in 1992. The currency component of M_2 (currency/M_2 ratio) followed a similar pattern, first declining from the 1960 level of 54 per cent to 35–8 per cent in the mid-1960s and gradually creeping back to 54 per cent in 1983–6, pointing to large currency holdings of money compared with holdings in bank accounts.[2] It was reduced to the previously attained low ratio of 35 per cent only in the early 1990s. A similar pattern was followed by the non-transaction demand for money, measured by the (M_2-M_1)/GDP ratio;[3] this declined to 2 per cent of GDP in 1983–4 and then recovered to 4–5 per cent of GDP in the early 1990s. Thus all indicators confirm that a process of financial 'shallowing' occurred between 1976 and 1983.

Although the ratios discussed above have improved since the mid-1980s, a

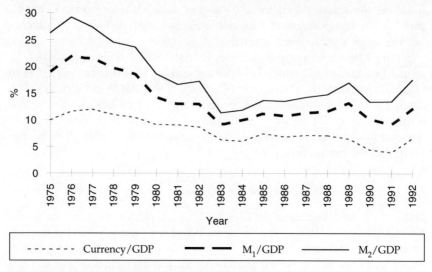

Figure 6(a) Financial deepening indicators Ghana
Sources: IMF, IFS, Bank of Ghana *Quarterly Economic Bulletin*

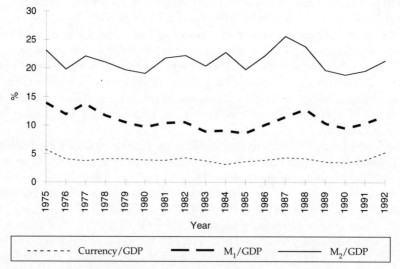

Figure 6(b) Financial deepening indicators Malawi
Sources: IMF, IFS, Bank of Malawi *Economic Bulletin*

significant recovery to the process of financial deepening has yet to begin.[4] After several years of financial liberalization and costly bank restructuring, the financial deepening ratios are still far from the levels attained in the second half of the 1970s. In addition, the ratios do not compare well internationally. The current M_2/GDP ratio attained in Ghana (17 per cent)

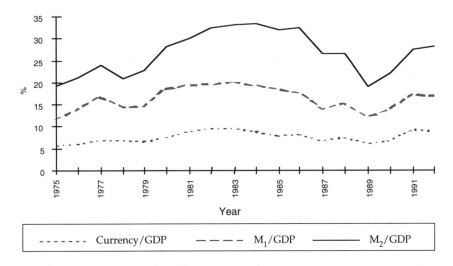

Figure 6 *(c)* Financial deepening indicators Nigeria
Sources: IMF, IFS, Central Bank of Nigeria *Economic and Financial Review*

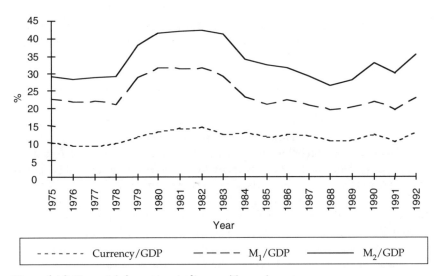

Figure 6 *(d)* Financial deepening indicators Tanzania
Sources: IMF, IFS, Bank of Tanzania *Economic Bulletin*

can be compared with 79 per cent in Malaysia, 46 per cent in Indonesia, 37 per cent in Kenya and 30 per cent in Zimbabwe. As discussed in Chapter 5, the maturity structure of banks' deposit liabilities is still weighted heavily towards demand and savings deposits,[5] which reflects the dominance of the transaction demand for money, with its low interest elasticity.

105

Fig.7(a) illustrates the dominance of the central bank's claims on central government in total domestic credit. Credit to the private sector by deposit-taking banking institutions (DMBs) has been increasing, reaching over one-third of total domestic credit in 1989–90. However, fiscal imperatives continue to dominate credit allocation, as is clearly shown for the early 1990s. Again, international comparisons are unfavourable. The size of private sector credit in relation to GDP is extremely low in Ghana, at 3–4 per cent, compared with 50 per cent in Indonesia, 75 per cent in Malaysia and 20–3 per cent in Kenya. There has not yet been a clear upward trend since the implementation of liberalization measures and bank restructuring to restore banks' commercial viability. Indeed, banks' asset portfolio management appears to have become more risk-averse after liberalization (see section 4.2 below).

4.1.2 Malawi

Measured in terms of M_2/GDP and $(M_2–M_1)$/GDP, Malawi has clearly achieved a higher level of financial depth than Ghana (Table 6 and Fig. 6(b)). In addition, it has not experienced such a dramatic turn in financial deepening indicators as Ghana. However, the process of financial deepening has not proceeded rapidly either. The M_2/GDP ratio fluctuated between 20 per cent and 25 per cent over the period 1975–92 without showing any definite trend (Fig. 6(b)). The currency/M_2 ratio declined from 36 per cent in 1965 to 20 per cent in 1980, and remained under 25 per cent throughout the rest of the period, which is much lower than in Ghana. Non-transaction demand for money (the difference between M_2 and M_1) has been higher, accounting for 10–14 per cent of GDP, which suggests a stronger preference for interest-bearing financial assets. However, as Chipeta and Mkandawire (1996b) note (see also our discussion below in section 4.2), the commercial banks' fear of the rising cost of funds had led banks to set lower interest rates on time deposits of twenty-four months than on those of shorter maturity. Indeed, time deposit facilities over twelve months have been practically withdrawn in the post-liberalization period (see Chapter 5). In the absence of these measures, a greater shift of deposits in favour of longer maturities might have been observed. With all these factors at work, despite relatively greater financial deepening than in Ghana, there is no evidence to show that the adoption of a policy of liberalization in Malawi has led to an upward trend in these ratios.

In Malawi the share of public sector credit in total domestic credit has historically been lower than in Ghana. Moreover, this share declined by ten percentage points in 1987–92 to just over 50 per cent (Table 6). Looking specifically at the credit extended by deposit money banks, it can be seen that the share of the private sector increased from around 60 per cent in the mid-1980s to over 80 per cent in the early 1990s. Over the same period the proportion of credit to central government and other public entities declined.

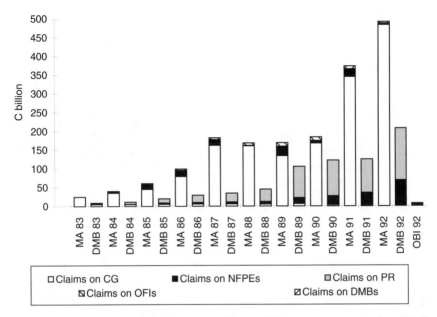

Figure 7(a) Credit extended, by sector Ghana. MA monetary authority, DMB deposit money banks, NFPE non-financial public enterprises, OBI other banking institutions, OFI other financial institutions, PR private sector, CG central government

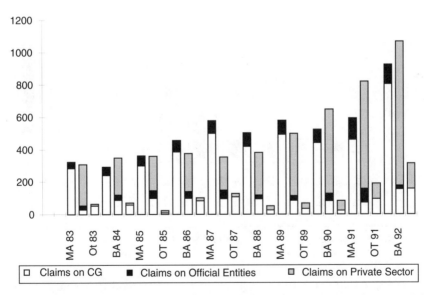

Figure 7(b) Credit extended, by sector Malawi. MA monetary authorities, BA banks, OT other banking institutions

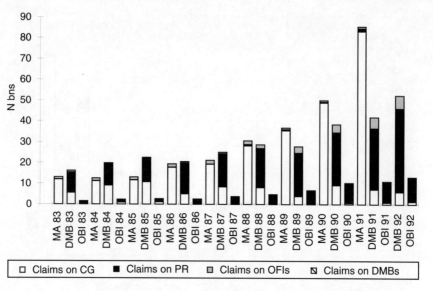

Figure 7(c) Credit extend, by sector Nigeria. CG central government, MA monetary authority, DMB deposit money banks, OBI other banking institutions, PR private sector

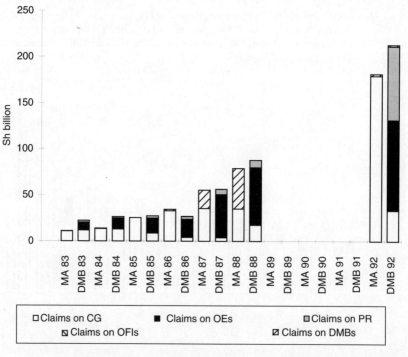

Figure 7(d) Credit extended, by sector Tanzania. CG central government, DMB deposit money banks, MA monetary authority, OE official entities, OFI other financial institutions, PR private sector

However, Table 6 shows that, as a proportion of GDP, credit flows to the private sector declined in the later period (1987–92) by almost five percentage points compared with the earlier period (1981–6). This marked contraction of private sector credit suggests an initial convulsion experienced by the banking sector in response to liberalization measures. However, loan advances have expanded rapidly since then, stimulated by import liberalization and the removal of credit ceilings. This has led to a substantial reduction in reserve holdings in early 1990 (see section 4.2). However, it is reported that an increase in the profitability of the main commercial banks since 1987 was due primarily to trade-related fees and income from foreign exchange dealings. Thus standard bank performance indicators, reflecting these short-term factors, may not reveal the viability of Malawi's banking system.

4.1.3 Nigeria

Historically, financial asset composition in Nigeria clearly shifted towards interest-bearing assets in the pre-adjustment period. The M_2/GDP ratio increased steadily from 19 per cent in 1975 to 33 per cent during the mid-1980s. The ratio of (M_2-M_1)/GDP showed a similar rise, although the currency/M_2 ratio remained around 26 per cent. However, the difficulties experienced by the formal financial system after 1986–7 were clearly evident in the financial deepening indicators. Figure 6(c) shows that both M_2/GDP and (M_2-M_1)/GDP ratios declined in the late 1980s. In particular, the abrupt drop of these ratios in 1989 reflects the government's decision to withdraw public sector deposits from the banking system in an attempt to absorb liquidity, discussed in Chapter 3. Although the ratios have since recovered, Nigeria's process of financial deepening appears to have stalled in the adjustment period, as the data in Table 6 and Fig. 6(c) confirm. Financial liberalization and deregulation had not led to an increase in deposits mobilized by banking institutions.

Table 6 also shows that in the earlier period (1981–6), Nigeria's banking system consistently allocated a smaller proportion of credit to the public sector than those of Ghana, Tanzania and Malawi. In the later period, the share of the public sector declined further to 50 per cent. However, when measured in relation to GDP, banking institutions mobilized fewer financial assets and granted less credit to the private sector in the adjustment period. Section 3.3 argued that financial liberalization was incorrectly sequenced, given the unstable macroeconomic environment and weak supervisory framework. Thus it is not surprising that liberalization has not produced any significant positive trend in the aggregate financial indicators. On the contrary, the number of distressed financial institutions and non-performing loans has grown rapidly, and this has led to a sharp contraction of credit to the private sector, since government financing requirements have first claim on credit (Fig. 7(c) and also see section 4.3 below). The assumed function of banking institutions in savings mobilization and intermediation for productive investment was severely circumvented with the adoption of liberalization and deregulation of the financial sector in Nigeria.

4.1.4 Tanzania

There was a marked increase in deposits mobilized by banking institutions in the late 1970s and early 1980s, when the M_2/GDP ratio rose to over 40 per cent. This was far higher than the ratio attained in the other three case-study countries and higher than the average ratio of 25 per cent for sub-Saharan Africa. However, this may reflect a condition of *monetary overhang*. As Collier *et al.* (1991) notes, financial assets held by the non-bank public sharply increased as a result of severe shortages of consumer goods in those years.[6] As economic reform and adjustment commenced and proceeded, and goods shortages eased in 1984–8, the banking system lost ground in savings mobilization. Currency accounted for over a third of M_2 and the non-transaction demand for money has declined noticeably.[7] Figure 6(d) shows that the composition of financial assets has begun to shift back to bank accounts since 1989, as economic recovery began. However, the private sector has still been allocated a very small share of bank credit in relation to GDP – just over 2 per cent, despite the declining share of the public sector in total credit allocation (Fig. 7(d) and Table 6). However, in Tanzania, where, apart from upward adjustments to interest rates in 1987, actual restructuring of the financial institutions was commenced only in 1991, it is imprudent to attribute these changes to financial sector reform as such.

4.1.5 Synthesis

In all four countries, the expected positive effects of liberalization, in savings mobilization and credit allocation, have been slow to emerge. Two of the indicators used to measure the degree of financial deepening, the M_2/GDP ratio and the private credit/GDP ratio, have not shown any clear upward trend in any of our sample countries. In Nigeria, where poorly designed reform was undertaken without the necessary prerequisites, both indicators showed a marked *deterioration* in the 'adjustment' period. Although the share of credit to the public sector has declined in all four countries, government and public enterprises continue to receive the largest proportion of bank credit.

Various explanations have been advanced to explain the apparent failure of financial liberalization programmes. Most frequently mentioned as an explanation of the disappointing outcome of financial liberalization in sub-Saharan Africa is the *partial* nature of reforms. The World Bank (1994a) ascribes continued poor financial performance to incompleteness and lack of progress in some of the reform measures. Certainly, it is too soon to assess the outcome of the financial sector reforms in Tanzania, where the actual reform process commenced only in 1991.

In Nigeria, incorrect pace and sequencing in the initial years of reform led to crisis and the eventual collapse of the financial system, necessitating several policy reversals, and policy consistency and credibility have become a critical issue. Policy changes in the course of reforms in a number of African countries are often assessed either as *ad hoc* responses to emerging events or a reflection of low government commitment to reform measures. In contrast, favourable evaluations of some Asian liberalization experiences have applauded the way that policy has been 'flexible and adaptable' while remaining firmly anchored in the strategy adopted by the implementing agencies. In these countries, policy responses to evolving circumstances have involved fine-tuning in the pace of reform measures rather than *ad hoc* changes. Certainly, in several countries, better design and implementation procedures might have attenuated some negative consequences of the reform.

However, in countries such as Ghana and Malawi, financial reforms have proceeded more gradually, but with few positive changes in financial indicators. These disappointing outcomes diverge from the optimistic assertions that were initially made about liberalization and reform, which had raised unfounded expectations about the time frame within which positive effects could be generated. As the World Bank Report (1994a) recognizes, 'In designing reform programs, African governments and external donors have sometimes placed too much faith in quick fixes. Reform programs over-estimated the benefits of restructuring balance sheets and recapitalizing banks – and underestimated the time it takes to improve financial infrastructure in an environment where the main borrowers (the government and the public enterprises) are financially distressed and institutionally weak' (p. 204).

More recently, the World Bank's Policy Review Note (1994b) argues that complete interest rate deregulation should be attempted only when more stringent criteria (than hitherto admitted) are satisfied. Besides stable macro-conditions and adequate regulatory and supervisory systems, these criteria include sophisticated and solvent banking institutions with positive net worth and 'contestable' financial markets. Where these conditions are not satisfied, the note argues, interest rates should not be subject to complete deregulation. Instead they should be managed as an interim measure, with the move to market-determined rates as an objective. These criteria, which have been acknowledged as necessary to prevent financial crises, are not met in many developing countries, particularly in sub-Saharan Africa. Thus the conditions facing the financial and non-financial sectors in Africa were not favourable for full-fledged liberalization and deregulation.

Despite some encouraging improvements reported in the adjustment period for some countries, the macroeconomic environment remains extremely fragile (see Chapter 3). Macroeconomic stability is difficult to maintain in the face of external shocks and political pressures, which erode fiscal and monetary discipline (see section 4.3). If inflation is not restrained, it is hard to achieve positive real interest rates, despite increasing nominal rates. Indeed, unstable and high interest rates have further destabilized macroeconomic conditions in many countries. In several Asian countries, rising interest rates engendered a shift to interest-bearing deposits with longer maturities. However, neither a marked growth in deposits nor a clear improvement in the maturity structure has been observed after increases in nominal rates in countries that have continuously experienced macro-economic instability (Nissanke and Basu 1992).

The second prerequisite for effective liberalization is also missing in many sub-Saharan Africa countries. Supervision and regulation of financial institutions remain grossly inadequate and ineffectual without genuine concerted measures to build the institutional capacity of regulatory systems, which are transparent, accountable and free from political interference and clientalism. Infrastructural support systems such as the legal framework and information base have not been developed.

Critically, banks' balance sheets remain equally precarious. Even in Ghana and Malawi, where reforms have been relatively orderly, most banking institutions have not had time to develop the capacity for risk management and operate with an inadequate information base. Under such conditions, they have become overly risk-averse in their asset management, resulting in a credit crunch. In comparison, in Nigeria and Tanzania, banks' net worth deteriorated in the adjustment period through imprudent asset management. These two contrasting trends observed in banks' portfolios in our case-study countries are what Caprio *et al.* (1994) describes as characteristic responses to liberalization attempts, where banking institutions had previously been shielded from market forces by government intervention. Caprio (1994) predicts two dramatically opposite reactions by banks – a retrenchment from all but the lowest risk or a reckless expansion of lending, even to insolvent clients.

It is now widely accepted that financial reform is a lengthy process, requiring critical progress in institution-building. For effective long-term reform programmes, it is important to gain a deeper understanding of banks' operating environment and their resulting behavioural characteristics. Unless the constraints that prevent improvements in banks' operational practices are reduced, it may take a long time for reforms to engender positive results. In the next section the behavioural characteristics of banks are discussed, particularly aspects of banks' balance sheets that have persisted despite radical policy changes.

4.2 Main features of the formal financial sector

Our review of the formal sector showed that many financial institutions have been established since independence in the sample countries, but commercial banks still dominate. As noted by Gertler and Rose (1994) (see Chapter 2.2), this dominance characterizes the formal segments of a financial system in the early stages of economic development. The government-sponsored creation of specialized financial institutions (see Chapter 3), has not increased competitive pressures for efficiency. Sometimes, lack of competition has been caused by a narrowly defined functional specialization that has guaranteed a virtual monopoly for each institution, as in Tanzania. Competition has also been limited by a high degree of interlocking ownership among financial institutions, as in Malawi and Nigeria. The absence of healthy competition for efficiency in mobilization and intermediation functions in Nigeria, despite reduced government ownership and a large number of institutions, suggests that neither public ownership nor paucity of institutions, in terms of both structure and number, may necessarily be the main source of inefficiency in the formal sector.

Instead, poor performance may be caused by the severity of operational constraints, fragmentation within the formal system, and the lack of opportunities for active portfolio management. This can be most clearly demonstrated by examining the main characteristics of financial institutions' portfolios: (1) the heavy concentration of their liability and assets in the short end of the market; (2) the prevalence of 'non-performing' term loans; and (3) the 'excess liquidity syndrome'.

4.2.1 Concentration on the short term

Banks hold their assets and liabilities predominantly in very short-term instruments, as is verified by empirical data for our case study countries (Chapters 5 and 6). Factors on the demand side that explain this concentration include: a short-term saving and credit cycle arising from the use of financial services to smooth consumption and income over the short-term horizon, rather than the longer horizon of production expansion or the life cycle; and a highly inflationary and unstable monetary environment, deterring many from entering into financial contracts except over the very short term. Given the short-term liability structure and the weak capital base in most cases, the portfolio management of the commercial banks is geared to matching the maturity structure of assets with the existing maturities of liabilities. Very little term transformation has taken place. Banks usually provide *de facto* 'term' loans by rolling-over short-term credit or overdraft facilities to their established clients.

However, the extreme bias towards short-term instruments is not restricted to the commercial banking sector but is found more generally in the formal sector as a whole. Thus the short-termism in question reflects the inability of financial systems to take on and manage risks associated with term loans and the maturity transformation. There are neither developed bond and equity markets nor mechanisms and instruments for financial systems at large to perform maturity transformations such as those in post-war Japan, where small and short-term postal savings were centrally mobilized in the Trust Fund Bureau of the Ministry of Finance. The maturity transformation was then effected by the use of these postal savings to purchase the coupon debentures issued by the long-term credit banks. This kind of mechanism can be viewed as a way of 'socializing' or 'externalizing' risks, when the risks are too high for the individual institution/unit to take on.

Critically, in sub-Saharan Africa, the inability of banking institutions effectively to perform maturity transformation is also closely related to the second and third of the portfolio characteristics listed above, to which we now turn.

4.2.2 Non-performing loans

The degree of distress permeating the formal financial sectors of the case-study economies is most clearly demonstrated by the high proportion of non-performing loans and low recovery rates. The problem is most severe among publicly owned financial institutions, though not exclusive to them. These characteristics are most pronounced where political interference in lending decisions was prevalent. The World Bank (1989a) suggests that well over 20 per cent of total bank loans are non-performing in developing countries. The situation in Africa is known to be much worse, with loan repayment rates often as low as 20–30 per cent. The World Bank (1994a) estimates that loan–loss ratios in sub-Saharan Africa approach 40–60 per cent, with banks in some countries showing bad debts for more than 90 per cent of their portfolios (p. 112).

As de Juan (1988) notes, proper bank disclosure has not usually been practised, and it is common for non-performing loans to be counted as 'current loans'. Unpaid interest may often be capitalized and accounted for as income. Thus the true extent of distress can be hidden for a long time. Meanwhile, banks continue to extend new loans to existing borrowers with repayment difficulties in order to avert their bankruptcy, thus exacerbating the problem and deflecting finance from new productive activities.

Our country studies reveal that there is a sharp contrast in portfolio management between those commercial banks expected to make their operational decisions on commercial considerations and those, often government-owned, whose operations are governed by non-commercial objectives (Aryeetey 1996; Bagachwa 1996; Chipeta and Mkandawire 1996b; Soyibo 1996a; see Chapter 6 for detailed discussion).[8] In Ghana and Malawi, commercial viability has increasingly become an important criterion governing the operational decisions of commercial banks in the adjustment period. Thus in Ghana, for example, after balance sheets had been cleaned through large-scale restructuring, commercial banks developed an extremely conservative lending profile, although the delinquency and default rates for DFIs remained high, and were still 70 per cent and 40 per cent respectively in 1988–90.[9] In Malawi the delinquency rate at the branch level centred around 19 per cent.

The conditions facing the Tanzanian banking system have been far worse. Tanzanian banks have long acted as a fiscal agent of the government in their lending operations, with little regard to creditworthiness or risk assessment. In section 3.3 it was argued that the delay in restructuring parastatals led to a serious deterioration in banks' loan portfolios in the adjustment period. For example, Tanzania's dominant commercial bank, the National Bank of Commerce (NBC), drew heavily on central bank facilities and continually extended short-term loans and overdrafts to its major clients, which were parastatals such as agricultural marketing boards and co-operative unions. The volume of loans extended in this way exceeded deposits mobilized for many years. In the 1980s, NBC's portfolio had long been technically insolvent, as the parastatals to which loans had been extended faced serious crises, with abrupt relative price changes and other shocks.

The Co-operative and Rural Development Bank (CRDB) also suffered from high delinquency and default rates on loans and overdraft facilities, as its main borrowers were the co-operative unions. In all these cases, from the outset there was little prospect of repayment. Yet the banks continued to provide loans, relying on implicit government guarantees. It is not surprising that our fieldwork found that the proportion of non-performing loans among commercial banks in Tanzania is 80–6 per cent (Bagachwa 1996). Assuming that the asset quality of the DFIs is equally poor, the non-performing assets of the major financial institutions on mainland Tanzania can be conservatively estimated at Tsh 200 billion, equivalent to 50 per cent of their total assets or 50 per cent of total government expenditure for 1993/4.

In Nigeria, both publicly owned banks and private banks are under considerable distress (NIDC annual report). As discussed earlier, there has been excessive proliferation of financial institutions following imprudent and premature deregulation. The problems of moral hazard, adverse selection and incentive effects have loomed large. The number of distressed banks doubled from eight to sixteen between 1991 and 1992. In 1992, 45 per cent of the total outstanding loans of the banking system were classified as non-performing. Among the distressed banks that are technically insolvent but continue to operate, 67–77 per cent of outstanding loans have been non-performing in recent years. The condition had considerably worsened by 1993, when twenty-four banks were classified as insolvent and a further twenty-six banks were recognized as distressed. Together they constituted two-third of total assets and three-quarters of deposits in Nigeria's financial system. In 1994 thirty-seven banks, accounting for one-third of commercial banks and merchant banks, were identified by NIDC as distressed, with non-performing assets. These statistics do not cover the non-performing loans of the DFIs, which are not licensed by the Central Bank. Their portfolio quality is believed to be even poorer, with non-performing loans amounting to over 80–90 per cent of total loans.[10]

The large proportion of non-performing loans in banks' portfolios can be attributed to many internally and externally generated factors. In the low-income, often commodity-dependent economies, financial institutions are frequently exposed to large external shocks. The adjustments then required far exceed the capacity of both the economies and the financial institutions to absorb these volatilities and manage the associated aggregate systemic risks. The portfolio structure of the institutions is often not very diversified, making it difficult to offset financial losses in one activity against the gains from another. A wave of loan defaults can be propagated throughout the financial system, owing to the high risk covariance.[11] Banks' net worth can rapidly turn negative in such circumstances. Thus financial systems in such economies are unable to deal with high systemic risks. In this context, we must remember that financial distress reflects a general crisis of the *real* economy, which impairs borrowers' net worth drastically, as well as the weakness of financial institutions in the absence of appropriate mechanisms, financial instruments and technology to overcome the problem.

Difficulties in coping with external forces are undoubtedly exacerbated by the internal weaknesses in many financial institutions, such as low capital adequacy ratios, poor asset quality due to inadequate loan appraisal and poor contract enforcement procedures, let alone political patronage and corruption. Inadequate bank supervision by the central bank makes it hard to arrest an accumulation of non-performing loans at an early stage. Without an adequate supervisory and regulatory environment, banks' mismanagement can progressively deteriorate from a stage of 'technical mismanagement', through 'cosmetic management' to 'desperate management' and 'fraud' (du Juan 1988).

It is difficult to disentangle external from internal factors as the cause of non-performing loans in our case studies; both have acted in *combination*. For example, the high incidence of non-performing loans in Tanzania's commercial banks can be traced to the crisis faced by marketing boards and co-operative unions. During the adjustment period (1984–91), higher demand for crop financing followed increases in producer prices, labour and input costs. It is also true that many publicly owned banks in sub-Saharan Africa have been routinely subject to pressure to grant political loans to certain categories of borrower without any credit assessment, such as marketing boards in Tanzania and state governments in Nigeria. Among Nigeria's commercial banks, the state-owned banks have performed worst, with non-performing loans amounting to more than 60 per cent of the total loan portfolio, followed by federal government-owned banks, with 40 per cent non-performing loans. The share of non-performing loans of private banks with foreign participation is known to average 20 per cent, even though they have lent the stipulated amount of 10 per cent of total credit to the high-risk agriculture sector (NIDC report).[12]

In many developing countries, the problem of non-performing loans is most pronounced among the development finance institutions (DFIs) and targeted credit such as agricultural credit schemes.[13] These institutions and schemes were established to alleviate two widespread forms of market failure in development finance, i.e. the dearth both of term lending and of rural and small enterprise credit. To achieve this, DFIs have been financed either by external sources or by the government. Most have not been involved, until recently, in mobilizing local savings to any significant extent, nor has loan recovery been given high priority, with the inevitable consequences.

Their portfolio position is further weakened by specializing in lending to high-risk areas such as agricultural finance.[14] Excessive exposure in high-risk sectors is compounded by generally poor risk analysis and inadequate assessment of debt capacity, excessive political pressure on lending decisions and limited opportunities for asset divestiture. DFIs are often constrained in risk diversification because of their stipulated specialization. Furthermore, they are frequently supposed to take on foreign exchange risks without appropriate hedging instruments (see Chapter 6). As a result, DFIs have experienced acute illiquidity and insolvency problems and have frequently suffered from non-performing portfolios with high default rates and bad debts.

Repeated recapitalization has not solved the underlying problem facing these financial institutions. This illustrates the failure of the standard 'supply-leading' approach, which has merely created financial institutions to meet the demand for term capital, i.e. to fill the perceived credit gap. The approach as adopted in many countries has not adequately addressed the critical bottlenecks that inhibit the viability of these specialized lending operations, namely high transaction costs and inadequate risk analysis and management.

It is important to recognize the tension that exists between the developmental objectives of the DFIs (and other specialized lending schemes) and their operational viability. Yet there are several examples of DFIs that have achieved better performance, by adopting a more flexible, pragmatic and commercial approach, and have also managed to meet development objectives. Good performers can be found not only in the more dynamic Asian economies but also elsewhere in sub-Saharan Africa. The Zimbabwe Development Corporation, the Agricultural Finance Corporation of Zimbabwe and the Botswana Development Corporation (BDC) have all been cited as healthy performers (Roe 1991). The first two of these DFIs have taken in local deposits as an important source of funds and have made constant efforts to diversify their portfolios. Meanwhile, the BDC has adopted public company status (rather than existing as a statutory corporation) and has enjoyed active equity participation in clients' companies. Generally, these three DFIs appear to have succeeded in both commercial and developmental objectives.

Comparing the performance of the relatively successful DFIs with those which have failed, there can be little disagreement on the recommendations suggested in Roe's (1991): the need for a DFI (1) to operate at arm's length from government, with greater emphasis on commercial judgement, and (2) to incorporate deposit-taking to lessen dependence on external funding and provide it with access to domestic savings.[15] This argument is similar to that put forward by the research group on rural finance at Ohio State University. The findings of this group support the conclusion that viable financial markets can only be built when each participating agency performs the integrated function of savings mobilization and lending operation (Adams et al. 1984; Meyer 1991). Clearly this recalls the debate on the most appropriate banking system, e.g. the 'universal banking system', in which all banks engage in commercial as well as developmental banking, or the 'specialized banking system'. While the first option has been taken up by many DFIs in sub-Saharan Africa, including Ghana, after financial reforms, we shall return to this critical issue in a more general context when we discuss different models of financial development in Chapter 8.

4.2.3 Excess liquidity syndrome

The term 'excess liquidity' refers to situations where banks voluntarily increase their holdings of liquid assets on a large scale, in response to a rise in perceived default risks, exacerbating recessionary tendencies resulting from reduced aggregate demand. The share of liquid assets in bank portfolios rises through a sharp retrenchment in bank lending. Therefore 'excess liquidity' in the banking system should be distinguished from 'monetary overhang', which occurs when non-bank public entities accumulate liquidity because of shortages in the goods market.[16] Caprio and Honohan (1991) report that this was also observed in the United States during the Great Recession of the 1930s as well as in the 'credit crunch' of 1990–1. In the earlier episode, for example, the share of liquid assets in the total assets of the US banking institutions is reported to have nearly doubled, from 35 per cent in 1929–30 to 65 per cent in 1935, then to have risen further, to 70 per cent, in 1940. The deep recession that gripped the major industrial economies in 1992–3 was also characterized by debt deflation on a global scale. The portfolios of banking institutions have been rapidly deteriorating, with increasing non-performing loans, and debtors/consumers have been adjusting over-leveraged positions due to excess borrowing in the previous period (UNCTAD 1992).

For many sub-Saharan countries, disequilibrium resulting from the 'excess liquidity' syndrome has been a widespread phenomenon of a more permanent nature.[17] The term is applied here to banking institutions, in particular those specializing in the short end of the market, such as commercial banks, holding liquidity well above the statutory level. Thus excess liquidity is defined here as the *net excess* of actual holdings of liquid assets (in cash and short-term government paper or other government securities) over minimum reserve requirements.

Minimum reserve requirements in developing countries are typically set as high as 40–80 per cent of total bank deposits. This compares with levels of around 10–15 per cent in industrialized countries (Kitchen 1986: p. 83). The high level of reserve requirements in developing countries is a commonly used instrument of 'financial repression', as the banking system becomes a captive source of government finance, pre-empting other potential borrowers (Kitchen 1986; Fry 1988; Chamley and Honohan 1990). Given these high statutory levels, the existence of substantial *excess* holdings of liquidity implies that total liquid assets can exceed 70 per cent of the total deposit liabilities of the banks. The banks hold excess liquidity of their own volition, either in cash with no return, or in treasury bills or government stocks, which until recently yielded low returns.[18] However, risk-adjusted returns on such bills and paper have been high enough to justify investment in them compared with alternative lending activities, which are perceived to be highly risky, as discussed below.[19] An analysis of the balance sheets of commercial banks in Ghana and Malawi demonstrates the nature and scale of this phenomenon with particular clarity (Fig. 8).[20]

Historically, the required minimum reserve requirements in *Ghana* have been set very high, indicating the excessive degree of 'repression' in the past. Reserve requirements were over 80 per cent of deposits in 1978 and 1979. The statutory level was gradually reduced to 23 per cent in 1986, before being raised to 57 per cent in the early 1990s. The actual level of bank reserves held in liquid assets was over 70 per cent in 1980–3, suggesting the existence of a 'low lending trap' in those years. During the 1980s, excess liquidity holdings fluctuated between 15 per cent and 25 per cent. While there was a temporary reduction in liquid reserves in 1987–8, an upward trend was again observed in the early 1990s. The share of liquid assets has returned to previous levels, at more than 70 per cent of total deposit liabilities. (We shall return to this recent phenomenon below.)

In *Malawi*, 45–50 per cent of the total assets of the commercial banks was held in cash or government paper between 1973 and 1975. As the minimum reserve ratio was set at 25 per cent, *excess* liquid assets held by the commercial banks amounted to 20–5 per cent of total deposits.[21] The late 1970s, however, brought a swift reduction in liquid assets. In this period, tobacco prices collapsed, and the commercial banks accumulated non-performing loans through their large exposure to the estate tobacco sector. Loan portfolios took

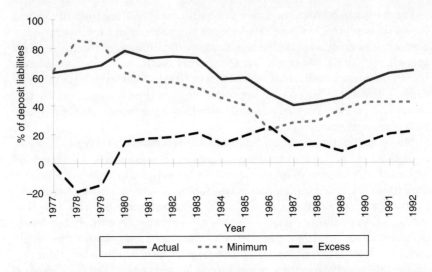

Figure 8(a) Liquidity ratios Ghana. Pre-1988 actual liquidity is a weighted average of primary and secondary banks; post-1988 figures represent commercial banks only.
Source: Bank of Ghana

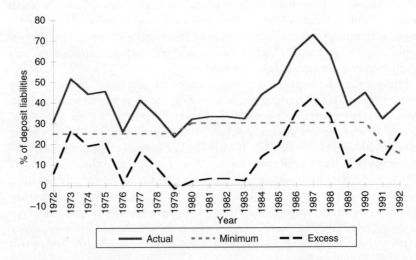

Figure 8(b) Liquidity ratios Malawi
Source: Reserve Bank of Malawi

some years to recover, making the commercial banks much more conservative in their asset management. Despite an increase in the minimum liquidity ratio to 30 per cent in 1980, the excess liquidity began to escalate after 1983.[22] By 1985 holdings of excess liquid assets were over 20 per cent. They increased throughout the period of interest rate liberalization of 1986–8.

Excess holdings escalated to 40 per cent, bringing the share of liquid assets to 70 per cent of total deposits in 1987. Trade liberalization measures taken in the late-1980s have since increased the loan/deposit ratio, as the banks have shifted to financing the import trade.[23] However, it is not yet clear whether the excess liquidity problem has been eliminated from the Malawian banking system altogether.

There are several explanations for the chronic prevalence of excess liquidity in these economies. First, it is certainly a reflection of the early stage of real sector development and a poor, often unstable, economic environment, with few investment opportunities for the private sector. Excess liquidity also mirrors the shallowness of financial markets, which is manifest in the paucity of financial instruments available to bankers to investment.

It is worth noting that banks' large reserve accumulation *per se* may not necessarily constitute a developmental problem, if the reserves held in government paper could be used effectively for economic development. As Courakis (1986) and Fry (1988) note, the funds obtained from required reserves could be channelled to specialized development finance institutions for *additional* lending. This would increase the total volume of loanable funds of the banking system, despite the rise in reserve holdings by commercial banks. However, such mechanisms to facilitate a smooth flow of funds from surplus units to deficit units within the financial sector, for example through interbank portfolio realignment, have been conspicuously absent in sub-Saharan Africa.

Part of the excess liquidity in banks' portfolios may simply reflect the inefficiency of banking operations, reflected in, for example, their disproportionately high intermediation and transaction costs, which could not be covered by normal ranges of spreads. Faced with high operational costs in lending, banks may turn to low-cost investment instruments, which are available only in government paper and stocks. This would result in the accumulation of such liquid assets by banks. Thus high transaction costs lead to the perception of poor investment opportunities and high default risks. Under such conditions, the opportunity cost of investing in government financial paper is estimated to be low on the part of bankers.

At the same time, the low returns that banks could realize on their assets, including liquid reserves, could encourage banks to increase the spread between lending and deposit rates. This is likely to happen where there is little effective competition or collusive agreements can be arranged among banks. It could set in motion a vicious circle, where excess holdings of poor-quality assets favour low return/high cost operations, which in turn lead to increases in low-risk asset holding.[24]

Excess liquidity is indeed closely related to the quality of assets. A high proportion of non-performing loans, with inadequate provision for bad debt, can result in an extremely high threshold for granting new loans, which forces banks to hold more liquid assets than would appear necessary. In particular, when economic conditions are worsening, or radical shifts in economic policy lead to high uncertainty about the future returns, the viability of existing assets becomes doubtful and bankers' perceptions of loan portfolios deteriorate. Thus the threat of dramatic increases in non-performing loans may be an additional reason to hold large liquid assets in their balance sheets, especially if they expect a rapid increase in depositors' demand for withdrawals. In such cases, excess liquidity is no longer perceived by bankers as *excess* but rather as a precautionary and prudent buffer stock, essential to safeguard their commercial interests. This situation then reflects not only bankers' conservative judgements but also the hard reality of the banking environment. In this 'credit crunch', banks' lending ability is severely impaired owing to changes in the value of their assets.

Further, excess liquidity contains *transitory* components as well as permanent ones. The former reflect time lags in bankers' response to changes in the banking environment, such as temporary external shocks (sudden changes in the terms of trade or a large influx of capital) that are not sterilized, or policy shocks such as devaluation or the monetization of large fiscal deficits that affect the money supply. Accordingly, these components should be viewed as short-term disequilibrium phenomena. The accumulation of liquidity in these cases reflects the slow speed of adjustment on the part of banking institutions and thus also a degree of operational inefficiency.[25]

Theoretical explanations for the more permanent components of banks' excess liquidity holdings can be derived from the two paradigms discussed in Chapter 2. First, in the framework of the financial repression hypothesis, it can be argued that the problem may stem partly from the government's excessive intervention in credit markets, through interest rate restrictions, credit ceilings and sectoral credit allocation policies. It is widely documented that low interest rates and directed credit allocation have had, to a varying degree, negative effects on the operations of commercial banks in sub-Saharan Africa, particularly savings mobilization.

Once banks had enough deposits to meet credit targets, savings mobilization was no longer actively pursued. Most 'priority' sectors, such as agriculture or small-scale enterprises (SSEs), designated under sectoral credit allocation policies are those that are identified by bankers as high-risk areas. Ceilings on lending rates have often inhibited banks from charging premiums to cover high risks and transaction costs. Since banks were not favourably disposed towards those sectors identified as priority credit recipients, they preferred to withhold loans and, consequently, did not feel compelled to mobilize additional savings. The 'repressive' policy environment may have contributed to passive banking practices with no active liquidity and asset management. Thus excess liquidity holdings in cash and government paper may partly reflect 'involuntary credit rationing' because of enforced credit targets and excessive government intervention.

Second, the imperfect information paradigm can explain the persistence of excess liquidity, particularly in the post-liberalization years, as the result of 'voluntary credit rationing' and self-imposed caution by bankers, who operate in a high-risk environment with imperfect and costly information. Bankers often explain a conservative lending policy by citing the absence of credit-worthy projects. However, it is not necessarily the absence of viable projects *per se* but the lack of banks' access to information with which risks and viability can be adequately assessed and of effective mechanisms to enforce repayment. Our fieldwork on banks' risk management mechanisms verifies this condition (Chapter 6 below). Liberalization policies have little impact on this particular cause of excess liquidity.

These explanations for excess liquidity have been conveniently summarized in a model proposed by Caprio (1992), wherein the Stiglitz–Weiss model is extended to explain the allocation of banks' portfolios between private sector loans and government paper in an environment characterized by policy uncertainty and information asymmetries. The first category of assets, private sector credit, is risky, and the riskiness increases as interest rates rise. This reflects the adverse selection and incentive effects and the moral hazard problem discussed in Chapter 2. The second category of assets, government paper, may be assumed to be virtually riskless. Figure 9[26] illustrates how a bank's portfolio decision is made under these assumptions.

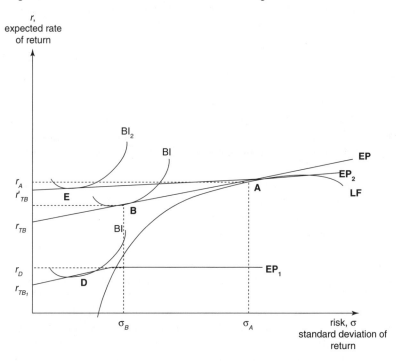

Figure 9 Efficiency portfolio

In this diagram, banks' loan risk–return frontier is drawn as *LF*. Note that *LF* reflects banks' perception of risks associated with private sector loans. Government's treasury bill offers r_{TB} with no risk ($\sigma=0$). Banks' preference for a risk–return mix of investment portfolio (the degree of their risk-averseness) is represented by a set of bank indifference curves (*BI*), the shape of which depends, among other factors, on banks' net worth. At a given risk, it is assumed that the required increase in expected return decreases as net worth rises. Thus *BI* becomes flatter as net worth increases.

A combination of efficient investment portfolio is shown by *EP*, which is tangent to both the *LF* and *BI* curves. The choice of investment portfolio depends on several factors affecting both *LF* and *BI*, and also the nature of the policy environment. Thus besides banks' risk aversion and net worth, already mentioned, these factors include: asset quality (i.e. the proportion of non-performing loans); intermediation efficiency, measured in terms of loan transaction costs; banks' risk assessment ability and endowment of information capital; and policy uncertainty and credibility.

Under a liberal policy environment (i.e. where there are no controls on interest rates or portfolio decisions), the interest rate on loans is given by the intersection at point *A*. Point *B* represents banks' portfolio choice between the riskless asset (with return r_{TB}) and risky loans (with r_A and σ_A). In other words, the average interest rate and riskiness of the chosen portfolio is given by *B*. If banks operate in an environment of financial repression with a ceiling on interest rates given by r_D, the optimal investment portfolio may be represented by point *D* on EP_1. The effect of interest rate liberalization would depend on changes in the other factors listed above with the shift in policy. There may be a reduction in the supply of loan funding if the policy change is accompanied by an increase in the return on treasury bills, from r_{TB} to r'_{TB}. This is shown by a shift of the chosen investment portfolio from *D* or *B* to *E*. We have observed such a portfolio shift as this, i.e. a flight to government paper and a reduction in the supply of loans to the private sector in many countries after liberalization, as shown below.

Thus excess liquidity can be explained in terms of 'rational' portfolio management from the banks' point of view. However, the persistence of this syndrome may have several implications for the efficacy of the financial system, as follows:

1. To cover high intermediation costs, the margin between deposit and lending rates must be sufficiently wide. However, in an environment of poor and costly information, there is a perceived absence of good investment opportunities at a high enough rate of return to justify the spread. Faced with few attractive lending and investment opportunities, the banks lack an incentive to mobilize additional savings. Banks have even regarded the shift to deposits with longer maturity as a negative trend which raises the average cost of keeping funds. Therefore, commercial banks in Malawi and Ghana, for example, are reported to have been turning depositors away,

in particular discouraging them from opening accounts bearing a high rate of interest.

Interest rate liberalization has had very limited impact on this phenomenon, which seems to frustrate its aim of increasing formal sector savings mobilization. This is illustrated by the reaction of Malawian banks to increases in interest rates in 1987–8, as a part of the financial sector reform (Chipeta and Mkandawire 1992a; Nissanke 1991). Interest rate rises coincided with a large increase in deposits due to buoyant income from tobacco. High lending rates discouraged borrowing, as shown by the sudden increase in excess liquidity holding in 1987 (Fig. 8(b)). Under the circumstances, the commercial banks found the cost of high-interest deposits unbearable. In response, it was decided that no new fixed or short-term deposits from any source and no savings deposits from companies would be accepted. To avert a possible financial crisis, interest rates were adjusted *downwards* in 1988.

In general, prudent bankers are constrained in their ability to raise the lending rate by considerations of adverse selection, incentive and moral hazard effects. Further, the interest elasticity of loan demand may be high. Therefore, even if the lending rate is raised to cover the intermediation cost after an increase in the deposit rate, the resulting reduction in demand for loanable funds may squeeze banks' profit margins and make interest-bearing deposits expensive. The financial repression school, on the other hand, assumes that liberalization will lead to a reduction in spreads through a drive for greater efficiency. However, this cannot be taken for granted, particularly in the short run, as our fieldwork revealed (see Chapter 5). In small countries, such as Malawi, a limit is set on domestic competition among financial institutions by the size of the financial market. Limited lending opportunities considerably dampen efforts at active savings mobilization by the formal institutions. Such experience suggests that interest rate liberalization alone has little impact on efficient savings mobilization when the financial intermediaries are awash with excess liquidity.

2. The 'low lending trap' engendered by the excess liquidity syndrome implies a serious deficiency in the bank-based system of financial intermediation for private sector development in these economies. UNCTAD (1991) notes that 'it is the power to create money, not the supply of loanable funds, which generates the power to command the use of real resources for investment purposes. This power lies in the decision of banks to grant loans, not in the decision of households to postpone current consumption' (p. 93). Excess liquidity means that banks do not perform this vital function of intermediation between the supply of loanable funds and the demand for investment funds. Instead, operating in an environment of high risk and imperfect information, they have shown high liquidity preference for risk-free government paper and stocks. Affecting very little of banks' risk perception, liberalization measures have not fundamentally changed the composition

of their assets. Thus the commercial banks in Ghana and Malawi have been very selective and discriminatory, exhibiting extreme conservatism in their portfolio management.

Owing to the absence of effective mediation between surplus and deficit units, potentially dynamic small-scale enterprises, which are thought to be important in generating self-sustaining growth, have had little chance of obtaining formal credit (see Chapter 7). Latent demand for credit by solvent borrowers may remain unsatisfied while the banking sector accumulates excess liquidity. From the commercial banks' point of view, there is little *effective* demand for credit from the private sector, and therefore the public sector automatically assumes an unchallenged position as a receiver of formal credit and as a vendor of financial paper. Thus excess liquidity can give rise to 'a low lending trap', impeding the emergence of vigorous entrepreneurship, as well as *de facto* crowding-out of private finance by public finance requirements in the post-liberalization period.

3. Monetary tightening is a standard policy response to excess liquidity in these economies. While it may succeed in reducing the growth of monetary aggregates, it fails to address the crux of the problem. In fact, the prevalence of excess liquidity may undermine the efficacy of monetary instruments for stabilization too. In the presence of excess liquidity, it becomes difficult to regulate the money supply via the required reserve ratio and money multi-plier, as postulated in the standard monetary base approach. It can be argued that monetary targeting and indirect monetary control are generally less effective in an environment in which the portfolio management of banks is conservative and reactive rather than dynamic.

This factor combines with several others to make it difficult for the monetary authorities to control the monetary base in many countries in sub-Saharan Africa. Net domestic credit is primarily determined by uncontrollable government borrowing requirements, while net foreign assets are inevitably susceptible to large exogenous shocks. In such conditions, adopting a pure floating exchange rate is often not a real option, as it can lead to a loss of the nominal anchor in monetary control. Without an effective sterilization policy, this could result in large fluctuations in the monetary base (see section 4.3 below). Furthermore, instability in the money supply can also originate in large fluctuations of the money multiplier. The money multiplier becomes unstable as a result of the prevalence of excess liquidity in the banking system. The presence of a large informal financial sector is a contributing factor to unstable monetary conditions, as substantial transactions take place outside the formal system and links between the informal and formal sectors are weak (Chapter 7 below).

When there is significant excess liquidity, an acute dilemma exists between the two objectives of monetary policy: stabilization and growth. The point can be illustrated by post-liberalization monetary development in Ghana. The Financial Sector Adjustment Programme was first implemented in 1987, and, since then, the financial sector has been subjected to a series of liberalization measures (see Chapter 3.3). By February 1988 all lending and deposit rates were decontrolled and left for the banks to set in accordance with market conditions, while a weekly treasury bill auction was instituted and new Bank of Ghana bills were introduced.

As shown in Fig. 10, when inflationary pressure increased in the post-liberalization years, 1989–93, Bank of Ghana bill rates were adjusted upwards from an initial rate of 26 per cent to 35 per cent first in January 1991 and again in March 1993. Increases in treasury bill rates followed, and bank deposit and lending rates were raised to compete with this paper. While the monetary tightening arrested the inflationary trend, it immediately shifted the composition of commercial banks' assets in favour of liquid assets (Fig. 11). With the rise in the required reserve ratio nearly doubled, from 29 per cent in December 1988 to 57 per cent in 1993, the actual liquidity ratio climbed from 42 per cent to 72 per cent during this period.

Cash reserve requirements were initially increased in steps from 20 per cent to 27 per cent in March 1990 and then were adjusted downwards gradually, reaching 5 per cent by the end of 1993.[27] The secondary reserve requirements, on the other hand, were raised continually, from 10 per cent in 1988 to 52 per cent in 1993.[28] As the commercial banks were temporarily not allowed to hold treasury bills directly, they switched to holdings of Bank of Ghana bills which were issued to regulate liquidity in the system. The rate of return on Bank of Ghana bills was the highest among alternative investment assets, as this rate has become a critical barometer of the government's monetary stance. Indeed, the banks' holdings of the Bank of Ghana bills were far in excess of the required level, pushing the actual level of liquid holdings by banks to over 70 per cent. This was similar to the level in the late 1970s and early 1980s, when 'repression' was blamed for the high level of this form of implicit taxation on financial intermediation.

Overall, the volume of bank lending to the private sector declined in relative terms in 1989–93. Banks did not engage in new lending, and were instead extremely risk-averse, investing in government securities and Bank of Ghana bills and extending overdraft facilities to established customers. While there was apparent success in absorbing liquidity in the economy through new monetary instruments, this episode suggests that increases in the rates on these bills and paper can make most lending operations to the private sector unattractive to banks, except for that which is very low-cost and highly remunerative, such as overdraft facilities. Following an increase in bill rates, deposit rates have to be raised to compete with these alternative financial instruments. However, the banks' transaction costs associated with their lending operations to the private sector are hard to cut in the short run. At the same time, banks are constrained in raising the lending rates and spreads without discouraging demand for loans and imperilling the risk composition of their loan portfolios. The increased return on government paper and bank

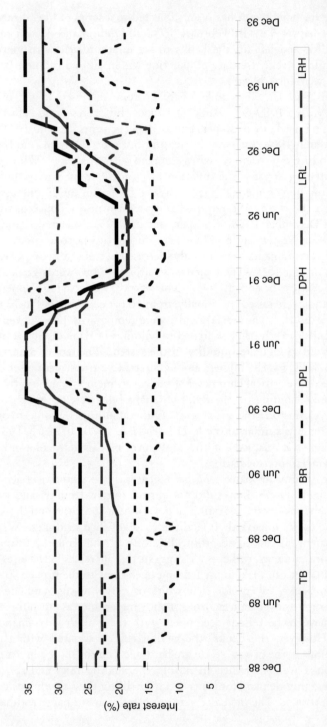

Figure 10 The structure of interest rate terms, Ghana. BR bank rate, DPL minimum three-month deposit rate, DPH maximum three-month deposit rate, LRL minimum manufacturing lending rate, LRH maximum manufacturing lending rate.

Source: Bank of Ghana *Quarterly Economic Bulletin*

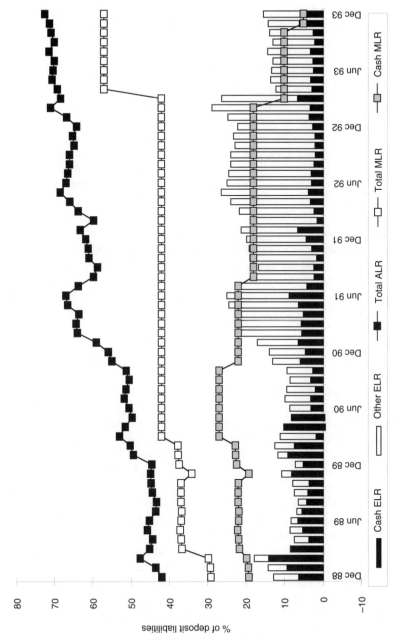

Figure 11 Monthly liquidity ratios, Ghana. ALR actual liquidity ratio returned, MLR minimum liquidity ratio returned; excess liquidity ration ELR = ALR − MLR.

Source: Bank of Ghana *Quarterly Economic Bulletin*

bills provides banks with an excellent alternative opportunity for high return/low cost/low risk investment. This results in a sharp decline of bank lending and the curtailment of financial intermediation between savings and private investment. Thus we observe a post-liberalization credit crunch.

4.2.4 Financial gaps

The preceding discussion suggests the considerable gap between effective securitized demand and notional unsecuritized demand for credit in these economies, where the private sector is dominated by small-scale enterprises, micro-enterprises or smallholders who have no physical collateral to offer.

Furthermore, it is worth noting that the characteristics of banks' portfolios highlighted here reflect not only fragmentation within the formal system but the serious mismatch of liquidity positions and the asset maturity structure demanded. While short-term money abounds in the form of excess liquidity in one segment of the banking system, within the economy as a whole there is an endemic shortage of capital, particularly long-term loan provision for productive investment and diversification. The near absence of functional interbank markets and transactions severely limits the ability of financial institutions to reduce or hedge risks associated with the maturity term trans-formation. No mechanisms and instruments are in place to generate funds for term investment within the domestic financial system. The intermediation function of the formal system has been seriously circumscribed.

Yet it has frequently been argued that the provision of long-term finance by the financial system is not necessarily such a critical condition of sustainable enterprise development so long as short-term working capital is in good supply, while retained profits and internally generated savings could be used for term investment. This implies that rapid industrial development can be financed without undue difficulty on the basis of retained earnings and short-term credit or overdrafts. However, the proposition can be challenged on two grounds. First, internally generated funds are often found to be inadequate when firms are required to grow rapidly (Nissanke 1996). A steady and sufficient supply of external funds to the business sector is one of the key characteristics of fast-growing economies, as in Japan and Korea. Secondly, term finance and short-term credit are fundamentally different so far as enterprise decisions about fixed investment are concerned.

In particular, in comparison with the financial needs of working capital and trading activities, fixed investment in manufacturing requires distinctly longer-term funds. As Bates (1996) notes, there is a clear distinction between commercial capital and industrial capital: commercial capital underpins the exchange and distribution of a flow of shipments, taking the form of short-term credit in an environment of multiple transactions. In contrast, the creation of industry often requires fixed sunk costs, i.e. long-term investment, and hence large commitments of 'lumpy' investible funds.

Mayer (1988) also emphasizes the critical difference between short-term debt that is rolled over and long-term debt finance. The latter involves a commitment by the bank that is absent from an overdraft facility. It is not difficult to perceive a real-world situation where investments that could be undertaken if a term loan were available may be rejected if only an overdraft is on offer. He argues that 'an explicit or implicit agreement to abide by a particular schedule of debt and equity servicing may induce lenders to participate in circumstances in which they otherwise would not' (p. 1179). In his view, what underlies the short-term concern is the lack of commitment on the part of market investors.

It is true that, in the earlier stages of economic development, there is generally little long-term financial provision relative to the need to finance capital-intensive fixed investment, owing to the short-term liability and little maturity transformation that will have taken place in financial systems. The relative scarcity of long-term finance is one of the commonly observed causes of *incomplete markets*, a condition arising from market failure in finance in the process of economic development (Teranishi 1996).[29]

However, there is strong evidence from late-industrialising countries such as Japan and Germany to support Gerschenkron's argument that the growth of enterprises may be much slower if fixed investment is solely dependent on retained earnings. Historical experience from fast-growing economies suggests that, in the absence of developed bond and equity markets where savings mobilized are directly available to investors, the provision of term finance by banking institutions for fixed capital has played a vital role in growth and economic transformation.

We shall return to this issue again in Chapters 7 and 8, when we examine the 'gaps' in financial services from the demand side. Meanwhile, in Chapters 5 and 6, we shall evaluate the factors that influence banks' portfolio investment decisions, including the characteristics of liabilities/assets, intermediation/transaction costs and risk assessment methods, as revealed by our fieldwork data.

4.3 Financial sector reforms and intersectoral financial flows

In this section we analyse the changes in intersectoral financial flows during the five-year period 1987–92. This period encompasses the adoption of financial liberalization measures in our case-study countries, despite country variations in the scope and sequence of reforms. Naturally, the variations detected in intersectoral financial flows during this period cannot be attributed solely to changes in the financial policy environment. These economies have undergone radical shifts in macroeconomic and other sectoral policies under Structural Adjustment Programmes. Furthermore, they are constantly subject to large external shocks. These factors alone tend to generate excessive instability in monetary parameters.[30]

Since macro-parameters exhibit large annual variations, it is hazardous to regard the flow of financial resources in any single year as a reflection of the typical structural features of these economies. With this caveat in mind, we shall analyse snapshots of the flow of funds for 1987 and 1991–2 in Ghana, Malawi and Nigeria.[31] A flow of funds account has been constructed, so far as data availability permits, in order to analyse these changes. A flow of funds account records the financial transactions between different sectors in an economy. The analysis focuses on the role of financial institutions in intermediating funds between deficit units and surplus units. The economy is disaggregated into (1) the consolidated public sector, which consists of the central government and public enterprises,[32] (2) the private sector,[33] (3) the foreign sector and (4) the formal financial system, which consists of the central bank, the deposit money banks and the other non-banking institutions. Thus financial flows are analysed using basic 'balance sheets – accounting identities' among these sectors.[34]

The data used are derived primarily from the combined balance sheets of different financial institutions, complemented by national account statistics, balance of payment data and estimates taken from other secondary sources.[35] While matrices, flow charts and detailed discussion of the analysis of the flow of funds in the public sector are presented in the Appendix 4.1, we present here the main findings of the analysis, which is divided into three parts: (1) the analysis of the flow of funds of the consolidated public sector, which is dominated by the fiscal stance of the central government and public enterprises (section 4.3.1), (2) the flows of funds intermediated by formal financial institutions (section 4.3.2) and (3) the flow of funds to and from the private sector, as official statistics reveal. For comparison, we also discuss here some preliminary estimates of the size of the informal financial sector in the countries studied (section 4.3.3).

4.3.1 Public sector finance

Public sector finance has long dominated financial flows in the official statistics of sub-Saharan Africa countries. In particular, the manner in which public sector deficits are financed has had profound implications for flows of financial resources. In general, government can finance deficits in three ways: (1) borrowing from the central bank, which amounts to money creation; (2) borrowing from the domestic bank and non-bank system through sales of government paper and securities; (3) borrowing abroad (external financing). To the extent that the rate of money creation exceeds the growth rate of the demand for money balances, the first deficit financing method is inflationary. It directly increases the monetary base, and is often referred to as an inflation tax.[36]

In contrast, the other two methods, though 'non-inflationary' in a direct sense, increase the government's debt obligation over time. This has

132

implications for domestic interest rates, credit rationing and future current account positions. Generally, in the absence of alternative sources, governments in sub-Saharan Africa continue to resort to the first method of deficit financing. Consequently the degree of monetization of budget financing remains high, as shown below. The non-inflationary domestic finance has not yet become a major financial source of funds to meet government's short-term budgetary requirements. Thus excessive fiscal deficits are thought to affect many of the key macro monetary parameters such as inflation, interest rates, real exchange rates.[37] While it is difficult to ascertain the effects of fiscal adjustment on economic growth, recent empirical evidence tends to emphasize that fiscal adjustment could make a significant positive contribution to growth by reducing macroeconomic instability (Schmidt-Hebbel 1994).

In view of these effects, the recent literature on public finance attempts to define a 'sustainable' level of fiscal deficit as the level that is financed without raising public liabilities for the feasible levels of growth, real interest and inflation rates that are consistent with macroeconomic equilibrium.[38] According to this definition, sustainable deficit levels may generally lie in the range of 2–6 per cent of GDP, which is equivalent to a primary deficit in the range of –2 per cent to 2 per cent of GDP for many countries (Schmidt-Hebbel 1994).

Burgess and Stern (1993) report that the averages of government deficits in industrial and for developing countries in 1986–7 were 4.5 per cent and 4.3 per cent of GDP respectively. Schmidt-Hebbel (1994) estimates that in 1986–7 the consolidated non-financial public sector deficit was 6.5 per cent of GDP for ten African countries, compared with 5.6 per cent and 3.5 per cent for thirty-six developing countries and eighteen OECD countries respectively. Clearly, fiscal deficits in sub-Saharan Africa tend to exceed the threshold level for sustaining a stable growth path.[39]

With these general features in mind, we turn now to three individual country cases. Figure 12 shows the trends in government budget profiles and deficit financing methods.[40] Tables 7–9 show the distribution of government debt stock by holders. Figure 15 illustrates the flow of funds centred around the consolidated public sector for 1987 and 1992.

4.3.1.1 Ghana

In 1984–91 the financial profile of the central government showed a significant improvement. On the revenue side, tax revenue increased and there was a steady inflow of foreign grants. The ratio of the combined income (tax revenue and grants) to GDP doubled from 8.8 per cent to 16.6 per cent during this period. The central government consistently generated savings amounting to 2–5 per cent of GDP in the second half of the 1980s. With controlled overall expenditure, this enabled the government to switch its overall financing position from a deficit, equivalent to over 6 per cent of GDP

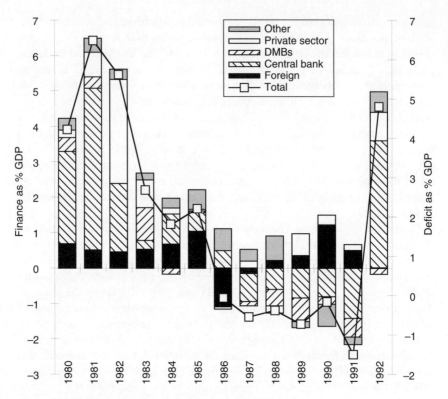

Figure 12(a) Financing the government deficit Ghana

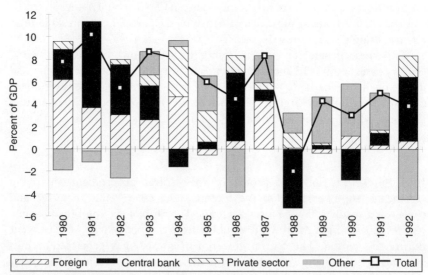

Figure 12(b) Financing the government deficit Malawi

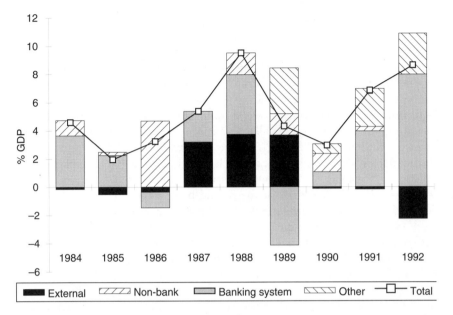

Figure 12(c) Financing the government deficit Nigeria

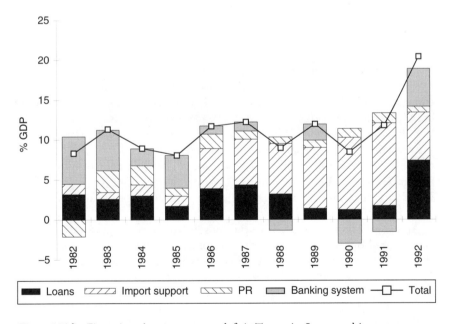

Figure 12(d) Financing the government deficit Tanzania. Loans and import support are both external sources

135

in the early 1980s, to a surplus in 1986 (Fig. 12(a)).

By the mid-1980s, external borrowing had begun to replace domestic sources of deficit financing in the early 1980s.[41] The degree of monetization of government deficit (the ratio of central bank credit to the government as a proportion of the government borrowing requirement) declined from 60–70 per cent in 1981–2 to 24 per cent in 1985. In 1987–91 external finance made it possible for the government to repay some of its debt to domestic creditors, including the banking system. Table 7 confirms this trend: the increase in government domestic debt stock had been controlled since 1984 and indeed the debt stock showed a significant decline in 1987 and 1991. In particular, inflationary financing, via money creation at the central bank, was sub-stantially reduced. The share of the central bank in government debt stock declined from 58 per cent in 1984 to around 30 per cent in 1991. In later years, central government outstanding debt was distributed relatively evenly between the Bank of Ghana, the SSNIT and other financial institutions.[42] As a result, the ratio of outstanding government domestic debt to GDP was reduced from 13 per cent in 1984 to only 2 per cent in 1991.

However, the government's finance requirements changed dramatically in 1992. In the period preceding the election, current and capital expenditure both escalated markedly. This increased the ratio of total government expenditure to GDP by three percentage points in 1992 and by four further percentage points in 1993. By 1992–3 the fiscal deficit had again risen to more than 5 per cent of GDP, requiring substantial recourse to domestic finance. The government's commitment to maintaining the level of deficit within the threshold of sustainability became questionable. Initially, the deficit was mainly financed by the central bank's overdraft facility, which was converted into long-term stock to be held by the bank. At the end of 1993 the central bank held C307 billion worth of government domestic debt, compared with a mere C16.7 billion in 1991. Thus substantial monetization of the government budget deficit did take place again, despite the stated shift in policy stance on deficit financing in favour of more market-oriented debt instruments. The degree of monetization of the budget deficit climbed back to 75 per cent in 1992, and total government domestic debt rose to 12 per cent of GDP in 1993. The stabilization issue was back on the agenda, and inflationary pressure stemming from monetization of the fiscal deficit once again became a critical issue.

An extension of our analysis to the consolidated *non-financial* public sector is hampered by the paucity of data on public sector institutions. It is known that there were 329 institutions classified as public enterprises in Ghana in 1990, seventeen of which were originally defined as 'core' public enterprises, accounting for 78,000 employees out of 200,000 and for 70 per cent of output in this sector.[43]

Between 1979 and 1983 the operating deficit of about 100 public enterprises increased significantly and the net flow of budgetary transfers

Table 7 Government debt: Ghana, 1984–93 (billion, end of period)

Debt	1984	1985	1986	1987	1988	1989	1990	1991	1992	1993
Total outstanding stock	34.6	40.7	56.1	51.9	53.4	61.2	53.8	48.4	227.0	473.0
of which										
Monetary authorities (Bank of Ghana)	19.9	21.6	27.3	23.5	22.0	13.7	13.7	16.7	155.1	306.9
Commercial banks	6.2	8.1	10.9	10.5	8.2	6.4	2.9	0.9	0.3	0.3
Social security fund (SSNIT)	2.4	2.4	6.1	7.3	14.5	11.9	18.4	18.4	32.3	94.5
Financial intermediaries [a]	1.5	3.5	8.0	6.0	0.0	5.2	10.9	12.5	39.3	71.3
Non-financial sector	4.6	4.5	4.1	4.4	8.9	24.0	7.9			
of which private sector	3.1	3.1	2.9	3.4	6.6	15.3				
of which public sector	1.5	1.4	1.2	1.0	2.3	8.7				
Memorandum items										
Domestic debt/GDP	12.8	11.9	11.0	6.9	5.1	4.3	2.6	1.9	7.5	11.9
Bank of Ghana bills	n.a.	n.a.	n.a.	n.a.	n.a.	n.a.	n.a.	142.3	148.6	334.5

Source: Bank of Ghana; World Bank (1994a), Ghana Financial Sector, 'Bringing savers and investors together', table 3.4
Notes:
a Data from 1991 onwards include financial intermediaries and the non-financial sector.
Stock data provided by the Bank of Ghana are not entirely consistent with financing flow provided by the Ministry of Finance.

to public enterprises was considerable, amounting to about 10 per cent of total government expenditure during the period. In the mid-1980s public enterprises continued to generate a loss, requiring considerable subventions from the central government (Islam and Wetzel 1991). The banking system was also an important means by which this operating deficit was financed. The central bank is known to have supported the substantial losses of these enterprises through a number of means: net lending at a low interest rate; and implementation of recapitalization or valuation adjustments on their net foreign liabilities stemming from devaluation losses.

Since 1988 the public enterprise sector had undertaken several measures aimed at improving operational efficiency and financial discipline. Yet many of the public enterprise sector's accounts remain unaudited. Most of its financial transactions with the central government lack transparency, are conducted through unpaid taxes, loan dividends and other implicit subsidies. In general, there remains considerable ambiguity in resource transfers between the central government and public enterprises.[44]

Snapshots of the flow of funds for 1987 and 1992 as shown in Fig. 15 (a–b) generally reflect these characteristics and trends, though neither 1987 nor 1992 can be regarded as a typical year. A number of general remarks can be made here, though the findings are discussed in detail in Appendix 4.1.

In 1987, having made a great improvement in its current budgetary position and generated considerable savings, the government reduced substantially its liabilities to the other sectors – the foreign sector and the domestic banking system. A significant reduction in its debt to the central bank was particularly noteworthy, with its important monetary implications. On the other hand, public enterprises remained a net deficit sector. However, their dependence on the domestic banking system declined markedly, largely thanks to credit available from foreign sources, and to a lesser extent from the government. The SSNIT had increasingly become a prominent creditor to the consolidated public sector.

However, this trend to reduced government dependence on the banking system was abruptly reversed in 1992. With a large emerging fiscal deficit, the government turned to the central bank's overdraft facilities once again, which resulted in the subsequent monetary tightening to combat the monetization effect of the huge fiscal deficit, and hence in the crowding-out of private finance, as discussed in section 4.2. Both the SSNIT and the private sector shifted their asset portfolio in favour of holding government paper too. The public enterprise sector's interaction with the commercial banks was intensified through the placement of cocoa bills while reducing its dependence on the central bank's lending facility.

A comparison of flows of funds in the consolidated public sector between the two end periods in Ghana demonstrate well how fragile the government's commitment to fiscal discipline can be and how the flow of financial resources in sub-Saharan economies can be essentially dominated by fiscal imperatives.

4.3.1.2 Malawi

Historically, foreign sources had been critical for financing government expenditure in Malawi. In 1981–6 foreign grants accounted for 12 per cent of government revenue (Table 5). However, since fiscal expenditure was maintained at over 30 per cent of GDP, much higher than in any other sample countries, grants combined with domestic revenue were not sufficient to cover this level of expenditure. Budget deficit borrowing requirements to fill the financial gap were over 8 per cent on average during this period (Fig. 12(b)). In the initial years (1980–3), foreign borrowing and credit from the central bank (the Reserve Bank of Malawi) were a predominant source of deficit financing. However, external loans had become increasingly expensive and scarce. As earlier loans fell due for repayment the government had to reschedule its external debt several times. In the circumstances it was forced to turn to domestic sources for financing, while it tried to stem an increase in expenditure in 1984–6.

The instability characteristic of the government budget position was amply demonstrated in 1987–8, when the overall fiscal position swung from a deficit equivalent to 8 per cent of GDP to a surplus of 2 per cent of GDP. However, since then the size of the fiscal deficit was contained at the level of less than 4 per cent of GDP, on average, for the period 1987–92. In the latter period, new foreign borrowing was discouraged and domestic finance through government debt paper (treasury bills and government local registered stocks) was endorsed. Yet, as shown below, the government resorted from time to time to the facility of 'advances' extended by the Reserve Bank.

Table 8 shows the distribution of treasury bills and local registered stocks by holders for 1982–93. In Malawi, local registered stocks have been a predominant instrument for financing government budget deficits. They are held mostly by NBFIs such as insurance companies and other financial intermediaries and banks, while the commercial banks are a dominant holder of treasury bills. Reflecting the improved fiscal condition in the later years, total government outstanding debt stock in relation to GDP halved from 14–15 per cent in 1984–6 to 7–8 per cent in 1991–3.

In the early 1980s the public enterprise sector (parastatals) consisted of seventy-six commercial statutory and non-statutory enterprises and approximately fifteen further non-commercial organizations, which operated in all major areas – agriculture, mining, transport and utilities, and industrial holdings as well as in the financial sector. Of these twenty-three were fully government-owned and thirty were government majority-owned through the main DFIs (Agricultural Development and Marketing Corporation, ADMARC, or the Malawi Development Corporation, MDC).[45] Adam *et al.* (1992) report that their financing has been largely supported by 'soft financing', i.e. net transfers from the government, representing an average of 6.5 per cent of government expenditure in the 1980s, as well as by borrowing from government and financial institutions.

Table 8 Government debt outstanding: Malawi, 1982–93 (K million)

Holder	1982	1983	1984	1985	1986	1987	1988	1989	1990	1991	1992	1993
Holdings of treasury bills												
Reserve Bank	1.4	0.5					0.5	1.4	1.4	6.3	6.6	6.6
Commercial banks	11.1	12.4	12.4	26.1	26.1	26.7	26.7	22.2	22.9	18.3	73.3	232.9
Insurance companies	0.8	0.3	0.3	1.6	1.3	1.0	1.0	0.8	0.8	0.5	37.1	23.6
Other financial intermediaries	0.2	0.2	0.2	0.2	0.2	0.2	0.2	0.2	0.2	0.2	0.2	32.5
Statutory bodies and local authorities	0.1	0.1	0.1	0.9	0.5	0.5	0.4	0.4	0.4			
Private sector	0.5	0.3	0.3	0.9	0.7	0.4	0.3	0.3	0.3	0.2		
Foreign sector		1.2	1.8	0.3	1.2	1.2	0.9			0.2		
Total	14.0	15.0	15.0	30.0	30.0	30.0	30.0	26.0	26.0	26.0	117.6	295.9
Holdings of local registered stocks												
Reserve Bank	24.7	13.7	16.6	37.0	36.2	11.5	8.2	11.5	15.0	13.3	19.7	43.4
Commercial Banks	13.6	15.6	72.9	71.2	70.9	67.9	67.1	62.6	62.6	60.1	90.1	97.5
Insurance companies	12.3	15.1	21.2	33.5	40.4	46.4	58.7	64.9	64.9	77.9	73.0	69.9
Other financial intermediaries	41.5	61.8	69.2	81.6	96.4	123.7	158.6	159.7	159.9	168.2	169.8	170.5
Statutory bodies and local authorities	2.9	2.9	3.3	4.0	4.5	4.5	4.4	3.5	3.5	5.4	4.8	2.1
Private sector	24.3	25.1	28.0	29.6	34.7	41.2	44.1	51.2	49.6	80.8	49.1	42.8
Foreign sector	1.6	1.2	4.0	2.5	2.4	1.8	1.7	0.1	0.1	0.1		
Total	132.2	146.0	227.1	272.9	299.7	309.7	356.5	360.5	360.5	410.2	409.2	427.8
Total	146.2	161.0	242.1	302.9	329.7	339.7	386.5	386.5	386.5	436.2	526.8	723.7
GDP	1245.0	1437	1707	1945	2198	2614	3418	4388	5079	6144	6669	8918
Total government debt/GDP (%)	11.7	11.2	14.2	15.6	15.0	13.0	11.3	8.8	7.6	7.1	7.9	8.1

Source: Reserve Bank of Malawi, *Financial and Economic Review*, XVII, 1 (1994), tables 3.3–4.

Domestic credit to this sector accounted for an average of 15 per cent of total domestic credit, since profits on the operations of non-financial parastatals in particular have been negligible throughout the 1980s. Adam *et al.* (1992) conclude that (1) the overall weakness in the financial performance of the parastatals was compounded by internal inefficiencies and poor public sector management; (2) the focus of the reform and privatization process of this sector initiated by Structural Adjustment Programmes has been on the strengthening of the 'troika' of ADMARC, MDC and Press Holdings through the asset swap and the ADMARC–MDC divestitures; and (3) the reform programme has not actively promoted the crowding-in of the indigenous private sector, except in the case of the sale of small estates by ADMARC, though a comprehensive monitoring structure for the sector has been established.

Flows of funds for the public sector, discussed in Appendix 4.1, show the significant difference in the pattern of financial flows between 1987 and 1992. In 1987 – a year recording large fiscal deficits, the central government was heavily dependent for deficit financing on foreign sources: foreign grants and loans drawn on to finance government expenditure were equivalent to 4.4 per cent and 9.1 per cent of GDP respectively (Fig. 15(c–d)). At the same time, a large proportion of government resources (4.8 per cent) were used to repay the early debt, so that net borrowing from foreign sources was equivalent to 4.3 per cent. To finance the remaining gap, the government used the Reserve Bank's advance facility extensively (5.5 per cent of GDP). Further, NBFIs and the private sector financed the rest of the deficit by increasing their holding of locally registered government stock. Parastatals, on the other hand, whilst still heavily dependent on budgetary transfers from the government, decreased their liabilities considerably *vis-à-vis* the foreign sector and the domestic banking system.

In 1992 the traditional source of government finance – foreign loans and grants – was drastically curtailed to hasten the democratization of the political regime. In response, current expenditure and capital expenditure were both cut to contain the level of deficit. However, non-bank public financial institutions, except insurance companies, also reduced their holdings of government paper. Under these circumstances, the domestic banking system inevitably became the main deficit finance source for the government. The Reserve Bank advanced to government the equivalent of over 5 per cent of GDP, while commercial banks increased their holdings of government bills and stocks (by 1.3 per cent of GDP). In contrast parastatals received a large injection of foreign finance (over 2 per cent of GDP). With this significant external finance available, they reduced their liabilities to the banking sector as well as their dependence on the government budgetary source.

4.3.1.3 Nigeria

Since oil accounts for over 75 per cent of the federal government revenues, Nigeria's fiscal time profile inevitably emulates the cyclical movement of oil prices. At the same time, government expenditure is also known to follow the cycle shaped by the political imperatives of the regime (Fig. 12(c)).[46] In 1984–5 the government deficit declined with a sharp retrenchment of expenditure. The oil price collapse in 1986, however, engendered a rising budget deficit in the next three consecutive years to over 10 per cent of GDP in 1988. The sharp increase in the deficit in 1988 was also a result of the 'reflationary' budget dictated partly by the need to arrest anti-Structural Adjustment Programme unrest.

The improved budget position associated with the oil price increase induced by the Gulf crisis in 1990 was short-lived and deficits increased again to 8 per cent of GDP in 1992. Critically, extra-budgetary spending, financed largely by special funds such as stabilization or dedication accounts, was reported to be as high as 60 per cent of total expenditure in the early 1990s. Stein and Lewis (1996) report that most of the oil windfall from the Gulf crisis-induced boom, amounting to US$3 billion, was diverted to off-budget accounts for consolidating military support, reviving several large capital projects or funding the programme with a view to the pre-announced transition to civilian rule.

The availability of external sources for financing the budget deficit had become increasingly uncertain amidst Nigeria's deteriorating credit position. Except for 1987–9, when external funding was made available through multilateral and bilateral loans or short-term borrowing from international capital markets, deficit financing had to rely heavily on domestic sources.

Table 9 shows public debt composition by debt instruments and holders. Treasury bills, certificates and more recently treasury bonds were continually issued by the federal government and held mostly by the banking system. The Central Bank underwrites the issues of these government securities and rediscounts, so that it often ends up holding most of them. The increasing level of debt resulted in a situation where interest payments on public debt, both domestic and external, accounted for more than 40 per cent of the total expenditure of the federal government by the early 1990s. The large devaluation of the naira since 1986 had the effect of accelerating interest payments on external debt, claiming over two-thirds of total interest payments on public debt.

Detailed flows of funds of the public sector are not constructed here for Nigeria on account of the quality of the data available on public sector finance and the discrepancies and inconsistencies observed among different sources.[47] Further, an analysis of the consolidated public sector is made difficult by the lack of adequate data on the state and local governments and on public enterprises. Some 1,600 and 1,700 federally and state-owned public

Table 9 Government debt: Nigeria, 1977–90 (N billion)

Debt	1977	1978	1979	1980	1981	1982	1983	1984	1985	1986	1987	1988	1989	1990
Total federal government debt	4.6	6.0	7.3	7.9	11.4	14.8	22.2	25.7	28.0	28.5	36.8	47.0	57.1	84.1
of which														
Treasury bills	0.7	0.8	2.1	2.1	5.8	9.6	13.5	15.5	17.0	17.0	25.2	35.5	34.1	25.5
Treasury bonds													11.4	20.0
Treasury certificates	0.9	1.8	2.3	2.7	2.3	1.7	4.9	6.4	6.7	6.7	6.7	6.8	6.9	34.2
Development stocks [a]	1.8	2.2	2.8	3.1	3.4	3.6	3.9	3.8	4.3	4.8	4.9	4.8	4.6	4.4
Ways and means advances	1.2	1.2	0.1											
Holders														
Banking system	3.4	4.4	5.0	5.8	8.2	11.2	16.8	19.7	22.2	22.9	27.6	35.6	42.2	65.8
Central Bank	1.7	3.2	2.5	2.9	6.0	8.0	11.3	10.7	11.5	17.7	19.2	27.7	38.4	56.6
Banks	1.7	1.2	2.4	3.0	2.2	3.2	5.5	9.0	10.7	5.1	8.4	7.9	3.8	9.3
Non-bank public	1.3	1.6	2.3	2.1	3.2	3.7	5.4	6.0	5.8	5.6	9.2	11.5	14.9	18.3

Source: Central Bank of Nigeria, Annual Report and Statement of Accounts, table D.2.
Notes:
a Development stocks included Banker's Unit Fund Investment.

enterprises were known to be in operation in the early 1990s. Their operations were poor and had been a heavy burden on the budget, accounting for 30–40 per cent of government expenditure (World Bank Country Economic Memorandum 1993). Owing to the heavy reliance on the banking system for budget financing, resource flows between the federal government and banking institutions are significant. This will be examined in the next section, where our analysis is based on the balance sheets of these financial institutions.

4.3.2 *Financial intermediation by the formal financial system*

This section analyses financial intermediation by *formal* financial institutions through a 'snapshot' analysis of the flow of funds for 1987 and 1992 (Fig. 16). Financial flows presented in this sub-section reflect changes in the balance sheets of formal financial institutions (the Central Bank, banking institutions and non-banking financial institutions).[48]

Reflecting the multiple functions assigned to it, the Central Bank's balance sheet typically consists of: (1) assets consisting of international reserves (net foreign assets, NFA_c), credits to the government and other public enterprises (CB_p), and credit to banking institutions (CB_b); (2) liabilities consisting of currency circulation (CU), bank reserves and deposits (CD_b).

Net foreign assets[49] reflect an economy's balance of payments position and the degree of willingness on the part of the central bank to maintain its exchange rate in the light of developments in the external account. The central bank's foreign exchange operations have counterpart effects on its liabilities, due to the involvement of banking institutions in foreign exchange operations.

Credits to government and other public institutions reflect the central bank's holdings of the public sector's deposits and government securities (treasury bills and bonds) or overdraft facilities extended to finance public sector deficit, as discussed in the previous section. Credits to banking institutions are issued against securities for which the central bank extends rediscount facilities. This creates borrowed reserves and appears on the asset side of the central bank's balance sheet. The central bank is supposed to influence the level of borrowed reserves through changes in its discount rate. In contrast, unborrowed reserves (banks' deposits at the central bank) appear on the liability side of the balance sheets. In order to affect monetary policy, changes in the level of borrowed and unborrowed reserves should be responsive to policy instruments such as changes in discount rates, reserve requirements or open market operations.

The assets/liabilities of the central bank, referred to as the monetary base or as high-powered money, are bounded through the following accounting identity:

$$MB = CU + CD_b = NFA_c + CB_p + CB_b$$

In the balance sheets of *deposit money banks*, the liabilities side consists of equity capital (the capital base, CAP) and bank deposits (demand deposits, DD_d, and savings and term deposits, DD_t), while the asset side consists of cash reserves and deposits held at the central bank (CD_b), short-term and long-term government debt (treasury bills and bonds, BC_g), and loans to private sector borrowers (BL).[50]

The assets/liabilities of deposit money banks are similarly bounded through the following accounting identity:

$$DD_d + DD_t = CD_b + BC_g + BL$$

In recent decades, banks in industrial countries have become increasingly involved in *active* liability/asset management. This has led to their greater involvement in money market operations, by issuing certificates of deposit, taking interbank loans or entering into repurchase agreements as to securities, or securitization.[51] Through these operations, banking institutions actively interact with each other and with other financial institutions in order to raise funds and extend loans. There is also an extensive flow of funds within the sector, through layering and 'off-balance sheet' activities.

However, in the absence of developed money or interbank markets where commercial paper and private securities can be actively traded, banking institutions in the case-study countries remain passive in their liability/asset management. In the face of mounting illiquid and non-performing loans to the private sector and the shortage of 'bankable' projects, banks have indeed turned to holdings of highly liquid government securities and bank bills in seeking a safe low-cost investment outlet. (See section 4.2 above.) Under these conditions, there are only limited flows of funds among financial institutions, except their direct links with the central bank. Further, banks holding chronically large excess liquidity, as in Ghana and Malawi, have rarely used the central bank's discount facilities (CB_b). These are some of the distinct characteristics of the flow of funds in the financial systems of sub-Saharan countries.

In conventional policy perspective, high-powered money/monetary base (MB) should form a basis for controlling the money supply. Indeed, one of the critical issues facing the central banks in the case-study countries is the controllability of the monetary base and the money supply, as the level of the money supply (M_1 or M_2) is linked with the monetary base through the equations:

$$M_1 = CU + DD_d = m_1 * MB \text{ or } M_2 = CU + DD_d + DD_t = m_2 * MB$$

where m_1 and m_2 are a money multiplier, the choice of which depends on the monetary aggregates selected as intermediate policy targets.

Figure 13 shows trends in the level and change of the monetary base in relation to GDP. Two different series of monetary bases are presented here: the monetary base as defined from the asset side (high-powered money calculated as the summation of the monetary authorities' net foreign assets and domestic credit) and from the liability side (reserve money).[52] These graphs confirm the presence of considerable annual fluctuations in the monetary base and net foreign assets, reflecting the large external and policy shocks. Figure 14 shows money multipliers, defined as ratio of M_1 or M_2 to reserve money. These also exhibit sizeable fluctuations.

Some key monetary indicators of the four countries, summarized in Table 10, verify this point. Overall, Table 10 shows that the average annual growth rates of the money supply and net domestic credit are extremely high, although this masks the large annual fluctuations observed in most of the countries in the pre-adjustment period. Further, their economies had to undertake massive exchange rate adjustments in the 1980s due to excessively overvalued currencies. The extent of exchange rate overvaluation is confirmed by the substantial parallel market premium during this period, defined as the black market exchange rate over the official exchange rate (World Bank 1994a). Parallel market premiums in these countries in the early period were much higher than those in nine other developing countries reported in Montiel *et al.* (1993). In the adjustment period (1987–92) these economies continued to devalue their currencies. The rates of exchange rate devaluation were substantial in Ghana, Nigeria and Tanzania, which, owing to the resultant loss of a critical nominal anchor, had undoubtedly had pervasive effects on price stability in these years.

Similarly, the seigniorage revenue that these governments have been able to extract from printing money has at times been significantly higher than the average for OECD countries and other developing countries, reported as 1.0 per cent and 2.1 per cent respectively in 1970–88 (Schmidt-Hebbel 1994).[53] It is abundantly clear that the financial institutions operate in a monetary environment of high volatility and instability. We shall now examine these features for Ghana, Malawi and Nigeria.

4.3.2.1 Ghana

The monetary indicators presented in Table 10 and Fig. 13(a) amply illustrate the extent to which large monetary shocks could have a deleterious impact on the real sector's performance. A number of inferences regarding Ghana's monetary parameters can be drawn from the data.

1. The monetary base had dominated the money supply and domestic credit for a long time, as indicated by the high ratio of the monetary base to GDP in 1975–87, compared with the money supply/GDP ratio shown in Fig. 6(a) and Table 6. The high level of the monetary base/GDP ratio in the pre-reform period is predominantly accounted for by the considerable credit

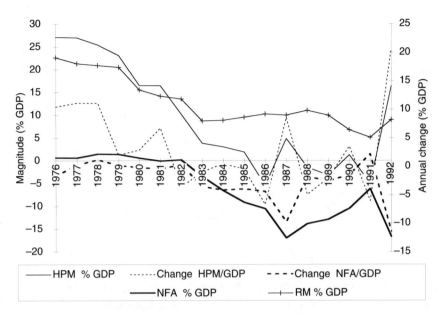

Figure 13(a) The monetary base Ghana. HPM high-powered money, NFA net foreign assets, RM reserve money

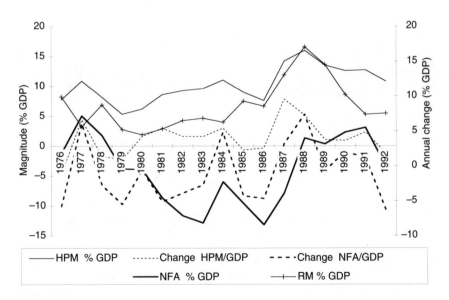

Figure 13(b) The monetary base Malawi

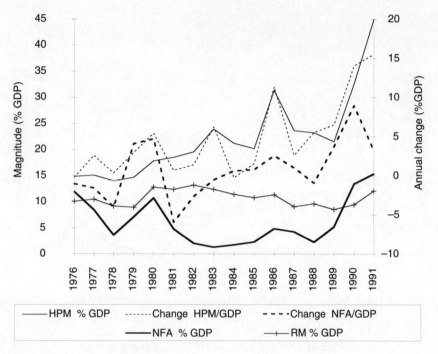

Figure 13(c) The monetary base Nigeria

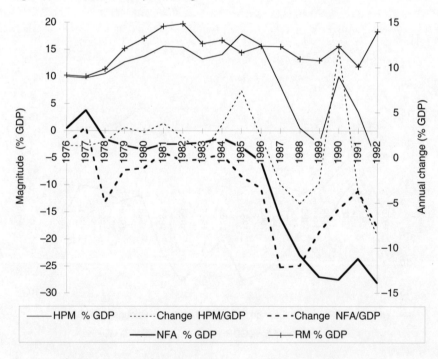

Figure 13(d) The monetary base Tanzania

Table 10 Monetary indicators for case-study countries

Monetary indicators	1981–6	1987–92
Ghana		
Reserve money as % GDP	9.7	7.9
Growth in reserve money (% p.a.)	15.5	12.0
Growth in money supply	42.3	41.2
Growth in net domestic credit, banking system (% p.a.)	51.35	37.15
Growth in private sector credit	73.09	57.08
Exchange rate changes (% devaluation, average p.a.)	217.78	40.78
Parallel market exchange rate premium (%) [a]	1098.2	3.4
Seigniorage [b]	3.3	0.4
Malawi		
Reserve money as % GDP	7.1	11.6
Growth in reserve money (% p.a.)	12.8	1.7
Growth in money supply	15.8	19.4
Growth in net domestic credit, banking system (% p.a.)	14.4	15.64
Growth in private sector credit	4.86	26.33
Exchange rate changes (% devaluation, average p.a.)	17.94	18.18
Parallel market exchange rate premium (%)[a]	53.6	29.4
Seigniorage [b]	1	1
Nigeria		
Reserve money as % GDP	11.9	9.75
Growth in reserve money (% p.a.)	2.4	14.7
Growth in money supply	9.2	27.8
Growth in net domestic credit, banking system (% p.a.)	18.88	15.16
Growth in private sector credit	13.67	15.74
Exchange rate changes (% devaluation, average p.a.)	62.99	39.34
Parallel market exchange rate premium (%) [a]	232.7	25.1
Seigniorage [b]	1.1	2.9
Tanzania		
Reserve money as % GDP	13.2	11.7
Growth in reserve money (% p.a.)	9.2	12.9
Growth in money supply	19.8	31.5
Growth in net domestic credit, banking system (% p.a.)	20.3	46.34
Growth in private sector credit	23.88	68.04
Exchange rate changes (% devaluation, average p.a.)	63.96	41.26
Parallel market exchange rate premium (%)[a]	248.8	74.5
Seigniorage[b]	3.8	7.6

Notes:

a Excess of parallel market exchange rate over official rate (%).

b $(M^1_t - M^1_{t-1})/GDP_t - g_t (M^1/GDP)_t$ where g_t is real GDP growth, except for Tanzania, where M_2 was used for the calculation of seigniorage in 1990–1.

extended to the central government by the central bank, as net foreign assets were marginal.

2. Large annual changes in high-power money, the money supply and domestic credit in the range of 40–60 per cent. In particular, high-powered money has been extremely volatile throughout the period, shown in Fig. 13(a) by its changes in relation to GDP. The high volatility of Ghana's monetary base is partially explained by the erratic trends in net foreign assets.[54] However, equally relevant has been the uncontrollable fiscal imperative imposed on the Bank of Ghana.

3. This excessive volatility continues to characterize the central bank's balance sheet, shaping in large part the monetary environment of financial institutions. The exchange rate – one of the key nominal anchors of price stability in the system – remains subject to large-scale devaluation in the adjustment period, 1987–92. The annual rate of devaluation in the second sub-period was 40 per cent, though there was a large reduction in the rate of devaluation from the first sub-period (1981–6), when massive exchange rate adjustments took place in the light of the excessive premium the parallel market commanded in those years. Overall, there is no sign that the volatility of the monetary environment declined in the more recent period. Financing of the large budget deficit by the central bank in 1992 pushed up seigniorage again, which recorded a decline in 1990–1 from 3 per cent in the early period.

4. A weak and unpredictable relationship between the annual changes in the monetary base and the money supply points to the difficulty of controlling the money supply through the application of conventional monetary policy instruments such as reserve requirements. The money multiplier has become highly unstable in Ghana in recent years (Fig. 14). Yet it takes some time to develop money markets so as to conduct open market operations with a view to effecting indirect monetary control.

Our flow of funds analysis of the financial system for 1987 and 1992 (Fig. 16(a–b)) underscores the monetary instability discussed above. In 1987, reflecting the improved fiscal condition, the Bank of Ghana experienced an increase in net resource inflows, with the consolidated public sector amounting to 1.1 per cent of GDP. On the other hand, the Bank of Ghana's balance sheet was dominated by transactions with the foreign sector, which were considerable in relative size in both liabilities and assets (a reduction by 6.6 per cent and 4.6 per cent of GDP respectively). By comparison, the bank's interaction with the banking system was marginal.

In 1987 the deposit money banks (DMBs, including all commercial banks and development banks) recorded an increase in savings mobilized from the private sector, equivalent to 2.5 per cent of GDP, while the flow of funds to the latter was just 1.5 per cent of GDP. This is far less than the 7 per cent of GDP for fourteen developing countries on average (World Bank 1989, p. 28). The DMBs had a net resource inflow from the consolidated public sector in 1987 (1.1 per cent of GDP), reducing their stock of government

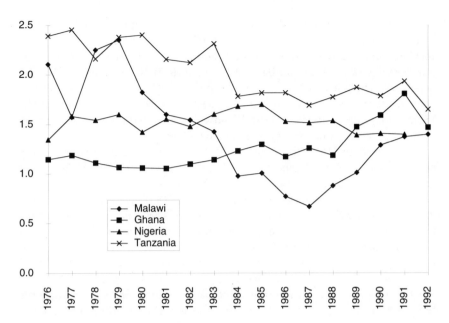

Figure 14(a) Money multipliers M_1

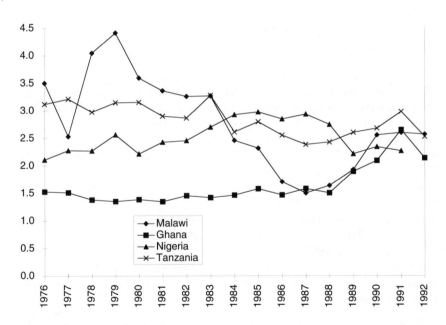

Figure 14(b) Money multipliers M_2

debt significantly. The SSNIT – one of the most prominent NBFIs, with a surplus amounting to 0.9 per cent of GDP – invested 15 per cent of its surplus funds in real estate, the rest being divided mainly between the purchase of treasury bills and Bank of Ghana bills (0.30 per cent of GDP) and deposits at the DMBs (0.45 per cent of GDP).[55] Thus in 1987 the SSNIT's investment portfolio was still heavily tilted towards the public sector. The SSNIT's deposits at banks were well above the level required for transaction demand, reflecting the paucity of other investment outlays.

In contrast, in 1992, the Bank of Ghana's assets were dominated by the need to finance the fiscal deficit, recording an increase in credits to the central government, equal to 4.6 per cent of GDP. The counterpart of this on the liability side was an increase in foreign liabilities (3.07 per cent of GDP) and in currency holding by non-bank public institutions (3.1 per cent). Furthermore, there was a major restructuring of the Bank of Ghana's liabilities between cash and Bank bills. As discussed in section 4.2 above, since the banks were no longer allowed to hold treasury bills, they held secondary reserves in Bank of Ghana bills, which were issued to counter the inflationary pressure resulting from the Bank of Ghana's financing of the large budget deficit.[56] The commercial banks increased their holdings of the Bank of Ghana bills by as much as the equivalent of 1.8 per cent of GDP.

In 1992 funds intermediated by banking institutions were equivalent to 6.4 per cent of GDP, less than the amount recorded in 1987 (8.8 per cent of GDP). Despite real deposit rate increases, overall private sector financial savings at the banking institutions remained similar to the level recorded in 1987 (2.3 per cent of GDP). Most of the deposits were indeed non-interest-bearing demand and savings deposits (Chapter 5). The banks' loans and advances to the private sector rose only very marginally, recording an increase in claims on the private sector equivalent to 1.8 per cent of GDP, compared with 1.5 per cent of GDP in 1987. This can be compared with the similar size of an increase in banks' holdings of Bank of Ghana bills. The banks also increased claims on public enterprises, which were largely accounted by increased holdings of cocoa bills. Thus the banks' portfolio structure shifted decisively towards low-cost, high-yielding, short-term paper, compared with high-cost and high-risk loans to the private sector (section 4.2).

The SSNIT remained a significant surplus unit in the economy, mobilising resources equivalent to 1.07 per cent of GDP, nearly half of savings mobilized by all banking institutions. It also shifted the composition of its liquid assets in favour of Bank of Ghana bills while reducing its holdings of treasury bills.[57] Further, the SSNIT increased flows to the private sector to C5.7 billion (0.19 per cent of GDP) through stock market operations. The emerging investment pattern shows that SSNIT is a significant participant in both money and capital markets.

4.3.2.2 *Malawi*

The data presented in Table 10 and Fig. 13(b) enable us to make a number of observations regarding the monetary indicators. First, the growth of reserve money, the money supply and domestic credit have been markedly lower than in Ghana, nor were there significant changes in these growth rates between the two sub-periods. Only credit extended by the banking system to the private sector grew faster in the second period.

Secondly, the average data conceal the presence of high annual fluctuations, observed in all these indicators. The relationship between the money supply and the monetary base, i.e. the money multiplier, is unstable, calling into question the controllability of money supply growth (Fig. 14(a)). As in Ghana, the monetary base dominated money supply and domestic credit in the early years, which was predominantly accounted for by considerable credit extended to the government and parastatals by the central bank, as net foreign assets held at the Reserve Bank of Malawi were negative in 1979–88. On the other hand, the annual fluctuations in the monetary base were accounted for more by the high volatility of the Reserve Bank's net foreign assets, as foreign liabilities and assets held by the RBM were both highly variable. However, on the whole, the degree of volatility of RBM's balance sheet has been lower than in that of the central bank of Ghana (Fig. 13(b)).

Thirdly, the required scale of exchange rate alignment was also far less than that observed in the other three countries. The parallel market premiums were lower and the rate of devaluation effected has been less dramatic. Seigniorage revenue was 1 per cent, the same level as for fifteen OECD countries noted above. On the whole, financial institutions in Malawi have operated in a less volatile monetary environment than those in the other three countries studied.

Our flow of funds analysis shows, under these monetary conditions, how financial institutions intermediated funds in 1987 and 1992 (Fig. 16(c–d)). In 1987, the RBM's operations were largely driven by the need to finance the fiscal deficit. Thus the RBM's advances to the government were equivalent to 5.5 per cent of GDP while also increasing foreign assets considerably during the year (2 per cent of GDP).

This asset increase of the central bank was backed up by a significant rise in deposits held by commercial banks (4.4 per cent of GDP) and the consolidated public sector (3.4 per cent of GDP) and foreign borrowing (1 per cent of GDP, inclusive of SDR allocation).[58] The two commercial banks, while reducing foreign liabilities significantly (1.6 per cent of GDP), increased deposits from parastatals and the private sector by amounts equivalent to 0.46 per cent and 4.7 per cent of GDP respectively. Three-quarters of these deposits were placed in term deposits. The significant increase in deposits by the private sector was caused by buoyant income from tobacco estates. However, the banks found it hard to increase loans in the face of the subdued demand for high-interest-rate loans upon the interest rate liberalization (section 4.2). Thus the banks undertook little intermediation for investment. While increasing deposits at the RBM (4.4 per cent of GDP), they reduced loans and advances to the private sector (1.18 per cent). This pattern of flow of funds confirms that, following liberalization attempts, the banks suspended their function as an effective intermediary for the economy.

Insurance companies, which raise current income through premiums from the private sector, invested their assets mostly through increases in deposits at the commercial banks (0.43 per cent of GDP), whose assets were largely kept in turn at the RBM in the absence of alternative investment outlets. The insurance companies switched their asset composition, divesting their holdings of government stocks and shifting to increasing investment in the private sector by almost an equal amount in 1987.

Other financial institutions,[59] mostly the POSB and the NBS, drew an increased flow of deposits from the private sector (1.79 per cent). Investment in government paper and stocks was a prevalent outlay by the POSB and the NBS (0.94 per cent of GDP), while loans to the private sector (0.72 per cent of GDP) were mostly carried out by the INDEBANK, the NBS and the LFC. A substantial proportion of cash holdings (0.54 per cent of GDP) was accounted for by the POSB.

1992. The RBM's liability structure changed significantly from that in 1987. It drew most resources from the foreign sector (K270 million, 4.4 per cent of GDP), while deposits from the government, parastatals and banking institutions were reduced by an amount equivalent to 2 per cent of GDP. The RBM further reduced its foreign assets by K187 million (2.8 per cent of GDP). The resultant net inflows of K458 million from the foreign sector were almost exclusively for lending-on to the central government, which required the RBM's credit facilities, equivalent to over 5 per cent of GDP.

While there was a significant increase in the foreign liabilities of the commercial banks due to the increase in trade-related credit, deposits mobilized from domestic sources by the commercial banks declined in relative terms. The flow of deposits from the private sector and parastatals to the banks' deposits reduced considerably to a level equivalent to 2.3 per cent and 0.22 per cent of GDP, compared with 4.7 per cent and 0.47 per cent of GDP in 1987. Further, the maturity structure of these deposits changed in favour of demand deposits. Nearly 60 per cent of deposits were placed in demand deposits as the banks discouraged term deposits (see section 4.1).

Investment by the insurance companies in 1992 was dominated by a portfolio shift to treasury bills at the cost of reductions in all other investment outlays. An increase in deposits mobilized by the POSB and NBS was equivalent to 1.34 per cent of GDP, a nearly two-thirds of deposits increase by the commercial banks. Apart from cash holdings (0.47 per cent of GDP), a rapid increase in loans to the private sector was recorded by the NBS, the

INDEBANK and the LFC, together accounting for 1.61 per cent of GDP, again nearly half the lending increase by the commercial banks.

4.3.2.3 Nigeria

The monetary parameters presented here enable us to make a number of observations. First, the monetary base and its components (both domestic credit and net foreign assets) have shown high volatility (Fig. 13(c)). The scale of annual variations is as large as in Ghana. The increased volatility of the monetary base in the 1980s was also evident in the higher average growth rate of the monetary base in 1987–92 than in 1981–6, shown in Table 10. This trend was also revealed in the higher average growth of the money supply in the second sub-period, though there was little change in the annual rate of credit expansion between the two sub-periods.

Secondly, the relative size of net foreign assets measured in relation to GDP followed the oil price cycle, showing a declining trend from the high level of 15 per cent of GDP in 1975 to 1–5 per cent of GDP in the 1980s. On the other hand, the substantial expansion of the monetary base in the 1980s was increasingly accounted for by Central Bank credit to finance government deficits.

Thirdly, as in Ghana, the large parallel market premium over the official rate in the first period was corrected by massive devaluations effected since 1986, which had a significant impact on relative prices and monetary development. Continuing reliance for budget financing on Central Bank credit raised seigniorage from 1 per cent in the first period to 2.9 per cent in the second sub-period. In short, there was a marked deterioration in the monetary environment in the adjustment period.

Our analysis of the flow of funds of the financial system shows how formal financial institutions intermediated resources in 1987 and 1991. In 1987, the Central Bank's balance sheet for the year was dominated by increases in foreign liabilities (3.2 per cent of GDP), mostly in trade-related short-term liabilities, and by increases in credit to the federal government (3.4 per cent of GDP). The latter was mostly accounted for by increased holdings of treasury bills.[60] At the same time, the commercial banks experienced very few liquidity problems as such.[61] Rather, with substantially increased deposits from the private sector (4.6 per cent of GDP), the commercial banks fled to increased holding of treasury bills (3.2 per cent of GDP), while increasing their foreign assets as well (1.25 per cent of GDP). The private sector received proportionately much less of an increment in loans and credits by the commercial banks, about one-third of savings mobilized from the sector (1.58 per cent of GDP). Further, the commercial banks recorded some two-way interbank transactions with merchant banks, presumably using deposit facilities reciprocally.

Though the merchant banks may have exerted some competitive pressure on the commercial banks, their additionally mobilized savings were one-fifth of those of the commercial banks. It is worth noting, however, that they were proportionately more inclined to provide loans to the private sector than invest in government paper. There are a large number of other banking and non-banking financial institutions in Nigeria (Chapter 3). What is revealed in Fig. 16(e–f) is an approximate size of their operations in its totality, despite the fact that they specialize in the provision of different financial services. The total size of their liabilities/assets is similar to that of the merchant banks. Inflows from the private sector to these institutions, in aggregate, were somewhat larger than those to the merchant banks, while they were providing fewer loans directly to the private sector.

In 1991 the dominance of budgetary financing requirements over the flow of funds intensified. Credit extended by the CBN to the federal government exceeded 10 per cent of GDP, though it was partially offset by a substantial increase in the government' deposits placed at the CBN (6.9 per cent of GDP). The CBN held government securities in treasury bills, certificates and a relatively new instrument, treasury bonds. Net foreign assets held by the CBN had risen, as the increase in foreign assets exceeded that in foreign liabilities.

Though the commercial banks continued to mobilize savings from the private sector nearly as much as in 1987 (4.45 per cent of GDP), their asset allocation became less transparent. There were larger items classified as 'other assets/liabilities', which were the single most significant one in their portfolio. This may be a reflection of severe deterioration in their loan portfolio. They continued providing a similar size of loans to the private sector in relative terms (1.44 per cent of GDP) as in 1987, while reducing substantially their holding of government paper and stocks. Instead, they placed more deposits at the CBN than in 1987.

The merchant banks, on the other hand, reduced their share of savings mobilization from the private sector, though maintaining their share of credit and loan allocation to the private sector. The balance sheets of commercial banks and merchant banks reveal also increased transactions among themselves. The actual size of interbank operations may have been even larger than shown here. The share of other financial sectors in savings mobilization and intermediation declined significantly between 1987 and 1991. On the whole, interaction between the private sector and formal financial institutions declined markedly during this period.

4.3.3 *Financial flows of the private sector*

As discussed in Chapter 2.6, private agents can hold an array of financial assets – currency in circulation, demand and interest-earning time deposits at banks, short and long-term debt papers, foreign currency (or foreign currency-denominated deposits), savings and credit with the informal sector, and so on. Thus flows of funds in the private sector should reflect changes and portfolio adjustment in the net financial wealth of the private sector. However, the flow of funds analysis of the private sector for the case-study countries is severely constrained by the limited availability of data on this sector's financial transactions. In particular, it is not possible at present to decompose the sector into household and corporate sub-sectors. This is increasingly unsatisfactory in light of the growing role played by private agents in business transactions. In the absence of a comprehensive survey of the private sector, all data are derived from the 'other side' of transactions. Many calculations, including the estimation of savings and investment, were made on a 'residual' basis.

Figure 17 illustrates different instruments and channels through which the private sector conducts financial transactions with other sectors. The private sector has been conducting transactions with the central government mainly as current payments through taxation and transfers. However, in recent years, the purchase of government debt paper has become a conduit of capital transaction between the two sectors. While the private sector's transactions with banks are made through deposit and loan facilities, savings mobilized by many other non-bank financial institutions are conducted as current transactions through contributions, premium income or other. However, the NBFIs in some countries have become involved in capital transactions with the private sector as capital markets have began to emerge and develop. The only capital account item with the central bank that directly involves the private sector is net changes in currency holding. The private sector interacts with the foreign sector through two channels: net borrowing from abroad and capital flight.[62]

Furthermore, we know that the majority of household financial savings are mobilized through informal financial agents or groups. Our case-study reports suggest that the magnitude of financial transactions between the private sector and the informal financial sector can be far larger than in other sectors. We present here our preliminary estimates to show some approximate measures of these transactions in relative terms. Owing to the data limitations, we restricted an evaluation of the flows of funds in the private sector to Ghana and Malawi.

4.3.3.1 Ghana

Using conventional 'residual' methods of calculation from national account statistics, the private sector's savings can be estimated at just over 6 per cent of GDP in both 1987 and 1992. Investment rates were 5.5 per cent in 1987 and 3.8 per cent in 1992. While these low and declining private investment ratios are cause for serious concern (as discussed in Chapter 3), a number of observations and assumptions can be made to derive some tentative estimates of various financial flows for this sector.

First, these savings ratios are supposed to be aggregate *total* savings, and so should include financial and non-financial savings. However, according to various survey estimates, the private household savings rate ranges from 20 per cent to 30 per cent of income (the Ghana Living Standard Survey) to 50 per cent in rural households (IPC 1988). The former study reckons that a quarter of savings are in financial assets, i.e. 5 per cent of household income is transformed into financial savings.

The second study estimates that 20 per cent of the total savings of rural households are held in financial assets, the remaining 80 per cent being held in various forms of non-financial real asset. This study suggests that there are marked regional variations: in northern Ghana, a larger proportion of these savings are held in the liquid form of stored produce (e.g. bags of maize) and live animals, while in the southern regions, where incomes are generally less seasonal, most rural savings are held in more illiquid forms, such as building materials, partially completed construction projects and cleared land. Overall, the savings rate is thought to be smaller in urban households, though a much higher degree of financialization of savings is observed. A survey of market women in urban areas (Aryeetey and Gockel 1991) revealed that their savings, predominantly in financial assets, form about 20 per cent of their annual income.[63]

Considering the dominance of rural households in the private sector, these household studies have led us to believe that the private sector savings ratios calculated from national account statistics are more suggestive of the size of household *financial* savings. This might be expected as non-monetized economic activities are not generally captured in official statistics.[64]

Second, the aggregate private savings data clearly do not cover financial savings conducted through informal financial units. Yet our country study suggests that: (1) 80 per cent of household financial savings were made informally; (2) the informal sector (excluding non-commercial transactions among friends and family members) is responsible for initially mobilising at least 55 per cent of total financial savings; (3) savings mobilization and lending operations have grown in recent years, as much as 50 per cent in 1990–1. These estimates are used to derive our tentative calculations of the size of the private sector flow of funds with the informal financial sector.

Third, a greater share of resources was made available by the household sector for the acquisition of financial assets in 1992 than previously. This may be indicative of further financialization of private savings as well as of some growth in the interaction of the household sector and the formal sector in general.

A comparison of the private sector flows of funds for 1987 and 1992 (Fig. 17(a–b)) allows us to make a number of interesting observations:

1   Between the two periods, the private sector reduced net flows to central government in current transactions in relation to GDP, while it

considerably increased claims on the government through purchases of government paper. During this period, the return on such paper increased significantly (section 4.2). It can be inferred from this that private sector financial savings as a whole could display a reasonable responsiveness to relative rates of return on different assets. The allocation of private financial savings with formal institutions appears to have shifted in favour of such paper. In 1992, 16 per cent of private financial savings were invested in treasury bills and 20 per cent in other securities, 48 per cent in savings deposits and 15 per cent in time deposits.

2   In this five-year period, there have been few changes in savings and credit flows between the private sector and the banking institutions. However, the SSNIT increased income from the private sector through contributions and property income threefold.

3   The private sector had very small foreign liabilities. However, the outflow from this sector to the rest of world can be of significant size and is highly volatile.

4   A large share of financial savings has been mobilized by the informal financial sector. It may be nearly double that mobilized by the formal banking sector. Furthermore, half of those savings mobilized by banks may be conducted through informal units and agents.

4.3.3.2 Malawi

National account statistics suggest that the private sector generated significant *net* savings, equivalent to 8.2 per cent of GDP in 1987. In 1992, however, the sector's position changed, with negative *net* savings (6.8 per cent of GDP). Thus these aggregate data show the very high volatility of the sector's net saving position. Although these estimates should be inferred with due caution because of the 'residual' method of calculation used, the flow of funds charts of the private sector corroborate the substantial yearly variations in resource flows in and out of the sector (Fig. 17(c–d)). A comparison of these charts for 1987 and 1992 provides us with some general observations, which can be summarized as follows.

1   In 1987 over three-quarters of the sector's net financial savings recorded in official statistics were mobilized by the commercial banks and the other NBFIs (4.7 per cent and 1.79 per cent respectively). However, the relative size of deposits mobilized by these formal financial institutions combined declined to 3.6 per cent of GDP in 1992, despite liberalization measures instituted.

2   The private sector received a little increase in net resources from the formal financial sector (only 0.7 per cent of GDP) in 1987, largely accounted for by a substantial decline in loans advanced by the commercial sector, as discussed in section 4.3.2. By 1992 the commercial

159

banks had become a net creditor to the private sector. As flows from the other NBFIs also increased markedly, the private sector increased net resource flows from the formal financial sector to 4.7 per cent of GDP, thus switching from a position of net creditor to that of net debtor.

3   However, the private sector is believed to have much more significant resource flows with informal financial units if non-commercial informal financial transactions are also taken into account. According to the estimate by Chipeta and Mkandawire (1991), both savings and credit flows with the informal sector exceeded 6.0 per cent of GDP in the late 1980s and have probably increased at least (by 10 per cent) in the early 1990s. Though most informal financial sector transactions take place within the household sector, these flows are separately shown in Fig. 17.

4   The private sector was a steady revenue source for the central government. Tax and non-tax revenue in both years was 17–18 per cent of GDP, the average for developing countries. However, the sector's holding of government stocks had shown large swings, indicating some significant switches of the sector's asset portfolios.

5   The private sector's foreign liabilities had shown some increases between the two periods. The sector's foreign asset holding is estimated to be of significant size.

4.4   Synthesis

Our analysis of the flow of funds, above, confirms that inter-sectoral financial flows, reflecting a pattern of intermediation by formal financial institutions, continue to be driven by fiscal imperatives in these economies. The relative size of credit flowing from the formal institutions, in particular from the central bank, to the government exceeds any other flows by a wide margin. Financial reforms have not induced discernible changes in this overall pattern of inter-sectoral flows. Formal financial institutions, many of which continue to operate in a highly unstable monetary environment, have not changed their behavioural characteristics in a significant enough way to affect the pattern of flows yet. The private sector continues to be marginalized by the formal sector. Financial transactions within the private sector are conducted largely in a circuit of informal finance.

Appendix 4.1   Flow of funds charts and analysis of the public sector

In Figs 15–17 financial flows are expressed as a percentage of GDP, for ease of comparison across countries and over time. Since our interest lies in capital account transactions, reflected in changes in the assets and liabilities of the various sectors, current account transactions between the sectors are shown by a broken line to distinguish them from capital account transactions, shown by a solid line.

Ghana

Flow of funds for 1987

The flow of funds of the public sector for 1987 elucidates the much improved fiscal position. In *current transactions*, the government increased tax and non-tax revenue to 13.2 per cent of GDP from the private sector, while receiving just under 1 per cent GDP in foreign grants (Fig. 15(a)).[65] With raised revenue, the government generated savings, equivalent to 4.1 per cent of GDP, surpassing the level of government investment and becoming a net surplus sector. Its transfer payments to the private sector were equivalent to 0.4 per cent of GDP. Net transfers to public enterprises were almost nil, as transfers were cancelled out by an equal amount of non-tax revenue raised by public enterprises.[66] Transfers and interest payments to the foreign sector (1.41 per cent of GDP) surpassed the size of external grants received (0.8 per cent of GDP).

Reflecting the overall strong budgetary position, *capital account transactions* of the central government showed a positive total resource transfer in 1987. The central government domestic debt to GDP ratio declined from 11–13 per cent in 1984–6 to 7 per cent in 1987 (Table 7). Thus one of most noticeable features of the flow of funds for the central government for 1987 is the reduction in net liabilities in relation to the other sectors. In particular, the central government reduced its total liabilities with the domestic banking system. The holdings by the central bank of central government debt in the form of stocks, treasury bills and overdraft facilities declined by 0.5 per cent of GDP, while the government increased deposits at the central bank by 0.28 per cent. Similarly, the deposit money banks' holdings of government debt declined by 0.05 per cent, whilst the government increased deposits with them by 0.07 per cent. Foreign liabilities of the central government also declined by 0.16 per cent.

The private sector and the SSNIT are the only ones which had increased their holdings of government paper. Thus during the year the private sector increased its stock of government debt (treasury bills and stocks) by 0.2 per cent of GDP, accounting for about 7 per cent of total outstanding government debt. The SSNIT increased its holding of government paper by 0.3 per cent of GDP in the year, increasing steadily its share as holder of government debt stock over the year (Table 7).

The public enterprise sector remained a net deficit sector. Its saving–investment gaps were financed by the foreign sector, which increased claims on state-owned enterprises considerably (by 2.4 per cent of GDP), and by credit from the central government (an increase of 0.7 per cent of GDP). However, it ceased to be a heavy drain on the resources of the domestic banking system. Although it continued receiving credit from SSNIT and the latter increased its assets to public enterprises by 0.06 per cent of GDP, the

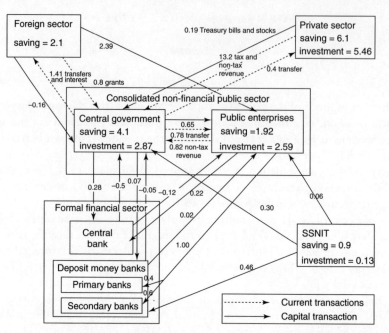

Figure 15(a) Flow of funds: the consolidated public sector Ghana, 1987. All figures are expressed as a percentage of GDP

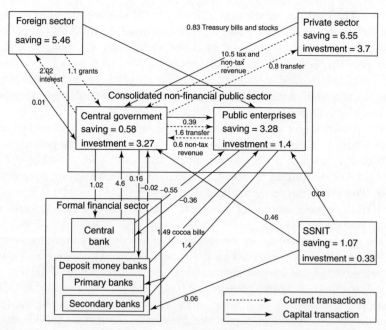

Figure 15(b) Flow of funds: the consolidated public sector Ghana, 1992

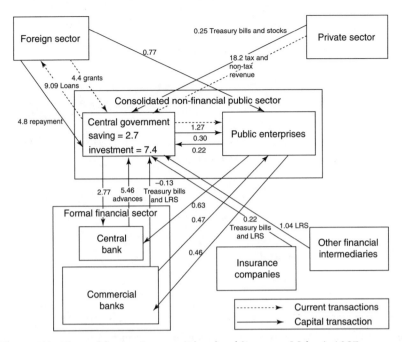

Figure 15(c) Flow of funds: the consolidated public sector Malawi, 1987

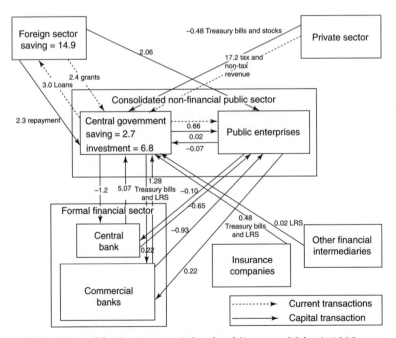

Figure 15(d) Flow of funds: the consolidated public sector Malawi, 1992

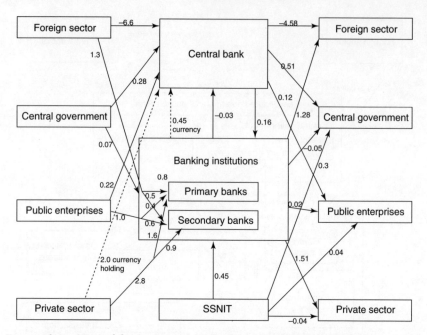

Figure 16(a) Flow of funds: intermediation by the financial system Ghana, 1987. All figures are expressed as a percentage of GDP

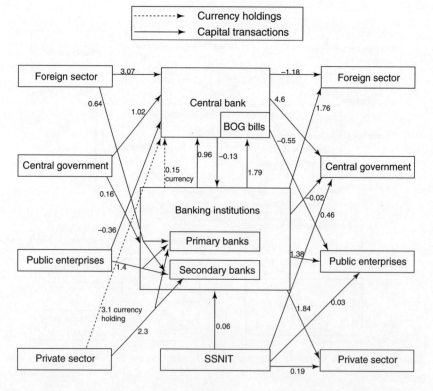

Figure 16(b) Flow of funds: intermediation by the financial system Ghana, 1992

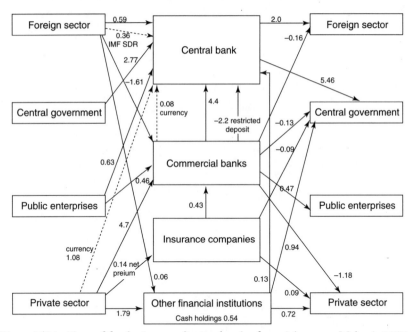

Figure 16(c) Flow of funds: intermediation by the financial system Malawi, 1987

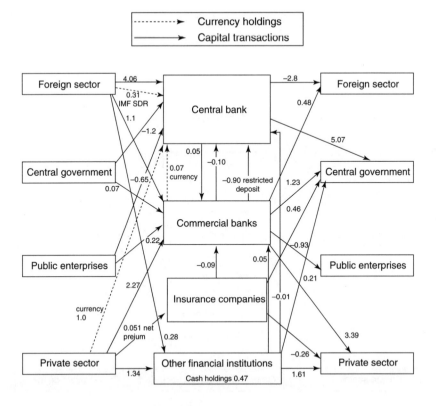

Figure 16(d) Flow of funds: intermediation by the financial system Malawi, 1992

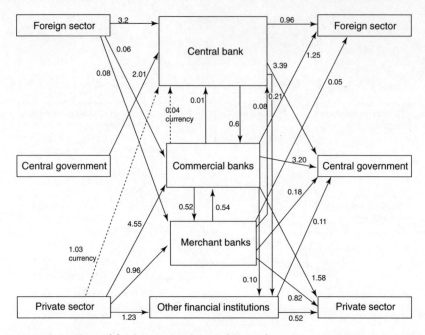

Figure 16(e) Flow of funds: intermediation by the financial system Nigeria, 1987

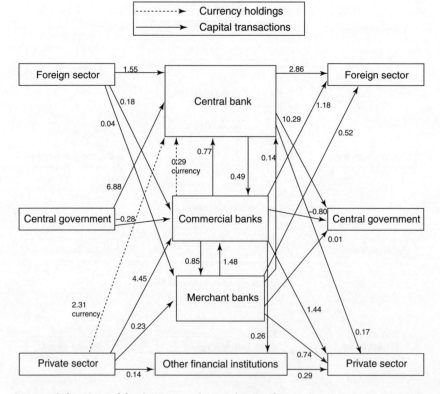

Figure 16(f) Flow of funds: intermediation by the financial system Nigeria, 1991

public enterprise sector increased deposits both at the central bank and with deposit money banks by 0.2 per cent and 1.04 per cent of GDP respectively.[67] In contrast, credit from the central bank increased only by 0.12 per cent and increased from deposit money banks marginally (by 0.02 per cent), resulting in an increase in their net assets with the banking system.

On the whole, in 1987, the central government reduced its liabilities by 0.19 per cent and increased its total assets by 1.0 per cent, resulting in a net resource position of 3.87 per cent of GDP.[68] The public enterprise sector's net resource position was, on the other hand, equal to 4.93 per cent of GDP, largely drawing on foreign resources in that year.

Flow of funds for 1992

The central government budget position worsened considerably in 1992, as both current and capital expenditure increased in the course of the election campaign. This resulted in a significant change in the flow of funds accounts from those in 1987. The central government savings declined from 4.1 per cent in 1987 to 0.6 per cent of GDP in 1992, while its investment rose from 2.87 per cent to 3.3 per cent of GDP.

Through *current transactions* the government raised just over 10 per cent of GDP in tax and non-tax revenue from the private sector, three percentage points lower than in 1987. At the same time, transfer payments to the private sector doubled. Further, the government had to make a net transfer of 1.0 per cent of GDP to public enterprises. To the foreign sector the government had to make a positive transfer of just under 1 per cent of GDP, with interest payments increased by 2 per cent of GDP against increases in grants equal to 1.1 per cent. Faced with this situation, the government was required to mobilize much larger resources for deficit financing through *capital transactions*.

Increasing foreign liabilities only marginally during 1992 (by 0.01 per cent of GDP), the government turned to domestic sources to finance an emerging fiscal deficit. Both the SSNIT and the private sector increased their holdings of government debt by 0.46 per cent and 0.83 per cent of GDP (Table 7). However, since commercial banks were not allowed to hold treasury bills,[69] by far the most significant source of deficit finance in 1992 was the overdraft facilities of the central bank. While government's deposits at the central bank increased by 1 per cent of GDP, credit from the central bank to the central government increased by 4.6 per cent of GDP, a dominant flow of funds in Ghana for the year. Direct interaction through capital transactions between the central government and other banking institutions remained relatively marginal.

The financial position of public enterprises improved in 1992 after several years of reforms, and the net savings position of this sector turned positive. In contrast to the situation in 1987, no capital transactions were recorded

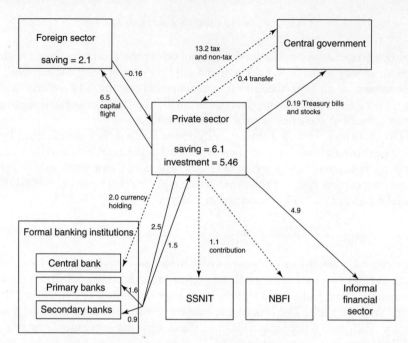

Figure 17(a) Flow of funds: the private sector Ghana, 1987

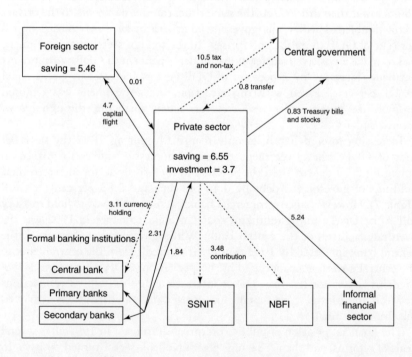

Figure 17(b) Flow of funds: the private sector Ghana, 1992

168

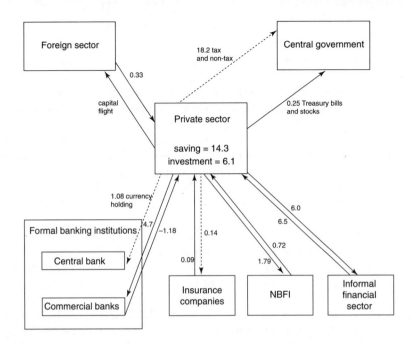

Figure 17(c) Flow of funds: the private sector Malawi, 1987

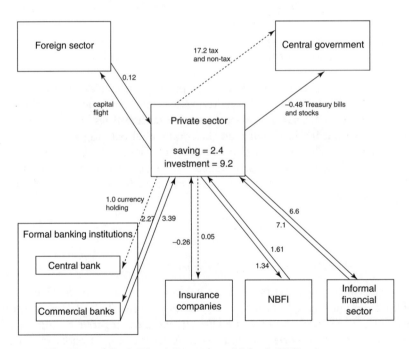

Figure 17(d) Flow of funds: the private sector Malawi, 1992

169

between public enterprises and the foreign sector in 1992.[70] Apart from the increase in net lending from the central government, the public enterprise sector also changed its relationship with the banking system. Transactions with deposit money banks increased, as public enterprises moved away from dependence on the central bank. In 1992 credit from the central bank to public enterprises decreased by 0.55 per cent of GDP, while deposits at the central bank fell by 0.36 per cent of GDP. Instead, public enterprises turned to commercial banking institutions for deposit and credit facilities. Deposits of public enterprises at banking institutions increased by 1.4 per cent of GDP,[71] and an equal increase was recorded for credit extended by DMBs to public enterprrises.

This shift, however, largely reflects changes in the finance of cocoa crop purchases. Before 1992 the Cocoa Board used to receive the bulk of agricultural credit and borrowed heavily from the central bank, which financed the purchase of about 80 per cent of total crop purchases. After liberalizing the marketing board and allowing private traders to buy cocoa, the central bank stopped lending to the Cocoa Board and 'cocoa bills' were issued instead. Indeed, most of the increase in credit was accounted for by commercial bank purchases of these cocoa bills in the money market. The equally marked increase in deposits of public enterprises can also be explained by the Cocoa Board's placement of resources mobilized by the Board through a syndicated loan facility of US$140 million (C126 billion) from the Euromarket.[72]

Overall, in 1992, the central government increased liabilities by 5.9 per cent of GDP, mostly through central bank overdraft facilities, and increased its general asset position by 2.5 per cent. This resulted in a net resource position of 6.5 per cent of GDP, which represents an increase of 2.5 per cent compared with 1987. The public enterprise sector's net resource position was also increased to 4.5 per cent, with a rise in total liabilities by 1.3 per cent of GDP, increasing its dependence on the commercial banking sector for cocoa crop financing. Thus the consolidated non-financial public sector as a whole mobilized a larger share of resources from the rest of the economy to finance the sector's activities in 1992. These changes were largely engendered by fiscal imperatives, discussed above.

Malawi

Flow of funds for 1987

The government received tax and non-tax revenue equivalent to 18 per cent of GDP, and foreign grants amounting to 4.4 per cent of GDP. However, this did not cover current expenditure entirely, yielding negative savings of 2.7 per cent of GDP in current transactions. With investment equal to 7.4 per cent, a deficit of significant proportions had to be financed by borrowing.

Foreign loans, amounting to over 9 per cent of GDP, were taken up. However, as repayments due on early loans were also of considerable size (4.8 per cent of GDP), net resources available from the foreign sector were much less.

The central bank made considerable advances available to the government, equivalent to 5.5. per cent of GDP, though net transaction between the government and the RBM was half this amount, with a marked increase in the government deposit at the RBM. The rest of domestic finance was made available through issues of treasury bills and locally registered government stock. The private sector, insurance companies and other NBFIs increased holding of locally registered government stock by 0.25 per cent, 0.22 per cent and over 1 per cent of GDP respectively.

Net resource flows in and out of parastatals were much smaller in 1987.[73] Their overall liabilities decreased, with a marked decline in foreign borrowing (investment) by this sector. While parastatals still received grants of considerable size (1.3 per cent of GDP, 4.1 per cent of government expenditure) from the government in current transactions, net lending from the government was much less significant (0.08 per cent of GDP and 0.27 per cent of government expenditure). Indeed, they increased deposits at the RBM significantly (0.63 per cent), whilst their resource balance with commercial banks was almost evenly netted out. Thus parastatals as such ceased to draw on the resources of the banking system in 1987.

Flow of funds for 1992

The year 1992 was a difficult one for fiscal management. The drought that hit the country was the worst in living memory. Besides the low tea prices commanded in the world market, aid from foreign donors was restricted for non-humanitarian purposes in support of democratization of the political regime. This condition was reflected in the flow of funds for the public sector for the year.

Though a reduction in domestic current revenue was marginal in relative terms, foreign grants indeed declined to 2.4 per cent of GDP. With the reduced level of current expenditure, however, the current transaction account yielded smaller dissaving. Additionally, in comparison with 1987, capital expenditure was halved in relation to GDP. The budget borrowing requirement was accordingly halved too.

Foreign loans taken out were reduced to 3 per cent of GDP. Indeed, external borrowing netted out repayment became a marginal source of budget finance. In contrast, dependence on the central bank as a major source of financing increased. The government drew on advances from the RBM (5 per cent of GDP) as well as reducing its deposits at the RBM by 1.2 per cent. The degree of monetization of the budget deficit was maintained high. Several sectors reduced holdings of locally registered government stock. For example, the private sector reduced such holdings by 0.5 per cent. Commercial banks, on the other hand, increased holdings of both locally registered government stock and treasury bills significantly (by 1.3 per cent of GDP), while insurance companies also switched their investment portfolio from locally registered stock to treasury bills. Thus government deficit financing in 1992 was significantly dependent on borrowing from the formal financial system on the whole, whose holdings of government debt paper increased by 1.8 per cent of GDP.

Parastatals further reduced their dependence on resources from the government as well as from the banking system. While net lending to parastatals from the government hardly changed from that in 1987 on account of the decline in their loan repayment, they received far less grants from the government in current transaction. Their liabilities to both the RBM and commercial banks declined markedly, though there was a considerable reduction in their deposits at the RBM. Their reduced liabilities to domestic institutions were, however, compensated for by a marked increase in their liabilities to the foreign sector (by 2.06 per cent of GDP).

Notes

1 Data on broader money, M_3, including deposits held by non-banking financial institutions (NBFIs) are not shown here, owing to the non-comparability of data for these countries.

2 The ratio of currency to M_2 can be estimated by comparing the currency/GDP ratio with the M_2/GDP ratio in Fig. 6.

3 This ratio can be represented as the difference between the graphs of M_2/GDP and M_1/GDP.

4 However, Duggleby et al. (1992) report that bankers estimated that the proportion of the national savings base held outside the banking system had declined from as much as 45 per cent of the national savings base to 25 per cent by 1992.

5 In Ghana a savings deposit account operates just like a liquid current account.

6 See below for the definition of monetary overhang.

7 By examining data on financial assets compiled by the Bank of Tanzania, Kimei (1994) notes that there has been a change in the structure of the financial assets held by the public. The share of currency and government securities in total assets has increased markedly, while there has been a corresponding decline in the shares of cheque accounts, savings and term deposits with non-bank financial institutions.

8 As argued below, those belonging to the first category have not been immune from frequent non-commercial (political) pressure in their portfolio decisions. In the context of sub-Saharan Africa, the demarcation is rather a matter of degree and scale. Harvey (1996) notes that while the commercial banks in Zimbabwe, including those owned by the government, such as Zimbank, managed to contain political pressure to lend on non-commercial grounds, there have been still many incidences of political loans and corrupt lending, though within manageable limits in relation to what has been observed in other African countries.

9 The delinquency rate is calculated as the proportion of loans which have not been paid after a specific period of time. The default rate is defined as the proportion of loans that have not been paid after a certain period of delinquency. Definitions of periods may vary across countries.

10 Stein and Lewis (1996) present the extent of the crisis affecting the banking sector by reporting the ratio of classified loans to shareholders' funds for different categories of institutions for the period 1988–92; it doubled to over 200 per cent for the merchant banks. It deteriorated from 500 per cent to 2,300 per cent for state-owned commercial banks. The ratio fluctuated from 150 per cent to 280 per cent for commercial banks. The average ratio for the NDIC-insured banks was 300 per cent, triple the minimum benchmark for classification as distress banks.

11 When economies are narrowly based, credit risks are highly correlated.

12 As noted in Chapter 3, however, the portfolio quality of many private banks, established after deregulation, is known to be grossly sub-standard because of the nature of their operations.

13 Adams and Graham (1981) note that most of the 160 or more agricultural credit programmes of the World Bank in Africa had failed to achieve sustainable and financially viable operations.

14 Agricultural lending is often regarded as one of the most costly and risky areas of financial activity, because of geographic dispersion, collateral problems, the small size of loans, and the risks inherent in farming (Adams *et al.* 1984). It is argued that these characteristics make loan transaction costs extremely high. Gonzalez-Vega (1990) attributes high transaction costs and high risks to fragmentation, limited market integration and incomplete institutional organization.

15 The World Bank policy study (1993) attributes the success of DFIs in East Asia to several practices: (1) the use of commercial criteria to select and monitor projects, even within the constraints of government priority setting; (2) the adoption of measures to contain wilful political interference in development banks; and (3) overwhelming dependence on domestic sources for finance.

16 'Monetary overhang' is a disequilibrium state resulting from the interaction between the money and goods markets. The disequilibrium literature advanced by Barro and Grossman (1971), Malinvaud (1977) and Muelbauer and Portes (1978) among others has long referred to this as 'repressed inflation'. Caprio and Honohan (1991) note the prevalence of this phenomenon in reforming socialist economies. We corroborated above the observation made by Collier (1989) with regard to the occurrence of monetary overhang in Tanzania in the early 1980s, when the economy suffered from a severe goods shortage.

17 Indeed, the syndrome is not confined only to countries in sub-Saharan Africa, but is widely observed in many LDCs, including the relatively open economies of small Pacific islands. See Nissanke and Basu (1992) for other examples in LDCs.

18 Treasury bills and government securities held as secondary reserves are not nearly as liquid as cash, particularly in the absence of active secondary markets for such paper.

19 The effect of the recent upward adjustments of the rate on government paper as a part of financial liberalization and monetary stabilization policies will be discussed below.

20 Excess liquidity in Nigeria has increased in recent years. Commercial banks have increased holdings of treasury bills in an attempt to improve asset quality, halving the loan/deposit ratio from over 80 per cent in December 1989 to just over 40 per cent in December 1993.

21 In the 1970s the largest component of liquid assets was held in government stock rather than in treasury bills.

22 During the 1980s most liquid assets were held as central bank deposits rather than as government securities, in contrast to the situation in the 1970s. These deposits at the central bank reflected the banks' liabilities for outstanding import payments awaiting externalization because of foreign exchange shortages.

23 In 1993 the delayed remittance of export earnings by clients, who had anticipated a devaluation of the Malawian kwacha, forced one of the larger banks to utilize the overdraft on its account with the central bank.

24 Indeed, it is often argued that high reserve *requirements* act as a heavy tax on financial intermediation (see Chapter 2.8). This tax is passed to private borrowers through an increased spread between the loan rate and the deposit rate (Fry 1988; Cottani and Cavallo 1993). However, Courakis (1986) argues that the *actual* effect of the reserve ratio depends critically on market structure, the characteristics of demand for loans and deposits and other conditions.

25 Most of the excess liquidity in Kenyan commercial banks in the 1970s appears to belong to this category. Here, banks have been more dynamic in savings mobilization and credit provision, and the minimum statutory required liquidity ratio has been at a lower level than in many other African countries.

26 This diagram combines Caprio's three diagrams (figs 1–3), with some modification.

27 While the cash reserves used not to earn any return in the early years, they were remunerated at 3 per cent to 5 per cent during 1990–3.

28 Instruments eligible for secondary reserves are government paper, Bank of Ghana bills, commodity bills and call deposits at the discount houses.

29 A missing insurance market for a high level of risk is another well known example of incomplete markets (Teranishi 1996).

30 Schmidt-Hebbel (1994) constructs an index of macroeconomic instability across regions, which encompasses four parameters: the inflation rate; the variation in real exchange rates; the external debt ratio; and the percentage black market premium. According to his estimates, the long-term (1970–90) regional average of the index for Africa is 1.22. This can be compared with the level of instability of 1.25 for Latin America and the Caribbean, 1.03 for other developing countries, and 0.26 for OECD countries.

31 Tanzania is not included in most of the analysis in this section, as data required for the analysis of inter-sectoral flows are either not available or of doubtful quality. For comparison, however, some basic indicators are estimated and presented in graphs and tables, though they should be evaluated with caution on account of the data quality. Our analysis of flow of funds for Nigeria is less comprehensive than for Ghana and Malawi, owing to the data problems.

32 There are several ways to define public sector composition (Schmidt-Hebbel 1994). As this study focuses on the role of intermediation of financial resources by financial institutions, the consolidated public sector here includes non-financial public enterprises in addition to the central government. Thus publicly

owned financial institutions are in principle excluded. However, owing to difficulties in obtaining accurate financial information on public enterprises in these countries, the estimates presented here should be viewed as preliminary.

33 Flow of funds analysis of the private sector in developed economies is usually subdivided into the corporate business sector and the household/non-corporate sector. Owing to data restrictions, we have not been able to accomplish this for our case-study countries. To the extent that public enterprises dominate real business activities in these economies, this might not have presented a serious problem to flow of funds analysis. However, this is increasingly unsatisfactory, as the dominance of public enterprises has considerably diminished in recent years, owing to economic reforms and in particular the privatization drive.

34 For a formal presentation of these inter-sectoral relationships see Johnston and Brekk (1991, pp. 105–8).

35 See Chapter 3 for the composition of the formal financial system, and Wall (1995) for detailed discussion of the method of estimation, data definition and other statistical issues.

36 It is argued that inflation acts as a tax through the effect on real money balances (see Chapter 2). It is also assumed that an increase in the monetary base will lead to an expansion of the money supply, which in turn results in inflation. This assumption is based on the premises of the monetary school, which assume a stable and predictable relationship between the monetary base and the money supply, and between the money supply and the inflation rate. The empirical validity of these premises has been challenged by numerous writers. Indeed, the money multiplier – the link between the monetary base and money supply – has been highly unstable in the case-study countries, as discussed in section 4.3.2. On the basis of empirical data from ten Asian countries, Gupta (1992) finds that the link between the monetary base and money supply is tenuous, which in turn casts doubt on the empirical validity of the direct relationship between the size of the fiscal deficit and the money supply.

37 Clearly a two-way causality exists in the relationship between fiscal deficits and other macroeconomic parameters, since foreign and macroeconomic shocks impinge on many components of public spending and revenue. (See Schmidt-Hebbel 1994 for a detailed discussion of the various channels of these causal relationships.)

38 Other definitions of the sustainable level of fiscal deficit include: (1) that which would not lead to the insolvency of the public sector as a result of developing a systematically higher debt–output ratio than the real interest rate; (2) that which is consistent with the intertemporal budget constraint of the public sector and the intergenerational consequences of fiscal policy.

39 As to our case-study countries, Ghana and Malawi had managed to reduce government deficits to sustainable levels in the adjustment period, while Nigeria's fiscal position continued to show large yearly fluctuations. It is clear that Tanzania's budget deficits had consistently exceeded a threshold of sustainability by wide margins.

40 The central government deficit can be measured in many different ways (Islam and Wetzel 1991; Schmidt-Hebbel 1994). As our primary objective is to estimate the public sector's net use of financial resources, the fiscal deficit here is

175

measured in terms of financing requirements, as reported in IMF government financial statistics.

41 Government deficit financing prior to the 1980s was dominated by central bank financing through money creation and financing by the Social Security Fund (SSNIT), which was required by statute to invest in government stock.

42 In this period, commercial banks were not allowed to hold treasury bills.

43 See Wall (1995) and Islam and Wetzel (1991) for the list of these enterprises.

44 Therefore, a number of assumptions have had to be made in order to construct a flow of funds account for the consolidated non-financial public sector (Wall 1995).

45 See Chapter 3 for the operational characteristics of ADMARC and MDC. In addition, the Malawian economy had long been dominated by a third prominent investment holding company, Press Holding, owned by its life President until very recent years. The structure of the public enterprise sector is discussed in detail in Adam *et al.* (1992).

46 As a federal state Nigeria has a multi-tiered system of federal, state and local governments. As federally collected revenue is passed to the lower-tier governments, the federal government retains only 55–70 per cent of federally collected revenues.

47 The Nigerian government has not published audited budgetary accounts since 1982. Hence, Nigeria's data are not reported in the IMF's government statistics. Furthermore, data on government accounts are inconsistent within the *Central Bank Bulletin* when the Central Bank balance sheets are cross-checked with the data presented in the section on government accounts.

48 The balance sheets data are checked against and supplemented by data on the financing requirements of the public sector, the current account balance, and changes in the net financial wealth of the private sector.

49 Net foreign assets are defined as total foreign assets minus foreign liabilities to non-residents.

50 These components of bank assets are also listed here in descending order of liquidity. As discussed in section 4.2, banks' holdings of treasury bills and other paper qualify as secondary reserves. Reserve requirements are expressed as the ratio of cash holdings (primary reserves) and holdings of secondary reserves to total deposit liabilities. Risk-adjusted capital adequacy requirements, increasingly used to measure illiquidity and insolvency, are calculated as the ratio of equity capital to total liabilities. This ratio illustrates the degree to which equity capital is able to absorb losses from risky assets.

51 Securitization is the transformation of an illiquid, non-marketable asset, such as a mortgage loan, into marketable liquid assets like commercial bills, which can be sold on the secondary market.

52 Although these two series should be identical through the accounting identity shown above, they diverge considerably when the IMF data are used for calculation. A key factor accounting for this divergence may be the fact that monetary authorities' operations with foreign assets and liabilities may not have corresponding counterparts in net issues of domestic currencies with the resultant changes in reserve money. Furthermore, for all case-study countries, the data on foreign assets and liabilities from IMF sources and from their central bank publication do not agree. This may be explained by different procedures used in

estimating the domestic currency equivalent of foreign assets/liabilities in the two series or differences in identifying the monetary authority. We use IMF data series for cross-country comparisons, while our flow of funds analyses are based on the data presented in the central bank publication.

53 The data are taken from World Bank (1994), where seigniorage is calculated as the increase in monetary growth in excess of that needed to satisfy the transaction demand for money. It is argued that seigniorage of more than 2 per cent of GDP is undesirable and that more than 3 per cent for several years indicates large macroeconomic imbalances.

54 According to the data in the central bank's balance sheets, reported in various issues of its *Bank Quarterly Economic Bulletin*, there was a significant change in the structure of high-powered money/monetary base in Ghana in 1988. It was caused by the fivefold increase in foreign liabilities, resulting in a sharp plunge in net foreign assets. In fact, the central bank's net foreign assets have been negative since then because of ever-increasing foreign liabilities, despite increases on the foreign assets side. However, this dramatic structural shift in the central bank's balance sheet was not borne out in IMF statistics which are used in our calculation of the time series data.

55 The SSNIT is a compulsory publicly owned provident fund and one of the most important non-bank financial institutions in Ghana (Chapter 3). By law it had been a captive source of government deficit financing, as it was required to invest solely in low-yielding treasury bills and other government securities. When these securities were not available, the SSNIT used to deposit the balance of any surplus with the Bank of Ghana (Islam and Wetzel 1991). Since 1986 it has moved into the real estate business, buying up residential and commercial property to lease or rent (Wall 1995). The SSNIT runs a surplus every year from its current operations, amounting to 0.9 per cent of GDP in 1987 (C6.7 billion). Its investment in real assets was just under C1 billion that year. The rest was invested in short-term financial assets, mainly treasury bills, Bank of Ghana bills and equity purchases, as well as deposits at the banking institutions.

56 Generally, central bank paper can be issued for liquidity management independent of government budgetary considerations. If an issue of Bank of Ghana bills is undertaken purely for liquidity management, it should only lead to restructuring of the central bank's liabilities between cash and other reserve assets, without having any corresponding increase on the assets side. In practice, however, it can be used as quasi-government debt paper, resulting in an increase in the central bank's credit to the government, thus altering the overall size of assets/liabilities. Therefore, in such circumstances, the net budgetary and monetary impact of using either central bank paper or treasury bills is similar. For example, Johnston and Brekk (1991) argue that the difference between the use of the two instruments is presentational, as 'for example, government budget finance would be affected at an equal rate with the net cost of issues of central bank bills through reduced central bank profits available for appropriation by the government' (p. 105). In the case of Ghana in 1992, there was strong pressure on the Bank of Ghana to finance the emerging budget deficit, and the Bank of Ghana bills were an attractive instrument to counter the resulting inflationary forces in the economy. Considering all these possibilities, Bank of Ghana bills

are presented as a separate category affecting flows of funds between the Bank of Ghana, the central government and the banks in Fig. 16(a–b).

57 In Fig. 16(b) this is shown as direct flows to the central government from the SSNIT, as the central government recorded C13.8 billion borrowed from the SSNIT. This is the net sum of the purchase of Bank of Ghana bills amounting to C19.6 billion less sales of government paper amounting to C4.8 billion.

58 The RBM reports a decline of 'restricted' deposits, 2.2 per cent of GDP, for which no clear definition is given.

59 These include the Post Office Savings Bank (POSB), the New Building Society (NBS), National Mercantile Credit Investment and Development Bank (INDE-BANK), and Leasing and Finance Company (LFC).

60 The Central Bank was, however, also known to have reduced its holdings of government paper for rediscount by an amount equivalent to 2 per cent of GDP. There was also a substantial increase in the federal government's deposits at the Central Bank (2 per cent of GDP).

61 While the commercial banks used very little credit at the CBN, a much larger increase was recorded (0.6 per cent of GDP) in the commercial banks' deposits at the CBN.

62 To derive flow data for these transactions, we have used numerous international and national secondary sources, including: national account statistics; the *Balance of Payment Statistical Yearbook*; the government financial statistics; and central bank publications (see Wall 1995 for detailed sources). In some cases, such as the estimation of capital flight, the data presented here inevitably remain speculative. (See Claessens and Naude 1993 for detailed estimation methods on capital flight.)

63 There are very few data on the financial conditions of the private business sector. The recent REPD study estimates that retained earnings of this sector averaged 19 per cent of the value of capital stock.

64 The World Bank (1994c) suggests that national account statistics underestimate private investment rates as well. Investment and saving activities are often difficult to distinguish in these economies, where savings are made in non-financial real assets yielding a low (negative) rate of return, with low levels of perceived risk. Data on private investment do not include, for example, the replanting of cocoa trees by small and medium-sized farmers. Yet Bateman *et al.* (1990) estimates that new plantings of cocoa under five years old involve 33 per cent of all the land under cocoa.

65 The size of tax revenue in relation to GDP was still significantly lower than 18 per cent, which is the average level for developing countries (Burgess and Stern 1993).

66 The data on public enterprises shown here are drawn from Islam and Wetzel (1991), which includes time series data on the net profits (losses) of the Cocoa Marketing Board (CMB, 1970–88) and the Ghana Industrial Holding Corp (GIHOC, 1970–86). The latter encompasses some profitable divisions, such as distilleries, canneries and pharmaceuticals, as well as continually loss-making sections, such as bricks, tiles and vegetable oils. The data on the Social Security and National Insurance Trust are reported separately, as it is one of the key publicly owned non-banking financial institutions in the Ghanaian economy. As such it demands analysis in its own right. The net profit position of the CMB

has historically been very unstable, generally producing a net operating deficit. In contrast, the GIHOC has generated net profits on the whole. Other non-financial public enterprises, except the Volta River Authority, are known to have made substantial losses or earned only meagre profits.

67 Public enterprises placed 40 per cent of deposits with primary commercial banks and the rest with secondary banks.

68 A sector's net resource position is calculated as the sum of total liabilities and savings, which should be equal to the sum of total assets and investment in the absence of any statistical discrepancy.

69 The commercial banks turned to holding Bank of Ghana bills instead (see sections 4.2 and 4.3.2 below).

70 This is remarkable, as foreign lending increased to C23 billion a year in 1989. In 1990, 8 per cent of public enterprise debt was foreign.

71 The increase is significant for both demand and time deposits in 1992. However, in the first six months of 1993 all the growth in deposits was in time deposits (Wall 1995).

72 Foreign currency loans contracted for cocoa purchases were sold on the interbank market, giving licensed Ghanaian buying agents access to the cedi proceeds. In 1994, out of the US$50 million loans secured for this facility, US$15 million went to four private traders and the remaining US$35 million to the public sector Produce Company – an autonomous agency (World Bank, Ghana Financial Sector, 1994).

73 Unfortunately, official statistics available do not separate data for financial and non-financial public enterprises. However, since financial parastatals' performance has been much better than non-financial ones (Adam *et al.* 1992), one can assume that most current and capital transactions presented here had gone to non-financial parastatals.

5

A MICRO-ANALYSIS OF MARKET SPECIALIZATION AND FRAGMENTATION

This chapter provides detailed information about portfolio management approaches in our case-study countries. We intend to link these factors with restrictions on the sphere of operations of lending units. To discuss this fragmentation in the financial markets, the chapter will characterize basic features of the operations of the different segments in terms of clientele, loan prices, loan purposes and maturity, as well as the accessibility of credit offered by the different segments.

In section 4.2 we made the general argument that portfolio management is often reduced to ensuring greater profitability, without necessarily expanding the volume of loans made to the private sector. While commercial banks have not been under any liquidity pressure in most sub-Saharan Africa countries, development banks have been more likely to suffer such pressures. Their restricted deposit base has led to increasing dependence on governments and international donors, which prevented a squeeze on their lending base until the early 1980s.

The relatively small amount of formal sector term lending to the private sector is often not the result of an inadequate lending base; it is instead a problem of the management of that base (Nissanke 1993a). The inability of lenders in sub-Saharan Africa countries to provide significant amounts of term financing varies for different institutions. For the formal sector, we intend to show that this inability is related to: (1) problems associated with maturity transformation of their liabilities; (2) difficulties in administering term loans, particularly regarding screening and monitoring for relatively small borrowers; (3) relatively high transaction costs, partly because of loan administration procedures and the relatively high risk of default; and (4) crowding-out by the public sector.

For the informal sector, on the other hand, the size of the lending base controlled by each unit is critical. It often depends either on deposits mobilized from a distinct group, as in a savings and credit association (SCA) or on the surplus funds of the lender from profits made either from lending or from other business activities. Ensuring a proper balance between their liabilities and assets often results in approaches that transcend the bounds of profitability, as we will see in Chapter 6.

Many semi-formal units have approaches to liability and asset management that lie between those of formal and informal units. For example, when credit unions in Africa occasionally administer credit provided by donor agencies, as in Ghana and Malawi, their management approaches are expected to contrast significantly from that used when they administer locally mobilized resources.

Following these observed differences in portfolio management, we show in this chapter that informal and semi-formal units have different asset/liability structures from formal units. In addition, they appear to manage these structures differently, though with the common goal of minimizing costs. We will investigate the extent to which lenders are able to finance their lending activities from deposits. Our analysis shows that banks have had difficulty matching their assets with their liabilities, despite widespread reforms and financial liberalization. This analysis is essential in explaining the poor trends in deposit mobilization and low levels of term lending.

The analysis is based on both secondary material and primary data from our surveys of formal and informal/semi-formal lenders. The survey data on formal institutions for Ghana were compiled for the period 1989–91, and for 1990–2 in the remaining three study countries. The selection of samples of bank branches was done within a stratified framework. The stratification was based on the type of bank (commercial, development, merchant, unit rural, community, etc.) and its location (urban or rural). In each country we attempted reaching at least 15 per cent of bank branches or at least fifty branches/unit banks. Without definite population characteristics for informal agents, we attempted to reach all types of known informal deposit mobilizers and lenders. Varying numbers of informal lenders were interviewed in each country. A minimum of 100 lenders were studied.

The chapter is presented in two main sections, looking first at the liabilities of formal and informal/semi-formal institutions in 5.1 and then at their assets in 5.2. We draw conclusions from these analyses in the last section. In each section, trends in the secondary data are discussed before proceeding with detailed survey results from branch-level interviews and other primary sources.

5.1 The liabilities of formal and informal financial institutions

Even after reform, the liabilities of many banks continue to be dominated by relatively liquid short-term instruments. For most commercial banks, deposits are the most important component of liabilities. However, these vary considerably in significance across banks, forming between 45 per cent and 85 per cent of total liabilities. As is to be expected, commercial banks generally have higher ratios of deposits to total liabilities than development and merchant banks. Commercial banks in Ghana on the average had deposit/ liability ratios of 60 per cent to 70 per cent in the 1980s. In contrast, development banks had ratios of between 50 per cent and 60 per cent, and the proportion of deposits in total liabilities was even lower in merchant banks. These deposit/liability ratios appear to be relatively stable in the short run.

An analysis of consolidated balance sheets of banks in our sample countries shows that deposits are closely followed in order of importance by 'other liabilities' (see the flow of funds analysis). These represent low-cost and short-term credit, margin requirements, and provision for taxation and payroll deductions. However, the proportion of short-term borrowing varies for many banks. While other liabilities formed as much as 20 per cent of total bank liabilities in Tanzania, they constituted only 9 per cent in Malawi.

As a category, 'other liabilities' is quite volatile. In Ghana, it grew steadily in the years of financial repression, constituting about 18 per cent of total liabilities in 1977 and rising to about 40 per cent in 1983. After the reforms, they declined rapidly, reaching 12 per cent of total liabilities by the end of 1991. This growth in the 1980s showed the reliance on borrowing in the face of shrinking business for development banks and a declining deposit base. Currently, short-term borrowing is almost non-existent in Ghana, even with the emergence of two discount houses. There is much more active business in short-term borrowing for banks in Nigeria than in the other countries studied, which could be attributable to greater competition. Long-term borrowing also is on the decline, as borrowing possibilities have shrunk with reforms. Only seven out of fourteen banks in Ghana had any long-term borrowing commitments in 1992, and they were mainly development banks.

Shareholders' funds seldom exceed 15 per cent of total liabilities in most countries. Nevertheless, many banks meet the capital adequacy requirements of central banks, except in Nigeria. Since reforms began, shareholders' funds have grown considerably, mainly because recapitalization of banks has been a major component of banking sector adjustment programmes.

In Ghana, capital adequacy ratios stipulate that shareholders' funds should account for a minimum of 5 per cent of liabilities. Until 1988 all state-owned development banks and a few commercial banks maintained ratios below this minimum. Since then, however, average ratios have been well above the minimum. Interestingly, state-owned development banks have some of the highest ratios of shareholders' funds to total liabilities, averaging 12 per cent, mainly due to recapitalization schemes. Malawian shareholders provided 12 per cent of the funds available to commercial banks in 1992, while the ratio was only 3.3 per cent for Tanzania. The low figure for Tanzania is a strong indication of the relatively slow pace of banking sector reforms.

In contrast, *informal* lenders' liabilities are narrower, being limited to deposits taken from a specific group of people or from surplus income earned by the lender from other economic activities. There is very little evidence that lenders borrow to lend to their clientele (see Chapter 7). In the few instances where lenders have borrowed or used 'external funding sources', the lenders have been semi-formal units, such as savings co-operatives and credit unions, that have been either capitalized or recapitalized by donor agencies.

Given informal lenders' dependence on deposits (except moneylenders), fluctuations in the availability of their funds are tied to membership sizes and the financial disposition of their members. Also, changes in general economic performance and real income appear to have more effect on the funds of informal lenders than they do on banks. Aryeetey and Gockel (1991) have reported examples of this from Ghana. In 1983 widespread bush fires in Ghana destroyed significant amounts of farmland. Moneylenders, who depend mainly on surplus income earned elsewhere, often lost their crop and, with it, the source of surplus income for lending. Many had to convert some of their lending capital into investments in their cocoa farms and working capital. Similarly, after staggering levels of inflation in the early 1980s, many SCAs and credit unions gave up their operations, as members could no longer afford to make the deposits that kept these institutions operational. In periods of high inflation, groups simply collapse.

5.1.1 *Deposit mobilization by formal institutions*

5.1.1.1 *General characteristics*

The deposits of banks in sub-Saharan Africa tend to be dominated by the holdings of the private sector, which in turn originate mainly from the household sector. However, there is some evidence that the share of deposits from the corporate sector has been increasing in the last decade in some countries. A feature of commercial bank deposits is that they are overwhelmingly short-term, and attract little or no return to the depositors. Depositors make relatively little use of the (often few) long-term deposit instruments that are available in sub-Saharan Africa countries. This dominance of short-term deposits is similar for informal lenders, as will be seen shortly.

In Ghana, approximately 70 per cent of bank deposits were demand deposits before 1983. By 1991, following reforms that began in 1985, demand deposits still accounted for 57 per cent of aggregate deposits. With savings deposits accounting for most of the rest, roughly two-thirds of bank liabilities were liquid instruments.[1] The trends in Tanzania, Malawi and Nigeria also varied in this period, although demand deposits continued to dominate total deposits. In Tanzania, where we observed the greatest growth in less liquid deposit instruments, the share of demand deposits in total commercial bank deposits dropped from 69 per cent in 1980 to 45 per cent in 1992. Simultaneously the share of time deposits went up from 23 per cent to 30 per cent, while savings deposits also increased from 7 per cent to 17 per cent. Evidently financial sector reforms and liberalization have altered this particular characteristic in many countries (see Fig. 18).

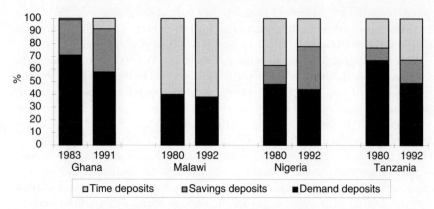

Figure 18 The composition of bank deposit liabilities before and after the reforms (% of total deposits)

There has been considerable growth in financial sector infrastructure over the last decade in Nigeria, where the structure of liabilities suggests a more even distribution of liabilities in the reform years, even though the proportion of time deposits fell by about 15 per cent in 1982–90. However, it must be noted that more than half of all time deposits in Nigerian commercial banks mature in three months or less. This suggests, as in many other sub-Saharan Africa countries, a strong preference for liquid assets.

Malawi has shown clearer and more sustained growth in interest-bearing deposit instruments over time. It was the only country in our study where such deposits dominated non-interest-bearing deposits. The share of demand deposits in total deposit liabilities was as high as 50 per cent in the mid-1970s, but decreased to 40 per cent in 1980. Over the same period, the share of time deposits increased from less than a third to more than half. The share of savings deposits remained relatively stable, owing to their wider distribution and the smaller amounts per depositor than demand and term deposit liabilities. This structure of commercial bank liabilities hardly changed in the reform years.

The trends outlined above suggest that reforms in these countries have had some positive effect on private sector portfolio allocation. Aside from the significant switch to treasury bills and other bonds, discussed earlier, there are problems with the flexible manner in which available term deposit instruments are operated. It is unlikely that the usual measure of financial deepening, the M_2/GDP ratio (discussed in Chapter 4), gives an accurate picture of how people wish to save. M_2 more clearly reflects the use of deposits for transactions than the demand for long-term savings. In fact, the monetary base has remained high in many countries, and has been not much less than the M_2/GDP ratio.

Given these trends, banks in Ghana, Tanzania and Nigeria would in principle have some difficulty in developing long-term assets. A normal function of banks is to achieve acceptable levels of maturity transformation, given these liabilities, and the important issue arising from this analysis of maturity structure concerns the possibility of achieving maturity transformation. Alternatively we may evaluate the scope for matching the maturity structure of bank assets with the existing maturities of their liabilities. We look now at how the above trends are reflected in branch-level analysis.

5.1.1.2 Trends in branch deposit mobilization after the reforms

Using survey data on the numbers of depositors and average deposit sizes from sample branches, we will investigate the trend of savings mobilization since the reforms began. Given the portfolio shifts described above, an upward trend in these indicators would be the clearest positive response to the incentives produced by reform. However, the survey data have shown inconsistent growth in the number of depositors and deposit sizes over a three-year period (1989–91) when reforms had already taken root in various countries. There has often been slow progress towards active deposit mobilization, which can be attributed to the excess liquidity syndrome that is evident in all sub-Saharan Africa countries (Nissanke 1993a and Chapter 4.2 above).

For Ghana, the numbers of depositors and deposit amounts generally changed slowly. The major sources of variation in deposits mobilized by bank branches were the type and location of the bank. A fall in commercial bank deposits in 1990 coincided with the first deterioration in economic performance since the beginning of the Structural Adjustment Programme, which suggests that income plays an important role.[2] The average number of urban commercial bank depositors fell in 1990 and rose again in 1991 (see Table 11), consistent with the decline in urban real incomes in 1990. For urban development banks there were only marginal increases in the number of depositors. Rural incomes, however, were sustained by rises in the producer price of cocoa in an attempt to boost exports, and rural branches showed significant rises. The significant growth in rural branch depositors was related

Table 11 Average number of depositors per branch/bank in Ghana, 1989–91

Type of bank	1989		1990		1991	
	Urban	Rural	Urban	Rural	Urban	Rural
Commercial	8,482	4,834	7,818	6,222	8,030	6,362
Development	4,517	5,189	4,692	8,077	6,647	7,122
Unit rural	–	4,799	–	5,730	–	6,550

Source: survey data.

to the increasing use of rural banks and branches for the payment of cash crop growers.

These changes in the numbers of depositors in Ghana were evenly matched by mobilized deposits, suggesting no significant changes in average deposits over the period. In interviews, bankers suggested that while some portfolio switches have occurred after the reforms, this has taken place from within the ranks of the traditional clientele of banks. Therefore, reforms do not appear to have drawn in significant numbers of new clientele, particularly in urban areas.

In Tanzania, deposit mobilization also improved marginally after the reforms began in 1986. Again, it varied according to the type of bank and its location. Commercial bank branches in Dar es Salaam saw their depositors grow eleven times as fast as in regional towns in the period 1990–2. In small rural towns, where the number of depositors grew faster again than in Dar es Salaam, rapid growth was partly the result of a government decision to pay salaries and farmers' payments through rural bank outlets. Many bankers believed that the most significant factor behind the rapid rise in the number of rural depositors was this new payment mode adopted by the government for agricultural export purchases. It should not, however, detract from commercial bank initiatives to increase savings mobilization.

Many people holding deposits at the banks did so under compulsion, as their salaries and other payments were channelled through the banks. These payments are usually kept in the most liquid deposit instruments, so we are again obliged to regard many such deposits as a reflection of transaction balances rather than a demand for savings (see Table 12).

Inconsistency in deposit growth is particularly evident in Malawi, where the number of commercial bank branch depositors grew by 39 per cent between 1990 and 1991. A year later, only 2 per cent growth was recorded in the number of depositors. Ironically, average nominal deposits of both urban and rural households actually fell between 1990 and 1992. Urban average deposits (bank balances) fell from US$1,496 in 1990 to US$1,047 in 1992, while those of the rural farmers fell from an average of US$741 in 1990 to US$497.

From Nigerian survey data, clearly the people's banks and community banks had the largest numbers of small depositors in 1990. However, their share began to fall as the commercial banks took on more depositors. Correspondingly, commercial banks recorded a significant growth in total deposits held by small depositors (see Tables 13 and 14).

That deposit mobilization by bank branches is often unstable and smaller than expected is partly a result of the absence of appropriate incentives. For example, branches are allowed to lend only certain fixed amounts decided by the head office, and this is often unrelated to the level of mobilized deposits. Bank branches usually transfer mobilized deposits to head office or appointed regional offices, and 'surplus branches', which mobilize more deposits than

Table 12 Branch-level deposit mobilization in Tanzania, 1990–2

Deposits	Dar es salaam			Regional towns			Rural towns		
	1990	1991	1992	1990	1991	1992	1990	1991	1992
Depositor per branch									
CRDB	950	11,241	11,241	7,970	8,989	9,054	21	805	835
THB	25,655	30,570	33,835	4,357	6,320	7,665	–	–	–
TPB	4,115	5,120	5,500	2,500	2,960	3,750	462	590	650
Total deposits, nominal (TSh million)									
CRDB	2,388	3,773	5,507	7,164	10,233	14,340	46	92	141
THB	895	1,168	1,000	2,604	2,750	3,460	–	–	–
TPB	16	29	27	6	12	18	8	15	15
Total deposits, real (TSh million)									
CRDB	120	155	185	360	420	481	2.3	3.8	4.7
THB	45	48	34	131	113	116	–	–	–
TPB	0.8	1.2	0.9	0.3	0.5	0.6	0.4	0.5	0.5

Source: survey data.
Note: US$1=TSh195.1 in 1990; US$1=TSh219.2 in 1991; US$1=TSh297.7 in 1992.

Table 13 Average number of depositors per branch/bank in Nigeria, 1990–2

	Type of bank												
	Commercial			Merchant			Community			People's		
Type of depositor	1990	1991	1992	1990	1991	1992	1990	1991	1992	1990	1991	1992
Small-scale enterprises	307	390	1,453	3	11	16	479	693	234	1,451	912	
Large-scale enterprises	440	558	2,057	4	9	14	216	677	553	784	831	624
Small-scale agriculture	316	454	558	3	18	23	185	817	550	2,418	1,647	580
Other	2,202	2,206	2,561	205	111	140	107	146	665	606	508	630

Source: own survey.

Table 14 Average amount mobilized by branch/bank in Nigeria, 1990–2 (N million)

Type of depositor	Type of bank											
	Commercial			Merchant			Community			People's		
	1990	1991	1992	1990	1991	1992	1990	1991	1992	1990	1991	1992
Small-scale enterprises	6.9	14.3	15.6	1.9	4.4	8.9	0.2	0.3	5.0	0.2	0.2	0.2
Large-scale enterprises	14.0	16.2	32.0	5.7	14.7	36.7	0.1	0.1	14.1	0.1	0.1	1.4
Small-scale agriculture	2.3	3.5	8.9	4.0	14.0	51.7	0.4	0.4	10.2	0.2	0.4	0.9
Other	20.6	22.1	38.9	22.2	15.2	30.3	0.2	0.5	1.2	0.1	0.2	0.3

Source: own survey.
Note: US$1=N8 in 1990; US$1=N9.9 in 1991; US$1=N17.6 in 1992.

they are permitted to lend, support 'deficit branches', whose requirements are met through inter-branch transfers. As this arrangement provides no room for branch management of reserves and no clear rewards for increased deposit mobilization, there is no incentive for branches to increase the number of deposit customers or the size of their deposits.

5.1.2 Trends in informal sector deposit mobilization

There is a growing consensus that informal finance has a crucial role in the achievement of integrated financial markets (Von Pischke 1991; Yotopoulos and Floro 1991). This conclusion is based on the high proportion of people who use informal financial facilities, and also the magnitude of transactions that take place within such units. It is worth noting that while the formal sector has shown considerable inconsistency in mobilizing deposits since the reforms, some informal agents have had consistently good performance. In spite of the acknowledged potential of informal units as deposit mobilizers, however, they have never been seen as having a key role in financial intermediation in the region. This is because units are seen as fragmented, with relatively small lending bases, and remaining untouched by government monetary and financial sector policies aimed at reform and liberalization.

5.1.2.1 Deposit mobilization by savings and credit associations

Savings and credit associations (SCAs) are known to operate in about half of all African countries (Miracle *et al.* 1980). Our surveys show, however, that their importance varies from country to country. We came across some SCAs that rotated payments to depositors (ROSCAs), while others did not. Indigenous SCAs, particularly ROSCAs, appear to have had a longer tradition in West Africa than in East Africa. Ardener's (1964) work shows the wide-spread use of ROSCAs in West Africa. Non-rotating groups are sometimes also called accumulating savings and credit associations (ASCRAs) or fixed-fund associations (Miracle *et al.* 1980; Bouman 1994, 1995).

These differences in the type of operation of SCAs (i.e. rotating or non-rotating) depend on the original operational goals of the association: whether they are pure savings and credit associations or mutual aid associations. In the first category, members join the group only for the purpose of saving and collecting from the pool of funds, while, in the second, clubs often combine general assistance to members with other communal obligations. Savings mobilization and lending are secondary in the latter. Since the principles of saving are quite similar in most cases, we consider rotating and non-rotating units together here, making appropriate distinctions where they matter.

The lending base of each SCA depends on membership size, the incomes of members and the frequency with which deposits are made. It is difficult to generalize about these, since SCAs vary in size both within and among countries. Limits are imposed on group size in order to contain risk and preserve the socio-economic values of group members.[3] Bouman (1977) noted a membership of between ten and thirty persons for associations in rural Cameroon. However, mutual aid associations, often non-rotating, tend to be bigger. Among *susu* groups in Ghana that did not rotate we observed an average membership size of thirty-seven, which was similar to the average for savings and credit co-operatives. For those *susu* groups that rotated, a size of twelve, corresponding to the number of months, was common. Thus non-rotating associations are usually larger than rotating ones. At the same time, urban SCAs generally tend to have larger numbers than rural ones. In Malawi the sizes of SCAs (all non-rotating) ranged from two to 250 people, with a mean of thirty-eight. The wide variation in membership sizes is evident.[4]

Individual deposit sizes are dictated by the personal purchase goals of members. Monthly contributions by individual members of SCAs in Ghana averaged about US$10, equivalent to 10 per cent of the monthly salaries of most public employees in Accra. Mean deposit sizes in Zambia, Tanzania and Kenya have also been estimated at 5–10 per cent of members' incomes (SODECON 1990). In both Tanzania and Ghana, some SCA members said that they were not willing to deposit more than 10 per cent of income in the ROSCA. As the nominal deposits did not change much in this period, only low inflation kept their real values significantly unchanged. For a long period most SCAs have maintained the proportion of income that they receive as deposits, and consequently their deposits have been more stable than those made at banks. The trends in Nigerian and Malawian SCA deposits have been quite similar. This stability is likely to be related to the tendency of members to 'target' deposits in order to yield a sum large enough for them to undertake purchases or to provide some working capital for business.

While we did not observe significant growth in the deposits made by individual members of SCAs in our study countries, indications of growth in deposits with SCAs are taken from the increasing number of operational SCAs in all countries. Although no data on the total number of associations exist, indications from interviews were that most operating associations were either new or have become active again after the reforms. In Tanzania the total volume of deposits mobilized by SCAs increased by 57 per cent in real terms from 1990 to 1992, with significant growth in the numbers of depositors accompanying the movement to a more liberal political and economic environment.

Similar to the commercial banks, the highly liquid nature of SCA deposits requires that ROSCAs minimize the intervals between payments into the common pool, especially where there are many members. Weekly and fortnightly contributions are very popular among traders, market women and other self-employed people.

5.1.2.2. *Deposit mobilization by savings collectors*

Our surveys established that, in Nigeria and Ghana, savings collectors were the most significant informal deposit mobilizers, measured by the number of depositors and the size of deposits. In Ghana, Aryeetey and Gockel (1991) came to the same conclusion after estimating that 77 per cent of market women in Ghana's three largest cities saved with *susu* collectors. Lelart and Gnansounou (1989) estimate that 45 per cent of market women in Cotonou save with a *tontinier*. USAID (1989) observed similar savings collectors in Senegal, and Shipton (1991) in the Gambia. Flammang (1989) described periodic deposits with trusted local individuals in Senegal.

Savings collectors' income (usually one day's deposit per month) depends on the number of depositors they can manage, as does the amount they have available to lend. These numbers have grown significantly since economic reforms were undertaken in both Ghana and Nigeria. *Esusu* collectors in Nigeria increased their depositors from an average of 250 in 1990 to 438 in 1992. Their counterparts in Accra raised their mean number of depositors from 155 in 1990 to 290 in 1992. The largest operations can involve up to 1,500 clients in a month, with several people engaged in the collection. The increase in clientele in Ghana was more rapid in urban areas than in rural areas; the number of urban depositors increased by 48 per cent in the period, compared with only 5 per cent in rural areas. In Nigeria, however, both urban and rural areas recorded significant increases.

With the increasing numbers of clients, mobilized deposits by savings collectors in West Africa appear to be growing rapidly after liberalization in comparison with other deposit-taking institutions. Our survey results suggest that deposit mobilization by savings collectors in both Ghana and Nigeria has grown considerably as the number of depositors has risen. Monthly collections for Ghanaian *susu* collectors (rural and urban average) increased from US$1,565 in 1990 to US$1,704 in 1992 (an annual growth rate of over 4 per cent). Aside from growth in number of depositors, collectors also attributed growth to larger deposit sizes in the three-year period. In the urban area of Accra the average amount mobilized in a month by a collector went up from US$6,410 per month in 1991 to US$7,918 in 1992, an increase of 24 per cent, and the average daily deposit of clients grew from US$0.76 in 1991 to US$0.86 in 1992. In rural areas, however, deposits mobilized grew only marginally, and mean daily deposits moved only from US$0.14 to US$0.15 between 1991 and 1992.

Although *esusu* collectors in Nigeria increased the number of their depositors by 75 per cent between 1990 and 1993, average deposits mobilized went up by only 51 per cent, indicating falling mean deposit sizes. As Nigeria has seen a proliferation of semi-formal financial institutions in the last decade, ostensibly to meet the financial needs of low-income groups, it is likely that these semi-formal institutions have drawn away potential clients with higher incomes. Thus the *esusu* collector has experienced an increase in the number of clients, but it has come from poorer groups.

5.1.2.3 *Deposit mobilization by co-operatives and credit unions*

Savings and credit co-operatives in urban areas are often known as credit unions and credit societies, and are usually part of organizations affiliated to the African Confederation of Co-operative Savings and Credit Associations (ACCOSCA). The confederation defines thrift and credit co-operatives as free associations of people with a common bond who save and lend money to one another at low interest rates, for use in productive and provident activities. Urban units deal mainly in consumer deposits and credit, while rural co-operatives are more involved in production finance, particularly in agriculture. Rural co-operatives tend to be very informal in their operations, while urban credit unions have more formal or semi-formal structures. For purposes of simplification, we shall use the expression 'co-operative societies' or 'co-operatives' for rural institutions and 'credit unions' for their urban counterparts.

Co-operatives and credit unions are probably the commonest non-indigenous informal/semi-formal financial units found in many sub-Saharan African communities. Saving and financing through co-operative arrangements appear to be more common in East and Southern Africa than in other anglophone parts of the region. However, they are also extensively present in francophone countries. We observed in Tanzania that the co-operative movement, or 'scheme', was the most significant form of informal deposit mobilization in rural areas. The movement operated initially as a set of urban arrangements, until the government encouraged it in rural and agricultural finance schemes. While most of these groups were initially spontaneous, the Tanzanian government later tried to influence their formation.

There are considerable variations in how co-operatives build up their funds in Tanzania. The funds are expected to come primarily from mobilized deposits, although the co-operatives sometimes receive financial support from international donor institutions. By law, they are permitted to raise funds through the issue of shares, as well as deposits. Urban societies are often able to do both, while rural schemes depend mainly on deposits.

In 1990 Tanzania had 438 rural-based co-operatives and 485 urban-based savings and credit societies or credit unions. The urban societies had 93,111 members, while the rural co-operatives registered 68,385 members. Together they mobilized about US$4.2 million worth of deposits, which was equivalent to 4 per cent of total commercial bank deposits in 1990. Membership and average deposit sizes have grown in the last few years, albeit inconsistently. The average size of rural groups was ninety-eight in 1992 and 281 for urban groups.

Savings and credit co-operatives operating in rural areas in Ghana had an

193

average membership size of thirty-seven in 1992, similar to the average size of a non-rotating SCA. Aside from the fact that rural co-operatives have been legally set up and registered, there is little distinction between their functions and those of the *susu* groups or SCAs. While urban credit unions have large membership sizes, averaging 390, they are not as widespread as individual *susu* collectors. In the Accra area, credit unions had an average of 1,166 members in 1992, a marginal growth of 6 per cent over the 1990 figure. Allowing for regional variations, the average monthly deposits of individuals in credit unions and in the *susu* system would be comparable, averaging 10 per cent of the monthly earnings of depositors in 1992.

In Nigeria, rural co-operatives appear to be much more vibrant than urban credit unions. The average size of a co-operative in Nigeria was more than five times the average size of a credit union. Mean deposit sizes in rural co-operatives were about twice those of urban credit unions. This may be related to differences in the purposes of saving, as rural members save to finance their investments, while urban depositors are targeting some consumption item. In addition, many rural co-operatives have been used to channel donor credit funds.

The ability of credit unions in many countries to mobilize deposits has fluctuated considerably over the past decade. In Accra they mobilized on average US$14,575 a month in 1992, but the flow of deposits had been erratic for some time, reflecting the general problems of credit unions in Ghana. Deposits had actually declined by over 50 per cent from the 1991 figure after a 40 per cent increase between 1990 and 1991, and the average size of monthly deposits made by individuals to *susu* collectors in Accra in 1992 (US$26) was significantly larger than those to credit unions (US$10). The smaller deposit sizes of union members are explained by differences in membership. Members of unions were mainly low-income public servants with relatively fixed incomes, who were saving towards consumption for a 'rainy day'. On the other hand, many market women saving with *susu* collectors were not merely saving towards consumption, they were accumulating their working capital for the next month.

5.1.3 *Increased competition and deposit mobilization*

In our study countries, it has generally been expected that competition would increase following the entry of new banks into the market and the re-structuring of existing banks and their financial products. However, the subsequent changes in competition have varied extensively across countries, from the very extensive increase in Nigeria to little change in Malawi. The situation in Tanzania is similar to that in Malawi, while in Ghana new institutions are quite clearly observable. Three new banks have been registered since 1988, and others are slowly emerging.

Increasing competition is important to induce innovations to attract depositors. Even where only modest restructuring had taken place, bankers interviewed in all countries suggested that they were experiencing increasing competition. Nigeria had the longest history of competition coming from the entry of new banks. Established banks in Ghana reported losing customers to the new merchant and commercial banks. The new commercial banks compete for deposit customers from the older banks, while the merchant banks take away larger corporate customers. There is no suggestion of significant new business being created, however. The older banks have indicated that the situation has forced them to adjust operations.

Most banks remain generally uninterested in adapting financial products to meet the needs of the majority of the saving public, and instead attempt to mould customers to the existing set of financial products. At best, traditional financial products (i.e. interest-free current accounts, savings accounts, time deposits and a selected number of bonds) have been repackaged by some banks. Nigeria probably offers the largest variety of banking sector products, and Nwandike (1990) has identified 151 such products, although this may overestimate the extent of variation. Often, seemingly different products are simply the same products with different packaging. The entry of a new commercial bank in Ghana led to the introduction of a new interest-bearing current account, a feature that was previously unknown in the country.[5]

Innovation after reform in Tanzania is reflected less in the financial products themselves than in banks developing more innovative ways of reaching customers. The largest commercial bank has introduced the mobile agency scheme, under which branches offer regular banking services to the public, using rented premises in selected centres. Another bank uses mobile vans with audio-visual equipment to attract customers. By far the most significant innovation here has been the introduction of the deposit link insurance scheme to cover small depositors. This arrangement is not widely found in sub-Saharan Africa, and may be expected to provide a strong boost to deposit mobilization.

Malawian banks also employ mobile vans in the attempt to reach more deposit customers. For the two commercial banks that operate this service, however, there are indications that mobile services are rather costly, and they are pursued only under a directive of the Ministry of Finance. This would suggest that competition among banks is currently low, and does not seem to have engendered any innovative approaches to increase market shares. This may be attributed to the fact that government institutions hold significant shares in the two major commercial banks. New entrants into the financial market have been limited to semi-formal institutions that offer banks little competition, given their limited range of services (see Chapter 7).

Given the limited effect of reform on competition and innovation, it is not surprising that deposit mobilization has not grown as rapidly as expected. At best, new banks steal customers from old banks and force them to repackage old products. Hardly any new products are developed to reach untapped segments of the financial market. The dearth of more innovative financial products from the banks is exemplified by the current popularity of treasury bills in many countries. Ironically, this preferred portfolio choice of many savers under the new liberal environment does not help banks to build a strong and stable lending base using their liabilities.

5.2 Assets of formal and informal financial institutions

As might be expected, there is greater variety in the assets of formal institutions than in the informal sector. The composition of formal financial assets also varies considerably across countries, with considerable variation in fixed and other assets (see Table 15). Ghanaian and Tanzanian commercial banks had an average of over 30 per cent of their assets allocated to fixed and other assets between 1988 and 1992, compared with only 14.6 per cent of Malawian commercial bank assets. The most important reason for this difference is the pervasive branch networks of the large, state-owned commercial banks in Ghana and Tanzania. Branch networks are not found on a similar scale elsewhere. The differences can partly be explained by greater government pressure on state-owned banks to expand their branch networks. In Nigeria commercial banks' assets were even more heavily dominated by fixed and other assets (49 per cent in 1992). This is explained by the significant expansion of the banking infrastructure, as the number of new banks was increasing rapidly.

Except for fixed assets, 'other assets' are mainly in highly liquid form and other self-liquidating assets with acceptable collateral. Although claims on government and the public sector have fallen in significance for commercial banks, they still form a noteworthy proportion of total assets.

The relative freedom of commercial banks in Malawi to manage their own portfolios may explain the much larger claims commercial banks have on the private sector than in other countries. While claims on the private sector have increased considerably in the reform years in the other countries, they still lag far behind the other claims of banks. The difficulties in increasing lending substantially to the private sector are discussed below.

In many countries with large formal financial systems and with significant participation of government in the ownership of banks, the most significant change in the composition of bank assets since the reforms began has occurred within the development banking sector. Prior to reform, development banks had the greatest difficulty in matching assets with liabilities, so it is not surprising that they have carried out more extensive revisions of their asset structure. There has been a gradual diversification in portfolios, and development banks have significantly reduced the proportion of term loans. In Ghana the volume of loans with maturities over three years has been

Table 15 Composition of commercial bank assets, 1992 (%)

Country/asset	Ghana	Malawi	Tanzania	Nigeria
Claims on private sector	20.00	57.4	21.5	22.0
Claims on government	0.04	10.0	8.9	3.0
Claims on other public sectors	9.80	1.4	26.4	0.0
Other assets[a]	35.50	14.6	32.4	49.0
Foreign assets	23.30	2.9	2.9	11.0
Cash and deposits with central bank	11.30	13.5	4.9	15.0

Note: [a]Fixed and office assets.
Source: computed from various annual reports of relevant central banks.

reduced by over 20 per cent since 1988 in favour of short-term loans. This is in line with the attempt to create 'universal banks'. The trend is similar in Nigeria, where short-term financing is increasing with new merchant banks. Loans with maturities over one year declined from 69 per cent of merchant bank portfolios in 1980 to 46 per cent in 1990. After 1986 Tanzania experienced a similar trend.

5.2.1 *Trends in formal sector lending*

5.2.1.1 *General characteristics*

After reform, banks had been expected to increase the volume of lending to competitive sectors of the real economy. Such lending is determined by the risks associated with projects and the expected rate of return on loans. Thus it was anticipated that some benefit would accrue to those sectors of the economy that suffered from policy biases under financially repressive regimes, such as private small-scale manufacturing. However, this has not happened on the scale anticipated (World Bank 1994a).

In Tanzania and several other countries, lending to the public sector dominates total lending from commercial banks, although private sector lending by commercial banks is on the increase. Lending to the private sector in Tanzania has been low for a long period. This can be attributed to the country's socialist history and large losses in the years of financial repression (Chapter 4). While private sector lending has increased, it still accounts for only about a quarter of total commercial bank lending. Since 1989 the trend in Ghana has shown considerable change in favour of the private sector. In Nigeria also, while lending to the private sector is reported to have increased, there have also been recent switches by the banks to increased government lending as, in Ghana and Tanzania (see Table 16). Comparatively, Malawi has had a better distribution of commercial bank loans and advances, and the private sector has tended to be favoured in lending.

Table 16 Private sector lending in total commercial bank lending, 1986–93

Year	Ghana	Malawi	Nigeria	Tanzania
1986	13.6	39.4	47.2	7.2
1987	10.6	29.0	54.3	7.8
1988	16.9	35.5	51.9	12.9
1989	37.0	48.2	n.a.	9.6
1990	27.6	52.5	63.5	14.6
1991	30.1	59.0	54.1	11.8
1992	30.9	63.0	40.8	23.0
1993	35.8	40.4	44.9	27.1

Source: computed from various annual reports of relevant central banks.

Within private sector portfolios, there is considerable variation in the distribution of domestic credit according to economic sector. Financing agricultural exports dominates the sectoral allocation of credit in both Malawi and Tanzania, where it takes more than 50 per cent of total credit. Small producers are less likely to receive these sectoral allocations. In Tanzania, for example, only 5 per cent of credit goes into agricultural production itself, and as much as 58.5 per cent goes into the marketing of agricultural produce, which was handled by a loss-making public entity. The choice of this activity was therefore dictated by government. In Malawi the bulk of agricultural credit finances tobacco production on large commercial farms and the activities of tobacco merchants as they buy from local auction floors, process, pack and export tobacco. This is the mainstay of the economy and the banking system has been designed to meet the need. The dominance of credit in Ghana and Nigeria by 'Other' shows the strong influence of domestic traders, mainly importers and retailers. For economies that are anxious to expand and diversify their production bases, the relatively low allocation to manufacturing is striking. Indeed, it is often only the largest manufacturing firms that receive credit from banks in Africa (see Table 17).

Table 17 Sectoral allocation of credit, 1992 (%)

Sector	Ghana	Malawi	Nigeria	Tanzania
Agriculture	11.4	53.6	15.8	68.1
Mining	1.6	0.1	1.4	
Manufacturing	25.0	12.1	35.4	22.1[a]
Construction	17.8	0.9	10.6	2.0
Other	44.1	33.3	36.8	7.8

Note: [a] Includes mining.
Source: computed from annual reports of relevant central banks.

Aside from the bias towards specific sectors, there is clearly a preference for large-scale activities. In Ghana, only one out of three applications submitted by micro-enterprises to banks has any chance of success, as against one in two applications by larger firms (Aryeetey *et al.* 1994). We use our survey data to explore the extent of the bias against small borrowers below.

5.2.1.2 *Trends in bank branch lending after the reforms*

The analysis here focuses on the characteristics of loans made by formal sector institutions to different categories of borrowers. Despite reforms, banks' ability to diversify loan portfolios has not improved significantly. After demonstrating their bias in lending to large and other low-risk borrowers here, we will investigate the reasons for this behaviour in the next chapter.

Loan applications There is some variation in the sectoral composition of loan applications received by different banks in the study countries. In Ghana the most loan applications came from sectors other than manufacturing and agriculture. Within the manufacturing sector, small borrowers also dominated loan requests. The largest number of small manufacturing applications per branch (fifty-five) in 1991 went to development banks, while the smallest number (twenty-two) went to unit rural banks. In 1991, on average, banks received only nine applications from large-scale enterprises, thirty-five from small-scale enterprises, 100 from the agricultural sector, and 156 from others, mainly commerce, construction and households. The pattern in Malawi is similar.

In Nigeria, the people's banks have undoubtedly become the largest recipient of loan applications. Most bank branches received no more than 100 applications from each sector, but applications to the people's banks exceeded 2,000 for all sectors in 1990 and 1991. By 1992 branches were receiving almost 6,000 applications on average, but with a significant decline in the number of large-enterprise applications. In Tanzania an average of 220 loan applications were received by branches of the Co-operative and Rural Development Bank, rising to 380 by the end of 1992. Other banks experienced similar increases in the number of applications, particularly from micro-enterprises. In all countries, there are significantly more loan applications from small enterprises than from large enterprises, indicating their strong demand for finance at liberalized interest rates. At the same time, applications from 'Others' often far exceed those from the 'productive sectors' of the economy.

Branch sectoral allocation There is also considerable variation in loan approvals by bank branch. In Tanzania, for example, only 10 per cent of loan applications in regional urban branches were approved in 1992.[6] In small rural towns, less than 3 per cent of applications for bank credit facilities were approved.

While our secondary data for Tanzania show the dominance of lending to large public enterprises, there are indications from branch data that more attention is now being paid to small borrowers. Unlike the situation in other countries, where loanable funds are not in short supply, Tanzanian banks are constrained in meeting the demand for finance from larger state-owned enterprises, and there are hardly any medium-sized private enterprises.

While large manufacturing enterprises in Ghana tended to be relatively few in the number of loan applications, they have dominated credit allocations to the private sector. For commercial bank branches, large enterprises took as much as 74 per cent of their total loan portfolio for the private sector, while agriculture had less than 5 per cent. In addition, large firms took more than 50 per cent of loans extended by development banks. Ironically, the lending portfolio of the unit rural banks was dominated by lending to traders and public servants, at 61 per cent of total loans. Even in rural areas, small manufacturing enterprises received fewer loans than their urban counterparts. Evidently, rural banks have come to prefer lending to 'others' at the expense of small agriculture and small manufacturing/repair service sectors.

In Malawi the greatest improvement in loan numbers occurred in the small enterprise sector. However, the contrast in loan amounts is striking. While 21 per cent of all loan approvals were earmarked for the small enterprise sector in 1992, it received only 15 per cent of total loan volumes. Large enterprises, with 10 per cent of loan approvals, received 63 per cent of total loans disbursed.

Nigeria appears to exhibit much greater access to loans for small enterprises. Small enterprises are more likely to be successful in their loan applications than elsewhere, with 83 per cent of their loan applications to commercial banks approved during 1990–92. Also, total portfolio allocations to the small and large enterprise sectors show less disparity, although large enterprises continue to receive a greater share of total loans disbursed. In general, banks in Africa devote much greater proportions of their loan portfolios to large borrowers.

Trends in loan interest rates since the reforms After adopting financial sector adjustment programmes, many governments expected that banks would set lending and deposit rates in response to credit supply and demand conditions. This would entail an initial increase in the spread between lending and deposit rates, as banks needed time to reshape their cost structures within the changing environment (see Fig. 19). However, it was expected that the spread would narrow as more efficient business practices were adopted in the face of increasing competition and as credit demand stabilized. Banks were also expected to increase the volume of lending to competitive sectors of the real economy.

However, lending rates have not only risen sharply during the reform years in all countries, their rise has been much faster than that of deposit rates.

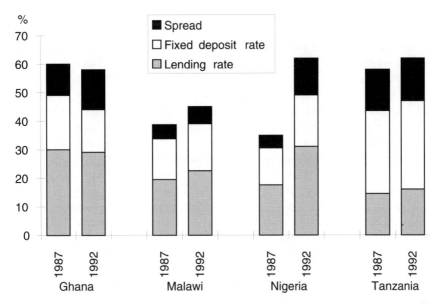

Figure 19 Interest rate spread in sample countries

While there is no universally accepted time frame for the reduction of spreads, a criterion that could be used is the period required to restructure ailing banks. Three years is usually an acceptable turn-round period. However, in most cases, increases in spreads have been maintained more than seven years after the reforms began.

Our survey results from Nigeria showed that lending rates for small enterprises varied between 22 per cent for people's bank and 44 per cent for merchant bank loans. Most Nigerian lending rates were between 29 per cent and 33 per cent in 1992. To show how fast lending rates rose, it may be noted that prime lending rates for commercial banks climbed from 23 per cent in March 1992 to end the year at 29.8 per cent. By mid-1992 in Ghana banks' base rates ranged from 26 per cent to as high as 32 per cent for unsecured loans.

It is not obvious what factors currently drive interest rates. Interviews with head office staff in many banks suggest that banks set lending rates according to market competition and the average cost of funds. Administrative costs were mentioned only as a third determinant. However, the present cost of funds to banks does not appear to justify current spreads. It is generally expected that an increase in transaction costs would encourage lenders to push up their lending rates to maintain profits, depending on the structure of the market. In contrast, Hoff and Stiglitz (1990) argue that there is a limit to the ability of lenders to increase their rates, as 'at some higher interest rate the greater risk and thus higher incidence of default will offset the increased interest income from the loan portfolio' (see Chapter 2). Instead lenders try to keep a 'favourable risk composition of projects'. Banks in many developing economies consider a favourable risk composition to be one that is heavily weighted against small-scale enterprises and the agricultural sector.

Variations in the base rate for loans by sector have almost disappeared in many countries after the reforms. Differentials continue to exist in the *total* cost of loans by sector, but they are usually marginal. Thus for example, on top of the nominal rates advertised, many banks in Ghana impose commitment and servicing fees on lenders. In 1992 these usually added about 2 per cent to the advertised rate. Indeed, most commercial and development bank managers interviewed said they had such additional fees for all categories of borrowers. So did most of the unit rural banks studied. However, the rates vary for different borrowers. Interestingly, small agricultural loans were the least likely to attract other charges. In an unusual case, one development bank's base charge for SMEs was 30 per cent. Borrowers were also charged 1 per cent for legal documentation, a 1 per cent fee for the appraisal and valuation of collateral, a 2 per cent servicing fee and a 1 per cent commitment fee, yielding an effective rate of 35 per cent. While variations in nominal rates for different sectors are vanishing, effective rates still suggest discrimination against small producers.

Following the liberalization of interest rates in 1990, the head offices of Malawian commercial banks set minimum lending rates. These were advised to their branches, which had discretion in deciding the addition to this minimum rate. The addition is largely influenced by the length and quality of the relationship with the customer, as well as by the risk and the type of collateral security offered. The more liquid and readily realizable the security the fewer the percentage points added to the minimum interest rate. Small firms are likely to receive loans with the largest additional charges. Nigeria and Tanzania exhibited similar charges on top of base rates.

Trends in loan maturities after the reforms   There are considerable differences in the maturity of loans between the case-study countries. The shortest average maturities we observed were in Malawi, where most loans mature in less than ten months. Given this, small enterprise credit has the shortest average maturity period of three and a half months, while agricultural loans have longer maturities, averaging nine months to coincide with the farming cycle. The longest maturities that Malawian commercial banks will make available are for twenty-four months to large-scale manufacturers. These maturity characteristics do not appear to have changed with the advent of reforms.

Tanzanian banks have much longer loan maturities than in Malawi. Indeed, the Tanzania Housing Bank still has thirty-six-year loan facilities. The Co-operative and Rural Development Bank has a portfolio dominated (99.6 per cent) by medium and long-term loans for financing farm machinery, equipment, expansion or improvements in ranch development. The largest portfolio of short-term loans (one year) is available from the National Bank of Commerce. Portfolio restructuring for development banks has not had appreciable effects, as public institutions continue to be the largest borrowers from state-owned banks.

Loans from commercial banks in Ghana generally have longer maturities than those of other banks. It is interesting that, for all banks, there were hardly any distinctions in loan maturities by location. Maturities are not very negotiable, and thus the maturity of rural loans does not differ from those of urban loans. The longest loan maturity we observed for bank lending to the small enterprise sector was seventeen months in 1991. For the large enterprise sector, the longest maturity for a commercial bank loan was eighteen months. It would appear that banks did not generally use different maturities to discriminate between borrowers within a sector. But there were sectoral differences: hardly any agricultural loans had a maturity beyond twelve months for all banks.

In Nigeria, SME loans from commercial banks had an average maturity of nine months, and loans to large enterprises had an average maturity of fourteen months. Loans from merchant banks had longer maturities than commercial bank loans. In this case, the merchant banks play the typical role of term lending institutions. The maturities of loans from the people's banks were found to be shortest.

5.2.2 *Trends in informal sector lending*

The discussion of financial products here is intended to highlight the segmented nature of the market. This segmentation is related to different strategies by lenders to overcome moral hazard and adverse selection. We defer discussion of the actual process of asset management to Chapter 6, and here look at the financial products of the different informal agents. For each informal unit, we consider the characteristics of borrowers, the volume of lending and the nature of the loans themselves. In all cases, we consider trends since the implementation of financial reforms. For moneylenders, we analyse the sources of their funds, since they do not generally mobilize deposits. In view of the similarities between the facilities offered by rural co-operatives and SCAs, we discuss them together.

5.2.2.1 *Lending by savings and credit associations and rural co-operatives*

Like certain other informal financial activities, SCA lending has experienced considerable growth, both in the numbers of clients and in their diversity. Although the scope of SCA activities has broadened with time, the socio-economic principles underlying their operations do not appear to have altered. Rather, greater diversity has been induced by the changing socio-economic circumstances of their clientele and by changes in the national economy.

In view of the extensive variation in size of SCAs and co-operatives, it is difficult to compare loan volumes across regions. We will, therefore, measure growth in the volume of lending by measuring the proportion of loan applications that are actually successful. This has been complemented with information on loan size. There appears to have been significant growth in the lending of many SCAs and rural co-operatives. In Nigeria, for example, the average number of loan applications to SCAs averaged thirty in 1990, with 60 per cent success. The applications more than doubled to sixty-three in 1992, and the success rate rose to 76 per cent. For Nigerian co-operatives, while the number of both loan applications and loans granted increased significantly, the success rate dropped only marginally. There is also evidence of growth in SCA lending in Tanzania, as the number of loan applications increased by 61 per cent and the success rate remained constant. Interestingly, in Ghana, growth in SCA loan applications was not uniform throughout the country. The fastest growth occurred in poor regions, as these experienced a significant boost in economic activity following structural adjustment and also lacked sophisticated financial structures. Malawian SCAs granted loans to each applicant. This failure to observe normal turn-down rates suggests that supply may exceed creditworthy demand.

It is well known that SCA credit facilities are widely used for consumption. They may also be used by farmers requiring seasonal assistance. In Malawi the use of SCC loans for financing agricultural working capital outweighs their consumption use. These loans are used mainly for fertilizer purchase and payment for farm labour (Chipeta and Mkandawire 1991). Evidence from Malawi and elsewhere shows that these small, short-term loans are suited to activities which have a quick turnover, such as cereal production. In rotating associations, borrowing in urban areas is usually aimed at the acquisition of consumer durables that cannot be financed directly from monthly incomes, while in rural areas agricultural implements and other farm inputs, such as seeds, are purchased.

Loan sizes are often directly related to the size of the groups and their deposits. Therefore, larger groups offer larger loans. Chipeta and Mkandawire (1991, p. 26) have observed in Malawi that the 'amount a member is allowed to borrow per month is expected not to be in excess of his salary, which sets an upper limit on his known debt-servicing capacity, since the standard credit period is one month'. We observed average loan sizes of US$320 for an average period of four months in 1992, and this had been growing for some time. In many countries, within a twelve-member ROSCA, early drawers from the fund could secure as much as US$100-US$200 loans (with varying 'maturities', depending on their position in the rotation).

In Ghana, the average amount granted to successful applicants by SCCs and SCAs was about US$130. This figure, which is certainly not large, lay between the amounts that could be borrowed from *susu* collectors and moneylenders. Loans could be extended beyond six months only under unusual circumstances, such as bereavement. The largest loan amount observed for an SCC in Ghana was US$1,000 and the smallest US$3 in 1992. However, few potential borrowers have access to SCC/SCA funds, as membership is a prerequisite.

Although large sizes ensure larger loan amounts, the sizes of the groups must be kept at levels that can be effectively managed. Membership is an essential tool for screening loan applications and for ensuring that contracts can be enforced. For many SCAs, limitations on size are imposed, as it is expected that risk will increase with numbers and that homogeneity will be lost as the group expands. The resilience of ROSCAs appears to rest in homogeneity, as described in Slover's study (1991) of ROSCAs in Zaire. Homogeneity provides members with a sense of familiarity that engenders mutual trust. ROSCA members often suggested that their associations were not keen on 'mixing people with too different backgrounds and interests', which signifies the importance attached to homogeneity in socio-economic status. However, ethnicity, which is often assumed to be an important factor in association membership, may be losing its importance in the selection procedure. In many large African cities, SCAs are often based in offices and market places where there are high levels of ethnic diversity, and they become relatively 'cosmopolitan' in character. Nevertheless, the founder of a ROSCA may initially attract people with similar ethnic backgrounds.

Limits on the size of loans restrict the use of SCAs to those borrowers whose demand for loans is not regular (e.g. those requiring a loan to purchase a relatively expensive consumption item). In some associations in Ghana, however, market women and traders who need larger loans co-ordinate funds with *susu* collectors and SCAs. The deposits returned by *susu* collectors are placed in the SCA and allow them to multiply significantly the size of their loans. Lelart and Gnansounou (1989) have described a similar combination scheme in Benin in which a *tontinier* collects a daily deposit from twenty-one clients and distributes the accumulated pool (minus fee) every ten days to each client in turn over 210 days. Although such joint arrangements were previously reported by only 1 per cent of respondents (Aryeetey and Gockel 1991), they are reportedly increasing in popularity among West African traders (presumably larger ones who are less constrained by day-to-day liquidity requirements).

In general, annualized informal sector interest rates appear high by comparison with formal sector rates, and this is also true of co-operatives and SCAs. However, annualizing interest rates may not be appropriate in making comparisons. For example, when co-operatives or SCAs lend to their members, they expect to use the return on the loans to finance the entire operations of the group. These objectives go beyond the accumulation of loanable funds, and the welfare aspects of their operations are thereby catered for. In 1992 mean interest on the loans of co-operatives in Ghana was about 5 per cent per month for their six-month loans. This was similar for SCA lending to members who expected to be paid a dividend out of interest profit earned. Interestingly, when SCAs lent to non-members their lending rates were comparable to those of regular moneylenders, as members expected to be paid dividends at the end of the deposit cycle.

For Tanzanian SCAs and SCCs, we observed a mean monthly interest rate of about 2.6 per cent. This was comparable to the 31 per cent per annum charged officially by the state-owned commercial bank, and co-operative bodies claimed to base their lending rates on formal sector rates. This stands in sharp contrast to interest rates in other countries. In Malawi the mean monthly interest rate for co-operatives was 13 per cent, which is much higher than the formal sector rates discussed above. Interestingly, this rate was also higher than those of the SCAs.

In rotating schemes, no explicit interest is paid, and, to ensure that all members receive interest-free loans, cycles of saving and lending are usually arranged. Such cycles ensure that each member will obtain an interest-free loan at frequent intervals. In contrast, loans from rural co-operatives are often packaged to coincide with the farming cycle. Depending on the mix of crops grown, in many areas maturity will be from four to nine months. Co-operatives are sometimes willing to extend term loans (up to twenty-four months in Tanzania), if they are secured by land. SCA loans, which are often for consumption, have shorter maturity periods, seldom exceeding six months.

5.2.2.2 Lending by savings collectors

Periodically, savings collectors grant 'advances' to some of their trusted clients, and Ghanaian savings collectors said that there was a very high demand for such 'advances'. An average of 60 per cent of their clients request credit each month. Out of these, 50 per cent are judged to be 'bankable', reflecting the ability to repay from cash flow (Steel and Aryeetey 1995). Collectors usually lend at the beginning of each month out of deposits mobilized in the first few days, in the hope that borrowers will complete repayment within the month so that other depositors can receive the full value of their deposits. Any outstanding loans on the last day of the month may prevent them from meeting their obligations.

Savings collectors believe that the more credit they grant the higher is the likelihood of finding deposit customers. Nevertheless the limits on the maturity of loans and their lack of any capital or credit to fall back on prevent them from granting additional advances in proportion to loan requests. Although 50 per cent of loan applications may be bankable, no more than 15 per cent of applicants are successful. In the Accra area the average *susu* collector received 1,584 loan requests throughout the year in 1990, 1,692 in 1991 and 1,860 in 1992, an average annual increase of over 8 per cent. In both years the success rate of applications varied little, ranging between 13 per cent and 15 per cent of applicants. Nigerian *esusu* collectors had on average fewer loan applications, because of the larger number and variety of credit suppliers. Applications per collector rose from forty-one in 1990 to 130 in 1992, and, during the same period the number receiving loans in Nigeria also rose from thirty-three to eighty-three. As with other lenders, there is a greater success rate for applications than in Ghana.

Over 90 per cent of the loan applicants of savings collectors are their deposit clients. The remainder are likely to be other traders in need of short-term credit. Most people applying for credit from a collector regard their request as urgent. When collectors lend to non-deposit clients, the terms are often different from those of their deposit clients; they tend to behave as moneylenders. In providing 'advances' to clients, savings collectors are generally guided by the size of the daily deposits of those clients. We estimated that the average loan size was US$30 to regular clients in 1992 in Accra. Loan sizes in rural Ghana were half the size of urban loans. A similar amount, US$38, was estimated for average loan sizes in Nigeria. Collectors ensured that only a part of the maximum deposit of a depositor (they often mentioned 50 per cent), could be taken as an 'advance'. The largest monthly advance reported for 1991 was US$300 in Ghana.

While there is usually no explicitly stated interest payment agreed with the borrower, collectors apply relatively high effective charges.[7] Interest payments are built into the service fees that all depositors pay. However, the rate of interest for any amount is usually uniform and related to the daily payments/deposits of clients. Thus, for borrowers who take an 'advance' less than the equivalent of their monthly savings, the service fee may be equated with an interest payment, i.e. 3.3 per cent per month. In cases where borrowers take an 'advance' in excess of the normal monthly accrued deposits, they are obliged to raise the daily deposit to amounts that ensure that repayment can be completed in a month.

In situations where interest is paid over the usual service fee, we observed rates of about 40 per cent for three months. Many collectors suggest that explicit payments of interest are not common, since they undermine the confidence of clients. It would appear that an increase in the volume of 'advances' and a subsequent increase in 'service fees' appropriately compensates them for the loan services they provide. Considering that they derive interest income *without* lending, the incentive to increased lending is the expected rise in the number of clients, which in itself would ensure additional 'service fees' or 'commission'.

Savings collectors do not usually allow clients to repay 'advances' over periods beyond a month. When relatively large amounts are lent, however, a maximum of three months is sometimes permitted for the completion of repayment. Short maturity is the major characteristic of these 'advances', and that makes savings collector loans unattractive to people desiring longer-term facilities, for either working capital or fixed investment.

5.2.2.3 Lending by moneylenders

The definition of 'moneylender' employed for our study was 'anyone whose business (either full-time or part-time) is to lend money on a regular basis in expectation of a return'. The lender may or may not have any other business relationship with the borrower. In many countries, the extent of other business relationships leads to certain forms of 'specialization' within this category. For example, moneylenders include trade creditors and supply creditors. In these situations, lenders sometimes show interest not only in the outcome of the credit facility but also in the related activities of the borrower, leading to interlinked transactions. We look here at the commercial moneylender whose relationship with a client does not go beyond the present loan facility, even if he/she operates only on part-time basis.

In Nigeria the clientele of moneylenders is wide, including farmers, market women, other traders, both senior and junior public servants, self-employed craftsmen and businesspeople. The profile of borrowers is similar in Ghana and Malawi. Farmers usually borrow from moneylenders during the planting season to maintain their households until the next harvest. They may also borrow for expenditure on funerals and other social events (Adegboye 1969). Our survey data suggest that public servants are the most important clients of urban moneylenders in Nigeria. In urban areas, borrowers often live or work in the same community as the lender. In many rural areas, however, long distances may have to be travelled; the average distance covered to reach a moneylender in rural Ghana was about 50 km. These distances introduce another element of risk in rural areas, which we analyse in Chapter 6.

Credit from moneylenders is not attractive for investment purposes, for a number of reasons to do with the conditions of the loan and its quantity and type. Initial funds for lending are usually surplus income from other economic activities, and the growth of these funds is entirely dependent on profits from lending and the other economic activities. Traditionally, moneylenders do not mobilize deposits and therefore cannot expand their lending base that way. The limited supply of funds (often held by a monopolist lender) has to be allocated among different borrowers within set geographical areas in a manner that permits the lender more information about the borrower's ability to repay.

There is some evidence of increases in the number of loan requests going to moneylenders in several countries, although the increases are not as large as those observed for other informal lenders. Loan applications in Ghana rose by 21 per cent over the three-year period 1990–2. Rural moneylenders appear to receive more applications in a year than urban lenders, and there is certainly more competition in urban areas. In 1990 a moneylender in Ghana extended an average of seventy loans, corresponding to 82 per cent of their loan applicants. The proportion of applicants receiving loans in 1991 and 1992 was 71 per cent and 82 per cent respectively. In Nigeria, also, similar growth in the number of applications and approvals was observed. The average *katapila* in Malawi received forty-four applications for loans in 1990, the figure rising to seventy in 1992. Only fifteen applications could be honoured in 1990, and twenty-four in 1992, however. It is evident that small borrowers applying for informal loans have a higher likelihood of success than those applying to formal lenders.

The size of loans from urban moneylenders in our case-study countries ranges between US$50 and US$1,000, with a median value of about US$250. For Ghana as a whole, the average loan among moneylenders in 1992 was US$172. Urban loans are significantly larger than rural loans: in Accra the average loan was about US$340, as against US$30 in rural Ghana.

In general, loans from moneylenders are larger than from other informal lenders. While loan sizes observed in Nigeria were not much different from those in Ghana, the loans granted were significantly smaller than the amounts applied for (by about a third). There does not appear to be any clear rationale for this discrepancy, except the possibility that Nigerian borrowers have exaggerated expectations. While moneylenders usually strive to accommodate the loan requirements of borrowers, lenders do not always feel obliged to offer the amount requested. In situations where the lender does not know the borrower well, the loan amount is often limited.

The interest rates of moneylenders are often one of the least understood features of informal lending. Much of the literature describes them as 'usurious', in spite of considerable variation among and within countries. Moneylenders' rates are usually reckoned on a monthly basis, but apart from that, rates and terms vary from one moneylender to another. Credit from moneylenders is often the most expensive credit available, and so the demand is usually from people without other options. The interest rates of *katapila* in Malawi appear to be higher than in other countries, and Chipeta and Mkandawire (1991) have reported rates sometimes as high as 100 per cent per month. Such rates have been applied for many years in Malawi, and interestingly, in both Malawi and Ghana, moneylenders insist that interest rates have been established 'by tradition'. The expression *katapila* is derived from the term meaning 'returning substantially more than originally borrowed' (Chipeta and Mkandawire 1991). In many countries, the interest rates of moneylenders exceed formal lending rates by at least 50 per cent per annum (see Fig. 20).

In spite of 'tradition', the reform years have seen some evidence of a reduction in moneylender interest rates in some countries. It is not obvious whether it is a result of a decline in demand due to competition with other informal lenders or a change in moneylenders' own supply situation. Quite

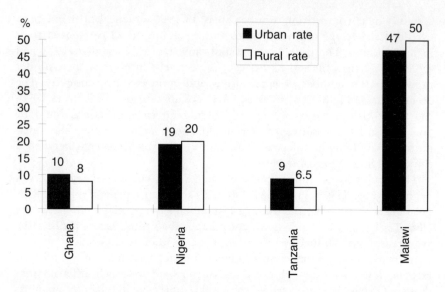

Figure 20 Moneylenders' monthly interest rates, 1992 (%)

likely it is a consequence both of competitive market forces and of some structural change on the demand side arising from economic reforms and subsequent growth in those countries. Moneylenders are having to change the scope of their lending business in response to changes in the financing needs of their traditional clientele. Consumption credit demand is falling in significance, and there is increasing pressure on lenders to provide more credit for working capital at longer maturities. Moneylenders indicated during interviews in Accra that 'our clients have difficulty paying 100 per cent on loans for up to three months, so we have to be sympathetic'. Moneylenders' loans have an average maturity of three months. Few loans in Ghana go beyond six months, even though the maximum period a lender would permit is one year. However, it is common to roll over one-month or other short-term loans.

Interest rates are influenced by several factors, which vary according to local conditions. Ghate (1990) has identified four components of moneylender interest rates: the risk-free element in the rate of interest (that is, the opportunity cost of funds); a premium for risk; a premium to cover the transaction cost; and an element of monopoly profit. Usually, the relatively high interest rates of moneylenders are explained by their overestimation of the risk element involved, leading to a high risk premium. But moneylenders' perception of high risk may be justified on the grounds that they do not have the sanctioning authority that other informal lenders enjoy – by operating, for example, among well known groups of people. Another possible explanation is that borrowers lack information about cheaper sources of credit. Our analysis of costs later will show, however, that the element of monopoly profit is also very high. The illegality of moneylending in most countries reduces lenders' sanctioning power and increases their monopoly status.

Evidence of the use of interest rates to discriminate among borrowers is inconclusive. While almost all moneylenders we studied in Ghana indicated that they did not use interest rates to differentiate among borrowers, the opposite was found in Nigeria, where large interest rate differentials existed for new customers. New customers paid as much as 8 per cent more than existing customers did.

5.2.2.4 Lending by credit unions

Lending by credit unions in many African countries has been problematic in the last decade, owing to widespread difficulties in sustaining lending programmes. Many unions would hardly survive without the support of various donors and NGOs (Chipeta and Mkandawire 1991).

More than half of credit union members in most countries apply for loans each year. Records do not indicate as much growth and vigour in the activities of credit unions as we have seen among informal lenders. Thus unions in Ghana received on average 133 loan applications in 1990, 137 in 1991 and 123 in 1992. The figures for loan applications per union varied considerably by location; in larger cities, total loan applications were over twice those in smaller towns. This is attributable to the relative sizes of the unions.

Union lending in many places is erratic. For example, in Ghana, application success rates have varied extensively from year to year. Only 55 per cent of applicants in 1990 were successful, in contrast with 83 per cent in 1991 and about 95 per cent in 1992. This can be accounted for by the external support credit unions received in the latter years to boost their lending activities. The trend is quite similar in Malawi, although Tanzanian unions appear to be financially much stronger.

The by-laws of credit unions allow them to determine each year the maximum loan amount for each member. Most credit unions fix an amount that is twice the value of the savings held for the member. Others have larger loan limits, depending on whether the projects to be financed are deemed to be income-generating or not. The smallest loan amount from the credit unions we studied in Ghana was US$2.5 and the largest US$7,500. On average, however, loan amounts were about US$112 in most urban areas. The difficulty that credit unions have with lending in Ghana is shown by the fact that loan amounts were significantly smaller than the amounts requested by applicants. In Nigeria the average loan amount of US$58 in 1992 was 85 per cent of the amount requested. Credit unions had the smallest loan sizes among the informal/semi-formal units studied in Nigeria.

It would appear that the interest rates of credit unions are intended to be close to formal sector rates for lending. The philosophy of unions is not to provide subsidized loans, and rates are often set to be either on a par with or marginally below the minimum lending rates of commercial banks. While unions in Ghana charged a mean rate of 3 per cent per month on the outstanding balance at the time of our survey, Nigeria unions charged 2 per cent for the same period. The data from Malawi and Tanzania were not much different.

Credit union loans generally have longer maturities than those of other informal lenders. In many countries, maturity is usually for a period of six to twelve months. The only exception in our case-study countries was Tanzania, where union loans had a relatively short average period of three months. An average maturity of seven and a half months was observed in Nigeria. In Ghana, however, the most frequently indicated loan maturity was twelve months at the time of the survey. Credit unions are able to provide loans at longer maturities only when a small proportion of members are eligible for loans in any one year. Their portfolio management problems are related to the difficulties they have had in adhering to guidelines on eligibility from year to year.

5.3 Synthesis

We have shown in this chapter that the deposits and credit facilities of both formal and informal/semi-formal financial units display specific differences in structure and packaging. This makes it possible to associate their demand and use with distinct socio-economic groups. In Chapter 6 we analyse the rationale behind the choices lenders make, while in Chapter 7 we explore in greater detail the structure of the fragmented market that results from these characteristics.

Notes

1 In many countries, even though savings deposits may be withdrawn only within seven-day intervals, branch managers often exercise a wide degree of discretion, depending on their liquidity position. This allows many savings customers to operate savings deposits as demand deposits (without chequebooks), thus making such accounts highly liquid.

2 The performance of branch-level deposit mobilization in Ghana parallels changes in the M_2/GDP ratio. This ratio rose from 12 per cent in 1984 to 17 per cent in 1987. After a decline in 1988, it rose to 16 per cent in 1989, only to fall again in 1990 to 14 per cent (see Chapter 4).

3 We discuss limits on size further in section 5.2.

4 Elsewhere, members have been observed to range from 'a handful to several hundred' (Ardener 1964). The *iqqubs* in Ethiopia have an average of eleven members (Aredo 1993).

5 Account holders are expected to keep a minimum balance of US$800, which attracted a minimum interest payment of 18 per cent in 1993. Interest is

subsequently calculated on daily cleared balances and varies in line with prevailing rates. Other interest-bearing accounts normally attract interest only on the minimum balance within a quarter. For this type of account, withdrawals are restricted to a maximum of six cheques per month. It remains the only major interest-bearing current account in the country. One older commercial bank has only allowed interest on current accounts where the balance exceeds US$3,080 in a quarter, and this attracted an interest payment of 5 per cent to 8 per cent in 1993.

6 This proportion had risen from 6 per cent in 1990.

7 When lending to non-deposit clients, there are usually *explicitly* stated interest payment obligations.

6

INFORMATION, TRANSACTION COSTS AND RISK MANAGEMENT AMONG DIFFERENT INSTITUTIONS

There is a growing theoretical literature on credit and savings in economies characterized by incomplete markets and imperfect information (e.g. Alderman and Paxson 1994). These works help us analyse the institutional arrangements through which financial transactions take place in sub-Saharan Africa. Aside from playing the core role of intertemporal allocation of resources, credit transactions reflect the economic environment within which they occur. As this study has shown, the environment in sub-Saharan Africa is usually characterized by objective risk, with unpredictable variations in income as a result of weather and other exogenous processes. In the absence of complete insurance markets, credit transactions take on a special role in allowing resources to be transferred in response to income shocks. The costly acquisition and asymmetrical distribution of information are essential aspects of this environment. Risk and information take on a special role in credit transactions, an analysis of which provides an important insight into intertemporal transfers of resources.

When discussing financial market segmentation, it is important to distinguish between normal specialization, resulting from the differentiated attributes of risk and cost, and fragmentation, in which the differences in risk-adjusted returns occur across segments (see Chapter 2). Specialization is characteristic of well developed markets where the risk-adjusted returns are comparable for the different suppliers. In fragmented markets, on the other hand, the prices that lenders charge for their services reflect their own different perceptions of access to information and of the risks involved. Hence, different lenders may offer similar products at different prices to different borrowers (Jones et al. 1991). Even where financial products (credits) are perceived to be different, the fungibility of money ensures that differences in product are not too wide to entirely preclude substitution, in spite of substantial price differentiation.

On the supply side, some nominally similar products may have significant variations in contracts by different lender types serving different market segments – banks, finance houses, credit unions, moneylenders, savings and credit co-operatives, savings and credit associations, traders, landlords, savings collectors, money guards, friends and relatives. When these different segments have relatively little interaction, the prices of each category have little or no bearing on the operations of others.

On the demand side, the clientele can be approximately divided into large established firms that have access to banking facilities, and individuals, small-scale businesses and the agricultural sector, which rely mainly on informal finance (Adams and Fitchett 1992). These types of demand are not necessarily exclusive, as demand for the products of both sectors have specific and non-specific elements. In most rural areas, where the demand for credit cannot be satisfied by formal channels, the demand for informal finance is likely to be specific or exclusive, and informal products may be considered as a substitute for what the formal sector could have offered. In urban areas, where much of the demand for credit is non-specific, issues of information asymmetry gain prominence and issues of complementarity and substitution become obscured.

This chapter highlights the methods by which formal and informal lenders attempt to mitigate the problems of moral hazard and adverse selection which arise out of information asymmetry. In coping with these problems, lenders develop special organizational features that demarcate the boundaries of the various market segments. Our objective is to show that, after various adjustments to their costs, the returns to many different categories of lenders are hardly comparable, even when account is taken of the differential risks they face. We analyse lenders' perceptions of risks in financial transactions, looking at how they manage risk, and the transaction costs involved, using primary data gathered on the assessment of risks by banks and other informal lenders. Processes for loan screening and their associated costs are reviewed, as are loan monitoring and contract enforcement. In carrying out these reviews, we seek to answer the questions of how the differential risks and incentives of different lenders and borrowers are affected by uncertainty. These evaluations help in assessing the comparative advantages of each segment, thus helping to explain why they choose to lend to particular borrower categories.

Our analysis of practical approaches to contain risk have been guided by some of the recent theoretical work in this area, as presented in Appendix 6.1. The theory emphasizes the importance of lenders' ability to impose penalties on defaulting borrowers and suggests that lenders will not make loans if penalties are unavailable, regardless of the apparent availability of arbitrage opportunities. Hence, the absence of strong legal enforcement mechanisms in financial markets in sub-Saharan Africa is an important possible explanation for financial market segmentation. In that situation, lenders will lend only if pressured for non-economic reasons (for example, by governments), as often happens in many sub-Saharan Africa financial systems. We thus seek to ascertain empirically the validity of these and other theoretical positions in this chapter.

6.1 Differences in risk assessments by lenders

Do different lenders have the same perception of the level of risk associated with each borrower? The discussion in our earlier chapters would suggest that they do not. Formal lenders tend to see small borrowers as riskier than large borrowers, while informal lenders appear to assess borrowers on criteria other than size. We consider briefly the empirical evidence.

6.1.1 *Variations in risk by borrower for formal lenders*

From the country surveys, it was clear that a significant number of formal lenders attributed variations in interest rate by borrower to differences in perceived risk. In Nigeria, for instance, the effective SME interest rates from merchant banks were significantly higher than effective rates for other sectors. In Ghana 70 per cent of bank managers offered similar explanations for higher rates. We noticed, in Chapter 5, that bank branches in Malawi set margins on the base rate that were dictated by perceived risks, among other factors. These margins were often particularly high for small borrowers.

Formal lenders suggest several reasons why small borrowers are riskier: it is more difficult to obtain accurate information about them – partly because they are often geographically remote; frequent illiteracy among borrowers makes it less likely that they understand contract terms; and their incomes are often erratic, making repayment sources unclear.

6.1.2 *Variations in risk by borrower from informal lenders*

If informal lenders also attached different risks to borrower types, then we would again expect to observe different interest rates. This tends to happen when informal lenders lend to people outside their normal set of borrowers, at which times they act much like moneylenders. However, this behaviour is atypical. In most interviews, informal lenders contended that they did not attach different risks to borrowers within their usual clientele. Membership requirements for these clients necessarily mean that borrowers have been pre-selected. It is, therefore, the broader objectives and functions of these lenders which dictate their perceptions of risks in lending. In Tanzania, for example, ROSCAs and savings and credit societies do not perceive different levels of risk for borrowers, because of group membership selection criteria. Similarly, traders who lend only to people they have a trading relationship with are less concerned about the return of cash lent than about gaining access to the produce of the client. Cost of acquiring information is also reduced because of transactions with the client in other markets.

In sum, the methods of client selection used by informal lenders effectively reduce the risk of dealing with small borrowers. Thus their clientele may be thought of as low-risk, even though they would be perceived as high-risk by formal lenders. We discuss later some of the methods informal lenders employ to reduce the risk associated with small borrowers.

We mentioned above that the only type of informal lender who regularly deals with a wide range of different types of borrowers, i.e. who does not lend to a distinct group of clients, is the moneylender. However, in Ghana even they insist on charging similar interest rates for different borrowers. Although they often did not think that lending to small and microenterprises was profitable, none of the Ghanaian moneylenders we interviewed indicated that he used interest rates to differentiate among borrowers. For instance, it was observed that new customers were charged similar rates to old customers. The minor differences observed in informal interest rates for different borrowers in Nigeria may be attributed to differences in administrative requirements rather than to variations in risk perceptions. It is possible, in the absence of formal regulations, that there may be social norms about socially acceptable rates to charge.

6.2 Empirical approaches to uncertainty and risk management

In Chapter 2 we discussed the problems of formal contract enforcement due to the inadequacy of legal infrastructure and secondary markets for seized collateral. It is not surprising, therefore, that both formal and informal lending institutions attempt to minimize risk through loan administration practices that place greater emphasis on loan screening than on loan monitoring or contract enforcement. While this may suggest greater concern with adverse selection than with moral hazard, our surveys provide other evidence that indicates that moral hazard remains a major problem in the information asymmetry that lenders confront. Section 6.2.1 will deal with formal sector attempts at risk minimization, while section 6.2.2 will discuss the situation of informal lenders.

6.2.1 Loan administration and risk reduction by formal lenders

Under reform programmes, many banks have been restructured. Banks have been required to restructure their portfolios and write off bad assets, tighten credit analysis standards, and increase project equity requirements (Chapters 3 and 4, and Popiel 1994). Following the central bank's decision to remove sectoral lending ceilings, banks have attempted to spread their risks by diversifying into different sectors. Some banks have sought to improve portfolio performance by reducing over-concentration in sectors that are subject to high foreign exchange risk. Loan administration procedures have been changed in order to improve credit growth and recovery management, and have resulted in greater centralization of loan processing and supervision. Restructuring in many countries has also tended to increase banks' risk aversion, contrary to the hope that market liberalization would reduce their risk aversion towards small borrowers.

We consider here some of the methods banks in the study countries use to screen and monitor loans and to enforce contracts. This enables us to examine how project analysis is conducted to contain risks in the absence of reasonable loan insurance to provide risk coverage.

6.2.1.1 *Loan screening by banks*

Our theoretical framework relies on the development of repetitive inter-actions in a one-period 'stage game' (see Appendix 6.1). The contention that lenders are more likely to enter into repetitive games was partially borne out in the study countries by bank lending patterns. Many Nigerian banks, for example, had long-standing relationships with their large clients, which they rarely had with small borrowers. First-time borrowers, therefore, are unusual compared with repeat borrowers. The pattern was accentuated with small borrowers, among whom only 30 per cent of those borrowing from Nigerian banks in 1992 were first-time borrowers. This proportion rose to 55 per cent for community banks, which dealt mainly with small borrowers. In Ghana in 1991, first-time borrowers accounted for 64 per cent and 75 per cent of those receiving small agricultural loans from commercial and development banks respectively. However, less than 1 per cent of large enterprise borrowers were borrowing for the first time. The pattern was again repeated in Malawi, where only seven out of eighty-six small loans went to first-time borrowers. These observations would suggest that most lenders incorporate their historical relationships with borrowers into the screening procedures for the granting of loans.

Screening procedures for loans were very similar in all the study countries. Typically customers visit the local branch of their bank where their account is held and submit a loan application together with recent financial statements, cash flow projections and other financial details. In the case of a short-term loan, prospective borrowers are already likely to have overdraft facilities with the bank, and past records of these will be scrutinized. The bank's project officers and accountant will consider the loan application and assess ability to repay. If the amount of the loan requested is within the predetermined limit the decision on whether to grant the loan rests with the branch manager. Otherwise it is passed up to the next authorizing officer, usually the regional loans board or committee.

The main source of variation in this procedure is in the size of the lending limits for branch managers, which tend to be low. Account history is an important part of the procedure. In Malawi, for instance, banks require that deposit accounts are held with them for six to nine months before a credit request is considered. Nigerian commercial banks that grant rural loans often first match them to current account deposits, for which they have an account history. This minimizes the informational gap between the banks and their rural clientele (World Bank 1995).

The reliability and comprehensiveness of bank information about lenders and their proposed projects is of crucial importance. The majority of bankers indicated that the most important information for lending decisions should be obtainable from feasibility studies of the proposed projects. However, in practice these are often inadequate and banks are compelled to seek additional information about the personal characteristics of the borrower.

Where feasible, banks in the study sought information about potential borrowers from other sources. For Ghanaian commercial and development banks, this amounted to asking other bankers for references. In Nigeria, merchant banks prefer to use referees, which they sometimes identify themselves, but which are sometimes nominated by the borrower. However, while bankers' references may occasionally yield vital information, in the majority of cases potential borrowers do not hold a bank account with any other bank.

Bankers do not wait for all the information they have sought before making loan decisions, especially when it is unlikely to yield useful material. In Nigeria, 85 per cent of banks grant loans without receiving a complete set of responses to requests for information from third parties. For group lending schemes, now a popular form of agricultural lending, bankers consider references from other banks irrelevant.

In all the sample countries, banks sought information about current indebtedness. Indeed, more than 70 per cent of bank managers interviewed mentioned it. This bit of information was followed in order of importance by the personal integrity of the borrower, but this is the area about which banks feel least well informed. When this information is lacking they resort to information about the feasibility of the project itself, using both project documentation and their personal knowledge of the proposal.

Although many banks request information from third parties, they tend to use the customers themselves as their main source of information. Most bankers said that they 'tested' loan applicants in screening them. The tests normally took the form of interviews with clients, during which both the proposed project and the financial position of the applicant would be discussed. Interviews were very important in the screening of both small and large enterprises, but rarely mattered when considering small agricultural loans. Bankers considered interviews to be routine. Across all the sample countries, more than 80 per cent of enterprise loan applicants went through such interviews.

Other forms of 'test', such as the provision of a small initial loan, were rarely applied, though this process is known to be applied by many NGO lenders and group lenders who use peer monitoring as collateral substitute. Less than 10 per cent of bank managers in Ghana said they had provided initial advances to any type of borrower. The limited use of this technique may suggest that the theory of repetitive interactions may be of limited relevance to formal lenders, in spite of the dominance of repeat borrowers. They are probably less cautious in the first interaction than is generally expected, and this could be because greater emphasis is given to the quality of projects than to the personality of the borrower.

For many banks, it was standard practice to visit the project sites of particular clients as part of the screening process. Generally, visits were favoured for small agricultural and large-enterprise projects; such visits were less common with small enterprises. In Nigeria, commercial and merchant banks were particularly keen to visit small agricultural projects. In small Ghanaian towns and rural areas, bankers said they were likely to be acquainted with projects already, making screening visits unnecessary.

6.2.1.1 Assessing project creditworthiness during screening

We asked bankers to list the most important indicators of project viability and to state how they were measured. Most bank managers said that the return on projects was the most important criterion for assessment. Although collateral was not mentioned as the *most* important factor in assessing creditworthiness, it was invariably mentioned as one of the top four factors by all the bankers we surveyed.

In Tanzania, as in other study countries, the requirements for accepting an application were similar across banks. The major considerations in order of importance were: (1) economic viability, the financial and technical feasibility of the project as reflected in a detailed feasibility study; (2) a pledge of tangible, legally accepted and convertible security in real property, stocks or fixed assets; (3) an equity contribution of at least 15–25 per cent of the fixed assets; and (4) a licence and/or certificate of registration.

It is important to note that the criteria used by banks to appraise large and small-enterprise loans were much the same. Similarly, the criteria for new and older firms did not differ greatly. Banks gave higher priority to the business experience of new customers, often because they had little information on which to base a judgement of the character and reputation of the customer. Some banks do not require collateral for large established firms.

Banks undergoing reforms appeared to be searching for ways of improving information for the assessment of project viability. For many, this necessitated seeking alternative ways of screening project applications. We observed some interesting attempts to improve creditworthiness assessment, but they were often expensive and not always worth while. Many banks recognized the problems caused by the absence of credit reference bureaus and poor interbank co-operation. The lack of good market information about supply, demand and costs also hinders the assessment of project viability. Time spent in verifying information for project analysis, with its associated salary and support costs, was cited as the largest single impediment to lending to small borrowers.

Recent reforms do not appear to have introduced any significant new approaches to the appraisal of creditworthiness. Some bankers said they were placing more weight on the character of small borrowers than they did before, because they were more aware of the financial and technical inability of many of these borrowers to supply the documentation and financial information demanded by project appraisal. Banks said that most small entrepreneurs applied for loans without any feasibility studies, audited accounts or documentation of collateral. However, despite greater interest in character-based assessments, a number of banks in the study countries still did not consider them a suitable alternative to project analysis and would only rely on them if there were compelling reasons in individual cases.

The mention of collateral in the lending criteria of nearly all lenders suggests that it is probably used as a substitute for effective appraisal of the entrepreneur and project. Interestingly, while banks insist that they consider the viability of projects the most important criterion in assessing applications, many small borrowers believe that their loan applications were usually rejected because of lack of collateral. Furthermore, assessing collateral is not without problems. The foreclosure of landed property is difficult in many African countries, as discussed below. Given the ambiguities surrounding property rights, banks said that they were looking for alternatives to landed property. They have begun to check for a variety of other forms of security, including blocked accounts, letters of undertaking and pledges of other financial instruments. However, houses remain the dominant form of collateral, even though banks find them difficult to confiscate, and collateral remains a major tool of risk reduction.

6.2.1.3 Loan monitoring by banks

Frequent on-site monitoring of project loans is generally regarded as an effective way of ensuring that borrowers do not divert resources away from the purpose for which the money was lent. These checks are additional to the monitoring by branch office staff, with monthly reporting to head office. At least, this is what banks claim to do. In practice, we found little evidence of extensive loan monitoring in our bank branch surveys. In most places, greater emphasis is placed on the monitoring of accounts than on monitoring the projects themselves. In Ghana, for example, while 65 per cent of bank branch managers interviewed said that they always monitored small enterprise loans, only 32 per cent visited projects regularly and 24 per cent did so only occasionally. The pattern was similar for small agricultural loans. Even less project visit monitoring was observed with larger loans. By far the dominant form of loan monitoring is a close study of the account.

Even though visits to project sites were not generally widespread, commercial banks showed a greater likelihood of paying such visits than other banks. Commercial banks in Ghana visited on average seventeen out of the thirty small enterprise projects they initiated in 1991, while development banks visited only nine of the fifty-five projects approved the same year. The data from Tanzania show similar trends. Nigerian commercial bank branches visited twice as many projects as did merchant bank branches and also twice as many times as their Ghanaian counterparts. Malawi was even more different, as we will describe below. As we note later, differences in loan administration practices correlate with cost structures.

The failure of banks to make extensive project visits is not necessarily an indication of less concern about the moral hazard involved in lending to small businesses.[1] Rather, it is often due to pressure on banks to cut their costs as they try to reform. Also, many banks in Africa lack the requisite equipment for regular project visits. While most project officers know that they are required by internal regulations to visit projects regularly, they were constrained in doing so by lack of transport. This was particularly true of state-owned banks.

In Tanzania there appear to be few control mechanisms in place for the monitoring and supervision of credit. The largest commercial bank (NBC) set up a unit for monitoring and supervision only in 1992. The Presidential Banking Commission in Tanzania (1990) has pointed out the following weaknesses in the way that loans are monitored:

(1) A large number of NBC's borrowers in the parastatal and co-operative sectors had a poor repayment history, unsound financial conditions, abused loan terms by diverting sales proceeds away from overdrawn accounts, lacked up-to-date financial information, and were characterized by poor management,
(2) Some public sector borrowers exceeded agreed credit limits as interest accrued on earlier years' opening facilities,
(3) Although overdrafts were granted for short-term working capital requirements, in practice there was an increasing tendency to roll it over as a substitute for permanent or long-term capital,
(4) There were difficulties in the valuation of security, especially of stocks.

In Malawi the monitoring of loans dominates the loan administration process, taking up half the loan administration time. The business premises or farms of many borrowers are regularly visited. We believe this is, in part, because a large number of agricultural borrowers are large plantation owners and are within easy reach of urban bank branches.

6.2.1.4 *Loan repayment and contract enforcement by banks*

Loan repayment trends tend to vary considerably across bank types. While most banks studied had some problem with defaults, such defaults tended to occur in different sectors in different countries. We found some of the most disappointing bank loan repayment records in Tanzania, where poor loan repayment and contract enforcement characterize the banking system. An analysis of four-fifths of the NBC's credit portfolio showed that 94 per cent of it was sub-standard, doubtful or rated as loss by end-December 1991 (Eriksson 1993). About 91 per cent of the total contingent liabilities were adversely classified, with 63 per cent rated as loss. The twenty-five NBC clients with the largest loans outstanding at the end of June 1991 comprised ten co-operatives, twelve parastatals, two private enterprises and one belonging to the ruling party. In this case small-enterprise borrowers were not the worst debtors. This is partly, of course, because they carried only a small share of the loans portfolio. But it contrasts with the situation in other study countries where small borrower default is significant.

While loan defaults are also quite high in Ghana, greater variation by borrower type and bank location is observed. Repayment default is most acute among small agricultural loans. For the years 1988–90 about 55 per cent of delinquent loans were in the name of small agricultural borrowers, and 35 per cent were attributable to small entrepreneurs. Default by large enterprises represented 5 per cent of repayment defaults, while 'others' made up the remaining 10 per cent. Small agricultural loan defaults were much more pronounced in development bank branches and the unit rural banks. Together they had over 70 per cent of the total number of borrowers who failed to repay their loans on time between 1988 and 1990. In view of the larger loans that large enterprises attract, it was not surprising that, even though they had lower default *rates*, they held as much as 55 per cent of the loan *amounts* in default by the end of 1991. Amounts in default by small agricultural borrowers represented 25 per cent of the total.

Poor repayment rates for small borrowers were also observed in Malawi, even though Chipeta and Mkandawire (1996a) suggest that loan default is not a major problem for Malawian banks. They described the level of outstanding loans and interest as 'low' for 1991 and judge that delinquency was a more significant problem than actual default, as most delinquent loans tended to be paid within twelve months of becoming overdue. Delinquency was highest among households and other non-business borrowers; in 1991 19 per cent failed to repay loans on time. Delinquency among small-enterprise borrowers was 16 per cent for the same period. Interestingly, only 5 per cent of agricultural loans were delinquent or in default, a figure comparable to the 2 per cent for large enterprises. We attribute the low default rates for agriculture to the fact that the loans are directed at large plantation owners.

As in Ghana, loan repayment rates in Nigeria tend to vary considerably across banks and location. Some of the worst performances observed were those of large commercial banks engaged in rural lending. 'Despite the emphasis on group formation as the main platform on which the majority of the rural loans are granted, the performance of the beneficiaries in terms of rate of loan repayment has been very dismal. The reliance on peer pressure and group sanctions to effect compliance and loan repayment have obviously not had any significant impact, considering the high rate of loan default under the two rural credit schemes. In 1993, UBA had 40 per cent of its outstanding rural loans as non-performing, while the corresponding figures for 1991 and 1992 were 48 per cent and 38 per cent respectively' (World Bank 1995). Merchant bank lending in rural areas had similar experiences. Remarkably, the merchant bank loans were for large projects in those areas, including some sponsored by government agencies. Nigerian community banks did not report any major problems with loan repayment, at the time of field work.

We would expect that, under conditions of information asymmetry, contract enforcement mechanisms would play a significant role in loan administration. But, as indicated earlier, formal channels for legal contract enforcement are inadequate in many countries. Note, for instance, that despite relatively large incidences of default, no bank branches studied in Ghana foreclosed on any collateral in 1991. In Malawi, likewise, there were very few attempts at foreclosure on collateral security. Legal suits are relatively rare, which is not surprising considering the lower rates of delinquency and default in Malawi. Why do banks decline to enforce contracts and what do they do under such circumstances?

In Tanzania, where default rates are high, contract enforcement is 'difficult' and legal cases are very rare. Despite the high default rates, only two out of the thirty branches surveyed indicated that legal action had been taken against any of their defaulters. Most branches studied in Tanzania (60 per cent) threatened legal action without actually carrying it through. In six of the thirty branches they provided management assistance to forestall default and ensure payment. Tanzanian bankers blame banking laws that make it difficult to foreclose on security or realize value from such assets once foreclosed. During the country's socialist past the law was often designed to prevent banks from 'making individuals destitute'. Further difficulties arise with the time it takes to complete foreclosure through the legal system, which could be as long as four to six years. Even then, since most fixed assets owned by parastatals have little or no second-hand value, it is not always easy to sell the assets once foreclosed. Tanzanian banks have no power to appoint liquidators, receivers or administrators for borrower companies in difficulties.

Part of the difficulty in enforcing contracts in Tanzania is the cross-indebtedness of public sector borrowers. Most of the delinquent parastatals and co-operative unions are technically insolvent. There is a lot of political pressure on banks not to foreclose, as this could lead to many of the clients ceasing to operate or being forced into liquidation. There are sometimes fears that refusal to lend to co-operatives, for example, could cause undue hardship for peasants who are dependent on the co-operatives to purchase their produce.

Reasons for high loan delinquency and default in Nigerian commercial and merchant banks are broader than the absence of a proper administrative machinery. Quite a number of bankers believe that some default is wilful, although they also acknowledge that natural calamities, particularly for agricultural loans, are important. The World Bank (1995) also suggests that collusion between borrowers and some bank officials prevents delinquency and default from being reported for relatively long periods.

The first line of action to forestall default is often to persuade delinquent borrowers by written communication to resume their repayments. This is often followed up shortly afterwards by a threat of legal action. The fact that few cases end up in court may be because lenders expect most delinquent borrowers to pay within twelve months. In contrast to Nigeria, most Ghanaian bankers did not believe that the most frequent cause of delinquency was wilful default. Most believed instead that poor returns on investment were the most important reason for delinquency and default. They attributed poor returns to bad management of projects, particularly among small-enterprise borrowers. As many as 85 per cent of Ghanaian bank managers sometimes refinanced projects in the hope that they would revive and repay.

In the context of our theoretical model (Appendix 6.1), it would appear that there is a relatively high probability of banks playing 'lend' in the game, even under sub-optimal conditions, as long as they have information to believe that borrowers will not play 'no repayment'. This information is available only to a restricted number of clients at any one time, to whom the banks therefore direct most of their lending. It is clear, however, that even when there is not enough information about projects, other considerations, including political and social ones, sometimes make a decision to lend inevitable.

6.2.2 *Loan administration and risk reduction by informal lenders*

We analyse here how informal lenders assess and cope with risk. Different categories of informal lenders have different objective functions and hence different perceptions of risk. This has led some lenders to use such techniques as quantity rationing (as in many group schemes) or allocating credit on a wider set of criteria than those dictated by the market. We look at techniques used in screening applications, the role of information in the loan admin-istration process and how it is obtained. In doing so we are interested in the conditions under which lenders will lend or not within our theoretical framework, and, in particular, in whether repeat borrowing is an important part of the screening process.

6.2.2.1 *Screening practices and information used*

Screening in the informal sector relies extensively on personal knowledge of borrowers, as Udry (1990) has noted. It is often suggested that the development of personal ties and the use of proximity in decision-making are mechanisms for countering the effects of adverse selection and moral hazard. But there are some geographical and other variations in the significance of these ties. They vary as between group arrangements and individually managed arrangements. Responses from the Tanzanian survey indicate that an average of 86 per cent and 63 per cent of urban and rural informal lenders respectively always personally knew the people who were applying for loans. The figure was 100 per cent for ROSCAs, where only members received loans. Most of the remainder sometimes knew the people who were applying for loans. In general, more than two-thirds of successful applicants were personal acquaintances of lenders before they submitted their application. Repeat loan applicants were more likely to be successful than new ones with informal lenders, who prefer to deal with known, long-standing clients in order to mitigate the problem of moral hazard. Familiarity between lenders and borrowers as a factor in the functioning of informal credit markets is stressed by Yotopoulos and Floro (1991).

In community or group-based arrangements, screening practices are based on groups' observations of individuals' habits and groups' obligations towards applicants. In savings and credit associations (SCA) or rural co-operatives the associations are aware that members' principal reason for joining was the possibility of borrowing, which places them under an obligation to meet the expectation. In 'screening' applicants, therefore, the emphasis is not necessarily on whether members can pay back loans they have taken, but on the commitment of members to the group's goals and their general trustworthiness. Since they normally have similar incomes and similar credit requirements, the major criterion in answering these questions is an assessment of the individual's character.

Credit unions tend to have adequate information from their records about loan applicants, since they must be a member of the union. In most cases, therefore, third parties are not consulted for information. Where information is sought, it is about the character of the applicant. Referees are normally other members of the union who know the applicant. In workplace unions, it is generally easy to obtain information from colleagues and superiors. Credit unions do not visit project sites in screening loans, which is hardly surprising, since most loans are for consumption purposes.

Unlike the situation in East and Southern Africa, where most informal lending in our sample countries was based on personal ties, there is greater diversity in the kinds of relationships that exist between lenders and borrowers in West Africa. Knowing the client personally was considered beneficial but not essential for 83 per cent of our sample moneylenders in Ghana. In 92 per cent ethnicity and religion were unimportant.

Only 25 per cent of sampled Nigerian moneylenders had a working relationship with their borrowers. For over 60 per cent of moneylenders in Ghana and Nigeria, borrowers were usually recommended by their existing clients. For those lending to public servants, it was common to establish a working relationship with the accounts offices of various departments, which made it possible for individual applicants to be recommended by colleagues in those offices. Being a 'first-time' applicant with a moneylender did not necessarily put a loan applicant at a disadvantage. The proportion of successful 'first-time' loan applicants in 1992 (68 per cent) was not significantly different from that of 'repeat' applicants (74 per cent). Indeed, it would appear that the repetitive relationship becomes important in informal lending only if the lender has no other means of obtaining and verifying information about a borrower.

Most moneylenders studied in Ghana and Nigeria said they did not require a business relationship with applicants for decisions to be made about applications. In Ghana the sample was equally divided between those who made enquiries of third parties about applicants before granting loans and those who did not. More Nigerian lenders tended to seek third-party information. When they did so, the most important information was about the character of the applicant, although some wanted to know about the applicant's wealth. This contrasts sharply with bank managers, who mostly sought information on possible indebtedness. Moneylenders usually waited for information before granting loans, and referees were often people who worked with the applicant. In many cases, the word of the person recommending or introducing the applicant was sufficient. We noted that when lending to micro-entrepreneurs, moneylenders seldom visited the project sites of applicants.

The issue of repeat versus first-time borrowing does not appear to be very important to savings collectors in West Africa either. Survey results in Ghana and Nigeria suggested indifference as between 'first-time' and 'repeat' borrowers. This is mainly because the key item of information is whether cash flows are sufficient to make daily deposits possible. Screening generally involves a casual look at the ledger card of a loan applicant. 'Lots of empty spaces or blanks against days of the month suggest irregular payment of deposits' – an indication that an applicant cannot be trusted or may have cash flow problems. Given that a collector feels financially able to advance credit to a client, regular payment of deposits is the sole criterion in deciding on an application. Non-deposit borrowers (i.e. those who are not saving with the collector) must be personally known to the lender in view of the high-risk nature of such lending. About 98 per cent of *susu* collector respondents in Ghana indicated they would not lend to people they did not know.

Most people seeking loans from informal lenders in Africa do so verbally. The only major exceptions we observed were with urban credit unions. In Nigeria, however, moneylenders and *esusu* collectors were increasingly turning to written applications. In Ghana, as many as 66 per cent of money-lenders and 85 per cent of *susu* collectors indicated that verbal applications were the norm. Loan applications from credit unions and the Tanzanian SCS usually required an application letter and the completion of a standard form. The informal manner in which applications are made is a reflection of the personal nature of screening and other loan administration procedures.

The more rural the environment, the greater the need for personal ties to overcome information asymmetry. This is consistent with Udry's (1990) observation in northern Nigeria that agricultural lending among relatives, acquaintances, neighbours, etc., was the norm. The evidence of our surveys suggests that different lenders have different ways of confronting information asymmetry. In choosing among different loan applicants, the key question for most lenders is 'Which of these potential borrowers will it be least costly to persuade to repay?' In this situation contract enforcement mechanisms become very important. When relations are personal, whether it be through the extended family, friendship, kinship or other social relations, they become instrumental in engendering trust between transacting parties, and therefore as a potential tool for ensuring repayment. Mechanisms such as peer pressure and social stigmatization achieve this and are often used in group-based arrangements. In the absence of such mechanisms, lenders have to consider what sanctioning authority they possess. Collateral security then becomes important, as we discuss in section 6.2.2.3.

Many informal lenders make no pretence of evaluating projects. They accept the fact that they do not have adequate information to form clear judgements about the outcomes of particular investments, except in exceptional cases. They are also aware that most of their borrowers have no intention of using the borrowed funds in any economic venture. As a consequence, creditworthiness criteria appear to be relatively simple for many lenders. Group-based schemes, including credit unions, which are not particularly interested in 'investment' lending, have not developed any significant creditworthiness criteria. Their approach in lending appears to be one of rationing among members. Some commercial lenders sometimes attempt to develop criteria for assessing credit need. However, as many as 67 per cent of Ghanaian moneylenders studied indicated they were not interested in the return borrowers made on their 'investments'. A further 25 per cent were only 'sometimes' interested. They often remarked that the type of activities that their borrowers were involved in could be easily judged. A moneylender who trades can easily assess whether a loan to buy more stock of a consumer item is sensible or not.

6.2.2.2 *Loan monitoring by informal lenders*

When there is a strong fear of moral hazard, we would expect lenders to exhibit greater interest in loan monitoring. Indeed, it is often suggested that the opportunity for frequent and easy loan monitoring is one way by which informal lenders are able to reduce the incidence of default below that of formal institutions (Yotopoulos and Floro 1991). Contrary to this notion, we observed little attempt in many places to monitor the use of loans. This is not surprising in view of the fact that most of the loans were expected to be used for consumption expenditure. Half the credit unions in Ghana never monitored any loans and only a quarter always monitored loans. Monitoring among credit unions is more common in rural areas, where most lending is to farmers, and occasional visits to farms take place.

In Tanzania, only two of the ten ROSCAs studied and two of the nineteen SCSs reported any form of loan monitoring. Similarly, only two of the twenty-two trader lenders and only three of the eight sample landlords said that they visited clients for purposes of loan monitoring. The situation is similar in Nigeria, where little monitoring takes place. Our data suggest that Nigerian moneylenders do not bother with monitoring. In Malawi, while moneylenders and traders evinced no attempt to monitor loan use, almost all estate owners said that they did. However, the actions of Malawian estate owners are not strictly loan monitoring, since their loans are part of inter-linked market arrangements that require regular interaction between lender and borrower. Among West African savings collectors loan monitoring is taken for granted, because visits to clients for deposit collection ensure that loans are monitored daily.

Indeed, Udry's (1990) position on free information flow suggests that informal lenders have little need to explicitly monitor loans. Where such monitoring does occur, it is the result of an interaction necessitated by other related matters. Our conclusion from observations of the limited monitoring activities of informal lenders is that low default rates cannot be attributed to close or explicit monitoring of loan use.

6.2.2.3 *Loan repayment and contract enforcement by informal lenders*

There is a general belief that delinquency and default rates in the informal sector are relatively low (Udry 1990). Our surveys tend to confirm this view. Here we consider loan repayment rates and attempt to explain them in terms of the contract enforcement mechanisms we observed. In contrast to banks, 77 per cent of our total sample of informal lenders in Ghana had no delinquent borrowers in 1990 and 70 per cent had none in 1991. Among those who had, they were usually less than 5 per cent of borrowers. The largest proportions of defaulting borrowers were observed in a couple of rural credit unions and co-operatives where defaulters averaged 30 per cent of borrowers. These were large bodies with hundreds of members.

While Malawian and Tanzanian default rates were also low, such rates were slightly higher among some lenders in Nigeria. The survey results showed that 14 per cent of borrowers from moneylenders were delinquent, as were 17 per cent from savings and credit associations and 20 per cent of *esusu* collector borrowers. In accordance with Udry's (1990) findings, default rates in rural Nigeria were significantly lower than those in urban Nigeria. As in other countries, all lenders believed that delinquent borrowers would repay within three months of the loan maturing. They tended, therefore, not to regard default as a big enough problem to cause them serious cash flow problems.

Informal lenders gave various reasons for default or delinquency in the repayment of loans. But lenders' perceptions of the causes of delinquency and default may in part be at odds with their *actual* loan screening practices. Many of the screening practices described above show concern about the possibility of a 'strategic default' in which the borrower simply decides not to pay back (hence the concern about character), rather than the possibility of default through the failure of the project associated with the loan. In rural areas, non-payment is often attributed to borrowers' cash flow problems, while many urban lenders think it is a mixture of cash flow problems and low commitment on the part of borrowers to settle debts. Cross-tabulating perceptions of the causes of default with loan end use suggests, however, that lenders providing loans mainly for consumption purposes and trading tend to be more concerned with strategic default than those lending to farmers. The latter are more concerned about failed projects leading to default.

The different reasons lenders give for default are reflected in the different ways they attempt to enforce contracts. There are various ways of scheduling repayments to informal lenders. These include daily payments (as with *susu* collectors), monthly payments of interest and principal over an agreed period, and the bulk payment of principal and interest at the end of an agreed period. With the exception of *susu* collectors, who invariably stick to the first, and credit unions, which have regular monthly repayments, lenders tend to be flexible in their approach. We noted, for example, that while money-lenders usually accept a bulk payment of interest and principal at the end of a period, a number of them would rather receive only monthly payments of interest up to the end of the maturity of the loan, when the principal would be paid back in a lump sum. When this approach is adopted, lenders may not worry much about when the principal will be repaid so long as the interest payments are regular. With this approach, moneylenders seldom mention default if interest payments are being made. Short-term loans often get rolled over into long-term loans, with monthly interest rates often remaining unchanged.

There are a number of possible reasons for the relatively low default rates, some of which can be linked with contract enforcement mechanisms. Bagachwa (1995) has suggested that lenders prefer to lend to relatives or friends. Proximity reduces information costs, and kinship ties exert social pressure to repay. Similarly, there is a well established tradition of mutual help as a social obligation. Bagachwa, therefore, does not find it surprising that most loans among relatives and friends require no guarantee or collateral. It would appear that the social pressure to repay is given much attention by lenders, and default endangers future loans. We consider this to be more typical in rural areas and among small group-based arrangements. It is obvious that, where lenders cannot depend on moral suasion only, they apply other mechanisms.

In rural areas, the role of interlinked markets is more observable. In Tanzania, where we observed the largest use of interlinked transactions, Bagachwa (1995) has indicated that the interlinkage of contracts has the advantages of: (1) helping to increase information and improving contract enforcement; (2) reducing uncertainty by improving the lender's forecast of individual behaviour and thus the lender's ability to select risk appropriately from several potential borrowers; and (3) expanding the control variables and strategies available to a lender, enabling the lender to influence the borrower's actions. An interlinked transaction can thus be treated as a disguised form of collateral and may help mitigate moral hazard or adverse selection (Udry 1990). There is, however, an additional reason why Tanzanian lenders may be interested in land-based credit market interlinkages; it is the simplest way of acquiring the usufructuary rights to land in the absence of an effective land market. This situation gives rise to a lending game in which borrower defaults are favourable to the lender.

Where we do not find extensive use of interlinked markets, in Ghana and Nigeria for example, collateral seems to play a greater role in risk management. Far more Ghanaian lenders demanded collateral security than their Tanzanian counterparts. Variations among lenders arise mostly from the type of preferred security. About 83 per cent of Ghanaian moneylenders required security against loans, just as 76 per cent of credit unions did. Hardly any such requirement existed for other community or group-based institutions, including the co-operatives and both kinds of *susu* system. They took security for granted because of the nature of association. Among Ghanaian moneylenders there is a lot of variation in the most preferred form of collateral security. Two-thirds of the sample preferred physical assets such as buildings, farmland and undeveloped land. The remainder preferred non-physical securities such as guarantees from friends, relations or employers. When lending to a public servant the moneylender usually requires an understanding between himself and the borrower's paymaster. It must be pointed out that moneylenders were generally prepared to lend in the absence of collateral if other guarantees, including verbal pledges from extended family heads, were provided.

Collateral pledged in exchange for loans serves three important functions: (1) directly reducing cost to the lender of a loan default; (2) adding an incentive for the borrower to repay, thereby reducing the moral hazard; and (3) mitigating the problem of adverse selection by enabling the lender to screen out borrowers most likely to default (Udry 1990). We therefore hold the view that the general demand for collateral in combination with other contract enforcement mechanisms does deter default.

It is interesting to consider informal lenders' actions when default and delinquency arise. Some action is not dissimilar to that of banks. Just as banks would write letters to defaulters, informal lenders would go to the homes of their clients to deliver verbal warnings. When asked to indicate what they would do to forestall default by delinquent borrowers, some Ghanaian lenders said they would do nothing but hope the lender paid (20 per cent), while some would threaten to do the borrower bodily harm or damage his property (30 per cent). The remainder had an assortment of possible reactions, ranging from confiscating collateral to dismissing the borrower from the group. Group or community-based institutions have no effective means of dealing with defaulters other than relying on the social stigma of defaulting or denial of a future loan. Ironically, when the number of defaulters in a rural co-operative arrangement is large, the sanction of stigmatizing an individual fails to be effective.

The situation in Nigeria is similar to that described for Ghana. In Malawi, as in other countries, we found little evidence of informal lenders attempting to use the legal system to enforce contracts. Chipeta and Mkandawire (1996a) have observed that 'they do not rely on legal suits, which are expensive, nor do they normally confiscate collateral, make personal threats, or restrict inputs. Rather, they rely more on legal threats, the control of outputs (especially among moneylenders), and other techniques.' In Ghana we observed a total of only seven cases (8 per cent) of lenders seeking legal assistance to redeem loans. This low number was mainly due to the relatively small number of defaulters, but was also partly owing to reluctance to seek legal assistance because they believe it to be costly. We learned of cases where lenders had sought the assistance of security agents to compel borrowers to repay loans, albeit illegally.

Although some lenders demand collateral security before loans are granted, very few lenders (less than 4 per cent in Ghana) suggested that their first course of action in case of default was to foreclose on collateral. Instead, they seize the collateral where possible until the loan is eventually repaid. In many cases this yields no direct utility to the lender, unless interest is recalculated on the outstanding amount. However, such action entails loss of utility to the borrower and hence may render a stronger incentive to repay. In sum, we believe that informal lenders continue the loan as long as they are assured that they are receiving some cash from the borrower during the period when the principal is not yet fully paid, and as long as interest payments are being made. Holding on to collateral guarantees the loan. Banks are unable to seize collateral, as the storage and maintenance costs can be prohibitive. It is certainly easier and cheaper, for instance, for a cocoa farmer to hold a confiscated cocoa farm indefinitely than for a bank to do so. Hence borrowers would not treat the threat of collateral confiscation by an informal lender as lightly as a similar threat from a formal lender, and this could affect their attitude to repayment as between the two sectors.

6.3 Risk management and lending transaction costs

The different perceptions of risk attached to borrower categories by different types of lender has been shown above to feed through to risk management practices. One would expect these different practices to be apparent in the cost structures that determine price or, at least, to influence price determination. In this section we relate the risk management practices outlined above to transaction costs measured for different types of lenders lending to different categories of borrowers. The transaction costs of lending are simply the costs of administering credit and the costs of the risk of default. The administrative cost component includes the cost of information-gathering, recording systems for transaction processing, ensuring that loans are used as intended, and monitoring and enforcing contracts. These costs are mostly wage and salary expenses and other administrative costs such as printing, stationery, rent, travel, etc. The second component, default risk costs, is defined as 'those expenses for the risk of loan default incurred by the lending institutions, for example, provision for loan losses, the loan guarantee fees paid, and the actual bad debts incurred' (Saito and Villanueva 1981). Transaction costs are usually expressed as a percentage of the total loan amount. They form a major component of the effective cost of credit to any borrower. In the case of banks we expect that the effective rate on lending is derived from a summation of the net pure profit (returns on stockholders' equity), the cost of funds or interest cost, and the bank's transaction cost. Thus if we held the net pure profit and the cost of funds stable, any widening of the spread between lending and deposit rates could be attributed to transaction costs. By this reasoning, the trends described earlier in Chapter 5 for formal institutions could be attributed to still high and growing transaction costs, a point which we will establish here.

6.3.1 *The transaction costs of banks*

Most banks base transaction cost calculations on their standard overhead costs. They do not estimate the actual costs of administering each individual loan. Their usual assertion that small loans cost more to transact than credit to larger enterprises is based on the expectation that relevant information will be more difficult to collect. Apart from the possibility that absolute costs for small and large loans may not differ (which would therefore make transaction costs on small loans proportionately higher), small loans may be more expensive because: less is known about borrowers, and information is harder to come by; small borrowers are spread over wide geographical areas, making contact with them more difficult; frequent illiteracy among small borrowers means that more time may be required in dealing with them; their incomes are erratic, thus making repayment sources unclear; and special programmes for small borrowers (e.g. group-lending schemes), require additional administration at the initial stage, though group lending schems are intended to be cost-reducing in the long run.

Saito and Villanueva (1981), who developed the first known measurement of transaction costs for a developing country, suggest that 'in percentage terms, costs of administration are expected to rise as the size of the loan falls, the duration of the loans shortens, and accounting services are expanded in order to cope with a large number of small-scale borrowers. Costs of risks and defaults incorporate an element to cover losses through default. The more careful the loan appraisal, supervision of loans and pursuit of delinquents the higher the administrative costs are likely to be.'

There is clearly an assumption that small loans require more careful handling, but the previous sections do not suggest that small loans actually receive such 'special treatment'. Since we did not observe any major differences in the approaches banks adopted in screening, monitoring and enforcing loan contracts for the different categories of borrowers, we did not expect any significant differences in the administrative cost component of transaction costs among the different borrower categories.

6.3.1.1 *The cost of screening loans at banks*[2]

Screening costs are made up of the costs of assembling information in relation to loan applications, analysing such information in order to arrive at decisions, and processing the loans which ensue. We looked at personnel costs, stationery costs and transport costs. By far the most important marginal cost component in screening loans was the personnel involved. We found the lowest screening costs (as a proportion of total administrative costs and loans) in Ghana and Malawi. They tended to be much higher in Nigeria and Tanzania, where many more man days were required for the same activities. There were variations across countries and by bank type.

In Ghana, on average, a full man-day was required by commercial banks to screen a small-enterprise loan application properly. It takes several months for a loan to be approved and disbursed. The process involves a feasibility study, credit analysis and loan structuring. A similar exercise for a small agricultural loan takes a quarter of a man-day, while an average of two man-days is required for a large enterprise loan. In rural areas, about 50 per cent of the working time of loan staff at branches is devoted to screening and monitoring small agricultural loans. Only about 10 per cent of their time is devoted to a similar exercise for small enterprise loans and another 3 per cent for large enterprises. In larger urban centres, time spent on small agricultural loans remains under 10 per cent, while 60 per cent is spent on small enterprises and trading loans. Loans to large enterprises take about 30 per cent of their working time.

In Malawi, far less time is spent on screening small-enterprise loan applications than on large-enterprise loans. Consequently, more of the working time of bank officials was devoted to appraising large enterprise loans. They attributed this to the fact that the amounts sought by small enterprises often fell within the lending limits of branch managers. Branch personnel therefore saw 'little need for rigorous appraisal by the branch' to convince itself of whether or not to approve the application. Also, if a branch officer wishes to carry out a rigorous appraisal, he is constrained by a lack of available data about SSEs, including a lack of cash flow projections.

Feasibility assessment for a small enterprise loan in Nigeria is estimated to take two man-days in commercial and community banks, credit analysis taking a further two man-days. Credit analysis is estimated to take five man-days in Nigerian merchant banks. They all spend an additional two man-days structuring small-enterprise loans. Loan screening for small enterprises takes one week, after which decisions can be made. Contrary to expectations, banks indicated that they required more time to screen larger loans – two days, on average. We attribute the longer screening processes to the fact that decision-making tends to be more centralized in Nigerian banks than in most Ghanaian banks. Nigerian banks with centralized structures and large branch networks also tend to have relatively larger overheads than their Ghanaian counterparts. However, even though Nigerian banks spent more time than Ghanaian banks on loan screening, screening costs in Nigeria tended to form a significantly lower proportion of total loan administration costs than in Ghana (Table 18). This was probably because Nigerian banks attach more importance to other aspects of loan administration such as monitoring than to screening.

In both Nigeria and Ghana, for which our data enabled more detailed studies of costs, we observed some relation between the type of bank and total screening cost. A relationship was also observed between the location of the bank and these costs. The more centralized the bank the higher the

Table 18 Loan screening cost as a proportion of loan administration costs (% of total costs for each applicant type)

| Country | Type of enterprise/applicant | | | |
	SSE	LSE	SSA	Other
Ghana	67.6	58.4	42.2	60.3
Nigeria	14.5	16.4	13.7	25.4

Source: survey data.
Note: SSE small-scale enterprise; LSE large-scale enterprise; SSA small-scale agriculture.

probability of high screening costs. The World Bank (1995) study of rural financial institutions in Nigeria endorsed the view that Nigerian commercial banks operate with very high overheads. The lowest-cost banks in Nigeria were the community banks and the people's banks, largely because of their unit and hence decentralized structures. Decentralization significantly lowers the average screening cost to Nigerian banks of lending to small enterprises and the agricultural sector (Table 18). Nigerian merchant banks engaging in commercial lending to small agricultural and enterprise sectors have some of the highest costs we observed anywhere in our sample countries.

6.3.1.2 The cost of monitoring loans at banks

Detailed information about the cost of monitoring is available only for Nigeria and Ghana. For both Malawi and Tanzania, there is some indication that monitoring does not constitute a major item in bank administrative costs, even though considerable monitoring takes place in Malawi, involving mainly visits to projects not far from urban branches.

We observed in Ghana that, with the exception of small agricultural loans, most bank branches devoted less than 20 per cent of their administrative expenditures to monitoring loans. For small agricultural projects, all banks allocated an average of 40 per cent of the resources directed at servicing the sector to monitoring loans. Another peculiar feature of the activity levels with respect to loan monitoring was the unexpectedly low allocation of resources by development banks to the monitoring of loans to 'others'. Only 6 per cent of actual expenditures for the sector went into monitoring activity. This is attributed to the relative absence of adequately qualified persons and other resources to handle these activities. Banks explained that they put more monitoring resources into small agricultural projects because of the nature of the risks the sector was exposed to. In general, commercial bank branches devoted proportionately more resources to the screening and monitoring of loans than did development bank branches.

Table 19 Loan monitoring cost as a proportion of loan administration costs (% of total costs by applicant type)

| Country | Type of enterprise/applicant | | | |
	SSE	LSE	SSA	Other
Ghana	19.6	22.1	45.3	17.2
Nigeria	36.9	39.9	45.8	45.6

Source: survey data.
Note: See Table 18.

236

Close monitoring of agricultural loans is also found in Nigeria, where other studies (World Bank 1995) have indicated that monitoring takes up significant amounts of branch time. Our data suggest that Nigerian banks tend to spend almost twice as much on monitoring loans as they do on screening. Considering that this is dramatically different to patterns in the other countries, it is tempting to conclude that it is solely attributable to a higher fear of moral hazard in Nigeria.[3] But this would be to ignore the fact that quite a large proportion of the high loan monitoring costs occur in large commercial and merchant banks, which apply the same standard practices to small borrowers in remote rural areas as they do to others. They do it because they are better equipped (in terms of capital) than their counterparts in the other study countries (i.e. centrally placed loan officers have project vehicles to visit to small agricultural projects).

In both Ghana and Nigeria data plots revealed that type of bank and location each affected monitoring costs. There were no significant interaction effects. In Ghana, the average monitoring costs of commercial bank branches were more than 50 per cent higher than those of development bank branches for all categories of loans. Similarly, the monitoring costs of urban-located branches were more than 100 per cent higher than those of their rural counterparts.

Banks generally devote less of their loan-monitoring budget to small-enterprise loans than they do to large enterprises. However, the differences are not statistically significant in both Nigeria and Ghana. The differences in loan numbers suggests that monitoring costs per loan for projects tend to be higher for large-enterprise loans. Few small projects actually receive project visits.

6.3.1.3 The cost of enforcing contracts at banks

Contract enforcement costs relate to expenses incurred by banks in ensuring that contracts are adhered to. They include 'chasing' overdue loans through correspondence and/or visits, legal measures, and foreclosure on collateral. For many banks, some of these functions are performed at the head office in the banks' legal departments. In our analysis we have used actual expenses incurred by branches and weighted them to incorporate head office costs.

Table 20 suggests that Nigerian banks spent proportionately more on contract enforcement for all categories of borrowers, compared with Ghanaian banks. As with monitoring, the rather large appropriations for contract enforcement in Nigeria were due mainly to commercial and merchant banks. Trends were different for community and people's banks. This underscores the point that decentralization of decision-making is likely to affect lending practices and loan transaction costs. Similarly, in Ghana, the more centralized development banks had to spend more on contract enforcement, since they suffered more from loan defaults than other banks. Many commercial banks

Table 20 Contract enforcement cost as a proportion of loan administration costs (% of total costs by applicant type)

Country	Type of enterprise/applicant			
	SSE	LSE	SSA	Other
Ghana	12.0	19.4	17.3	20.9
Nigeria	48.6	43.7	48.17	31.1

Source: survey data.
Note: See Table 18.

would insist that a more thorough screening process results in relatively low default rates and choose this approach. But a thorough screening process by commercial banks often also resulted in relatively fewer loan approvals. It would appear that banks ultimately have to make a choice between more thorough screening and monitoring/contract enforcement. The costs shown in Tables 18–20 confirm the fact that, in both Ghana and Nigeria, banks' loan administration methods did not vary much by type of client.

Table 21 shows administrative costs as a proportion of total loan amounts. Loan administration costs for the small enterprise sector are much larger in Nigeria than in Ghana and Malawi. This is a cause for concern. High costs are mainly a result of merchant banks engaging in what would normally be considered as commercial bank activity. World Bank (1995) data for a sample of Nigerian commercial and merchant banks suggest that staff costs as a percentage of outstanding loans for a large commercial bank were in the region of 3 per cent to 5 per cent across the different borrower categories, but were 27 per cent for a large merchant bank. Indeed, total administrative costs for this merchant bank as a proportion of outstanding loans were as high as 54 per cent in 1993. However, this is probably unusual, particularly in systems

Table 21 Loan administration costs as a percentage of loan amount, by type of bank

Country	Type of enterprise/applicant			
	SSE	LSE	SSA	Other
Ghana	1.7	0.2	3.5	1.4
Malawi[a]	3.4	17.6	8.9	13.5
Nigeria	12.9	18.9	12.3	11.4
Tanzania[b]	12.4	–	–	–

Source: survey data.
a Based on staff time allocations.
b Not broken down by sector; reflects the global picture.

that are undergoing reform. The higher figures from Nigeria are an obvious indication of the slow pace of the financial sector reform programme in that country. The high administrative costs for Tanzania are a clear indication that costs have remained high where little financial sector reform has taken place.

The Ghanaian data show that development banks had relatively lower costs in administering large-enterprise loans. They also suggest that commercial banks are not geared to satisfying the small needs of farming communities. Analysis of variance in the costs of different banks showed that there was no significant difference in the mean total administration costs of bank lending to different types of applicant. More interesting was the relative significance of various factors in determining the levels and composition of these costs. Saito and Villanueva (1981) observed in the Philippines that lenders' annual administrative costs lie between 3 per cent and 4 per cent of loan amounts for lending to small-scale agriculture and small-scale industry. For lending to large-scale industry, an administrative cost component of 0.4 per cent of the loan amount was realized.

6.3.1.5 Default risk and total transaction costs

Data limitations made it impossible to estimate default costs for most of our study countries. The estimate from Ghana (Table 22) was mainly derived from data in the published profit and loss accounts of the banks, supplemented by information obtained in our interviews. For the development and commercial bank branches, we took the 'Provision for bad and doubtful debts' of each of the banks and allocated it proportionately to their branches.[4] We estimated default risk costs as percentages of the total loans made to the sectors by branches (Table 22).

A summation of the default risk costs and the loan administration costs yields the lending transaction costs of banks studied. In general, it was expected that administration costs would exceed default risk costs (Saito and Villanueva 1981). Table 23 shows transaction costs in Ghana and indicates

Table 22 Default risk costs as a percentage of total loan amount, by type of bank and applicant in Ghana

Bank type	Type of enterprise/applicant			
	SSE	LSE	SSA	Other
Commercial	2.0	1.5	1.7	1.6
Development	7.8	7.8	7.7	7.8
Unit rural	2.8	–	1.1	1.7
Overall	4.2	4.6	3.5	3.7

Source: calculated from bank balance sheets.

Table 23 Transaction cost of lending in Ghana as a percentage of total loan amount for sector, by type of bank

Bank type	Type of enterprise/applicant			
	SSE	LSE	SSA	Other
Commercial	3.2	1.8	6.4	4.1
Development	8.7	8.0	10.6	8.2
Unit rural	5.8	–	3.9	3.0
Overall	5.9	4.9	6.9	5.1

Source: calculated from survey data and bank balance sheets.

that costs were highest for development banks for all types of borrower. We attribute this to their loan administration methods, which put a considerable premium on default risk. It is significant that default risk costs added more to total transaction costs than administrative costs. Thus, even though development banks had the lowest loan administration costs per branch, their unusually high provision for bad debts significantly pushed up their lending transaction costs. Administrative costs generally dominated the total transaction costs of development banks in the Philippines, but the Ghanaian situation depicted the reverse. In a sense, the banks simply substituted manipulation of balance sheets for good banking practice. This is true of a number of banking sector reforms in African countries (Popiel 1994).

The average total lending transaction costs for small-enterprise lending (5.9 per cent) as a proportion of loan amount is comparable to that observed by Saito and Villanueva (1981) among similar borrowers in the Philippines (6.1 per cent from three classes of development banks). Similarly, the estimated average transaction costs of 6.9 per cent for small agricultural loans is only 0.6 percentage points higher than the 6.3 per cent they measured. The major difference arises in the averages for large enterprises: our measured transaction costs of 4.9 per cent of loan amount are more than twice their average of 2.1 per cent.

While we expect transaction costs in Nigeria and Tanzania to be much higher than those for Ghana, Malawian transaction costs should not be very different. Indeed, for most sub-Saharan countries undergoing structural adjustment and significant financial sector reforms, as is happening in the francophone countries, transaction cost structures should be similar to those we found in Ghana.

6.3.2 The transaction costs of informal lenders

Our hypotheses on the persistence of fragmentation among informal financial units lead us to expect significant variations in transaction costs with clients.

Such costs include administration and the cost of funds. We consider here the variation in the two. We followed the same method of calculating lending transaction costs for informal lenders as we did for formal lenders. What emerges is the consistent result across study countries that informal transaction costs are much lower than in the formal sector. We attribute this to differences in approach to screening, monitoring and contract enforcement. The practices outlined earlier suggest that one of the advantages informal finance has over formal finance is its ability to substitute proxy measures where it cannot find suitable information. The practice of selecting certain types of people and avoiding those that particular lenders believe they are ill equipped to do business with is reflected in the structure of transaction costs presented below.

6.3.2.1 Screening costs of informal lenders

As described earlier, screening is the most important component of the lending process in the informal sector. Hence, associated costs form the major component of overall transaction costs. An analysis of variance for total screening costs in Ghana in 1992 suggests that the most significant source of cost variation was again lender type, while covariates of region and type of settlement were not always important. Ghanaian urban moneylenders had an average variable cost for screening each loan of about 1.4 per cent of the loan amount. In rural areas, moneylenders' costs were about 2.5 per cent of the loan amount. The difference in screening costs, as a proportion of loan amount, for rural and urban lenders was found to be significant at the 5 per cent level, possibly because of the big differences in urban and rural loan sizes. For Nigeria, we estimate that screening costs for rural moneylenders were 2.7 per cent, quite similar to those of their Ghanaian counterparts. The trader-lenders who were studied in Tanzania had screening costs of 1.3 per cent and 2 per cent of loan amounts in urban and rural areas respectively. In Malawi, where we observed the lowest costs, moneylenders' screening costs were only 0.6 per cent of the loan amount.

These results for variation in the importance of screening costs by type of lender can be illustrated by an analysis of the cost for *susu* collectors. In Accra, *susu* collectors had an average variable screening cost of 0.3 per cent of the average loan amount. In other urban areas it was 0.9 per cent of loan amount. There was, however, no significant difference between urban and rural screening costs per loan or per loan amount for the collectors. The per loan screening costs of *susu* collectors were significantly less than those of moneylenders (at the 5 per cent level). In Nigeria we found a comparable screening cost of 0.6 per cent of loan amount in urban areas, again much lower than that of moneylenders.

Co-operatives and savings and credit associations appear to have some of the lowest costs in most countries. For urban co-operatives in Ghana the screening cost per loan was about 0.1 per cent of loan amount. This came mainly from the stationery and transport costs of their administrative officers. This cost went up to 0.2 per cent of average loan size for rural co-operatives. Here also, the differences in urban and rural costs were insignificant. The cost for non-rotating *susu* groups were quite similar to those of co-operatives. Rotating *susu* groups had almost zero screening costs, as they claimed to 'pay for nothing' except for the notebook they entered payments in. In Malawi the screening costs of savings and credit associations were only 0.2 per cent of loan amount, while no costs were recorded for similar associations in Tanzania. The major departure here was in Nigeria, where their costs were estimated at more than 1 per cent of loan amount. The only explanation we could find for the relatively high screening cost is the observation that SCAs operated with greater record-keeping in Nigeria than we observed elsewhere.

In general, the more formalized the informal entities the greater were their unit costs. Thus formal credit unions in Accra on average spent twice the actual cost incurred by co-operatives in doing the same thing, which was 1.4 per cent of the average loan amount. Their screening costs in other urban areas more than doubled (averaging 3.2 per cent of the loan amount), which came mainly from the salaries of a full-time treasurer and watchman, as well as other office expenses. Even though the difference in aggregate costs between urban and rural unions was not statistically significant, rural credit unions tended to have significantly larger screening costs per loan amount (4.4 per cent) than the urban unions, as they used the same institutional structure for both urban and rural areas, despite the considerable variation in membership between the two.

It may be noted that the screening costs per loan amount of credit unions seem comparable to those of some formal lending institutions. In Tanzania, where they still had relatively low screening costs, the SCAs had the highest costs among informal lenders. Remarkably, however, they had relatively low screening costs in Nigeria, 0.5 per cent of loan amount. The low Nigerian costs arose from the relatively larger loan sizes they had and the much larger numbers per union.

6.3.2.2 *Monitoring costs of informal lenders*

Moneylenders have virtually no monitoring costs. Close to 75 per cent of our sample never monitored loans and the remainder only sometimes did. When loans were monitored, it usually involved less than 5 per cent of the loans extended in a year. We, therefore, estimate a virtually zero monitoring cost to moneylenders. They described the process of lending as one in which the lender paid out money to borrowers in his house and waited for them to come back and repay.

Among Ghanaian *susu* collectors loan monitoring is taken for granted, as daily visits to clients for deposit collection ensures that loans are monitored daily. Monitoring costs for *susu* collectors were estimated at 0.2 per cent of loan amount. *Susu* groups have no monitoring costs, and only 20 per cent of co-operatives actually monitored loans. In Nigeria very similar monitoring costs were observed. Similarly, in Tanzania, the monitoring costs of all informal lenders are estimated to be negligible. For Malawi, only estate owners would have any monitoring costs, but these were expected to be generally low.

6.3.2.3 *Contract enforcement costs among informal lenders*

In view of the relatively low rates of delinquency and default, contract enforcement costs tended to be generally low, averaging 0.2 per cent for all categories of lenders in many places. The most significant contract enforcement costs were observed among urban moneylenders in Nigeria, where they were 2.9 per cent of loan amount. They went up significantly only if large numbers of delinquent cases were observed. As indicated earlier, it is rare for lenders to seek legal assistance to redeem loans. Quite a number of informal lenders believe that such channels could be costly. In Ghana we learned of a few cases where lenders had sought the assistance of security agents to compel borrowers to repay loans, albeit illegally, and this sometimes cost lenders about 10 per cent of the loan amount. In Tanzania, it is estimated, contract enforcement costs would not exceed 0.6 per cent of the loan amount for landlords.

6.3.2.4 *Total transaction cost of informal loans*

Analysis of the determinants of total administrative costs (including screening, monitoring and contract enforcement) in the various study countries suggests that the most significant source of variation was the type of lender. For example, the administrative costs of credit unions in urban areas were significantly larger than those of other informal units, while the lowest costs were incurred by the indigenous group-based units (see Table 24).

Table 24 Mean loan administration cost, 1992 (% of loan amount)

Country	Moneylender		Susu collector		SCC		Credit union	
	Urban	Rural	Urban	Rural	Urban	Rural	Urban	Rural
Ghana	1.8	2.7	0.9	0.6	0.3	0.3	2.6	4.4
Malawi	0.6	0.6	–	–	0.2	0.2	0.4	0.1
Nigeria	3.2	2.7	0.6	0.6	1.0	0.6	1.9	0.6
Tanzania	1.7	2.6	–	–	0.1	0.1	2.5	3.0

Source: calculated from survey data.

There is some correlation between the degree of organization involved in the activity and the administrative costs incurred in lending. Very often, 'organization' involves the extent of paperwork required, as transport expenses were minimal for all units. This supports the popular notion that the less formal the activity the lower the administrative costs. It is hard, however, to attribute the phenomenal differences in interest rates charged across informal lenders to the differences in loan administration cost shown here.

For a more accurate picture on this question, it is necessary to estimate the cost of funds using data on interest payments on deposits and their handling costs (where they are applicable), returns on alternative investments (the opportunity cost of lending) and interest payments on loans taken for lending. Although we have only limited material from Ghana and Malawi on some of these parameters, a number of general points can be made. First, lack of access to the banking system for lending on means that there is no cost on borrowed funds. Second, for most informal financial units, the process of mobilizing deposits incurs insignificant costs. This suggests that the cost of funds is negligible for most informal financial units.

The opportunity cost of funds can be fairly low, though it depends upon where lenders would have invested otherwise. For ROSCA members, low opportunity cost can be inferred from the fact that their operations remain sustainable even though no interest is paid on the funds deposited by members. Savings collectors have a *negative* cost of funds. For example, Ghanaian *susu* collectors receive payment for taking deposits and avoid having to deposit them at the bank when these are lent out. They earned interest on their deposits (mainly demand deposits) with the bank only if their balances exceeded C1 million continuously for half the year, which meant that there was usually no interest forgone. We measured the cost of funds as the implicit daily interest rate on daily fixed deposits accumulated over thirty days, or –0.2 per cent, representing the collectors' fee. This was equivalent to –6.3 per cent of average loan amount per month, or –54.4 per cent per annum. Thus, for a typical one-month loan from a *susu* collector in Accra, the total transaction cost was equivalent to –5.3 per cent of loan amount. Given the monthly interest rate of 3.3 per cent, there is a substantially large spread of more than eight percentage points. For the other informal lenders, cost of funds was usually between 0 per cent and 0.1 per cent, giving them also substantial spreads. In Malawi, too, the cost of funds for all informal lenders was estimated to be insignificant.

The opportunity cost of funds for moneylenders may also be low. Although moneylenders may be able to earn higher returns on other business opportunities, they are known to lend out temporarily idle funds. Their repayment record suggests that their risks are effectively contained and that the costs involved are not high. In this case, the high returns received by moneylenders realized in the high interest rates could be interpreted as monopoly profit from operating in incomplete, uncompetitive markets. Thus wide differential returns across different segments of the informal market cannot be justified by risk differentials or cost differentials alone.

6.4 Synthesis

It is evident that the nature of financial market segmentation in sub-Saharan Africa is different from normal specialization, where risk-adjusted returns would be similar. In this chapter we have observed significant cost differences across segments, related to the methods employed in the transaction of loans. These are influenced by factors such as proximity to lender and extent of personal relations. Even where measured costs do not differ significantly, as within parts of the informal sector, the strength of such factors as social cohesion and community organization has influenced perceptions of risk and therefore pricing. We have not found examples where the risk-adjusted returns are comparable for the different suppliers. The different perceptions of risk, and the management techniques thus employed, clearly identify different lenders with specific market segments.

Appendix 6.1

Some theoretical conceptions in dealing with risk by borrower type

The application of the theory of economic behaviour under conditions of incomplete markets and imperfect information has transformed studies of credit transactions. Dominated by the work of Stiglitz and Weiss (1981), a large number of theoretical paper have explored the implications of imperfect information and incomplete markets for contracts in credit markets in low-income environments.[5] They are a step ahead of the simple paradigm of competitive equilibrium and provide a new theoretical foundation for policy intervention in efforts to correct market failure. There are two sets of relationships or interactions that should interest us. On the one hand is the interaction between lenders and borrowers, and on the other that among the different lenders. In this latter relationship, note particularly the interaction between banks or formal lenders (often not well informed) and informal lenders (usually better informed) as they relate to small borrowers.

A lot of the risk that lenders are exposed to in their dealings with borrowers can be characterized by principal–agent relations resolved within game theory frameworks. Suppose we equate a lender with the agent in such a relationship, and denote him as A, who must take a certain action a (to lend or not to lend) from some given set of actions {a}. The choice he makes x depends on another given set of states of the world {θ}, which is often uncertain. Since the outcome must generate utility to a second individual or borrower (the principal P), they must reach a contract to ensure that P makes a payment y to A. The utility that A derives from the arrangement will depend on y and the value of a. The theory seeks to characterize the optimal forms of such contracts, applying various assumptions relating to the information A and P possess.

Since we seek to find a 'payment' schedule which optimally trades off the benefits of risk-sharing against the costs of providing an incentive to the lender (agent), we can set out a general optimization model in which the value of the borrower's (principal's) action is arbitrarily fixed at a = a^0. If we could determine a and θ, so that y depended only on θ, the solution of the risk-sharing optimum by which a payment y*(θ) is made by the borrower (principal) to the lender (agent) may be expressed as

$$\max. \int_0^1 u\big(x\big(a^0,\theta\big)-y(\theta)\big)f(\theta)d\theta \tag{1}$$

$$\text{s.t.} \int_0^1 v\big(a^0,y(\theta)\big)f(\theta)d\theta \le v^0 \tag{2}$$

where v^0 is the minimum level of A's utility.

The solution for y*(θ) is characterized by the condition

$$-u'\big(x-y^*\big)+v_y = 0, \theta \in [0,1]$$

Following recent theorization of the interaction between commercial lenders and small or poor borrowers, Aryeetey and Udry (1994) have observed that lenders are essentially preoccupied with the question 'Will I be repaid?'. Borrowers, on the other hand, appear more concerned about their individual reputation and hence their chance of receiving future loans (mainly used to provide working capital). These two major concerns condition the interaction that leads to repeated relationships in a game played under sub-optimal conditions. Based on the empirical observations that are characterized in Chapter 6, Aryeetey and Udry (1994) have produced a modified version of the Stiglitz–Weiss model of credit allocation when adverse selection is a major issue. They show that credit rationing does not need to occur under competitive equilibrium with adverse selection. When they extend the analysis to the situation in many African countries, where formal legal enforcement mechanisms are often lacking, the question of why borrowers bother to pay back loans gains greater prominence in the modelling.

Two sets of ideas have gained prominence. The first is that borrowers repay loans for fear of losing access to future loans if they default (particularly in schemes involving groups). It leads to a 'self-enforcing contract'. The second is the availability of social sanctions to punish defaulters. The idea is that defaulters are generally sanctioned by the community as a whole, in addition to being denied access to future loans. These are highlighted in the model of a long-term relationship between borrower and lender when imperfect enforcement mechanisms apply.

Aryeetey and Udry (1994) illustrate the operation of the model with a farmer who typically has very low income during the pre-harvest period (Y_g) and relatively high income immediately after the harvest (Y_h). Without any financial transaction the farmer's (autarky) utility is $U_A \equiv U(Y_g) + U(Y_h)$.[6] $U(\ )$ is a conventional concave utility function, so the farmer would like to borrow to smooth consumption. If the farmer could borrow L and repay the loan immediately after harvest at interest rate r, her utility is $U_{LR} \equiv U(Y_g+L)$ $+ U(Y_h-(1+r)L)$. Because $U(\ )$ is concave, there is a positive L for which $U_{LR} > U_A$. They then restrict attention to some particular combination of L and r such that the farmer strictly prefers taking the loan to not taking the loan. A problem arises, however, if the farmer decides to default, bringing her utility to $U_{LD} \equiv U(Y_g+L) + U(Y_h)$. Taking a loan and not having to repay may indeed be the best option for the borrower in the short run.

We may suppose that the lender is a profit-maximizer and has access to capital at zero opportunity cost. If the loan is made and indeed repaid he receives $\prod LR \equiv rL$. If no loan is made, the lender gets $\prod_A \equiv 0$, and if the loan is defaulted the lender earns $\prod_{LD} = -L$. The lender chooses one of two strategies: to lend or not to lend. The borrower chooses either to repay or to default. The normal form of the game is shown in Table 25.

The unique Nash equilibrium of this game is 'Don't lend; default'. Since the lender knows that the borrower will default, he refuses to lend. The result is the absence of a credit market. To create and sustain a credit market in these circumstances of no formal enforcement mechanisms requires other institutional arrangements. Such arrangements often rely on the development of repetitive interactions in this one-period 'stage game' in view of the borrower's fear of being cut off from future access to credit. If the lender and borrower interact over a number of years, with a constant probability of δ that the two will continue to interact next year, a Nash equilibrium with lending in the repeated version of this game may be possible.[7]

A number of strategies could be used to solve the problem. For example, the lender lends to the borrower unless the borrower has a history of default,

Table 25 Determinants of lending and repayment

Lender	Borrower	
	Repay	Default
Lend	$U_{LR} \equiv U(Y_g + L) + U(Y_h- (1 + r)L)$ $\prod_{LR} \equiv rL$	$U_{LD} \equiv U(Y_g + L) + U(Y_h)$ $\prod_{LD} \equiv -L$
Don't lend	$U_A \equiv U(Y_g) + U(Y_h)$ $\prod_A \equiv 0$	$U_A \equiv U(Y_g) + U(Y_h)$ $\prod_A \equiv 0$

Source: Aryeetey and Udry (1994).

in which case the lender never lends again. If, however, the borrower repays the loan but the lender does not make another loan, the borrower might default on any future loan. If δ is large enough, this will be a Nash equilibrium. For it to hold, both the lender and the borrower must play their best response to the other's strategy. In the case of the lender, if the borrower plays the 'repay' strategy, he makes a profit by lending. If the borrower plays 'default', the lender does best by not lending. The borrower's case is a little more complicated. If the lender plays 'lend', it is not obvious that playing 'repay' is in her best interest.

Aryeetey and Udry (1994) suggest comparing the expected utility achieved by the borrower if she repays with what she achieves if she defaults, assuming that the lender is playing the 'lend' strategy until a default and 'don't lend' for ever afterwards. If the borrower defaults, she gets U_{LD} in this period and U_A for ever more. If she repays, she gets U_{LR} this period and U_{LR} continually in the future. So the question is, is the gain achieved by the borrower by defaulting this period $(U_{LD}-U_{LR})=U(Y_b)-U(Y_b-(1+r)L)$ less than the future gain in utility that she gets by paying back the loan (which, in each period, is $U_{LR}-U_A$)?[8] Formally, the borrower will repay if

$$U(Y_h) - U(Y_h - (1+r)L) < \sum_{t=1}^{\infty} \delta^t (U_{LR} - U_A) = \frac{\delta}{1-\delta}(U_{LR} - U_A) \qquad (3)$$

$U_{LR}-U_A>0$, so this inequality will be satisfied for δ close enough to 1. In other words, if there is a high enough probability of the relationship continuing with a low discount rate for the borrower, the borrower will repay the loan. Once the lender knows this, he will indeed grant the loan and a credit market will exist even in the absence of external enforcement mechanisms.

This approach strongly suggests the importance of penalties in credit markets in Africa. Particularly in schemes that involve groups, loan repayment is enforced through the exclusion of defaulters from access to future credit transactions. This, of course, works if the relationship between borrower and lender is exclusive, which is so in many rural markets and in most group arrangements that involve poor people. Aryeetey and Udry (1994) indicate, however, that external enforcement makes it easier to sustain lending. Suppose that the penalties faced by borrowers are not restricted to exclusion from future access to credit, but can include exclusion from other financial transactions (such as informal insurance) or other economic or social penalties.[9] Suppose that these additional costs can be summarized by a utility cost of $D>0$ which borrowers must pay in the event that they default. The borrower's utility in the event of (Lend, Default) being played is now $U(Y_g+L)$ + $U(Y_b) - D$, and the left-hand side of inequality (3) now has an additional D subtracted. This makes it possible to sustain larger loans at lower values of δ than before. Hence, the availability of social sanctions is definitely positive for the sustenance of a credit market. These social sanctions, of course, are available only in reasonably cohesive social groups, providing yet another reason for the propensity to transact credit between friends, family, and neighbours. Since social sanctions do not often trigger similar responses on formal sector loans, this may contribute to the inability of many formal sector institutions to reach significant proportions of the population.

Notes

1 Indeed, one of the most intricate monitoring designs we have observed has been with the people's banks in Nigeria: 'As part of loan monitoring, field officers are required to visit the premises of the borrower every week to ensure proper utilization, offer technical assistance, where necessary, and document any improvement recorded in the business as a result of loan utilization. Other aspects of loan monitoring include weekly feedback to Branch Manager, fortnightly feedback to the State Representative on loan performance, fortnightly returns to the head office on loan repayment performance and periodic evaluation and reviews' (World Bank 1995).
2 Detailed costs are available for Ghana and Nigeria only. Discussion of trends in Malawi and Tanzania is based on the perceptions of bank staff and research associates.
3 Note that there is a more pervasive fear of wilful default in Nigeria.
4 The following criteria and weights were used. (1) Each bank's provision for bad debts was allocated to the small-enterprise sector, large-enterprise sector, small-scale agriculture and other sectors in proportion to total bank loans and advances going to the sector and weighted accordingly; these were distributed equally among all branches of each bank, giving an initial provision for bad and doubtful debt at the branch level (branch level default risk cost). (2) These initial provisions for study branches were weighted by the proportion of total bank loans and advances by branch and by the volume of advances they made to each sector. (3) The default risk costs were finally weighted according to the probability of default in each sector for each type of bank, estimated using our field data. For the unit rural banks, we averaged the total amount of banks' provision for bad and doubtful debts and allocated it among the various sectors weighted according to loan volume and the sectoral probability of default estimated from our field data.
5 Alderman and Paxson (1992) provide a useful bibliography of such studies.
6 To simplify, it is assumed that the farmer does not discount the future.
7 This will actually be a sub-game-perfect equilibrium.
8 We assumed earlier that L and r are such that the borrower prefers to borrow and repay than not to take the loan, so $U_{LR} > U_A$.
9 This is derived from the notion of 'interlinkage' usually used in the treatment of informal financial institutions, particularly in South Asia (Bell 1988).

LINKAGES BETWEEN SEGMENTS OF THE FINANCIAL MARKET AND GAPS IN FINANCIAL SERVICES

This chapter examines linkages between the formal and informal sectors of the financial market in each of the sample countries. Our flow of funds analysis (Chapter 4) has shown that interaction *within* the formal financial sector in these economies has primarily taken place through central banks or the passive use of commercial bank deposit facilities. At the same time, interactions *within* the informal sector are seldom observed because of the socially and geographically confined nature of such operations. In this chapter, we shall focus on interactions *between* formal and informal financial sectors. In particular, we will assess the benefits from such flows, and finally look into trends in these relationships after liberalization.

Following the framework developed in Chapter 2.3, linkages between sectors of the financial system are conceptually divided into *direct* and *indirect* links. The first two sections analyse direct institutional linkages in savings mobilization and credit allocation among different segments (sections 7.1–2). This will be followed by an evaluation of indirect or market linkages through demand relationships (section 7.3).

This analysis of financial linkages allows us to identify credit gaps, and we are particularly concerned to investigate gaps experienced by the small-scale enterprise sector (section 7.4). Finally, the chapter discusses the possibility of closing these gaps through the development of functional linkages within the financial system.

7.1 Analysis of institutional linkages in deposit mobilization

In Chapter 2.3 direct links between financial institutions were subdivided into deposit and credit links. Therefore, in assessing the direct links between formal and informal agents, we shall first discuss the extent of co-operation between deposit mobilizers in the course of their activities. While there is extensive evidence from our case studies that informal operators use the facilities of formal institutions during deposit mobilization, there is considerable variation in the scope and the rationale for such activity.

7.1.1 Nature and scope of linkages in deposit mobilization

In the countries we studied, all types of informal deposit mobilizers, except ROSCAs, operated accounts with the banking system. For example, only 18 per cent of the total sample of informal lenders in Nigeria did not have a bank account. *Esusu* collectors were the most likely to have a bank account. This was similar to our results from Ghana, where only 11 per cent of the sample did not have a bank account. Those that did not were mainly rotating *susu* groups, which do not need bank accounts because they disburse their collections immediately.

The use of bank facilities is generally more widespread among urban operators than among their rural counterparts, which is explained by urban bias in the distribution of bank facilities in many African countries. In Malawi, use of the banking system by informal deposit mobilizers was less frequent, and only a third of the co-operative savings associations had bank accounts. Informal deposit mobilization there is dominated by group-based associations that hand over most deposits to borrowers immediately after collection, as is done elsewhere by ROSCAs. In contrast, urban credit unions used bank deposit facilities extensively. In Tanzania, 97 per cent of urban operators had accounts, compared with 67 per cent of rural operators. The latter figure is relatively high because one of Tanzania's commercial banks, the CRDB, operates a long-standing rural savings and credit scheme, often used for deposits by individual savings and credit societies.

Usually bank accounts were used to ensure the safety of mobilized deposits.[1] While *susu/esusu* collectors invariably operated demand deposits with banks, other informal operators were more likely to have savings deposits. It would be difficult to measure the volume of informal deposits placed with banks, in view of the inadequate identification of the borrowers. Few informal lenders are identified as such by banks. However, we can be confident in asserting that informal financial operators are among the most frequent depositors that banks have, and, of these, by far the most frequent are savings collectors. Savings collectors in Nigeria make an average of eleven deposits and two withdrawals in a month. In Ghana they make approximately the same number of deposits, going to their banks on average three times per week. For many well established collectors, it is common to pay a daily visit to the bank to make deposits.

An illustration of the scope of the interaction that savings collectors in West Africa have with commercial banks is provided by our special study of the Greater Accra Susu Collectors' Co-operative Society (GASCCS) in Ghana.[2] At the time of survey (1992), *susu* collectors placed an average of 45 per cent of their entire deposits in a non-interest-bearing demand account for security.

This reflects the lack of alternative short-term financial instruments and investment opportunities. The remainder of deposits were invested in a trading business (40 per cent), lent to regular clients with low risk (9 per cent) or lent to non-clients with high risk and high returns (6 per cent) (Steel and Aryeetey 1995).

Members of the GASCCS have collectively undertaken to place their deposits with Ghana Commercial Bank (GCB),[3] which was chosen for two reasons. First, they hoped that a large volume of deposits with GCB would encourage the bank to grant GASCCS members various facilities, including credit at concessionary rates for on-lending and exemption from certain charges usually associated with demand deposits. Second, GCB has the widest branch network in the country. Some *susu* collectors operated accounts with other banks, especially when those bank branches were nearer to their areas of operation. Over 75 per cent have only a demand deposit account, while another 20 per cent operate both demand deposit and savings accounts.

Susu collectors usually chose branches of GCB within a 3 km radius of large markets, enabling frequent visits. All *susu* collectors maintained that, besides their association's requirement, the security of depositing money at a bank was the main reason for using bank facilities. This was quite similar to reasons provided by collectors in Nigeria.

Nevertheless, hardly any interactions in deposit mobilization exist among most informal financial agents. No deposit-takers interact directly with each other, although in some cases a link between two different types of deposit-takers is established via the depositor. Some market women with *susu* collectors redeposited the proceeds with a ROSCA, in order to multiply funds available, or with credit unions, in hopes of eventually obtaining larger loans.

7.1.2 *Magnitude of deposits mobilized through direct links*

The significance of informal deposit mobilizers to the banking system varies by country and by type of operator. We expect the largest deposits to be those of credit unions and savings collectors, in view of the number of depositors they serve. For credit unions, this conclusion appears to be valid throughout sub-Saharan Africa. However, the bank deposits of savings collectors are most significant in West Africa. To throw some light on the magnitude of informal deposits held at banks, we now turn to the relationship between GASCCS and GCB.

There were two major characteristics of the bank deposits made by Ghanaian savings collectors: (1) the individual balances of collectors rose steadily throughout each month, reaching their peak before the end of the month, and then dropping sharply as deposits were returned to clients; (2) in some bank branches, the balances of *susu* collectors towards month-end constituted substantial proportions of total balances of demand deposits held, as much as 40 per cent (Aryeetey 1992b).

While the deposit liabilities of several urban commercial bank branches in both Nigeria and Ghana are significantly influenced by deposits from savings collectors, this is not the case with *total* deposit liabilities of commercial banks. Collectors tend to be concentrated in only a few branches, which may not be the most significant for deposit collection. Similarly, the deposits of other informal operators, such as co-operatives and credit unions, may affect only certain branches significantly. Nevertheless, banks are beginning to recognize that a diverse spectrum of depositors, including traders and large estate owners, make a substantial contribution to deposits while simultaneously operating as informal lenders.

7.1.3 Benefits from direct linkages in deposit mobilization

Several benefits arise from the use of bank deposit facilities by informal agents. The positive effects are clearest for banks, as the only direct benefit to the depositors appears to be greater security. Credit unions also regard interest payments on their savings deposits as a benefit. The overall advantages can be summed up as follows:

1. These deposits would otherwise have remained outside the banking system.
2. Reduced cost of savings mobilization for commercial banks, which pay nothing for the services of informal finance operators.
3. Reduction in the transaction costs of depositors, who pay the savings collector's fee (3.3 per cent) rather than travel themselves to banks and queue up to make deposits and withdrawals.
4. The development of a 'savings habit' by the clients of informal operators.

Thus savings collectors play an important intermediary role between savers and the banking system, thereby creating the potential for enhanced financial intermediation. Savings collectors are, however, constrained in the amount of credit they can provide by the very short-term nature of their liabilities, as they cannot risk being short of funds to refund clients' deposits at the end of each month. Banks have not developed mechanisms and instruments of actively using these savings for intermediation so as to overcome difficulties arising out of this peculiar monthly pattern of accumulation and pay-out.

7.1.4 Trends in linkages for deposit mobilization since liberalization

In analysing trends in deposit mobilization, there are few indications that the use of bank deposit facilities by informal finance operators is likely to change. Security is the dominant rationale, and in many countries there are hardly any alternatives to regular deposits with banks.

An interesting development is the limited emergence of financial intermediation by informal and semi-formal agents, which allows them to bank a
smaller proportion of their deposits than previously.[4] A clear example of this
is the changing behaviour of members of the Greater Accra *Susu* Collectors'
Co-operative Society. In 1992 only 45 per cent of mobilized deposits were
actually placed with banks, whereas collectors surveyed in 1990 (Aryeetey
1992b) deposited as much as 75 per cent in bank accounts. Deposits with
banks fell substantially over the period 1990–2, and the proportion of
mobilized deposits lent to non-deposit clients increased. This trend is not
surprising. Increases in interest rates after liberalization did not affect the
return on the demand deposits generally held by *susu* collectors. Simultaneously, non-availability of bank credit to small borrowers ensured that *susu*
collectors faced a substantial demand from non-deposit clients for high-
return, very short-term credit. Such credit is often used to make one-time
payments, such as import duties. They responded to this demand by putting
more money to work, rather than just placing it in bank accounts for security.

Another interesting development that has occurred since the liberalization
of financial markets in Nigeria and Ghana is the emergence of new semi-
formal institutions that mobilize deposits and have relatively strong links
with the banking system. In Nigeria the emergence of *finance houses* illustrates
a new linkage between formal and informal finance. The *susu companies*
and later the *savings and loan companies* epitomize this development in Ghana.
We did not observe similar institutions in Malawi or Tanzania, however. We
discuss these developments in detail below.

7.2 Analysis of direct linkages in credit allocation

Regarding the second type of direct link, involving credit transactions, rarely
did informal financial units serve as conduits for formal credit in our sample
countries, even though these arrangements could potentially lead to lower
transaction costs for all parties (see section 2.3). Relatively few informal
lenders manage to borrow from the banking system to boost their lending
business.

7.2.1 *Magnitude of direct linkages in credit allocation*

Insignificant use of formal credit by informal lenders is due partly to the way
informal finance itself is organized. Many lenders (such as moneylenders,
traders and estate owners) run their lending operations together with other
businesses. Profits are often switched between the two, depending on relative
capitalization needs. For example, a farmer lender will seek formal sector
credit only if it is no longer possible to switch farm incomes into lending and
vice versa. Others require such credit only when they need to expand beyond
the size made possible by their deposits.

In Tanzania, only seven out of twenty-one trader-lenders had ever applied for bank credit. In Malawi only 23 per cent of all informal lenders had received bank loans. Furthermore, these individuals were predominantly estate owners who were not known to their bankers as lenders. And less than 15 per cent of those who had received bank loans used bank credit to boost their lending businesses, rather than their *other* businesses.

Similarly, only 20 per cent of the Nigerian sample of informal lenders had received bank credit. *Esusu* collectors had a higher likelihood of receiving credit than other lenders, and they were also more likely to use such credit to support their lending businesses. In Ghana, 66 per cent of our sample informal lenders had never put in an application for bank credit, and only 13 per cent had ever received such credit. Contrary to the Nigerian situation, while *susu* collectors in Ghana put in the most loan applications among informal lenders, they were the least likely to receive bank loans. This difference may reflect greater client orientation resulting from the greater competition in Nigerian banking.

Aryeetey and Gockel (1991) suggest that when informal lenders borrowed from banks to support their business, they could do so mainly because banks did not know they were going to lend the funds on. Lenders seldom reveal such information to bank officials, and many are not known to their bankers as informal lenders. The lending activities of as many as 40 per cent of sampled lenders in Ghana were not known to their banks. In Nigeria the figure was 64 per cent. Bank officials admit that they do not like to promote the lending-on activities of informal lenders, which they often regard as exploitative, as it involves an increase in the original interest rate. As a result, lenders who obtained institutional credit in various countries did so in their capacity as rich farmers, transport owners or big traders.

The situation is not very different from that observed in India. Bell (1990) noticed that moneylenders in India who were known to banks had less access to credit than those who were thought to be solely involved in other activities, such as trading. In 1952 only 4 per cent of village moneylenders in India borrowed from commercial banks, compared with 35 per cent of village traders. Similarly 25 per cent of urban moneylenders, who operate under many guises, borrowed from commercial banks. However, Bell concluded that the share of lending resulting from this type of intermediation was insignificant as a proportion of total household credit.

In the few situations in which banks knowingly provided facilities to informal lenders specifically for lending on, rural co-operatives were used by banks to channel agricultural credit to farmers. Where such co-operatives are weak, banks have been known to encourage farming communities to form small groups for credit allocation purposes. These were usually groups that came together temporarily for the specific purpose of receiving credit and disbanded after the credit line had been exhausted.

Group-based credit institutions in Africa more commonly depend on non-governmental organizations, which either provide credit directly or introduce groups to banking institutions. Many of the arrangements between banks and small groups involve donor-provided, guaranteed funds. Therefore it is not necessarily an indication of confidence that banks deal with these groups in order to reach individual borrowers. Instead, it is common that most of the risk is borne by the donor agency or the government.

7.2.2 *Benefits from direct linkages in credit allocation*

Bell (1990) argues in support of institutional lending through informal operators because of the potential to reduce the costs of funds. If money-lenders gained access to low-cost institutional credit, their cost of funds would fall, and that could lead to lower interest rates. To the extent that the moneylender faces competition, and marginal costs are constant, the gain from lowering the cost of funds would be captured by clients. Apart from assumptions about competitive market conditions, Bell's argument rests on the availability of 'low-cost institutional credit'. However, formal sector credit has ceased to be low-cost with the advent of financial sector liberal-ization in many countries. As we saw in Chapters 4 and 6, reforms have not reduced the cost of bank credit compared with informal credit, and very often bank lending has been restricted. Access to institutional credit continues to be a problem for many informal lenders, and a large number do not apply for formal sector loans because they perceive their chances of success to be very limited.

While Bell is correct in principle that such linkages could hold considerable welfare benefit for both lenders and borrowers, our research results suggest that it is unlikely to be significant under present market structures. In Ghana, moneylenders who admitted lending borrowed funds on said that they did not lower their interest rates when the cost of funds fell (Aryeetey 1992b). This was largely because of the monopolies they enjoyed and the low price elasticity of the demand for credit, which was generally required to meet emergencies.

Balkenhol and Gueye (1994) are also sceptical about directly linking formal and informal finance for purposes of credit allocation. Their argument is largely based on the incompatibility of formal and informal sector administrative requirements and transaction structure. After studying the potential for channelling formal credit through *tontines* in Senegal, they noted that 'in spite of the apparent desirability of linking *tontines* into the mechanism of mutual guarantee associations, the informality of *tontines* is unlikely to be compatible with bank regulations, and similarly, bank procedures are unlikely to meet *tontine* members' requirements of speed and flexibility'. As discussed in Chapter 2, the characteristics of the household/ non-corporate sector's demand for savings and credit (i.e. small size and high frequency) have largely precluded widespread formal financial involvement so far.

7.2.3 Trends in linkages for credit allocation since liberalization: emergence of new institutions

In both Nigeria and Ghana the most significant financial development has been the emergence of semi-formal institutions, such as finance houses and savings and loan companies, with strong links to the banking system.

Finance houses in Nigeria are privately owned investment companies (see also Chapter 3.2 for discussion of their evolution). They differ from banks in that finance houses are not allowed to take in regular deposits. They can only 'borrow' amounts greater than N100,000 from customers. They offer extremely high returns, with interest between 40 per cent and 50 per cent on borrowed funds. Finance houses create assets by granting credit, placing funds with other formal financial institutions and investing in business ventures. Their operational characteristics make it possible to take on a higher risk exposure by lending short and medium-term funds to clients who often would not satisfy the collateral requirements of conventional banks. Both small and medium-sized enterprises in Nigeria find finance houses useful and patronize them heavily. Registered as non-bank financial institutions under the companies code, they have been the target of considerable investment by both the bank and non-bank public. It is estimated that, at their peak, their assets became comparable in size to those of the banking system (Soyibo 1996a).

In Ghana there has been a significant increase in demand by businesses for finance. This is a consequence of the economic growth following reforms. While formal financial units have failed to satisfy this demand, there is an increase in demand for the services provided by informal units. *Susu* companies initially emerged as a new form of semi-formal finance, guaranteeing their depositors credit after six months of regular deposits. Following their failure to meet burgeoning credit demands, many folded. The authorities then attempted to regulate them and introduced the Financial Institutions (Non-banking) Law (PNDCL 328) in January 1993.

This new law establishes nine types of NBFIs that must meet minimum capital and other requirements. The requirements cover mainly formal NBFIs, such as leasing companies, discount houses and credit unions. The status of informal deposit-taking activities such as *susu* collectors is not addressed. Only two semi-formal institutions have succeeded in registering as 'savings and loan companies' under the NBFI law: Mutual Assistance Susu, of Women's World Banking, Ghana, and Citi Savings & Loan. The latter, which began operations in 1993, targets market women and other small businesses, as it believes that many market women control substantial financial wealth that normally remains outside the banking system. Informal finance-type strategies are used, such as sending collectors to the market women, a practice borrowed from the *susu* collectors. It also keeps long working hours to make banking convenient for market women. Its main functions include the acceptance of deposits from the public and loans and hire-purchase financing for account holders.

The company's financing instruments have been designed to satisfy a market niche that has not been met by banks, and the packaging of financial products appears quite innovative. Most clients are encouraged to open savings and current accounts and to deposit their daily turnover into the current account at the close of the market day, part of it to be withdrawn the following morning to meet daily running expenses. Many market women use the current account as an overnight safety deposit box at no cost. At the beginning of 1994, depositors received interest of 20 per cent on savings accounts and 28 per cent on twelve-month fixed deposits. These were higher than the deposit rates of commercial banks.

Customers can use their interest-earning savings accounts as collateral security for loans. While this may appear a standard bank facility, banks in Ghana generally require additional forms of security. Market women may also be provided with physical items for working capital in lieu of cash. The company intends in future to arrange for the bulk purchase of goods on behalf of traders. It currently extends credit to large traders (including 'market queens') to cover purchases of food items at the farm gate, with repayment expected within two to three days.[5] Such short advances are presently treated as overdrafts and attract a maximum interest payment of 0.75 per cent on the amount outstanding for each day the account remains in debit. For many market women this is a very satisfactory arrangement, as it evens out the flow of wares into their stalls and helps to regularize their income flows. Regular loans at present have an average maturity of three months. By the end of January 1994 eighty-two customers had benefited from such advances and loans and the amount outstanding was C86.5 million (US$121,148).

The main link between this savings and loan company and the banking system is its use of accounts with two commercial banks, on which the company issues cheques. Being a trusted client of those banks, it can in principle finance its lending to borrowers by overdrawing its commercial bank accounts. This facility allows 'large' customers to use company cheques to settle their indebtedness to large suppliers. The company is also negotiating with various formal creditors to become an on-lending agent, and it seems that it intends to play the role that it was anticipated the association of *susu* collectors would play.

As financial liberalization intensifies in other sub-Saharan Africa countries, similar institutions may be expected to emerge. However, it is critically important to address the issue of regulations governing such semi-formal operations. Optimal regulations must be devised that encourage prudential behaviour but will not debilitate their development. As witnessed in Nigeria and Kenya, without appropriate regulation on capital adequacy ratios and reserve requirements, their high risk exposure could lead to high failure rates, possibly destabilizing the financial system. In the absence of adequate prudential regulations, some of these newly established unregulated institutions tend to engage in a sort of 'pyramid scheme' to meet growing credit demands, resulting in severe liquidity problems and, eventually, collapse. We shall return to the regulatory issue in Chapter 8 below.

7.3 Indirect relationships between formal and informal finance

The relative importance of indirect relationships in sub-Saharan Africa credit markets can be assessed within the conceptual framework discussed in Chapter 2.3, where the degree of the substitutability of informal for formal financial products is one of key issues to be examined. A competitive relationship is one in which the expansion of one sector results in the contraction of the other. It implies that the financial products in question are substitutable, and the clearest indication of substitution would be a spill-over to informal operators when borrowers failed to secure formal credit. If this type of relationship predominates, informal credit is expected to expand rapidly under a repressive financial regime characterized by credit rationing. A corollary to this is that liberalization would lead to contraction of informal financial activities.

To analyse indirect interactions between formal and informal finance, we gathered information on financial decision-making by borrowers, who must make choices about sources and appropriate financial products. One question is whether borrowers choose a particular source because policy and structural bottlenecks leave no alternative. The role of the price of credit will be highlighted here, including the means by which prices in the formal and informal segments interact.

7.3.1 *The nature of financial products*

To assess the degree of substitutability of financial products offered by different agents, Adams (1992) suggests that 'informal finance is able to tailor contracts to fit the individual dimensions, requirements, and tastes of a wide spectrum of lenders and borrowers'. He suggests that lenders may grant several types of loan contracts to different borrowers, so that different financial products are likely to emerge even from a single lender. However, evidence from our country studies suggests that more variation exists in the types of contracts that emerge from different types of informal lenders than in contracts from a single lender. Indeed, some lenders said that they would not consider different loan contracts for different clients, as it would lead to mistrust and ill-feeling among them. This observation is even more valid in rural areas, where there may be greater flows of information between borrowers about loan contracts.

We have already shown in Chapter 5 that the contracts of different lender types often vary according to loan sizes, maturity, interest rates, mode of repayment and collateral requirements. When dealing with their usual clientele, different lender types usually have extremely different credit characteristics. However, the picture changes when they lend to others than traditional clients. Should an SCA, for example, lend to a non-member, or a savings collector lend to a non-deposit client, the terms are expected to be comparable to those of moneylenders. With this scenario, we conclude that loan contracts from different types of informal lenders may be similar *only* when they lend to non-traditional clientele. In this situation, the risks and costs involved become similar for most informal lenders. In contrast, contracts are not substitutable when lending to traditional clients.

In addition, informal contracts are seldom comparable to formal ones. Differences lie in the large size of formal loans, in the rate of interest (although the differentials have narrowed following liberalization) and in maturities. Taking the entire contract as representing the product, very few informal contracts can be compared with formal sector loans, except those of credit unions.

Further evidence of the low substitutability of the products of formal and informal finance is provided by the limited spill-over from those unsuccessful in the formal credit market. In Malawi, a sample of forty small businesses showed that it was relatively easy to secure bank credit, and among those who were unsuccessful only 35 per cent tried to use informal sources as alternatives. And when they did, they either turned to friends/relations or their suppliers for credit. They seldom bothered with proprietary lenders. A similar situation prevails in Ghana, where less than 50 per cent of a sample of fifty-five small firms were successful with their last bank loan requests, and yet more than half of those who failed to secure loans did not attempt to borrow elsewhere. Those who tried seeking other assistance invariably turned to their suppliers. The findings in Nigeria and Tanzania were similar.

7.3.2 *Trends in the use of formal and informal credit*

In postulating the effect of formal credit liberalization on total credit provision, it is popularly assumed that the expansion of formal credit leads to a contraction of informal credit on account of high substitution between formal and informal credit. There is little evidence to support this in our case-study countries. Aryeetey (1992b) reported that, when formal credit sources contracted in the years of repression, there was no apparent substitution of informal for formal credit. Business people either scaled down their level of activity or abandoned planned investments completely. Where it was possible, they financed investments and working capital with returns from other economic activities. Conversely, when the authorities tried to improve the availability of formal rural finance through the creation of unit rural banks, farmers' use of informal rural finance did not appear to diminish in any way. Thus these observations from Ghana do not support the idea that informal and formal credit generally substitute for each other, although there are obviously situations in which substitution might take place.

As indicated earlier, access to credit for the small enterprise sector has not become any easier following financial liberalization in our study countries. There have only been marginal improvements in total disbursements to the private sector. While formal finance has only marginally expanded with liberalization, informal finance appears to have increased its market share. We do not attribute the growth of informal finance to the policies of liberalization; rather, such growth is caused by the expansion of the real economy, which creates additional demands for finance and augments lenders' funds available from other sources.

7.3.3 Trends in the pricing of loans

Does the pricing of formal credit affect loan prices in the informal sector? One characteristic of financial liberalization in sub-Saharan Africa has been the steady nominal rise in formal lending rates. In the same period, however, most informal lending rates have not changed. The only exceptions have been moneylenders, whose rates have come down considerably in some places, and credit unions, which try to match bank lending rates.

Aryeetey and Hyuha (1991) provide a conceptual framework for analysing the interaction between formal and informal interest rates. Based on an analysis of the structures of demand and marginal cost curves facing the two sectors, they conclude that formal and informal prices cannot easily converge in view of strong institutional barriers facing borrowers and leading to market segmentation. A good example of an institutional barrier is the demand by the formal sector for immovable property as collateral. Marginal cost curves diverge because of different institutional frameworks and approaches in carrying out credit transactions, as seen in Chapter 6. The existence of these barriers and the resulting segmentation in operations suggests that informal lenders have little incentive to find out what prices formal lenders charge for their loans.

Our surveys asked informal operators whether they were always aware of prevailing bank lending rates. Most said that they were either never aware of such rates or only sometimes became aware. In Ghana only 29 per cent of the total sample of informal lenders claimed to be always aware of bank lending rates. As is to be expected, those that were most likely to know formal lending rates were credit unions, 90 per cent of which always knew what rates banks charged. Savings and credit associations were the least likely to know going rates. For almost 80 per cent of informal lenders in the sample in Ghana, their own rates were never consciously affected by those of banks. None of the moneylenders was affected by bank lending rates, although many credit unions indicated that they used the rates of banks as a guide. *Susu* collectors also frequently claimed to be unaffected by the rates of banks.

In Tanzania, also, only 35 per cent of sample lenders said that they knew official interest rates, and less than 15 per cent of all types of lender suggested that formal sector rates affected their own lending rates. Here also, most SCS or credit unions based their rates on those of the banks. Traders and landlords were the least affected, and they formed a substantial portion of the sample. Similarly, the Malawian data show that only 37 per cent of informal lenders kept note of bank rates, though as many as half of them said their rates were guided by those bank rates. This is due to the greater presence of credit unions and rural co-operatives in the Malawian sample. In Nigeria a larger proportion (57 per cent) of the sample knew the rates charged by banks at all times, but only 20 per cent (mainly credit unions) were guided by those rates in their own business. The greater competition among banks in Nigeria makes advertising by banks there much more common than in the other countries, thus increasing the probability that lenders get to know what goes on at the banks.

In conclusion, the interest rates charged in segments of both sectors of the market have little influence on each other, implying non-substitutability and fragmentation. The decrease in the interest rates of moneylenders in the post-liberalization era is attributable to changes in the demand and supply structures within their own segment of the market more than to changes in (generally higher) formal sector rates.

7.3.4 *Are there institutional barriers to the choice of lender?*

The above discussion implies relatively few spill-overs from formal finance into informal finance. *Institutional* barriers to such spill-overs go beyond the differences in products discussed above. In Africa today there are hardly any statutes that prohibit businesses and households borrowing from legally established lending agencies. However, interviews with firms for our borrowers' survey showed that only the smallest category of firms had ever tried to seek informal credit.[6] Besides suggesting that informal loans were not suitable for their finance requirements, medium-sized and large firms felt it was not 'proper' for them to borrow from non-institutionalized sources. This situation is quite different from Taiwan, where Biggs (1991) reported that medium-sized firms took loans from the kerb market.

Well established African business concerns appear to believe that their structure makes informal credit unacceptable. When we asked managers of medium-sized firms in Accra whether they would accept loans from moneylenders if the terms were acceptable (i.e. comparable to bank credit), they often indicated that their boards of directors would not permit the use of informal credit, since such lenders could not be trusted. Clearly this reasoning is partly based on prejudice. It removes the initiative for firms' managements to seek alternative funding, which could motivate innovation in both the informal and formal sectors.

Nevertheless, in both Malawi and Ghana, as many as 30 per cent of the sample SMEs surveyed had never applied for a bank loan. Similar conditions prevail in Tanzania. The low number of small borrowers who actively seek formal credit is directly attributable to the perception that banks would not extend credit to them. Many small businesses suggest that banks use the request for collateral security as a ploy to cut them off from the market, as they already know that the small entrepreneurs do not have such security. Small firms believe that they must grow to a certain size (in terms of turnover and employment) before banks will consider their loan requests positively. Their size acts as an institutional barrier to the formal segment of the financial market, and in their perceptions, profitable small firms have a smaller chance of success with banks than large loss-making enterprises.

7.4 Market specialization and credit gaps for enterprise development

In this section we discuss the extent to which the specialization of various segments in the market leads to an unsatisfied demand for financial services. Of relevance is the effect of narrow specialization and prevailing market fragmentation on financial product development. We shall first compare available financial products with the indications of more appropriate products given by entrepreneurs. The limitations of existing products are assessed in terms of their use for various enterprises and activities. This is followed by discussion of the financial services required for enterprise development. The section concludes with a description of the nature of the credit gap, indicating which potential borrowers remain unserved by existing financial services.

7.4.1 Financial products of various segments and their users

The empirical data in Chapter 5 show considerable variation in financial products. The liability structure of different segments of the financial system appears to dictate the types of assets generated. Thus the deposits and loans of both formal and informal financial units display specific differences in structure that associate their use with distinct socio-economic groups. In most cases, they appear to have been packaged to satisfy demand from specific groups only. For example, most bank deposits are short-term and do not earn returns. Deposit accounts are therefore attractive only to those organizations which are compelled to deposit funds by law, or can offset the transaction costs of making deposits in some way other than interest income (e.g. the receipt of a credit facility).

The fact that the deposit holdings of banks are dominated by households should not conceal the fact that most of these are transaction balances that provide little basis for asset transformation. The informal sector also contains segments that serve distinct market niches. While some of them may be willing to do business with any potential borrowers (e.g. moneylenders), their products are not always 'to the taste' of all borrowers, and are generally only desirable to the niche they serve.

Credit from banks is intended for businesses with good cash flow – usually large, well established and modern. Banks find it easier and more profitable to deal with this segment of the market, as risk is minimal and transaction costs are lower.[7] Their own management structures are also suited to transacting business mainly with relatively large corporate entities. As a consequence, potential borrowers without the desired track record have to look elsewhere.

Credit from *moneylenders* is often more expensive than other informal facilities, but such lenders remain the only source of informal credit that does not require borrowers to satisfy specific social obligations, such as membership of a group. Even though there is a high probability that loan requests will be granted, the short maturity periods and high interest rates do not make this credit attractive to those seeking working capital and fixed investment loans. The moneylender essentially meets the demand of those without many options, to meet social and economic emergencies.

Savings collectors serve low-income traders and others interested in very short-term working capital. Relatively low interest rates and the convenience of daily repayments make it attractive to those with a regular but small cash flow. Loan amounts are too small, however, for SMEs that wish to expand. At the same time, the fact that many micro-businesses do not have cash flow on a daily basis makes collectors apprehensive about their ability to meet debt obligations. The biggest constraint in their lending products is the monthly maturity profile of their liabilities. *Susu* collectors cannot lend for longer maturities at present because their lack of access to short-term credit inhibits more than extending limited advances to a few clients.

Savings and credit associations and co-operatives offer larger loans than savings collectors, while their charges are comparable. Membership of a group is essential, however, to ensure access to the facility. Membership is the group's only way of dealing with adverse selection and moral hazard, and they cannot expand size indefinitely because of the strain on group management. The weapons of 'social stigma' and 'peer pressure' become less effective in larger, more heterogeneous groups. Credit is mainly restricted to borrowers whose demand for credit is not regular and is instead for targeted expenditure, such as household appliances. Traders may also use it to complement their arrangements with savings collectors. While *credit unions* may have similar structures to rural co-operatives, their target group is the urban consumer, especially low-income public servants. Their semi-formal structures make it possible for them to be organized at public offices and among other institutionalized groups, such as churches.

Traders, landlords, estate owners, etc. are the best examples of interlinked credit in sub-Saharan Africa. They provide credit which is tailored to the specific needs of their clients, who have other contract relationships with them. Usually the objective of the loan is to facilitate the other contract obligations. For example, a trader or large estate owner provides credit to a farmer by financing inputs or payment for labour, and the farmer in return is obliged to sell all or part of his/her output to the trader. Such lenders will rarely lend to a person in whose output they have no interest and over whom they can exert no influence. Landlords can always ensure repayment of their loans, since default could easily mean eviction from land.

7.4.2 *Enterprise development and finance*

It is well known that, depending on the size of enterprises, there are considerable differences in financial services demanded and the constraints they face in gaining access to finance. At the same time, financial sector development is closely linked with real sector development and its evolution follows a certain sequence in response to demand for new kinds of financial services as the real sector develops (Gurley and Shaw 1967 and Goldsmith 1969). As Gertler and Rose (1994) note (see Chapter 2.2), an economy's financial structure follows an evolutionary path through demand–supply interactions as its enterprises grow and develop. However, this parallel evolution of financial and real sectors by no means promises a synchronized equilibrium path of demand–supply of financial services at each stage of enterprise development. Indeed, the demand–supply gap is known to be most pronounced for micro and small-scale enterprises.

At the same time, micro and small-scale enterprises are increasingly viewed as an important vehicle in providing productive employment and earnings opportunities for unskilled workers, often underemployed or unemployed otherwise, and hence in reducing poverty and inequality (Liedholm and Mead 1987). Fieldwork carried out in six developing countries over many years (Liedholm and Mead 1987)[8] shows that collectively small establishments account for the vast majority of industrial employment. An increasing focus on small enterprises in development policy discussion is also motivated by the general acceptance of the private sector as the leading edge of future development against a background of the general demise of publicly owned enterprises in developing economies (Steel 1996). Small-scale enterprises are viewed, in this argument, as a seedbed of entrepreneurs.

Studies such as those reported in Liedholm and Mead (1987) indicate some typical characteristics of these small-scale industrial firms in many developing countries. They are often located in rural areas and the majority of such firms are those with fewer than five workers and which are organized as sole proprietorships. Proprietors and family workers generally form the mainstay of the small-industry labour force. Many of these proprietors and workers do part-time work in industrial activities, often combined with farming. Farming and non-farming manufacturing activities are complementary over the agricultural production cycle. In some countries, particularly in West Africa, apprenticeship labour is also important, while hired workers form the smallest segments of small enterprise employment. The average wages paid to hired workers are significantly lower, usually of the order of half those paid to comparable hired workers in large-scale enterprises. Among the small producers, returns per hour tend to increase with the number of workers.

One-person firms often constitute over half the small establishments. Many of them operate as a jobbing workshop, producing to order with little marketing or management activity. One-person firms are often found on the margin of economic viability. Though there are many economically viable one-person entities, the difference in overall economic viability between the one-person firm and the small-industry firm is found to be striking. There is evidence to suggest that the slowest-growing segment is the one-person firm. Although, in aggregate, the absolute number of micro and small enterprises has been increasing in almost all developing countries, there are substantial changes taking place at the individual enterprise level. As Liedholm (1991) notes, 'not only are existing firms expanding and contracting, but many new firms are being created (births), while others are disappearing (deaths or closures)' (p. 3).

According to studies conducted in Africa (Parker and Liedholm 1989; Parker and Aleke Dondo 1991; Fisseha and Mcpherson 1991), birth rates and death rates are particularly high for micro-enterprises. About half the micro-enterprise deaths are attributed to business failure, i.e. their activity becomes financially unprofitable. Approximately half the entrepreneurs of closed firms eventually started new enterprises, while less than 20 per cent accepted paid employment elsewhere. The death (closure) rates are highest in the initial three years. After three years, however, the enterprises' chances of surviving increase markedly. Furthermore, if firms expand, they tend to do so in spurts, which tend to occur after the third or fourth year of the firm's life. However, the graduation rate from micro 'seedbed' into more complex 'modern' small and medium enterprises is not high, and in particular it is lower in Africa than in Asia and Latin America.

These findings on enterprise dynamics can be evaluated in light of numerous constraints small-scale industrial firms face owing to their operational characteristics, discussed above. Levy (1993) presents a comprehensive list of possible constraints on expansion: regulatory constraints; constraints on physical, technical and marketing inputs; cost constraints; and financial constraints.[9] Regulatory constraints include burdens on enterprise activities originating in tax regimes, bureaucratic procedure in dealing with government agencies, limited access to industrial sites, and labour regulations.

Because of the threshold at which the tax and regulatory requirements are imposed in some countries, this could prevent firms from expanding. In countries such as Tanzania, where enforcement is much more comprehensive, the bureaucratic burden (enterprise licensing and taxation) imposes substantial entry- and expansion-deterring costs on all enterprises.

Constraints on physical inputs include lack of access to raw and other input materials as well as lack of access to equipment and spare parts. The availability and cost of physical inputs could present as significant obstacles to expansion, while they tend to be sector-specific. Technical and marketing constraints usually score low in field surveys based on entrepreneurs' own perceptions, as these are evaluated in relation to their existing markets rather than as obstacles to expansion. Technical and managerial deficiencies are rarely mentioned as a problem by small proprietors. In reality, however, the most binding constraint on growth could be that of finding markets for increased output by upgrading the market niches they seek to serve, since when it comes to expansion and graduation the marketing and management skills of small enterprises are conspicuously deficient.

Most small-enterprise surveys conducted in developing countries (Steel and Webster 1991; Aryeetey *et al.* 1994) corroborate the findings reported by Levy (1993): *financial constraints*, i.e. lack of access to, and the cost of, finance, represent the binding constraint on expansion for small-scale industrial establishments. Liedholm and Mead (1987) report that the proprietors themselves typically perceive finance to be their most pressing input constraint. However, it is important to distinguish between demand for working capital and that for fixed capital, as the bulk of this perceived demand is typically for working rather than fixed capital. Indeed, small-scale enterprises tend to face constraints even in meeting working capital requirements for day-to-day operations. Yet working capital shortages are often the symptom of some other problem, such as an inadequate supply of other inputs, or managerial inefficiencies. For example, Boomgard (1989) argues that decisions to produce the wrong product for the wrong market at the wrong price are first felt as cash flow problems.

Carefully conducted survey work such as that cited above recognizes the tendency for entrepreneurs to overstate financial problems in surveys, while other problems, such as weak demand, supply problems or poor management, could be the real cause of their liquidity problems and lack of credit-worthiness. Boomgard (1987) reports cases where additional working capital loans, with no attempt to address constraints of management capacity, fixed assets or technology, had a negative impact on enterprise performance.

Despite this caveat, there are still enterprises for which growth in demand warrants expansion beyond the limits of self-finance. Lack of access to credit does curtail some SMEs' exploitation of highly profitable opportunities, and the growth of the SME sector could be accelerated if external financing were more readily available. For example, in Africa, survey data from fieldwork in

Ghana (Aryeetey *et al.* 1994) indicate that there are almost two SME applications for bank loans for each one awarded, and the ratio increases to 3:1 for microenterprises. The evidence also suggests that micro- and small-scale enterprises received much smaller loans than they had requested. Lack of credit for the purchase of capital equipment was cited as a critical constraint on business expansion by 37 per cent of the entire sample.

These statistics confirm the sizeable gap between the supply of and demand for enterprise finance. This gap is at least partly due to the problems of imperfect and costly information, high perceived risk and transaction costs, and enforcement problems associated with SME lending.

As far as banks are concerned, this may be consistent with prudent lending operations. Above all, as Little (1987) notes, 'institutional credit is better seen as a means of facilitating the expansion of firms that have passed the survival stage and have acquired at least the beginnings of a good track record' (p. 233). However, as Steel (1996) notes, in identifying the real causes of difficulties that banks encounter in dealing with small-scale entities, there is a need to distinguish weak incentives to serve small enterprise clients from the lack of adequate techniques for doing so. While banks often respond that there are not enough bankable SME projects, the real reason may lie in costly information and lack of incentives to develop new small clients. In many countries there is not enough competition in the banking system to ensure that banks have widespread networks that compete for new clients at the local level and bank managers are granted more autonomy in making small loans.

On the other hand, Aryeetey *et al.* 1994 reveal that SMEs in sub-Saharan Africa make very little use of informal finance, apart from start-up capital from family and friends.[10] For example, 8 per cent of the Ghana sample sought a loan from a moneylender and 3 per cent of them had approached a *susu* operator for a similar facility. Considering the relatively large number of rejected bank loan applications, these statistics indicate little spill-over of unsatisfied demand into informal segments of the financial market. This is partly due to the narrow specialization of each segment of the informal financial sector. This is also attributable to the nature of the financial products/instruments they provide – the relatively high interest rates, short repayment periods and limited loan size. These characteristics make informal sources less appropriate to regular business transactions than to consumption or emergency purposes. Many firms viewed borrowing from informal commercial sources as a last resort rather than a preferred means of regular finance.

The preceding discussion points to an important question: to what extent inadequate access to finance, informal and formal, may have impeded enterprise development. In addressing this issue, it is important to note that actual financial products demanded by enterprises may differ substantially in terms of size, frequency and maturity. This is partly related to the dynamic path of enterprise growth – the phases of formation, expansion and transformation/graduation into a larger and more sophisticated operation (Boomgard 1989). In this connection, it is critical to evaluate the type of external finance and financial facilities that are in short supply at each phase of development.

Thus Liedholm (1991) notes that 'the magnitude and composition of the small and micro enterprises' effective demand for finance will typically vary as they evolve. In particular, the relative importance of fixed and working capital as well as the overall magnitude of each will change as the firms age and grow' (p. 8). Further, 'the sources of finance available to a micro and small scale enterprise also change as it evolves. This evolution affects not only the relative importance of informal and formal sources of finance, but also the relative contribution of various types of informal finance' (pp. 14–15). In general, the following pattern tends to emerge from several studies which examine the evolving financial requirements and supply of micro- and small-scale enterprise dynamics (Liedholm 1991).

At the initial *formation* stage, capital requirements for start-up micro and small-scale industrial firms are usually modest in absolute size in most developing countries surveyed. However, evaluated in relation to the average *per capita* income of these countries, the initial capital barrier to small-scale industry is by no means insignificant, especially when compared with the capital required for commerce and trading. For example, in Bangladesh, the overall initial capital requirements amounted to six times the country's *per capita* income. While they are mostly for fixed capital, the complementary need for working capital tends to be underestimated at the initial stage. Further, whilst lack of capital is perceived by proprietors to be the most pressing initial constraint, their limited business experience coupled with other constraints discussed above may be binding for setting their operations into a viable path.

The micro-enterprise's primary financial need for start-up fixed capital at its inception is almost entirely obtained from personal savings or internal family sources such as gifts from relatives or friends. The relative proportion varies with enterprise size. In Ghana, survey data (Aryeetey *et al.* 1994) show that only 50 per cent of medium-sized firms used owners' savings as a primary source, as against 67 per cent for small-scale enterprises and 71 per cent for micro-enterprises. Gifts from relations ranked second after owners' savings as a source of start-up capital, prevalent among micro-enterprises and small-scale enterprises. This pattern is similar to those found in many other developing countries. Liedholm (1991) reports that these sources consistently accounted for 90–5 per cent of original capitalization.

Credit is rarely used to start up a business, as enterprises generally lack a track record to convince lenders of their reliability. Only 10 per cent of the Ghana sample had had access to bank loans to finance the start of their businesses (21 per cent of medium-scale firms, compared with 1 per cent for micro-enterprises). The use of suppliers' credit to start up businesses was observed for another 10 per cent (mainly small and medium-sized enterprises). Neither formal nor informal sources of finance play any significant role for micro-enterprises.

Once operations begin, the demand for working capital increases absolutely as well as relative to fixed capital, as the utilization of the initial fixed capital increases.[11] Lack of operating funds is frequently cited as primary business problem for micro-enterprises in this expansion phase. With the lengthening of the production and marketing period for material inputs and finished goods, associated with business expansion, obtaining adequate working capital was cited as a problem for rapidly growing micro-firms more frequently than for rapidly growing 'modern' small firms (Liedholm 1991).

The working capital needs are initially satisfied from firms' internal free cash flow and retained profits. However, as an enterprise expands, internal source becomes increasingly insufficient. A few sources of external finance become available for financing growing working capital requirements. Initially, it is supplied in the form of informal short-run finance such as advances from customers, other suppliers and trade credit. This type of informal finance can be developed into a steady source of financing through the subcontracting mechanism or regularly available trade credit, as in Asia. However, in Africa, where internal sources also dominate the financing of working capital, these forms of informal finance are often arranged for a one-off transaction or on a short-term contract. These cannot usually be regarded as secure sources on which to build up business. Both in Asia and in Africa, moneylenders are less used, except for working capital for a few days.

Overdrafts and bank loans are a popular and much more secure mode of financing working capital for those larger enterprises that have established a track record. For example, bank loans (usually overdrafts, which can be rolled over) are used by only 3 per cent of micro-enterprises, whereas they finance working capital for as many as 25 per cent of medium-sized firms.

However, for the *transformation* of micro-enterprises to a more complex modern small-scale enterprises, there is typically a sharp, discontinuous jump in the demand for fixed relative to working capital. While supplier credit and subcontracting arrangements could be a way of financing fixed capital, informal finance is typically well suited to providing short-term working capital, rather than to meeting the evolving fixed capital needs of micro- and small-scale firms. Therefore, at this stage of development, access to the other sources of external finance, notably to the formal financial market, becomes critical to meet the need for both fixed and working capital.

Our analysis above suggests that the scale and growth of enterprise operations are at present largely determined by the size of internal funds in all phases of enterprise development. While availability of external finance increases with firm size, internal finance is the dominant source of finance for the formation, consolidation and expansion of enterprises. Many small enterprises do manage to finance rapid growth from their own resources and equity capital from relatives and friends. However, the lack of external finance at a critical phase of enterprise development could be detrimental to micro- and small-scale enterprises with the potential for fast growth.

The prevailing pattern of finance also suggests the importance of adequate savings instruments and facilities. Further, insufficient finance for working capital can make daily operation very fragile, which may explain the high mortality among micro- and small-scale enterprises in sub-Saharan Africa. Under such conditions, enterprises use their retained profits to finance working capital for survival, rather than ploughing them back into expansion of capacity. Therefore, it is difficult to make the transformation from micro and smaller enterprises to larger units.

While informal financial arrangements are quite responsive to this evolutionary pattern, the diverse informal sources and services are not integrated and they are deficient for filling the gaps in the availability of both short and long-term funds at certain stages in a firm's evolution. Indeed, Bates (1996) goes further, to argue that informal organizations such as communities can support commerce and trade but not the creation of industrial capital, and that industrial capital formation requires appropriate formal institutions.

In order to assess the gap in financial services for enterprise development, we surveyed potential entrepreneurial borrowers in Ghana and Malawi on the characteristics of appropriate credit packages or financing schemes to meet the requirements of their businesses. Interestingly, while their responses on certain aspects of credit varied with the size of enterprise, their responses were often similar on other aspects.

In order to determine the range of interest rates acceptable to sample firms, we asked entrepreneurs to indicate how useful a loan at a relatively high interest rate (30 per cent in 1992) would be for new investment and for working capital. We then asked what they thought would be an appropriate interest rate, considering their expected returns and other market conditions. In Ghana, only 35 per cent of the entrepreneurs indicated that such loans would *not* be useful for new investment. The remainder found it either 'moderately useful' or 'very useful'. Differences among size classes were not significant. For working capital also, only 38 per cent of the sample thought that a loan at 30 per cent would not be useful. It was more likely that small firms (not micro-businesses) would consider a high interest rate useful for a working capital loan.

Irrespective of size, firms suggested that an interest rate of 18 per cent would be acceptable, after considering their expected returns and other market conditions. Minimum market rates at the time were eight percentage points above the preferred interest rate. In Malawi, most respondents thought a loan at 30 per cent was only moderately useful for both new investment and working capital, a situation not much different from our observations from Ghana. They also wanted to borrow at 18 per cent.

271

While many businesses find present interest rates quite steep, it is not the only significant factor motivating decisions on whether or not to borrow. For many small African entrepreneurs, a 30 per cent interest rate would be acceptable if they had sufficient market control to ensure that they could pass their increased costs on to consumers. In the early years of structural adjustment, when many firms enjoyed considerable monopolies and the flow of imports was limited, they tended not to mind high interest rates. Increased competition has made high interest rate loans difficult to service.

The greatest variation by firm size with respect to desired loan characteristics was in maturities. In Ghana, larger firms, often seeking fixed investment loans, preferred loans with longer maturities, averaging forty-eight months. Smaller firms were generally more interested in working capital loans that could be paid back within eighteen months. For the entire Ghanaian sample, the preferred average maturity of loans was twenty-four months. This is generally twice as long as the current average maturity of bank loans received by small and medium-sized firms and much longer than what is available from the informal sector. Similar results were obtained in Malawi also. Most borrowers would like to make regular repayments on a monthly basis – more than half in most countries.

While the demand for landed property as collateral by banks is often viewed as a binding constraint, a surprisingly large proportion of sample firms applying for bank credit were able to offer such collateral. In Ghana, less than 20 per cent of the sample could not offer any collateral at the time of the survey. As expected, micro-enterprises were the least likely to be able to offer property as collateral (30 per cent). Most owners of firms (70 per cent) without landed property suggested that banks could take a lien on their equipment, as an alternative source of collateral. A relatively small number of micro-enterprises suggested that the best alternative would be the savings account of a guarantor.

7.5 Conclusion

Direct institutional linkages between and within different segments of financial markets are insignificant and have little visible impact on the financial systems' capacity for mobilization and intermediation. There are direct links between banks and informal operators in deposit mobilization. The magnitude of deposits thus mobilized is not negligible, and the transaction costs associated with savings mobilization are significantly reduced for the banking system and individual savers. However, savings are kept in non-interest-bearing demand deposits for safe keeping and are hardly intermediated for investment. Banks do not engage in maturity transformation on any significant scale.

There are very few direct linkages in credit allocation between banks and traditional informal operators, despite potential benefits in the form of reduced cost of funds, transaction costs and risks. Instead, newly emerging semi-formal institutions have begun to develop specific market niches by utilizing informal practices while exploiting strong links with the banking system.

Indirect market links among different segments of financial markets are also weak. Little substitution and competition is observed in market relationships, so that spill-over effects from formal into informal finance remain limited. The weak linkages observed have a strong implication for the efficacy of financial and monetary policies. While policies are normally transmitted through formal segments of the market, their effectiveness is dampened by the significant number of financial transactions that take place outside those segments. The impact of policies would be enhanced and a broader range of financial transactions brought within their scope if informal segments were strongly linked with formal financial institutions.

Better integration can be achieved only if various segments are linked in such a way that they complement each other in those areas dictated by comparative advantage, while having access to the resource base of the entire financial market as a result of functional linkages. That is the essence of niche markets. If various segments fail to complement one another in the delivery of financial services as unrelated niches are developed, large sections of the real economy are left with inadequate financial services. The considerable gaps in financial services which have persisted are detrimental to real sector development.

Despite the large number of operating units in many countries and the assortment of lenders, few lending units meet the needs of borrowers interested in credit with the following characteristics:

1   small loan amounts (up to US$1,000);
2   interest rates far below 30 per cent per annum;
3   maturity of up to eighteen months.

These are the credit characteristics requested by small businesses in our survey. This illustrates the acute desire on the part of smaller enterprises to have access to capital and to overcome daily cash flow problems. The current situation explains why micro-enterprises wanting to expand in Africa are the most disadvantaged.

Figure 21 illustrates the situation where each lender satisfies the needs of a distinct niche in the market while none meets the needs of the potential borrowers, described above. The area between the niches (represented by the circles, which have not been drawn to scale) is an indication of the nature of the credit gaps that African economies have to contend with today. Obviously the scope of specialization of all types of lenders has been rather narrowly defined. Gaps embrace all those borrowers who cannot enter the circles of informal lenders because they do not find the packages/contracts attractive for

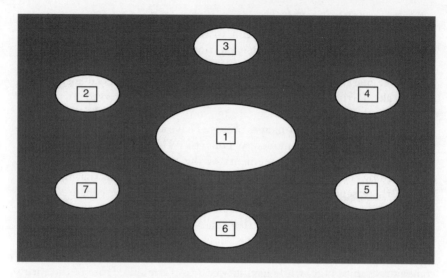

Figure 21 Market niches and credit gaps. 1 formal financial sector, 2 savings collectors, 3 savings and credit associations, 4 savings and credit co-operatives, 5 moneylenders, 6 credit unions, 7 non-governmental organizations. Shaded section shows credit gap

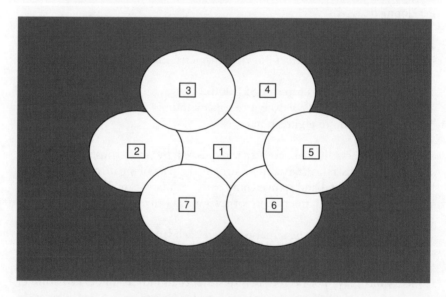

Figure 22 Financial integration among segments. 1 formal financial sector, 2 savings collectors, 3 savings and credit associations, 4 savings and credit co-operatives, 5 moneylenders, 6 credit unions, 7 non-governmental organizations

their business purposes, yet cannot gain access to the formal circles, as they are considered to be ineligible.

It is unlikely that either existing formal institutions or informal operators of the financial markets in sub-Saharan Africa can, on their own, make the necessary adjustments in structure to embrace those potential borrowers currently kept out. Our studies suggest that the dynamic institutions are those that have responded to market stimuli and developed semi-formal characteristics; keeping informal principles in their operations, but being flexible enough to accommodate some formal operational structures, including modern record-keeping methods. Hence, one issue that needs to be considered is the development of such semi-formal institutions to link informal and formal segments, as illustrated in Fig. 22. This may significantly aid the process of financial market integration. We shall return to the feasibility of this option in Chapter 8.

Notes

1 However, credit unions often indicated that they wanted interest payments on their deposits as a way of boosting lending capital.

2 In 1992 we conducted a survey of the relationship between GASCCS and Ghana Commercial Bank as a pilot study for this project (Steel and Aryeetey 1995).

3 Members of the society pay C1500 each week towards a security fund of the society. The intention is to use the fund to support members in difficulty. Out of this amount, C5,000,000 worth of treasury bills have been purchased through GCB. The individual contributions are recognized as shares held in the society.

4 We cannot draw a direct relationship between this trend and financial liberalization. It seems likely that the combination of renewed growth and comprehensive reforms has led informal financial operators to reorient their operations to satisfy new market niches, particularly demands from small investors.

5 It is assumed, for example, that when a market woman has been able to secure tomatoes to sell, she cannot hold them beyond two or three days. After the third day she should either be in a position to repay or be declared a defaulter, as the tomatoes will have gone bad through poor storage conditions.

6 Presumably firms view trade and suppliers' credit as part of business operations and hence do not regard it as informal credit.

7 This perception is invalid for large, unprofitable state enterprises. Poor bank portfolios have often been attributable to directed credit to parastatals that have proved to be very costly clients.

8 The countries are Sierra Leone, Jamaica, Thailand, Honduras, Egypt and Bangladesh. Their survey covered establishments with fewer than fifty workers engaged in manufacturing activities or related repair work, mostly engaged in the production of light consumer goods such as clothing, furniture, food and beverages.

9 His analysis is based on the fieldwork surveys conducted in Sri Lanka's leather industry and Tanzania's furniture industry.

10 Levy (1993) also reports that informal financing is less used by small enterprises in Tanzania than by those in Sri Lanka.

11 The increased utilisation is by no means guaranteed. Many micro- and small-enterprises operate with a substantial amount of excess capacity. Thus in Ghana, Steel and Webster (1991) report that 86 per cent of the enterprises operated at 50 per cent or less of capacity.

8

CONCLUSIONS AND POLICY IMPLICATIONS: TOWARDS GREATER FINANCIAL INTEGRATION

Despite extensive restructuring of formal financial institutions in many countries of sub-Saharan Africa since the mid-1980s, savings–investment performance remains poor and economic growth has been heavily dependent on official external finance. The aim of the present study is to explain the limited developmental effects of these financial sector reforms. Given the extreme fragmentation of financial markets, we set out a number of research objectives at the outset, including analysis of:

1   the extent of liberalization and financial sector reforms, and the effect of these policies on financial systems;
2   the causes of fragmentation and segmentation of financial markets;
3   the nature of market specialization by formal and informal segments;
4   existing and potential relationships between and within segments, including an investigation of gaps in financial services and credit for real sector development;
5   appropriate policy frameworks for financial sector development.

This chapter sums up key research findings and draws policy conclusions in the light of these research objectives. Section 8.1 presents a summary of our empirical findings, including a discussion of the conditions leading to 'specialization', where linkages exist between segments and each segment forms an integrated part of the financial system and can take advantage of the comparative strengths of others. On the basis of these findings, section 8.2 recommends integrative measures to improve flows of information and funds and to lower transaction costs and risks for the financial system as a whole. Recent developments in new financial institutions and instruments in the region are discussed in the context of appropriate policies for financial sector development.

8.1 Summary of findings

Three types of hypotheses – policy, structural and institutional – were proposed to explain financial market fragmentation in sub-Saharan Africa. These explanations are complementary rather than mutually exclusive. The policy hypotheses are concerned with the 'repression' and parallel markets arising from *government* failure, primarily through (often ineffective) financial policies and controls. In contrast, structural hypotheses emphasize *market failure* due to the inherent operational characteristics of financial transactions. Institutional hypotheses place market conditions in a broader historical context, and explain market fragmentation with reference to development of the real sector and a market-supporting infrastructure, such as legal institutions and information capital endowments.

To gain greater insight into the nature of financial market efficiency, we have also made a conceptual distinction between efficient *specialization* and market *fragmentation*. Specialization results from differences in risk and cost for segments of the formal and informal financial sectors, and occurs when risk-adjusted returns are comparable across segments and each segment performs according to its comparative advantage. In fragmented markets, in contrast, wide differences in risk-adjusted returns are observed across segments. Flows of funds and information are insignificant between segments, and access by clients to financial instruments is extremely limited, with little substitution or overlapping demand.

8.1.1 *Policy reform results*

To test the policy hypothesis, we examined the extent to which reform measures have affected the performance of each financial system. The general direction of the measures undertaken is similar for all four case-study countries, but there are important differences in initial conditions, policy sequence and the pace of reforms. These cross-country variations account, at least partly, for the differential outcome of financial sector reforms, in terms of interest rate volatility, bank portfolio quality and overall macroeconomic stability.

Despite these distinctions, the expected positive effects from liberalization, in terms of savings mobilization and private sector credit availability, have been slow to emerge in all four countries. Two of the indicators used to measure financial deepening, the M_2/GDP ratio and the share of private sector credit in GDP, have failed to show any clear upward trend. Indeed, in Nigeria, where poorly designed reform was undertaken without necessary prerequisites in place, both indicators show a marked deterioration in the 'adjustment' period. Though the share of credit to the public sector declined in all four countries, the central government and public enterprises continue to receive the dominant share of domestic bank credit.

Bank balance sheets remain precarious. Even in Ghana and Malawi, where reforms have been relatively orderly, most banking institutions have not yet developed the capacity for risk management. Instead, they continue to operate in an extremely constrained environment, with underdeveloped market-supporting infrastructure and a poor information base. Under such conditions, banks have become overly risk-averse in their asset management, resulting in a credit crunch. In Nigeria and Tanzania, banks' net worth had deteriorated in the adjustment period through imprudent asset management, albeit under different circumstances.

The portfolios of banking institutions have been continuously dominated by two characteristics: an extremely high incidence of non-performing loans and excess liquidity. The persistence of these conditions, despite radical changes in policy environment, can be explained by constraints that prevent improvement in banks' operational practice. Operational practice is a function of many parameters, such as risk-aversion, net worth, asset quality and intermediation efficiency measured in terms of loan transaction costs. In addition, it is affected by externally imposed factors, such as a poor information capital base and policy uncertainty and credibility.

These conditions explain the paucity of savings mobilization efforts, the 'low lending trap' in the presence of latent excess demand for credit and loans, and the *de facto* crowding out of private finance by public financial requirements. These factors have combined to form a general *post-liberalization credit crunch* in many countries, encouraged by the presence of high-yielding government paper or bank bills.

Indeed, our flow of funds analysis confirms that the pattern of inter-sectoral financial flows has not undergone substantial changes during the five-year period examined. The overall pattern of financial flows intermediated by formal institutions continues to be governed by the financial requirements of the public sector and the extremely volatile monetary environment. Formal financial flows to and from the private sector remain insignificant.

Instead, the size of flows circulated through informal finance within the household/non-corporate sector is estimated to be substantially larger than that of flows channelled through formal institutions. Furthermore, a significant proportion of household savings deposited at banks is known to be mobilized by informal groups and agents. Little of those savings are, however, intermediated back to the private sector. Thus our flow of funds analysis exposes the high degree of segmentation of financial flows. It also reveals how few interactions are observed among formal financial institutions, besides central bank operations or the use of bank deposit facilities by non-bank institutions.

Thus official statistics and secondary data tend to indicate that financial liberalization and other reform measures have so far had little effect on the performance of financial systems. However, our fieldwork data reveal some interesting financial developments in these economies.

In contrast to the disappointing responses of formal institutions during the adjustment period, the informal financial sector has invariably displayed dynamism and growth in its response to the increased demand for financial services. Certainly, this recent growth of the informal financial sector appears to contradict the theory of parallel markets, which views informal sector growth as a result of excessive government control. Instead informal finance has responded to the growing financial requirements of the informal segment of the real sector, which has been stimulated by greater trading and commercial opportunities in a more liberal political and economic climate.

8.1.2 *Structural characteristics*

In the light of unexpectedly slow responses to policy reforms, it is important to investigate financial market structures in these economies by examining the operational characteristics of each financial segment, namely the comparative advantages and constraints of different segments in terms of portfolio management and risk and cost characteristics.

The liabilities of banking institutions continue to be dominated by liquid short-term instruments after the implementation of reform measures. Their deposit base is volatile and no significant change has yet been observed in their liability structure. Few innovative instruments and products have been developed to reach untapped segments of the financial market. Nor have bank loan portfolios experienced any significant change. Banks continue to concentrate lending to their traditional clientele: large, established customers. Banks' preferred loan composition is heavily weighted against small-scale enterprises and small farmers. In spite of liberalization and the attempt to introduce greater financial competition, it is evident that formal financial agents have not become more accessible to a broad section of the real economy. Nor have the spreads between lending and deposit rates narrowed as expected, and generally loan maturity remains short.

The liabilities of informal units are narrower, limited to deposits taken from a specific group of people or to surplus income earned by the lender from other activities. Saving cycles in the informal sector are typically very short: weekly and fortnightly contributions are very popular among group-based schemes operating with traders, market women and other self-employed people. Facilities of savings collectors are used primarily to keep the deposits secure and savings are returned to the depositors within the shortest possible time. The functions of informal savings mobilization and credit allocation are often undertaken separately. Thus, in spite of the acknowledged potential of informal units as deposit mobilizers, they have never been seen as having a key role in financial intermediation in the region. The effective lending rates charged by commercial informal lenders are often too high for these funds to be used as a regular source of working capital. While many informal segments grew along with demand for their

280

services, they face difficulties in moving beyond their particular sphere of specialization.

In short, both formal and informal segments of the financial system serve a distinct clientele and a narrow *market niche*. Demarcation of the boundaries of this specialization is determined by each lender's attempts to mitigate the problems caused by information asymmetry associated with moral hazard and adverse selection, and to contain risks and transaction costs. We found that differential access to information led to varying perceptions of risks and transaction costs, arising from the screening of loan applications, monitoring and enforcement of contracts. Formal lenders associate small borrowers and informal agents with high risk and high transaction costs, and thus do not expand lending in these areas. Market-based reforms have not obviated the effects of this structural constraint, derived from poor information about small borrowers.

Informal agents are generally more effective at screening small loans. They can often rely on a relatively accurate communal information base. In particular, in attempting to minimize loan administration costs, many informal lenders tend to attach more importance to loan screening than to loan monitoring and contract enforcement. This suggests considerable appreciation of the problems of adverse selection by informal lenders, as they pre-select clients in the screening process. Their various methods of client selection effectively reduce the risk of dealing with small borrowers, who remain high-risk for formal lenders.

Many commercial banks place a similar emphasis on loan screening. For example, administrative costs, which include the cost of obtaining information and processing it, were measured for both commercial banks and informal lenders in Ghana. For both types of lender, these costs were largely composed of the costs incurred during screening. However, the types of information sought and available about small borrowers are relatively less reliable for banks and are different from that collected by informal lenders. Therefore, banks are often forced to devote relatively more resources to monitoring and contract enforcement than informal financiers. Loan monitoring and contract enforcement costs form a large proportion of administrative costs in Nigeria, where the problem of moral hazard is more pronounced. Further, transaction costs for banks are generally dominated by high default-risk costs, as loan repayment rates continue to be poor.

8.1.3 *Institutional constraints*

These structural factors are related in diverse ways to certain institutional constraints. The internal shortcomings of the financial system, such as inadequate supervisory and regulatory provision, are compounded by poor legal mechanisms for contract enforcement, increasing the riskiness of lending. Attempts to confront this increased riskiness resulting from the

weak internal and external environment have differential impacts on transaction costs and depend considerably on the lender's preference for using a
particular approach. For example, variations in collateral requirements can
become a source of market fragmentation, as formal and informal lenders can
handle only some types of collateral and not others.

In many respects, informal units enjoy considerable advantages in
information and transaction costs. However, financial systems as a whole have
failed to capitalize on these advantages effectively, and there has been an
absence of *functional linkages*. Instead, each segment appears to struggle with
its respective operational constraints.

Direct institutional linkages between and within different segments of
financial markets are rare. There are direct deposit links between banks
and informal agents/associations. However, the savings of informal agents
are kept in non-interest-bearing demand deposits for safe keeping, and, as
such, are seldom intermediated for investment, owing to conservative asset
management on the part of banks.

There are few direct linkages in credit allocation between banks and
traditional informal operators. Indirect market links among different segments of financial markets are also weak, with the extremely narrow range of
overlapping demand for financial services. Neither complementarity nor
competition is generally observed in financial market relationships. *De facto*
financial intermediation, which involves the lending on of formal funds
by large enterprises to smaller sub-contractors, has not been observed on the
scale found in some Asian countries. This appears to be a result of the limited
scope of backward and forward linkages in real sector activities in sub-Saharan
Africa. Nor has any extensive 'credit layering' of wholesale and retail provision of services been reported. With few linkages and interactions among
segments, the scope for information sharing has been limited. Consequently,
a mechanism for risk pooling and sharing across segments is also absent.

8.1.4 Financial gaps

The consequence of those policy, structural and institutional characteristics is
that financial units specialize in a very narrow range of financial products, so
not only do financial markets become too fragmented to allow risk-adjusted
returns to converge, but considerable gaps in financial services have also
emerged. The financing gaps absorb all those potential borrowers that fail
either to meet the lending criteria of various existing lenders or find their
products unattractive. They are either too large for the financing that informal
lenders can provide or at the same time too small for formal lenders.

These gaps appear to be detrimental to real sector development. If African
economies are to change their orientation away from trade and commerce
towards directly productive investments, improved availability of term funds
is desirable. Private investment in many countries suffers from a mismatch

between the short-term nature of most deposits and the longer-term requirements of productive investment. There is an identifiable 'credit gap', particularly affecting small and medium-scale enterprises. The financial gap thus identified is likely to correspond closely to the 'missing middle' extensively discussed in the literature on the enterprise development in Africa.

Financial sector reforms have not been very effective in closing this gap. Formal finance has not responded as expected, while the more positive response of informal finance has not led to significant increases in the flow of credit to dynamic small enterprises. Although informal units have the potential to lend efficiently to these businesses, their operations are limited by a restricted capital and deposit base. Importantly, the current range of financial products of the informal sector does not meet the requirements of small business. The use of informal finance may be confined to consumption purposes or working capital for small owner-operated businesses with little prospect of expansion.

Financial sector reforms and other liberalization measures, on the other hand, have encouraged the emergence of a number of non-bank financial institutions, including semi-formal institutions. These institutions have begun to develop specific market niches by reaching out to small savers and borrowers through the use of practices adopted from informal finance. At the same time, they actively exploit strong links with the banking system. These trends have led in some areas to competition, which, for example, has driven down the interest rates charged by moneylenders.

However, these new developments have not yet impacted positively on either market fragmentation or systems' performance in mobilization and intermediation on a visible scale. For example, there is little evidence that these positive developments will lead to a significantly greater supply of credit for expanding small businesses in the near future. The 'credit gap' facing SMEs remains the central problem for financial development in most sub-Saharan Africa countries. Filling this gap may require incentives for the banking sector to solicit smaller clients and support for informal and semi-formal institutions to expand into this market.

Meanwhile, financial market segmentation in Africa clearly exhibits a greater tendency to fragmentation than to functional specialization. Risk-adjusted returns are not comparable across segments for similar products. Interest rates diverge significantly, while flows of funds and information between segments are insignificant and ineffective.

8.2 Policy implications: towards greater financial integration

Our study examined the constraints on closer interaction between different segments of the financial market in sub-Saharan Africa. It clearly demonstrated that the achievement of financial market integration is constrained by a range of factors. In particular, our findings corroborate the generally agreed position that financial liberalization by itself would not create a solid basis for the integration of financial systems. Financial sector development is closely linked with real sector development, and its evolution depends on responses to demand for new kinds of financial services as the real sector develops. The performance of the financial sector also reflects conditions prevailing in the real economy. The strong response of informal finance in Ghana provides excellent testimony to the influence of a vibrant real sector on financial sector development.

The study findings imply that close co-ordination of financial policy with prudent 'real sector' policies is important to enhance the creditworthiness of borrowers. The study advocates a demand-driven strategy for financial development that is sufficiently flexible to accommodate innovations in products, instruments and institutions. Supply-driven approaches to formal financial sector development have not worked well in Africa.

Our findings also reveals the limited progress so far made by financial sector reforms in Africa towards improved savings mobilization and inter-mediation. This can be principally accounted for by two factors: (1) the implementation of reform programmes has been either incomplete or under-taken under inappropriate conditions, i.e. in the absence of the prerequisites for deregulation, in an incorrect sequencing or time frame; (2) programmes have not adequately addressed underlying institutional and structural constraints.

On both counts, the original design of the financial reform programmes should be reassessed.

The necessary prerequisites for successful liberalization – macroeconomic stability and a prudential regulatory and supervisory framework – are not yet firmly embedded in many countries in the region. A stable macroeconomic environment is undeniably an essential precondition not only for general economic development but for financial sector development. While a high degree of uncertainty may have an ambiguous direct effect on savings, it would definitely have a deleterious effect on productive investment, which would lead to lower rates of growth and savings. Unstable macroeconomic conditions together with political instability are known to engender a large-scale resource leakage through capital flight, flight to non-financial assets, or even a rapid reversal of the monetization process. Thus a stable macro-economic environment is an essential condition for generating a virtuous circle of high savings–investment–growth.

Further, an unstable monetary environment – high and variable inflation rates, and large fluctuations in exchange rates and interest rates in both nominal and real terms – elevates the intensity and scale of moral hazard and contributes to the propagation of insolvency among financial institutions and business enterprises. In the light of the close correlation between the loss of control over public sector finance and monetary instability in Africa (Killick and Mwega 1990; Easterly and Levine 1994), the maintenance of both fiscal and monetary discipline cannot be overemphasized.

In reality, all monetary aggregates, i.e. the monetary base with its two components (net foreign assets and net domestic credit) and money supply (M_1 to M_3), continue to exhibit high volatility in many African countries in the adjustment period. This prevailing condition has its root in the difficulty facing the monetary authorities in African countries of controlling the fiscal deficits and attenuating the effects of external disturbances on monetary condition.

Our study elucidates the process by which private investment is crowded out. This occurs through a shift in bank portfolios in favour of high-yielding government paper, issued to meet government financing requirements, or in favour of central bank bills, used for monetary stabilization. In addition to policy shocks, these economies continue to be susceptible to frequent and large external trade shocks, which give rise not only to recurrent disequilibrium in their fiscal and external balances but to highly volatile monetary conditions. Yet monetary authorities in the region are not yet equipped with an effective mechanism to deal with external shocks. In this light, the question of an appropriate exchange rate regime and the sequencing of deregulation of capital account transactions should be re-examined (Chapter 4). Where a clean floating exchange rate regime which entails the loss of a vital *nominal anchor* for the price level is not a realistic option, a strong case can be made for monetary authorities to institute and develop financial instruments such as 'stabilization bonds' for the sterilization purpose in coping with external shocks more effectively.

The second prerequisite for liberalization – an effective prudential regulatory and supervisory system – is also missing in African countries. It is regarded as an absolute requirement in all circumstances, since financial transactions through the banking system involve a significant externality through the act of offering deposits and money creation. Monetary authorities should maintain the solvency of deposit institutions and the stability of the monetary system through regulation of reserve requirements or risk-adjusted capital adequacy ratios or supervision of the maintenance of the quality of banks' assets and portfolios. In Africa, supervision and regulation over financial institutions remain grossly inadequate, while infrastructural support systems such as a legal framework are deficient, and banks' balance sheets remain equally precarious.

Furthermore, as discussed in Chapter 4, besides stable macro-conditions and adequate regulatory and supervisory systems, sophisticated and solvent banking institutions with positive net worth and 'contestable' financial markets are required for liberalization to yield positive results (World Bank 1994b). In the absence of these conditions, full-fledged liberalization and deregulation are not desirable. This position corroborates the view expressed earlier that 'the presence of strong institutions and markets (and of competitive industries) proved to be essential preconditions for successful liberalization' (UNCTAD 1991, p. 113).

A gradual move towards flexible interest rate management in the light of evolving macro-conditions and financial developments is a more promising strategy to ensure long-lasting positive results. As noted in Chapter 1, this approach has been summarized as 'cautious gradualism on deregulation of interest rates and portfolio restrictions, but prompt moves on institution building' (Caprio *et al*. 1994), and it appears to be the most sensible way forward for financial reform in Africa.

While freeing interest rates in a situation of macroeconomic instability is problematic, with moral hazard complications with prohibitively high real interest rates, the effect of interest rates on savings is ambiguous, owing to counteracting income and substitution effects on theoretical grounds (Nissanke 1991). Empirical evidence amassed on this subject for Africa also shows that the real interest rate is not an important determinant of total saving but an increase in real deposit rates results in increased financial saving for some African countries. Again, it is important to note that the second condition can be achieved on a sustainable basis only when macroeconomic and political stability is upheld and public confidence in financial institutions' operations is firmly established. Indeed, precipitate moves towards full liberalization in conditions of macroeconomic disequilibrium and without appropriate prudential regulation and supervision, coupled with often misplaced reliance on imperfect market forces, could destabilize an economy and weaken the financial base of its indigenous productive units and financial institutions. Furthermore Montiel *et al*. (1993) note that increases in interest rates could have *contractionary* macroeconomic effects through the impact on parallel markets.

Furthermore, there is no blueprint for correct financial policies of general applicability to all economies. Policies should be flexibly designed to take account of the prevailing and dynamically evolving conditions and circumstances in a particular country in a specific historical context. The validity of different theoretical paradigms has to be re-evaluated in relation to the conditions prevailing in Africa, when they are employed to base practical reform measures and procedures for the financial sector. In this regard, it should be recalled that the high degree of *flexibility* and *adaptability* to the changing circumstances, anchored in a firm and well thought-out development strategy, is a key to the sustained economic growth and macroeconomic stability attained in East Asian countries.

Clearly, extensive efforts at institution-building on all fronts are required to achieve sufficient market depth and improve the efficacy of macroeconomic and financial policies. While reforms undertaken have focused on the formal sector, our research shows that the relatively low transaction costs of informal agents and groups indicates that they provide a relatively efficient solution to the information and enforcement problems that characterize African economies. Their existence does not depend simply on avoiding government control and regulation or the costs of taxation.

This does not, however, mean that the informal sector can most efficiently supply financial services to the bulk of the economy in the long run. With lower-cost access to information and contract enforcement over time, formal institutions will be able to achieve lower costs and better risk management through risk pooling or sharing by means of portfolio diversification, economies of scale in portfolio management, and improving their capacity for maturity transformation. However, until the costs to formal institutions of acquiring information and enforcing contracts are significantly reduced, informal financial institutions will retain a comparative advantage in their market niches. In the interim, the efficiency of the financial system as a whole can be significantly improved by enabling informal and emerging semi-formal institutions to function better and by integrating them with the rest of the system. Accommodating the role of informal institutions is important both to increase the access of the broader population to financial services and to reduce high interest rates attributable to their localized monopoly power.

In the light of these findings, a number of integrative measures can be suggested to overcome the current state of market fragmentation and restrictive specialization. In this respect, particular attention should be paid to the fact that a reform that does not improve the informational base of lenders and reduce the riskiness of portfolios to different borrowers will not have a significant impact on client selection procedures.

The new approach to advance significantly on institution-building could include measures to improve the financial technology of both informal and formal finance to widen the scope of their operations. The restricted range of operations of financial agents is one of the factors that has engendered market fragmentation and credit 'gaps'. This narrow range of specialization has been dictated by variations in the risk profile assigned by lenders to potential borrowers. Innovative technology could induce changes in these risk profiles and, therefore, create an improved incentive structure for lenders.

Further, the intermediation efficiency of financial systems as a whole could be achieved through measures to develop various mechanisms for intensifying linkages among various segments through increased information and funds in both deposit mobilization and credit allocation. Finally, developing an appropriate regulatory and incentive framework is required to encourage the development and expansion of existing formal and informal institutions/units as well as of new semi-formal institutions. Therefore, institution-building measures we propose can be divided into:

1   measures to deepen financial markets in the context of alternative institutional arrangements;

2   measures to strengthen market-supporting financial infrastructure;
3   a new regulatory and incentive framework to advance market integration;
4   measures to improve the financial technology of both informal and formal finance to widen the scope of their operations;
5   measures to develop linkages among segments.

8.2.1   Measures to deepen financial markets in the context of alternative institutional arrangements

There is strong evidence pointing to the lack of effective interactions among formal institutions and the chronic mismatch of their liquidity and portfolio positions in Africa. No extensive flow of funds takes place between banks (Chapter 4). This calls for the creation and development of interbank money markets to facilitate rapid realignment of their liquidity positions. Since the 1970s, money markets in industrialized countries have been increasingly used for active liability and asset management by banking institutions (Chapter 4). Development of deep and highly liquid money markets could facilitate a shift of enterprise financing methods from indirect financing to direct financing. In the latter, firms could obtain funds directly by borrowing from surplus units (banks, pension funds and others) on the financial markets through commercial bill financing. This trend has also created new concepts of finance, such as securitization, or retail and wholesale banking.

In Africa, since the financial reforms were initiated, efforts have been made to develop interbank and money markets. Over twenty countries in sub-Saharan Africa began actions for treasury bills and central bank paper. However, these markets are still typically illiquid. Government stocks and bills are treated by financial institutions as 'risk-free' assets and often constitute a major component of their liquidity holdings (Chapter 4). Other instruments such as CD, commercial paper and interbank lines exist in a few countries but are used to lesser extent. Camen *et al.* (1996) report that interbank markets for local currencies exist only in Kenya, South Africa, Zimbabwe and in the West African Monetary Union at the regional level. The development of secondary markets for short-term securities has been very slow. Liquid secondary markets exist only in South Africa, and to a limited extent in Zimbabwe. Efforts to deepen money markets should therefore be an integral part of the development of a market-based financial system, in particular in the light of the well recognized mutual reinforcement between the operation of indirect monetary controls and deeper money markets, and the potential of money markets in providing banks with means of active portfolio management.

However, it can be argued that the gap that exists in the liquidity position of different banking institutions is of a structural nature which cannot be eliminated simply by activating short-term interbank transactions. There is little long-term loan provision, owing to the short-term liability and little maturity transformation takes place in financial systems, as noted in Chapter 4.

The question as to whether government should act to alleviate the effect of this kind of market failure, and if so, what are appropriate forms of intervention, remains unsettled. Many have argued that the provision of long-term funds by the financial system is not necessarily such a critical condition for sustainable enterprise development, so long as short-term working capital is in good supply. The experience of Korea and Taiwan is often cited, where rapid growth has been financed without undue difficulty on the basis of short-term credit or overdrafts. However, it should not be forgotten that in these countries, funds for long-term investment have largely been generated by rapidly generating internal savings and retained profits, which is only possible in circumstances of economic growth.

One of the popular measures adopted to overcome the problem of dearth of long-term funds in many developing countries in the early years was the supply-leading approach, whereby many specialized institutions such as DFIs were created (Chapter 2). However, in recent years, with the generally observed demise of development financial institutions, capital markets are seen increasingly as a credible alternative source of long-term investment financing. Indeed, in the light of the gap in the maturity structure of financial assets in the economies and the shortage of long-term loan provisions, many policy-makers have turned to the capital market development as a potential conduit for channelling long-term funds into the productive sectors while the banking system provides short-term finance to investors.

Conceptually, the capital market allows banks, other financial institutions such as pension funds and life insurance companies and corporations to take on long-term investment through the sale of long-term financial assets to the surplus units of the economies, either directly to households or via pension funds or insurance companies which mobilize contractual savings. Hence, an active and broad-based capital market is thought to mitigate the acute shortage of term loans and equity financing, and transform and lengthen credit maturities as well as reduce the credit risks inherent in transactions among individuals.

Therefore, Cottani and Cavallo (1993) argue that some specialization is possible: in an efficient capital market, stocks could channel very risky and highly productive projects, while banks, due to the non-contingent nature of bank loans, are left with financing of investments that are more secure and provide lower expected revenues.[1]

It is suggested that the capital market, by providing efficient and transparent price signals and liquidity in the secondary market for equities and bonds, could be used for vigorous portfolio arbitrage of bond- and shareholders.[2] With a liquid developed secondary market, investors with a strong preference for holding short-term liquid assets could participate in markets for long-term securities and bonds, with the knowledge that these long-term assets could be easily disposed of on the secondary markets. In the presence of these necessary conditions only, the maturity transformation can be performed effectively and capital markets are thus seen as a mechanism allowing the public easy asset and portfolio allocation and diversification and which can inject a higher degree of competition into the financial system.

In recent years, the need for a broad-based capital market is increasingly debated in the context of privatization programmes. For many, it appears that successful privatization and capital market development are mutually reinforcing.[3] In particular, privatization through capital markets is preferred over divestiture through direct sales in ensuring more efficient resource mobilization, equitable distribution of asset ownership, better policy transparency and performance monitoring (Adam *et al.* 1992).

In the light of these perceived benefits, capital market development has become an essential component of the Structural Adjustment Programmes. However, capital markets take time to develop and mature and often fail to perform many of the functions ascribed to them in the short-term. The paucity of financial instruments and potential participants inhibits deepening the market. In many countries government long-dated securities and bonds tend to be placed outside the market with quasi-public institutions and held to maturity. In most cases the market in corporate bonds or other private share stocks is at a very early stage of development in economies where the public sector has hitherto dominated. Many family-owned indigenous enterprises are understandably reluctant to go public. Tax policy in favour of deposit income over dividends is also seen as impeding a transfer from a bank-based financial system to a capital market-based one.

The development of functioning markets requires not just a broadening of the range of instruments and an increase in the number of market players, but also deeper trading to allow realistic portfolio adjustment and risk management. It also demands more effective monetary and fiscal policy management and a stable macroeconomic environment. Financial markets, like any other markets, can develop only if the environment is sufficiently stable and predictable for agents to assess price information accurately and take calculated risk positions. If markets are subject to extreme variability in supply and demand then prices will be unable to transmit information efficiently; where markets have few players and few counters, then prices do not convey real opportunity costs and values; and where markets are volatile and highly covariant, effective risk management is constrained.

Clearly, the failure of markets to cater for term lending must be examined in the context of these constraints and not simply in terms of creating additional instruments. Hence, the sustained development of these markets requires a system which is capable of intermediating risks. Further, an appropriate regulatory and supervisory framework should be in place to prevent damaging practices such as insider trading or illegal take-overs and mergers.

In general, financial systems and organisational arrangements are conventionally classified into bank-based financial systems and capital market-based financial systems. The latter are often referred to as the 'Anglo-Saxon' financing model, where the stock and bond markets play a prominent role. In terms of sequencing financial sector development, many argue that the capital market can play its full potential only at the later stage of economic development (Aoki and Patrick 1994). Collier and Mayer (1989) suggest that the relative importance of banking finance and capital market-based finance in economic development is related to the life cycle of firms and economies. In their early years, when screening and monitoring are important, before establishing a reputation, firms are heavily dependent on bank finance. Later, as the economy and firms mature and problems of asymmetry of information become less pronounced, bank finance dwindles in importance relative to securities markets, which will take on an increasing proportion of corporate risk.

In view of this historical evolution of financial systems, it is unrealistic to expect discernible benefits from capital market development in the immediate future for many low-income developing countries. Underdeveloped capital markets are not capable of assessing and intermediating risks. They cannot be expected to provide significant sources of new capital. Moreover, banking institutions are typically main participants and providers of liquidity at the initial stages of capital markets. Meanwhile, bank finance will remain the major source of external financing of investment for some years to come. As policies are introduced to encourage capital markets, the improvement of banking institutions' operations should be given due attention so that the economies can eventually benefit from the advantages of both bank-based finance and capital market-based finance.[4] After all, sound and dynamic banking and financial institutions are a critical constituent in the development of capital markets that could intermediate risks effectively.

Indeed, there are several ways of organizing the financial system, alternative to the 'Anglo-Saxon' financing model. For example, Aoki and Patrick (1994) point that there are a variety of institutional arrangements for banking institutions: state mono bank (e.g. the system adopted in the former Soviet Union and Eastern European countries), state commercial banks (common in sub-Saharan Africa before reform), private group banks (found in pre-1982 Mexico and in Japan under the *zaibatsu* during the 1940s), main banks (in post-war Japan), universal banks (the German model), arm's-length banking (the Anglo-Saxon model) and *laissez-faire* banking (e.g. as found in post-1989 Russia). These arrangements vary considerably in a number of critical aspects, including: banks' relationships to the securities market; ownership and control of banks; degree of government control over credit allocation and interest rates; monitoring and governance of corporations by banks. Much recent literature (Aoki and Patrick 1994; Stein 1996; Singh and Hamid 1992) asserts that the performance of the Anglo-Saxon financing model should be assessed in the comparative perspective of these alternative arrangements.

The universal bank system, adopted by Germany, combines investment banking with commercial banking services. Universal banks provide the usual banking services as well as investment and securities business. They can be subdivided into commercial banks, savings banks and co-operative banks. The last two groups of banks specialize in providing services to small and medium-size firms. Both short-term financing and long-term funding are organized within the banking system.[5] The system is known to have considerable advantages in the supply of cheaper and longer-term loans to firms and in better corporate governance, as banks are typically providers of debt as well as equity finance. Strong and direct control by banks is executed in return for fixed interest lending. Banks do monitor closely corporate performance and play an active role in corporate governance via their supervisory board representation. Thus Edwards and Fischer (1994) argue that 'Universal banking and bank representation on supervisory boards enable German banks to exploit economies of scale in costly information collection, and economies of scope between various different forms of information collection and the exercise of delegated control rights' (pp. 45–6).

In Japan too, short-term financing, long-term lending and equity holding have long been organized through the banking system rather than in the capital markets, under the main banking system.[6] Aoki and Patrick (1994) and Stein (1996) summarize a number of the key features of the system as follows:

1 The banks have widely dispersed ownership, providing considerable managerial autonomy. Corporations are lent money by many banks and own equity in a number of financial institutions. However, one bank takes responsibility as main bank, which takes the lead in arranging financing and owns a significant proportion of shares. It plays a big role in the *ex ante*, interim and *ex post* information-gathering, taking on the main functions of monitoring the corporations. In times of distress, the main banks take the responsibility for reorganisation, liquidation or the appointment of new management and therefore assume contingency governance.

2 Public and quasi-public long-term banks participate with private sector banks in financing investment and in extending the time horizons of loans. They often lead a consortium of banks which has extended term loans to firms. These term loan syndicates can diversify risk, while allowing the concentration of ongoing monitoring in the main bank under a system of reciprocal delegated monitoring. The long-term credit banks which mobilize funds by selling debentures to city banks and the Trust Fund Bureau of the Ministry of Finance are capable of assessing the validity of projects with a high concentration of technically competent experts. Their technical experts reduce risk and uncertainty.

3   Securities and bond markets tend to be poorly developed.[7] Banks are prohibited from engaging in underwriting functions. The government, keeping a close relationship with banks, plays an extensive role in setting sectoral priorities and in providing subsidized credit through the central bank. Interest rates are carefully regulated with spreads sufficient to guarantee profits to the banks. (Stern 1996, p. 13).

Both Teranishi (1996) and Stein (1996) underscore the critical role performed by the main bank system, in particular, by the system of creation and rationing of long-term funds for generating Japan's impressive investment record. Instituting effective mechanisms of maturity transformation in the financial system is probably one of the most critical contributing factors to the ever accelerated rate of fixed investment by large industrial firms in the modern sector during Japan's high-growth period.[8]

As discussed in Chapter 4, small and short-term postal savings were centrally mobilized in the Trust Fund Bureau of the Ministry of Finance. The maturity transformation was then effected by the use of these postal savings for purchase of the coupon debentures issued by the long-term credit banks. Financial debentures of long-term credit banks and corporate bonds, both issued at interest rates lower than market rate, were also rationed to city banks, which in turn were subsidized by a flexible supply of central bank discount facilities. The Bank of Japan provided funds by accepting the debentures as collateral for central bank loans to the city banks. Short-term deposits at city banks were thus converted into long-term credits (Teranishi 1996). This kind of mechanism can be viewed as a way of 'socializing' or 'externalizing' risks, when risks are too high for an individual institution/unit to take on.

These systems functioned under considerable state control with mild financial 'repression'. Reciprocity and contingent *ex post* monitoring were an important feature governing the relations between banks and private firms, while publicly-owned financial institutions provided critical technical expertise and information. A series of mechanisms of risk-sharing was instituted, which enabled firms to operate on a long-term horizon. This generated a systematic and higher incentive for firms to concentrate on capital accumulation and technological progress (Teranishi 1996). Through this system, Japan has been able to channel savings into long-term productive investment by mitigating the adverse selection problems arising out of information asymmetries, reducing uncertainty and providing a balanced mix of incentives and regulations (Stein 1996). Risks are minimized through various risk-sharing mechanisms and thus effectively socialized, which has engendered a critical condition for sustaining high economic growth.

Stein (1996) and Singh and Hamid (1992) present an interesting comparison of performance between the bank-based system along the German and Japanese models and the Anglo-Saxon system. The former system, by reducing the variability of lending flows to borrowers, allows firms to formulate and execute long-term plans. It allows the debt/equity conflict (the agency conflict) to be internalized. Firms' performance is closely monitored by banks and measured against long-term profit and growth objectives, rather than by quarterly earnings.

By contrast, the Anglo-Saxon system is dominated by 'short-termism' at both ends, since bank loans are short-term, and long-term outside funding is obtained from capital markets, whose price movements are often dominated by speculation, news and consideration of short-term capital gain. Cycles of booms and bust are characteristic of many stock markets experiencing frequent speculative bubbles around the world, including Japan and Korea in 1986–96.[9] Furthermore, in the case of equity finance, there is no effective built-in mechanism for monitoring or controlling management to solve the agency conflict between managers and shareholders (Blommestein and Spencer 1993). Hence, the Anglo-Saxon system often has to rely on the hostile take-over mechanism to monitor and replace inefficient managements.

Harris (1995) notes that in the United States and Britain, the stock market in the 1980s acted as a 'market for corporate control' to finance mergers and acquisitions. Yet the take-over process can be seriously detrimental over a longer-term horizon through discouraging capital formation and risk-taking for productive improvement. Singh and Hamid (1992) argue that widely practised take-overs 'lead to short-termism, i.e. shorter time horizons for corporate investment decisions . . . the expected rates of return on investment – dictated by the quarterly or six-monthly earnings-per-share requirements of the Anglo-Saxon stock markets – are too high' (p. 8).

Thus Crotty and Goldstein (1993) observe that there were few systematic economic gains from mergers and acquisitions through the highly leveraged corporate restructuring boom in the United States during the 1980s. 'Rather than mergers increasing productive efficiency, the search for speculative financial gain increasingly replaced productive efficiency as their motive force as the decade evolved. And instead of pricing assets and allocating credit optimally, deregulated financial markets poured a trillion or so dollars of credit into this speculative asset shuffling' (p. 253).

Evaluated in relation to corporate governance and industrial development, the Anglo-Saxon financing model with its heavy reliance on bond and equity markets is not necessarily the best way of generating long-term funds or mobilizing domestic savings. A variation and extension of the system of bank-based finance incorporating a feature of the universal bank system or the main bank system presents a possible alternative way of organising financial systems. If proper care is taken to prevent excessive controls by banks and collusive behaviour through prudent regulation, it could be argued that close and long-term relations between banks and firms can result in greater predictability in the availability of funds and lower the cost of finance for firms, thus allowing firms to take the long view in designing their business strategies.

8.2.2 Measures to strengthen market-supporting financial infrastructure

One of the fundamental long-term institutional measures is to strengthen market-supporting infrastructure such as the information base and the legal system. Enhancing the information capital base would reduce the cost of acquiring reliable information on both systemic and idiosyncratic risks for credit assessment. This can be achieved by developing a general economy-wide information network and increasing the transparency of operations of public institutions as well as listed companies at both national and local levels, as well as by developing agreed accounting and auditing systems and financial (money and capital) markets. Our research findings suggest that difficulties in obtaining reliable information and managing risks cause fragmentation. They raise the costs to formal institutions of entering market segments of household and small business. This provides local monopolies to informal agents who have developed individualized information and social networks. Specific measures to address this kind of problem through improved information flows concerning borrowers could include credit reference bureaus, registries for recording secured debt, and audits available to small businesses at reasonable cost.

Establishing and strengthening the legal infrastructure would be also a critical condition for market-based financial systems to function efficiently. It would lower the costs and risks associated with contract enforcement, and hence lenders' risk perception and the premium for external finance. This could, in the long run, encourage formal financial institutions to help dynamic small and medium-scale enterprises fill the 'missing middle'. Such measures would involve, for example, the legalisation of property and contract rights and the introduction or enaction of special commercial laws and an enforcement body. Commercial law should delineate clearly the rights, the responsibilities and the nature of liability for firms, managers and shareholders. The enforcement body such as the courts should be autonomous, removed from political influence, and empowered to enforce the law and capable of carrying out sanctions (Blommestein and Spencer 1993).

In certain cases, measures are needed to facilitate taking collateral in forms other than landed property, not only because land title remains uncertain or not transferable in many countries but because few small borrowers possess land. Laws and courts that facilitate strict contract enforcement, e.g. seizure of equipment and stock in case of default, would encourage leasing arrangements and working capital loans, especially to small businesses.

8.2.3 New regulatory and incentive framework to advance market integration

The importance of instituting an effective system of prudential regulation and supervision over banking institutions has been emphasized. However, our research suggests that regulatory measures required in building a market-based financial system in sub-Saharan Africa should also encompass measures to advance market integration. Currently, most African countries do not have specific regulatory or policy positions on the development of informal and other non-bank financial institutions. As part of financial sector reforms, a number of countries, particularly those fairly advanced in carrying out structural adjustment programmes, are attempting to introduce legislation to guide such activity. In Ghana, for example, the Non-bank Financial Institutions Law (PNDCL 328) and the Leasing Law have become operational. The Ghanaian NBFI Law specifies nine categories of institutions that are subject to a minimum capital requirement and regulation by the Bank of Ghana.

The fact that informal financial units are not mentioned among the nine types of NBFIs permitted by law to operate often leads to the interpretation of the law to mean that informal finance is outlawed in Ghana (Aryeetey 1994). However, the central bank takes the position that the operations of such agents are not illegal and simply adopts a passive attitude towards informal finance. However, acknowledgement by public agencies, including the central bank, of the role played by informal finance is important for the development of an integrated financial system, as it provides a signal to the formal sector of the significance policy-makers attach to informal finance.

Formal institutions will require explicit assurances before putting in place their own arrangements for interacting more closely with informal finance. As financial sector legislation is enacted in various countries, it is important for the governments' position on the operations of informal and semi-formal finance to be clarified. However, this does not suggest necessarily that governments and central banks must regulate the informal sector. Direct regulation of *susu* collectors as they are now, for example, is unnecessary, given the small, short-term nature of their deposits and the negligible impact that individual defaults have on the financial system. In other cases, it is almost impossible to regulate effectively in view of the ambiguous nature of activities in informal finance, often household or home-based group activities.

Indeed, most African administrative structures know little about informal 'institutions' and therefore frequently apply repressive instruments designed to coerce a response out of them. Attempting to directly regulate what cannot be easily regulated does not help the credibility of the authorities. Instead, policy-makers should generally adopt a more positive attitude towards informal finance. To illustrate how this might yield positive results, Biggs (1991) has noted that 'Faced with a difficult credit intermediation problem,

Taiwanese authorities pressed market forces into service of their financial policies by acquiescing to the unrestricted development of an active curb market as an efficient adjunct to regulated credit institutions' (p. 180). He explains further that the government permitted a series of credit 'markets' that had different borrowers and different types of loans. Government sometimes went as far as intervening to support the kerb markets.

The approach requires a 'light touch', as well as a differentiated regulatory structure, so that informal agents are encouraged to mature gradually and not be intimidated by regulation. Just as there are different degrees of formality among different types of financial agents, the regulatory system should be differentiated accordingly.

Thus reforms of the regulatory and supervisory systems should not only address formal institutions but should treat different tiers of the financial system according to the types of regulation that can be applied effectively. Regulations should be differentiated to apply with gradually increasing stringency as institutions rise in size and formality.[10] This may mean un-fettered operation at the lowest informal market niches – for example, closed membership groups such as ROSCAS and small bilateral transactions such as those of savings collectors and moneylenders. Self-regulation and some registration requirements may be appropriate for small semi-formal activities such as savings and credit associations and NGOs providing credit.

Full registration and prudential regulation become important when non-bank financial institutions are large enough and sufficiently connected with the formal financial system that their failure could have an important effect. At this level, it is critically important to devise optimal regulations that are prudential but will not debilitate their development. As witnessed in Nigeria and Kenya, without appropriate regulation on capital adequacy ratios and reserve requirements, high risk exposure of non-bank financial institutions could lead to high failure rates, destabilizing the entire financial system. In the absence of adequate prudential regulations, some of these newly estab-lishing unregulated institutions tend to engage in a sort of 'pyramid scheme' to meet growing credit demands, resulting in severe liquidity problems and, eventually, collapse.

An appropriately designed differential regulatory structure permits more innovation outside the formal sector and makes it easier for successful institutions to move to higher levels. The objectives of regulation must be clear, so that the interventions do not become counter-productive. A delicate balance is needed between encouraging the types of innovative institutions that are emerging and regulating those that are sufficiently large to come within the purview and competence of formal financial authorities.

In devising an appropriate regulatory structure, it may be important to take into account that, in many countries, central banks are not geared to dealing with informal and semi-formal financial units. In this situation, the regulation and supervision of semi-formal financial institutions could be made the responsibility of a body that understands the procedures of informal finance and its operational goals. One possibility could be the establishment of semi-autonomous regulatory agencies outside the banking system, directed by representatives of each type of informal/semi-formal financial institution as well as central government and the central bank. The promotion of appropriate self-regulating and prudential behaviour among the less formal institutions will need to take place to encourage such developments.

In Ghana the central bank has recently tried this approach with unit rural banks. In addition, the recently formed Association of Non-bank Financial Institutions in Ghana is applying for recognition of its role as a regulatory body, for which it believes it is better equipped than the central bank. Where possible, associations of informal operators could play a self-regulatory role by accrediting their members and encouraging the public to deal with accredited agents, although in some cases it may not be appropriate to give any one group a monopoly of licensing. For example, the Greater Accra Susu Collectors' Co-operative Society has requested such authority. To advance the process of institutional development, associations could develop their relations with banks and with non-bank financial intermediaries, who could become lenders of last resort to agents such as *susu* collectors (individually or as a group). In countries where such links are weak or non-existent, such as many African countries, regulation should seek to strengthen or create them. Indeed, closer linkages between the formal banking system and informal agents would be a more suitable means of dealing with the informal sector than direct regulation, which would drive informal agents underground and restrict their financial services.[11]

Eventual regulation of some of the less formal institutions will depend on how these institutions evolve. Some amount of self-regulation is possible and it will also require specialized training of the supervisory authorities so they can provide appropriate advice and guidance.

The best time to introduce direct regulation of institutions at the margin of the financial system is when such institutions are undergoing expansion. Regulation may then be introduced to control the instruments they trade in, the management of reserves and the size of the operation at a given time. The approach of stepping in when they can no longer operate simply on the strength of personal relations calls for consistent monitoring of developments in informal finance.

It should be emphasized again that there are no specific approaches to regulation that might be universally employed, since specific country characteristics are crucial to policy success. In general, however, regulation should be designed with a view to encouraging the expansion of deserving informal units into semi-formal financial institutions, while providing incentives for banks to channel credit through such semi-formal units. At this level, the passive attitude advocated for mainstream informal finance ceases to be appropriate. Governments must adopt a more 'proactive' approach towards these developing agencies. It 'consists of providing a legal, regulatory and prudential framework that fosters and, when possible, accelerates financial market development. This framework supports the setting up of mechanisms, institutions and instruments that promote and facilitate this development as the economy grows and market functions expand' (Popiel 1994, p. 92).

Regulation should steer away from restrictive laws and focus on removing the obstacles to financial market development. Thus restrictions on the types of asset banks may hold could be modified to encourage them to invest in semi-formal financial institutions. This requires the diversification of formal sector instruments. 'Commercial bills and bankers' acceptances based on co-operative or "mutualistic" guarantees should be developed to establish a link between semi-formal and formal financial institutions' (Popiel 1994, p. 93).

It should be emphasised here that new institutions require appropriate incentives to go into 'new niches', as financial development strategies should be demand-driven and sufficiently flexible to accommodate innovations in products, instruments and institutions. That is one promising way to fill the identified credit gaps. Supply-driven approaches to formal financial sector development have not worked well in Africa. At the same time, sufficient supervision is required to avoid problems such as insider lending (as has occurred with some community banks in Nigeria) and misuse of funds or inadequate capital to meet obligations (as happened with some *susu* companies in Ghana).

8.2.4 *Developing appropriate financial technology*

Our study suggests that the restricted range of operations of financial agents is one of the factors that has engendered market fragmentation and credit 'gaps'. Thus the scope of operation of both formal and informal segments must be widened through the infusion of improved financial technology. This narrow range of specialization has been dictated by variations in the risk profile assigned by lenders to potential borrowers. Innovative technology could induce changes in these risk profiles and, therefore, create an improved incentive structure for lenders.

Financial agents must reduce risks and transaction costs in dealing with borrowers at the margin, in order to mitigate constraints in dealing with non-traditional clientele. Such changes will necessarily involve internal management restructuring, which would lead to improved appraisal of risk and the development of tools for containing risk, such as risk-sharing and pooling.

At the formal end of the market, it is critical to make small-scale deposit-taking and SME lending cost-effective at the margin. To do this, formal institutions will have to adjust the way in which borrowers are identified, approved and supervised. Duggleby (1992) has noted that 'financial institutions that have been more successful in extending and recovering credits to

SSEs have often based their lending operations on an in-depth market assessment at the design stage, allowing them to determine actual patterns of demand and to identify and address the relative levels of risk involved' (p. 34).

In recent years we have observed several successful 'innovative' financial service programmes for income-generating activities and micro-enterprise development, such as the Grameen Bank in Bangladesh or the Badan Kredit Kecamatan (BKK) in Indonesia (Levitsky 1993; and Rhyne and Otero 1991). Christen *et al.* (1994) and Yaron (1994) conducted detailed studies of the common features of successful programmes for reaching 'the poor' in the field of 'microenterprise finance' and 'poverty lending'.[12] They assess the performance of these programmes in terms of two criteria: outreach and financial sustainability. 'Outreach' measures performance by the number of poor people who gained access to superior financial services as a result of the programme, while financial sustainability refers to the programme's independence of concessional funding.

These studies note advances in risk minimization in the provision of credit to small borrowers. These include: the use of groups; social pressure and unconventional collateral to motivate repayment; short-term working capital loans; and relatively high (i.e. cost-recovering) interest rates. In particular, peer pressure and group dynamics are used not only as a way of reducing the transaction costs of micro finance but as a mutual guarantee mechanism to ensure a high level of repayment without demanding collateral. Successful programmes instituted a number of other practices, including: (1) the inclusion of savings services as a short-term source of liquidity and a long-term reserve for emergencies; (2) the availability of services on an ongoing basis, i.e. through methods such as small, increasing repeat loans and borrower groups; and (3) an allowance for fungibility of money. These elements are akin to methods used by informal finance which are effective in minimizing screening, monitoring and enforcing costs and risk of default.

Indeed, if the risk of lending to small borrowers were reduced, using the approaches outlined above, the cost of *default risk*, which forms part of transaction costs, could fall significantly. However, these approaches could increase another component of transaction cost – administrative costs, if they are adopted and initiated by formal banking institutions. If administrative costs were to increase significantly, many commercial and development banks in sub-Saharan Africa would find it difficult to make the necessary adjustments to accommodate such innovative approaches in the short run without internal cross-subsidies or externally funded subsidies.

Many studies provide evidence to the contrary, however. Saito and Villanueva (1981) note that administrative costs do not rise that rapidly, and Duggleby (1992) has documented successful finance institutions that have reduced transaction costs while maintaining manageable levels of risk. Each of the financial institutions surveyed by Duggleby has attempted to standardize its credit extension procedures to reduce processing costs.

Christen *et al.* (1994) suggest that lending to small borrowers should be no more costly than lending to large borrowers, and they emphasize the financial viability of the programmes they studied. Loan size was not one of the factors that made lending to micro-enterprises more expensive among successful micro-enterprise lenders. For example, Christen *et al.* (1994) note that 'ten out of the eleven [programmes studied] are operationally self-sufficient and five have crossed the hurdle of full self-sufficiency, now generating returns on assets that would be considered adequate by private banking standards' (p. 19).[13]

However, the programmes selected for their study are rather an exception among the large number of programmes in the world which remain heavily subsidy-dependent, requiring constant injections of donor funds. Programmes operating in sub-Saharan Africa have incurred high costs, in particular. For example, Bagachwa (1995) discusses the difficulties of the Presidential Trust Fund for Self Reliance (PTFSR), which has adopted the Grameen Bank model. In 1991 the PTFSR extended TSh4.3 million in loans against a cost of TSh5.6 million. As of June 1992 it had issued TSh9.6 million in loans, yielding interest income of TSh0.99 million against an operating cost of TSh7.7 million. Savings are reported to have been only TSh1.01 million.

It is not surprising that many studies stress the need for competitive interest rates (Buechler 1995). To be profitable, financial institutions lending to small borrowers must earn enough to cover the cost of funds and operational costs. There must be some degree of flexibility in setting interest rates in order that they are able to maintain profits. However, the main limit on rising interest rates is the overall impact on macroeconomic balances and the problem of adverse selection, as discussed in Chapter 2. Furthermore, excessively high interest charges in relation to returns from project activity could leave the borrower in a state of perpetually increasing indebtedness. They must therefore strike a proper balance between risk management and loan-revenue.

After evaluating the operations of eleven innovative schemes for micro-enterprise finance, Christen *et al.* (1994) concluded that the two keys to financial viability were higher real effective interest rates and lower average salary compared with *per capita* GDP. Our study of different market segments suggests that reductions in administration costs are possible if the following management approaches are applied:

1   Devolution of decision-making and supervision to local levels. This ensures that information is relevant, timely, easy to obtain and relatively cheap, while transport expenses are kept low.
2   Increased application of character-based creditworthiness criteria for small enterprises compared to project-based criteria. This helps to reduce screening costs through minimal information requirements.
3   Use of information possessed by informal and semi-formal lenders, which

301

may be inexpensive and informative. Closer interaction between formal financial institutions and informal/semi-formal agents in deposit mobilization and lending has great prospects in facilitating transaction cost reduction while expanding the lending base and reducing risk borne by banks.

4   Use of other NGOs in screening and preparing SME loan applications. Institutions such as Women's World Banking and small business associations might be assisted to do this.

Many of these innovations have, in fact, been developed by semi-formal institutions in their attempts to use both formal and informal methods of intermediation. Since we are not sure that banks can adopt these without incurring high costs, practices of risk-sharing and information-sharing become highly valuable. For example, where expanding financial services in non-traditional financial market segments is viewed as risky, it is likely to be more effective to induce banks to link up with semi-formal or informal institutions that use appropriate methods than to lend directly.

Banks which link up directly with semi-formal lenders can use the screening mechanisms of the latter to supply credit to small borrowers. In situations where informal finance is well organized, informal units could also be used for screening, monitoring and contract enforcement. Thus proposals for risk-sharing will be central to our proposal, as we discuss how the institutional framework and policies will best accommodate greater financial integration.

8.2.5   Measures to develop linkages

The integrative measures proposed above aim to address the present state of market fragmentation, where there are weak interactions between different segments. In most sub-Saharan Africa economies, 'deficit' units and 'surplus' units within the financial system have little direct or indirect interaction. Apart from developing financial markets to allow greater interaction among formal institutions, as discussed above, this condition points to the need to develop a mechanism that permits non-formal units greater access to the surplus financial resources of formal institutions. Informal and semi-formal units could use formal credit to enable them expand their lending operations and meet the needs of the expanding real sector. However, this has not taken place in many countries because reforms so far have offered formal institutions no incentive to link up more closely with informal/semi-formal lenders and deposit mobilizers.

Greater integration can enhance the comparative advantage of each segment of the financial system, and consequently eliminate gaps in financial services. Integrative methods must overcome both structural constraints and those emanating from internal and external institutional practices. These constraints lead to perceptions of high risk and high transaction costs in lending to small borrowers in the absence of adequate information about prospective borrowers. The availability and quality of information about borrowers vary considerably among segments of the financial system. At present, there is little sharing of information between segments and there is certainly scope for ensuring that information relevant about various transactions becomes more readily available.

Developments in Ghana offer some ideas about the means by which information could be shared. There, semi-formal institutions with functional ties to commercial banks have contracted out deposit mobilization activities to *susu* collectors. The informal deposit collector appears to make use of his knowledge of the small depositor in the service of the semi-formal organizations. In turn, the semi-formal agent places deposits with the commercial banks. The specialized information that the informal operator possesses is available at relatively little cost to formal and semi-formal operators.

The semi-formal agent can bridge the information gap between the informal and formal sectors, and this is a role that credit unions and some NGOs seek to play (Christen *et al.* 1994). So far, many NGO-driven credit programmes have operated largely in isolation from the rest of the financial system, often without any co-ordination with similar programmes. This has made their impact on the financial sector development minimal. However, in recent years some pioneer programmes have moved either to develop links with existing banking institutions or to become full-fledged financial intermediaries themselves.[14]

Development of such institutions could help fill financial gaps and provide financial services at the wider population. Direct support to them should be performance-based and oriented towards building institutional capabilities and helping institutions through the transition to efficient methods and optimal scale.[15]

Buechler (1995) documents other occasions when semi-formal agencies are used as intermediaries to link the formal and informal sectors, thereby acting as conduits for information. She highlights the role of NGOs, credit co-operatives and small local banks as intermediaries between the informal real sector and national development banks. In some instances, the transformation of NGOs into profit-making entities has enabled them to use the facilities of commercial and development banks, as well as the money market. While they do not often deal with informal *financial* operators, NGOs have borrowed from informal practices in dealing with clients. However, semi-formal institutions often face higher costs when dealing directly with small clients than when they channel operations through informal operators (Aryeetey 1992a). This suggests multi-layering as a possible alternative.

8.2.5.1 Forging links in deposit mobilization

Banks should be encouraged and given incentives to enter into closer relationships with informal agents such as savings collectors and savings and credit associations, as well as non-governmental organizations. They have the potential to become an effective mechanism by which to mobilize deposits from and deliver credit to the household and micro-business sector. These agents can bulk up small savings at relatively low cost and could retail more credit to the informal sector if backed up by access to bank credit.

Indeed, banks could be encouraged to offer informal deposit mobilizers preferential deposit rates, higher than the rates of return on their other assets or activities. This would encourage informal agents to use the facility more and would also confer recognition of their role in savings mobilization.[16] The waiving of all or part of charges and fees on the demand deposits of informal deposit mobilizers by banks would be seen as encouraging an institutional link between the two.

While the establishment of direct contact between banks and informal deposit mobilizers will be important, there is also considerable potential for the semi-formal institutions, such as savings and loan companies, well functioning finance houses and credit unions or newly emerging institutions to act as intermediaries. Roemer and Jones (1991) have suggested that 'when markets are fragmented, the best policy is to develop new institutions that will integrate markets, and only then to regulate' (p. 220). In a satisfactorily operating market-based economy, governments need only be supportive, as the development of such new institutions is likely to take place if the demand for additional financial services exists.

8.2.5.2 Forging links in credit allocation

One of the ways to link credit allocation between financial segments is the development of an *agency* relationship in which bank loanable funds are channelled through informal lenders for lending on. For example, savings collectors could expand credit to their clients if they had recourse to a commercial bank line of credit, and the resulting expansion in collectors' business would increase the savings that they could mobilize for deposit in commercial banks. Technical assistance and a partial guarantee might be needed to establish mutually satisfactory arrangements.

Here also the operations of *susu* collectors in West Africa provide some valuable insights into the development of such arrangements. Indeed, Steel and Aryeetey (1995) have proposed an approach for linking the Greater Accra Susu Collectors' Co-operative Society with Ghana Commercial Bank in a scheme that could increase the proportion of *susu* depositors who gain access to credit facilities from their *susu* collectors. We would expect access to *susu* credit to rise from 9 per cent at present to 30 per cent if the scheme was implemented. It simply involves the availability of an overdraft facility from the bank to cover up to about 50 per cent of the shortfall in anticipated lending if *susu* collectors are to increase the average number of depositors from 420 to 600, the number they believe they can conveniently handle. The scheme was based on the observation that increased lending by collectors often leads to an increase in the number of depositors.

The realization of the full potential of informal finance units lies in the identification of similar links between formal and informal units. We recognize that the potential for financial integration is much stronger in some countries than in others. In East and Southern African countries, as well as in francophone countries, the relatively well developed co-operative organizations could be the ideal informal institutions for developing such linkages. Special incentives could encourage banks to develop twinning arrangements with semi-formal or non-bank financial institutions, providing them with management support as well as funds. For example, funds lent on to microfinance intermediaries could be rediscounted at a concessional rate to increase the profitability to banks, or tax incentives could be provided to compensate for the costs and risks of developing small-borrower portfolios. Or a partial guarantee of a line of credit to an NGO or association of informal agents for lending on in small amounts would make more sense than banks' guaranteeing direct small loans.

This would lead to the layering of credit supply through different intermediaries, involving a number of 'shock absorbers'. This is a principle quite well-known in informal financing arrangements that involve interlinkage with traders.

Examples of the successful channelling of credit through informal agents by banks are to be found in the Philippines. Yotopoulos and Floro (1991) have reported three schemes that have been successfully used to channel credit to farmers. 'The End Users/Input Suppliers' Assistance Scheme extends production loans to farmers, using traders, rice millers (end users), and input dealers (input suppliers) as intermediaries. The latter have access to subsidized government loans (at 6 percent per annum inclusive of service charges), which they re-lend to farmers at 15 percent per annum' (p. 165).

While we support the principle of channelling credit through informal sources, we are more cautious about the use of informal agents as conduits for such lending. We would rely more on well established agents who operate from within recognized bodies, such as associations, co-operatives, companies, unions, etc. These have greater credibility than individuals. However, in a number of countries, individual moneylenders with good long-standing relations with banks could be useful for the purpose. Yotopoulos and Floro (1991) defend the policy of channelling formal credit to informal lenders 'on the grounds of efficiency and increased financial integration, especially among small farmers. Informal lenders can build a personal relationship with their borrowers that can ensure an extremely low loan default rate' (p. 165).

Encouragement of subcontracting in the real sector would also generate greater financial linkages in parallel. For example, if leasing companies could pass on tax benefits to banks to obtain better credit terms, they could in turn pass on more finance to their clients. Biggs (1991) presents a good illustration of subcontracting in Taiwan.

8.3 Synthesis

In this concluding section we have argued that rather than restrictive regulation of less formal agents, financial policy-makers should primarily concern themselves with forging a closer link between informal and formal finance in terms of both deposit mobilization and credit allocation. We have also suggested that, to achieve integrated financial development, there is an obvious need for national policy frameworks that have appropriate levels of incentive and regulatory policies. Such frameworks should provide a developmental platform for financial institutions by helping them to reduce and share risk within an acceptable incentive structure. In turn, greater flows of funds and information between segments would help equalize risk-adjusted returns across segments and hence increase market efficiency by drawing on the comparative advantages of each.

Notes

1 The non-contingent nature of bank loans allows successful investors to keep any profits that are left and failed investors to transfer their losses to the banks.

2 According to the efficient markets hypothesis, the share prices on stock markets do always fully reflect all available information about the economic fundamentals. In practice, however, this hypothesis is often rejected even for highly developed markets.

3 Adam et al. (1992) review this proposition critically. They argue that whilst privatization can make a major contribution to the deepening of equity markets, a positive outcome from concurrent implementation of the privatization programme and capital market development is by no means automatically assured.

4 Blommestein and Spencer (1993) argue that instituting investment funds – a hybrid of the banking system and capital markets – may be a practical way forward for transitional economies, which typically face conditions such as a shortage of domestic savings, rudimentary capital markets and inadequate capacity in evaluating risks.

5 However, Baums (1994) argues that the description of the German corporate governance system as bank-oriented is somewhat misleading.

6 Aoki and Patrick (1994) define the term 'Japanese main banking system' as an informal set of institutional arrangements and behaviour that constitutes a system of corporate finance and governance.

7 The Japanese securities markets, however, grew rapidly in the 1980s with the deregulation and internationalization of corporate financing. Many large

corporations have turned to their main banks to facilitate bond issuance (Campbell and Hamao 1994).

8 It is important to notice the duality of the system. Teranishi (1996) notes that funds for investment by small-scale firms relied mostly on roll-over short-term credit or supplier's credit as well as internal accumulation.

9 The stock market in both countries experienced spectacular expansion in the 1980s, when these economies had undergone the process of financial and trade liberalization and all-encompassing deregulation. Substantial liquidity flowed into stock markets and real estate. As Patrick (1994) notes, 'speculators used gains in each market as collateral both to pyramid and to invest in the other market' (p. 347). Each market found itself in a speculative bubble in 1989–90, which inevitably resulted in an equally dramatic crash in the 1990s.

10 South Africa has adopted a multi-tiered system along these lines recently.

11 Over the past two decades, there have been frequent examples of official inter-vention driving informal activity underground in countries such as Tanzania and Kenya. Bagachwa (1995) observed a lot more informal financial activity in Tanzania than Hyuha et al. (1993) did in their survey, undertaken four years earlier.

12 Micro-enterprise finance centres on poor people with enterprises of their own, including the self-employed. Poverty lending tends to concentrate on lending towards income-generating activities.

13 Operational self-sufficiency refers to the ability of programmes to cover all non-financial expenses (salaries and administrative costs, depreciation of fixed assets and the cost of loan principal lost to default) out of programme fees and inter-est charges. Programmes are viewed to have reached full-self sufficiency if their revenues cover both non-financial and financial costs on a commercial basis.

14 For example, the Mennonite Economic Development Associates' Micro-enterprise Business Development Programme in Tanzania and Kenya Rural Enterprises Programme (KREP) are trying to transform into banking institutions so that they can mobilize voluntary deposits, expand to a more efficient scale, and complete the transition to full self-sufficiency.

15 Such support may include institutional development grants, fixed assets, time-limited coverage of operating or expansion costs, and lines of credit or capitalization grants for institutions with high levels of performance in terms of loan recovery, self-sufficiency, outreach and sound management (Committee of Donor Agencies 1995).

16 In many West African cities where transactions at bank branches take unusually long periods, 'special' clerks or tellers could be assigned to frequent depositors, as such as savings collectors, in order to reduce the length of time they spend at bank counters.

REFERENCES

Adam, Christopher S., William P. Cavendish and P.S. Mistry (1992) *Adjusting Privatization*, London: James Currey.

Adam, Christopher and Stephen A. O'Connell (1997) *Aid, Taxation and Development: Analytical Perspectives on Aid Effectiveness in Sub-Saharan Africa*, Working Paper Series WPS/97-5, Oxford: Centre for the Study of African Economies, University of Oxford.

Adams, Dale W. (1992) 'Taking a Fresh Look at Informal Finance' in Dale W. Adams and Delbert A. Fitchett (eds) *Informal Finance in Low-income Countries*, Boulder: Westview Press.

Adams, Dale W. and Delbert, A. Fitchett (eds) (1992) *Informal Finance in Low-income Countries*, Boulder: Westview Press.

Adams, Dale W. and Douglas H. Graham (1981) 'A Critique of Traditional Agriculture Credit Projects and Policies', *Journal of Development Economics* 8: 347–66.

Adams, Dale W., Douglas H. Graham and J.D. Von Pischke (1984) *Undermining Rural Development with Cheap Credit*, Boulder: Westview Press.

Adegboye, R.O. (1969) 'Procuring Loans by Pledging Cocoa Trees', *Nigerian Geographical Journal* 12, 1–2: 63–76.

African Development Bank (1994) *African Development Report 1994*, Dakar: ADB.

Alashi, S.O. (1995) 'A Brief on the Nigerian Community Banking Scheme', paper presented at International Workshop on Financial Integration and Development in Africa, London: School of Oriental and African Studies, 18–19 May.

Alderman, H. and C. Paxson (1992) 'Do the Poor Insure? A Synthesis of the Literature on Risk Sharing Institutions in Developing Countries', in E. Bacha (ed.) *Economies in a Changing World 4, Development, Trade and the Environment*, London: Macmillan.

Aoki Masahiko and Hugh Patrick (eds) (1994) *The Japanese Main Bank System*, Oxford: Oxford University Press.

Ardener, S. (1964) 'The Comparative Study of Rotating Credit Associations', *Journal of the Royal Anthropological Institute*, 94, 1–2: 201–29.

Aredo, D. (1993) *The Informal and Semi-formal Financial Sectors in Ethiopia: a Study of the Iqqub, Iddir and Savings and Credit Co-operatives*, AERC Research Paper 21, Nairobi: African Economic Research Consortium.

Aron, Janine, Ibrahim Elbadawi, Benno Ndulu *et al.* (1997) 'State and Development in sub-Saharan Africa', background paper for the World Bank *World Development Report 1997*.

Aryeetey, Ernest (1992a) 'The Complementary Role of Informal Financial Institutions in the Retailing of Credit: Evaluation of Innovative Approaches', paper presented at the UN regional symposium on 'Savings and Credit for Development in Africa', Abidjan, 27–30 April.

Aryeetey, Ernest (1992b) 'The Relationship between the Formal and Informal Sectors of the Financial Markets in Ghana', Nairobi: African Economic Research Consortium, research paper, October 10.

Aryeetey, Ernest (1994) *Financial Integration and Development in sub-Saharan Africa: a Study of Informal Finance in Ghana*, Working Paper 78, London: Overseas Development Institute.

Aryeetey, Ernest (1996) *The Formal Financial Sector in Ghana After the Reforms*, Working Paper 86, London: Overseas Development Institute.

Aryeetey, E. and F. Gockel (1991) *Mobilizing Domestic Resources for Capital Formation in Ghana: the Role of Informal Financial Markets*, Research Paper 3, Nairobi: African Economic Research Consortium.

Aryeetey, E. and Hyuha, M. (1991) 'The Informal Financial Sector and Markets in Africa: an Empirical Study', in A. Chibber and S. Fischer (eds) *Economic Reform in sub-Saharan Africa*, Washington DC: World Bank.

Aryeetey, E. and C. Udry (1994) 'Informal Financial Markets in Africa', paper presented at the Plenary Session of the Research Workshop of the African Economic Research Consortium, Nairobi, December.

Aryeetey, E., A. Baah-Nuakoh, T. Duggleby, H. Hettige and W.F. Steel (1994) *The Supply and Demand for Finance among SMEs in Ghana*, Discussion Paper 251, Africa Technical Department, Washington D.C: World Bank.

Asian Development Bank (1990) *Asian Development Outlook 1990*, Manila: Asian Development Bank.

Bagachwa, M.S.D. (1995) *Financial Integration and Development in sub-Saharan Africa: a Study of* Informal Finance *in Tanzania*, Working Paper 79, London: Overseas Development Institute.

Bagachwa, M.S.D. (1996) *Financial Linkage and Development in sub-Saharan Africa: a Study of* Formal Finance *in Tanzania*, Working Paper 87, London: Overseas Development Institute.

Bagachwa, M.S.D. and A. Naho (1994) *A Review of Recent Developments in the Second Economy in Tanzania*, Special Paper 16, Nairobi: African Economic Research Consortium.

Balkenhol, B. and E.H. Gueye (1994) 'Tontines and the Banking System – is there a case for building linkages?', *Small Enterprise Development* 5, 1: 47–55.

Barro, R. and Grossman H. (1971) 'A General Disequilibrium Model of Income and Employment', *American Economic Review* 61, 1: 82–93.

Bateman, M., A. Muraus, D.M. Newbery, W.A. Okyere and G.T. O'Mara (1990) *Ghana's Cocoa Pricing Policy*, Working Paper series 421, Washington DC: World Bank.

Bates, Robert (1996) 'Institutions as Investments', plenary paper presented at the AERC biannual workshop, Nairobi, 25–30 May.

Baums Teodor (1994) 'The German Banking System and its Impact on Corporate

Finance and Governance', in M. Aoki and H. Patrick (eds) *The Japanese Main Bank System*, Oxford: Oxford University Press.

Bell, C. (1988) 'Credit Markets, Contracts and Interlinked Transactions' in H. Chenery and T.N. Srinivasan (eds) *Handbook of Development Economics*, New York: North-Holland.

Bell, C. (1990) 'Interaction between Institutional and Informal Credit Agencies in Rural India', *World Bank Economic Review* 4: 297–327.

Besley, Timothy, Stephen Coate and Glenn Loury (1993) 'The Economics of Rotating Savings and Credit Associations', *American Economic Review* 82: 792–810.

Bhatia, Rattan J. and Deena R. Khatkhate (1975) 'Financial Intermediation, Savings Mobilization, and Entrepreneurial Development: the African Experience', *IMF Staff Papers* 22, 1: 132–58.

Biggs, Tyler S. (1991) 'Heterogeneous Firms and Efficient Financial Intermediation in Taiwan', in Michael Roemer and Chris Jones (eds) *Markets in Developing Countries*, San Francisco: ICS Press.

Binswanger, Hans and Mark Rosenzweig (1986) 'Behavioral and Material Determinants of Production Relations in Agriculture', *Journal of Development Studies* 22, 3: 503–39.

Blommestein, Hans J. and Michael G. Spencer (1993) 'The Role of Financial Institutions in the Transformation to a Market Economy', mimeo, Washington DC: IMF.

Bolnick, Bruce R. (1992) 'Moneylenders and Informal Financial Markets in Malawi', *World Development* 20, 1: 57–68.

Boomgard, J. (1989) 'AID Microenterprise Stocktaking: Synthesis Report', Bethesda MD: Development Alternatives.

Bottomley, Anthony (1975) 'Interest Rate Determination in Underdeveloped Rural Areas', *American Journal of Agricultural Economics* 57, 2: 279–91.

Bouman, F.J.A. (1977) 'Indigenous Savings and Credit Societies in the Developing World', *Savings and Development* 1, 4.

Bouman, F.J.A. (1994) 'ROSCA and ASCRA: Beyond the Financial Landscape' in F.J.A. Bouman and O. Hospes (eds) *Financial Landscapes Reconstructed*, Boulder and Oxford: Westview Press.

Bouman, F.J.A. (1995) 'ROSCA: on the Origin of the Species', *Savings and Development*, 19.

Buechler, S. (1995) 'The Key to Lending to Women Microentrepreneurs', *Savings and Development* 6, 2: 12–14.

Burgess, R. and N. Stern (1993) 'Taxation and Development', *Journal of Economic Literature* 31, 2: 762–830.

Calgagovski, Jorge, Victor Gabor, M.C. Germany and C. Humphreys (1991) 'Africa's Financing Needs in the 1990s' in I. Husain and J. Underwood (eds) *African External Finance*, Washington DC: World Bank.

Camen, Ulrich, Mthuli Ncube and Lemma Senbet (1996) 'The Role of the Financial Systems in the Operation of Monetary policy in Africa', paper presented at the AERC Collaborative Programme Workshop, Nairobi, May.

Campbell, John and Yasushi Hamao (1994) 'Changing Patterns of Corporate Financing and the Main Bank System in Japan' in M. Aoki and H. Patrick (eds) *The Japanese Main Bank System*, Oxford: Oxford University Press.

Caprio, Gerard (1992) *Policy Uncertainty, Information Asymmetries and Financial Inter-mediation*, Policy Research Working Papers 853, Washington DC: World Bank.

Caprio, Gerard, Jr and Patrick Honohan (1991) *Excess Liquidity and Monetary Overhangs*, Washington DC: World Bank.

Caprio, Gerard, Jr and Ross Levine (1994) 'Reforming Finance in Transitional Socialist Economies', *World Bank Research Observer* 9, 1: 1–24.

Caprio, Gerald, Jr, Izak Atiyas and J. Hanson (eds) (1994) *Financial Reform: Theory and Experience*, Cambridge: Cambridge University Press.

Chamley, Christophe and Patrick Honohan (1990) *Taxation of Financial Intermediation: Measurement Principles and Application to Five African Countries*, Working Papers Series 421, Washington DC: World Bank.

Chandavakar, Anand G. (1985) 'The Non-institutional Financial Sector in Developing Countries: Macroeconomic Implications for Savings Policies', *Savings and Development* 2: 129–41.

Chang, Kevin and Robert Cumby (1991) 'Capital flight in sub-Saharan Africa' in I. Husain and J. Underwood (eds) *African External Finance*, Washington DC: World Bank.

Chipeta, Chinyamata (1994) 'The Links between the Informal and the Formal Financial Sectors in Malawi', *African Journal of Economic Policy* 1, 1: 159–84.

Chipeta, C. and M.L.C. Mkandawire (1991) *The Informal Financial Sector in Malawi: Scope, Size and Role*, Research Paper 4, Nairobi: AERC.

Chipeta, C. and M.L.C. Mkandawire (1992a) 'Domestic Savings Mobilization for African Development and Diversification', mimeo (processed), Oxford: International Development Centre.

Chipeta, C. and M.L.C. Mkandawire (1992b) *Links between the Informal and Formal/Semi-formal Financial Sectors in Malawi*, Research Paper 14, Nairobi: AERC.

Chipeta, C. and M. Mkandawire (1996a) *Financial Integration and Development in sub-Saharan Africa: the Informal Financial Sector in Malawi*, Working Paper 85, London: Overseas Development Institute.

Chipeta, C. and M. Mkandawire (1996b) 'Financial Integration and Development in sub-Saharan Africa: the Formal and Semi-formal Financial Sectors in Malawi', London: Overseas Development Institute.

Cho, Yoon Je and Deena Khatkhate (1989) 'Lessons of Financial Liberalization in Asia: Comparative Study', *World Bank Discussion Papers*, Washington DC: World Bank.

Christen, R.P., E. Rhyne and R.C. Vogel (1994) 'Maximizing the Outreach of Microenterprise Finance: the Emerging Lessons of Successful Programs', Consulting Assistance for Economic Reform (CAER) paper (draft), Washington DC: International Management and Communication Corprations (IMCC).

Christensen, Garry (1993) 'The Limits to Informal Financial Intermediation', *World Development* 21, 5: 721–31.

Claessens, S. and D. Naude (1993) 'Recent Estimates of Capital Flight in Developing Countries', Working Papers, Washington DC: World Bank.

Cole, David C. and James S. Duesenburry (1994) 'Financial Systems' in D. L. Lindauer and M. Roemer (eds) *Development in Asia and Africa: Legacies and Opportunities*, Cambridge MA: Harvard Institute for International Development.

Collier, Paul (1994) 'The Marginalisation of Africa', mimeo, Oxford: Centre for the Study of African Economies.

Collier, Paul and Jan W. Gunning (1991) 'Money Creation and Financial Liberalization in a Socialist Banking System: Tanzania 1983-88', *World Development* 19, 5: 533–38.

Collier, Paul and Jan Gunning (1997) 'Explaining African Economic Performance', Oxford: Centre for the Study of African Economies, University of Oxford.

Collier, Paul and Colin Mayer (1989) 'The Assessment: Financial Liberalization, Financial Systems, and Economic Growth', *Oxford Review of Economic Policy* 5, 4.

Collier, P., D.L. Bevan and J.W. Gunning (1991) 'Income and Substitution Effects in Models of Peasant Supply Response under Rationing', *Oxford Economic Papers* 43 (2): 8.

Committee of Donor Agencies for Small Enterprise Development and Donors' Working Group in Financial Sector Development (1995) *Micro and Small Enterprise Finance: Guiding Principles for Selecting and Supporting Intermediaries*, Washington DC: Private Sector Development Department, World Bank.

Corbo, Vittorio and Jaime De Melo (1985) 'Overview and Summary', *World Development* 13, 8: 863–66.

Corbo, Vittorio and Jaime De Melo (1987) 'Lessons from the Southern Cone Policy Reforms', *World Bank Research Observer* 2, 2: 111–42.

Cottani, Joaquin and Domingo Cavallo (1993) 'Financial Reform and Liberalization', in Rudiger Dornbush (ed.) *Policymaking in the Open Economy*, Economic Development Institute, Series in Economic Development, Oxford: Oxford University Press for the World Bank.

Courakis, Antony (1986) 'In what Sense do Compulsory Ratios reduce the Volume of Deposits?' in Charles A. Goodhart, David Currie and David T. Llewellyn (eds) *The Operation and Regulation of Financial Markets*, London: Macmillan.

Crotty, James and Don Goldstein (1993) 'Do US Financial Markets allocate Credit efficiently? The Case of Corporate Restructuring in the 1980s', in Dymski *et al.* (eds) *Transforming the US Financial System: Equity and Efficiency for the Twenty-first century*, Economic Policy Institute Series, Armonk: Sharpe.

Deaton, Angus (1989) 'Saving in Developing Countries: Theory and Review', paper presented at the first annual World Bank Conference on Economic Development, Washington DC, April.

de Juan, Aristobuo (1988) 'Does Bank Insolvency Matter? And what to do about it?', mimeo, Washington DC: World Bank.

Delancey, V. (1978) 'Women at the Cameroon Development Corporation: How their Money Works: a Study of Small-scale Accumulation of Capital by Women in Cameroon', *Rural Africana* 2: 9–33.

Diaz-Alejandro, Carlos (1985), 'Good-bye Financial Repression, Hello Financial Crash', *Journal of Development Economics* 19: 1–24.

Dornbusch, Rudiger and Alejandro Reynoso (1993) 'Financial Factors in Economic Development', in Rudiger Dornbush (ed.) *Policymaking in the Open Economy*, EDI Series in Economic Development, New York: Oxford University Press for the World Bank.

Duggleby, T. (1992) 'Best Practices in Innovative Small Enterprise Finance Institutions' in William F. Steel (ed.) *Financial Deepening in sub-Saharan Africa: Theory and Innovations*, Industry and Energy Department Working Paper, Industry Series Paper 62, Washington DC: World Bank.

Duggleby, Tamara, Ernest Aryeetey and William F. Steel (1992) *Formal and Informal*

Finance for Small Enterprises in Ghana, Industry Series 61, Washington DC: Industry and Energy Department, World Bank.

Easterly, W. and R. Levine (1994) 'Africa's Growth Tragedy', mimeo, Washington DC: World Bank.

Edwards, Jeremy and Klaus Fischer (1994) *Banks, Finance, and Investment in Germany*, Cambridge: Cambridge University Press.

Eriksson, Gun (1993) 'Incidence and Pattern of the Soft Budget in Tanzania', Macroeconomic Studies 44/93, Stockholm: SIDA Planning Secretariat.

Faruqee, Rashid (1994) 'Nigeria: ownership abandoned', in I. Husain and R. Faruqee (eds) *Adjustment in Africa: Lessons from Country Case-studies*, World Bank Regional and Sectoral Studies, Washington DC: World Bank.

Fisseha, Yacob and Michael Mcpherson (1991) 'A Country-wide Study of Small-scale Enterprises in Swaziland', GEMINI Working Paper, Bethesda MD: Development Alternatives.

Flammang, R.A. (1989) 'Informal Financial Markets in Senegal and Zaire', paper presented at seminar on 'Informal Financial Markets in Development', Washington DC: Ohio State University/USAID, October.

Frischtak, Claudio (1990) 'Adjustment and Constrained Response: Malawi at the Threshold of Sustained Growth', Industry and Energy Department Working Paper, Industry Series Paper 41, Washington DC: World Bank.

Fry, Maxwell J. (1982) 'Models of Financial Repressed Developing Economies', *World Development* 10, 9: 731–50.

Fry, Maxwell J. (1988) *Money, Interest, and Banking in Economic Development*, Baltimore and London: Johns Hopkins University Press.

Galbis, Vincente (1977) 'Financial Intermediation and Economic Growth in Less Developed Countries: a Theoretical Approach', *Journal of Development Studies* 13, 2: 58–72.

Germidis, Dimitri, Denis Kessler and Rachel Meghir (1991) *Financial Systems and Development: What Role for the Formal and Informal Financial Sectors?* OECD, Development Centre Studies, Paris: OECD.

Gerschenkron, A. (1962) *Economic Backwardness in Historical Perspective*, Cambridge MA: Harvard University Press.

Gertler, Mark and Andrew Rose (1994) 'Finance, Growth and Public Policy', in Gerard Caprio, Jr, Izak Atiyas and James Hanson (eds) *Financial Reforms: Theory and Experience*. Cambridge: Cambridge University Press.

Ghate, P.B. (1988) 'Informal Credit Markets in Asian Developing Countries', *Asian Development Review* 6, 1: 64–85.

Ghate, P.B.(1990) 'Interaction between the Formal and Informal Financial Sectors', paper presented at UN International Conference on Savings and Credit for Development, Copenhagen 28–31 May.

Ghate, P.B. (1992) 'Domestic Savings Mobilization: an Issue Paper', paper presented at Economic and Social Commission for Asia and the Pacific seminar of Mobilization of Financial Resources, Bangkok, January.

Giovannini, Alberto and Martha de Melo (1990) 'Government Revenue from Financial repression: Policy, Research and External Affairs', Working Papers Series 533, Washington DC: World Bank.

Global Coalition for Africa (1993) 1993 Annual report, Washington DC: African Social and Economic Trends.

Goldsmith, Raymond W. (1969) *Financial Structure and Development*, New Haven and London: Yale University Press.

Gonzalez-Vega, Claudio (1990) *Evaluating the Validity of Agricultural Development Banks: Methodology*, Economics and Sociology Occasional Paper 1759, Columbus: Department of Agricultural Economics and Rural Sociology, Ohio State University.

Grilli, E.R. and Yang M.C. (1988) 'Primary Commodity Prices, Manufactured Goods, Prices, and the Terms of Trade of Developing Countries: What the Long Run shows', *World Bank Economic Review* 2, 1: 1–47.

Gupta, K.L (1992) *Budget Deficits and Economic Activity in Asia*, London: Routledge.

Gurley, J.G. and E. Shaw (1967) 'Financial Structure and Economic Development', *Economic Development and Cultural Change* 15, 3: 257–68.

Harris, Laurence (1995) *Corporate Finance*, London: School of Oriental and African Studies External Programme, University of London.

Harvey, Charles (1996) 'The Limited Impact of Financial Sector Reforms in Zimbabwe', IDS Working Paper, London: IDS.

Hettige, Hemamala (1992) 'Toward Financial Deepening in sub-Saharan Africa: an Analytical Framework', in W. Steel (ed.) *Financial Deepening in sub-Saharan Africa: Theory and Innovations*, Industry Series Working Paper Washington DC: Industry and Energy Department, World Bank

Hoff, Karla and Joseph E. Stiglitz (1990) 'Imperfect Information and Rural Credit Markets – Puzzles and Policy Perspectives', *World Bank Economic Review* 4, 3: 235–50.

Hussain, M.N. (1993) 'Savings, Economic Growth and Financial Liberalization: the Case of Egypt', background paper to *African Development Report 1994*.

Hyuha, M., Ndanshau, M.O. and Kipokola, J.P. (1993) *Scope, Structure and Policy Implications of Informal Financial Markets in Tanzania*, Research Paper 18, Nairobi: AERC.

Integriertes Projekt Centrum (1988) 'Rural Finance in Ghana: a Research Study on behalf of the Bank of Ghana', Frankfurt and Accra: IPC.

Islam, Roumeen and Deborah L. Wetzel (1991) *Macroeconomics of Public Sector Deficits: the Case of Ghana*, World Bank Working Papers (Policy, Research and External Affairs) 672, Washington DC: World Bank.

Johnston, B. and O.P. Brekk (1991) 'Monetary Control Procedures and Financial Reform: Approaches, Issues and Recent Experiences in Developing Countries' in P. Callier (ed.) *Financial Systems and Development in Africa*, EDI Seminar Series, Washington DC: World Bank.

Jones, C., D.L. Lindauer and M. Roemer (1991) 'Parallel, Fragmented and Black: a Taxonomy', *Markets in Developing Countries: Parallel, Fragmented and Black*, San Francisco: International Center for Economic Growth and Harvard Institute for International Development.

Kessides, Cristine, Timothy King, Mario Nuti and Catherine Sokil (eds) (1989) *Financial Reform in Socialist Economies*, EDI Seminar Series, Washington DC: World Bank.

Khatkhate, Deena (1980) 'False Issues in the Debate on Interest Rate Policies in Less Developed Countries', *Banca Nazional del Lavoro Quarterly Review* 133: 205–24.

Killick, T. and F.M. Mwega (1990) *Monetary Policy in Kenya, 1967–88*, Working Paper 39, London: Overseas Development Institute.

Kimei, C.S. (1990) 'Institutional Development: the Case of Tanzania', paper prepared for the International Conference on Savings and Credit for Development, United Nations and Danish Savings Banks' Association, Copenhagen.

Kimei, C.S. (1994) 'Financial Structures, Reforms and Economic Development: Tanzania', background paper to *African Development Report 1994*, Abidjan: African Development Bank.

King, Robert and Ross Levine (1993) 'Finance, Entrepreneurship, and Growth', paper presented at the World Bank Conference, 8–9 February.

Kitchen, Richard L. (1986) *Finance for the Developing Countries*, Chichester: Wiley.

Lelart, M. and S. Gnansounou (1989) 'Tontines et tontiniers sur les marches africains: le marché Saint-Michel de Cotonou', *African Review of Money, Finance and Banking* 1, 89.

Levitsky, Jacob (1993) 'Innovations in the Financing of Small and Microenterprises in Developing Countries', Small Enterprise Development Programme, Geneva: ILO.

Levitsky, J. and Prasad R.N. (1987) *Credit Guarantee Schemes for Small and Medium Enterprises*, Washington DC: World Bank.

Levy, Brian (1993) 'Obstacles to Developing Small and Medium-Sized Enterprises: an Empirical Assessment', *World Bank Economic Review* 7, 1: 65–83.

Liedholm, Carl (1991) 'Small and Micro Enterprise Dynamics and Evolving Role of Finance', paper presented at conference on 'Small and Micro Enterprise Promotion in a Changing Policy Environment: a Special Focus on Africa', The Hague, 30 September–2 October.

Liedholm, Carl and Donald Mead (1987) *Small Scale Industries in Developing Countries: Empirical Evidence and Policy Implications*, International Development Paper 9, East Lansing: Department of Agricultural Economics, Michigan State University.

Liedholm, Carl and Joan Parker (1989) *Small-scale Manufacturing Growth in Africa: Initial Evidence*, MSU International Development Working Paper 33, East Lansing: Michigan State University.

Little, I.M.D. (1987) 'Small Manufacturing Enterprises in Developing Countries', *World Bank Economic Review* 1, 2: 205–35.

Maizels, Alfred (1992) *Commodities in Crisis*, Oxford: Oxford University Press.

Malinvaud, E. (1977) *The Theory of Unemployment Reconsidered* Oxford: Blackwell.

Mans, Darius (1994) 'Tanzania: Resolute Action', in I. Husain and R. Faruqee (eds) *Adjustment in Africa: Lessons from Country Case Studies*, World Bank Regional and Sectoral Studies, Washington DC: World Bank.

Mayer, Colin (1988) 'New Issues in Corporate Finance', *European Economic Review* 32: 1167–89.

McKinnon, Ronald I. (1973) *Money and Capital in Economic Development*, Washington DC: Brookings Institution.

Meyer, Richard (1989) 'Financial Services for Microenterprise: Programmes or Markets?' in J. Levitsky (ed.) *Microenterprises in Developing Countries*, London: Intermediate Technology Publications.

Meyer, Richard (1991) 'Rural Finance Research: Priorities, Dissemination and Policy Impact', paper presented at the fifth SACRED meeting Rome: FAO.

Miracle, M.P., D.S. Miracle and L. Cohen (1980) 'Informal Savings Mobilization in Africa', *Economic Development and Cultural Change* 28: 701–24.

Montiel, Peter (1994) 'Financial Policies and Economic Growth: Theory, Evidence and Country-specific Experience from sub-Saharan Africa', paper presented at the African Economic Research Consortium biannual workshop, Nairobi, May.

Montiel, Peter J., Pierre-Richard Agenor and Nadeem Ul Haque (1993) *Informal Financial Markets in Developing Countries: a Macroeconomic Analysis*, Oxford: Blackwell.

Muelbauer, J. and Portes, R. (1978) 'Macroeconomic Models with Quantity Rationing', *Economic Journal* 88: 788–821.

Mwega, Francis M. (1996) 'Saving in sub-Saharan africa: a comparative analysis', paper presented at the plenary session of the African Economic Research Consortium workshop, Nairobi, May.

Nayarajan, Geetha, Christine David and Richard L. Meyer (1992) 'Informal Finance through Land Pawning Contracts: Evidence from the Philippines', *Journal of Development Studies* 29: 93–107.

Neal, Craig R. (1988) 'Macro-financial Indicators for 117 Developing and Industrial Countries', Washington DC: World Bank.

Nissanke, Machiko (1993a) 'Excess Liquidity Syndrome in the Banking System in Low-income Developing Countries', working paper, London: School of Oriental and African Studies, University of London.

Nissanke, Machiko (1993b) 'Savings and Financial Policy Issues in sub-Saharan Africa', in Y. Akyuz and G. Held (eds) *Finance and the Real Economy*, UNCTAD/ UN ECLAC/UNU Santiago: World Institute of Development Economics research.

Nissanke, Machiko (1996) 'Raising Finance for Private Enterprise Investment', background paper for UNIDO's *Global Report 1997*.

Nissanke, Machiko (1997) *Africa: Institutions, Policies and Development*, Tokyo: International Development Centre of Japan.

Nissanke, Machiko and Priya Basu (1992) 'Improving Domestic Resource Mobilization in LDCs', background paper to UNCTAD *LDC Report 1992*.

Nissanke, Machiko (1991) 'Liberalization Experience and Structural Impediments to Savings Mobilization and Financial Intermediation', mimeo (processed), Oxford: International Development Centre, University of Oxford.

Nwadike, Comfort I (1990) 'New Products in Banking Industry', M.Sc. (Banking and Finance) project report, Ibadan: Department of Economics, University of Ibadan.

Park, Young Chul (1994) 'Concepts and Issues' in Hugh T. Patrick and Yung Chul Park (eds) *The Financial Development of Japan, Korea, and Taiwan*, Oxford: Oxford University Press.

Parker, Joan and C. Aleke Dondo (1991) 'Kenya: Kibera's Small Enterprise Sector', GEMINI Working Paper 17, Bethesda MD: Development Alternatives.

Patrick, Hugh (1966) 'Financial Development and Economic Growth in Developing Countries', *Economic Development and Cultural Change* 14, 2: 174–89.

Patrick, Hugh (1994b) 'The Relevance of Japanese Finance and its Main Bank System', in M. Aoki and H. Patrick (eds) *The Japanese Main Bank System*, Oxford: Oxford University Press.

Popiel, P.A. (1994) *Financial Systems in sub-Saharan Africa: a Comparative Study*, World Bank Discussion Paper 260, Africa Technical Department Series, Washington DC: World Bank.

Presidential Banking Commission (1990) *Financial Sector Restructuring in Tanzania*, report to President of the United Republic of Tanzania, 19 July, Dar es Salaam.

Rhyne, Elizabeth and Maria Otero (1991) 'A Financial Systems Approach to Microenterprises', GEMINI Working Paper 18, Washington DC: Development Alternatives.

Roe, Alan R. (1991) 'Financial Systems and Development in Africa', conference report of an EDI Policy Seminar held in Nairobi, 29 January to 1 February 1990.

Roe, Alan and Nii K. Sowa (1994) 'From Direct to Indirect Monetary Control in sub-Saharan Africa', paper presented at the African Economic Research Consortium biannual workshop, Nairobi, December.

Roemer, Michael and Christine Jones (1991) *Markets in Developing Countries: Parallel, Fragmented, and Black*, International Centre for Economic Growth, HIID, San Francisco: ICS Press.

Saito, K.A. and Villanueva, D.P. (1981) 'Transaction Costs of Credit to the Small-scale Sector in the Philippines', *Economic Development and Cultural Change* 29, 3: 631–40.

Schmidt-Hebbel, Klaus (1994) 'Fiscal Adjustment and Growth: in and out of Africa', paper presented at the African Economic Research Consortium biannual workshop, Nairobi, May.

Seck, D. and Y.M. El Nil (1993) 'Financial Liberalization in Africa', *World Development* 21, 11: 1867–81.

Seibel, Hans Dieter (1989) 'Linking Informal and Formal Financial Institutions in Africa and Asia', in J. Levitsky (ed.) *Microenterprises in Developing Countries*, London: Intermediate Technology Publications.

Seibel, H.D. and M.T. Marx (1987) *Dual Financial Markets in Africa*, Breitenbach: Saarbrücken.

Shaw, Edward S. (1973) *Financial Deepening in Economic Development*, New York: Oxford University Press.

Shipton, Parker (1991) 'Time and Money in the Western Sahel: a Clash of Cultures in Gambian Rural Finance', in *Markets in Developing Countries: Parallel, Fragmented and Black*, San Francisco: International Centre for Economic Growth and Harvard Institute of International Development.

Singh, Ajit and Javed Hamid (1992) *Corporate Financial Structures in Developing Countries*, International Finance Corporation Technical Paper 1, Washington DC: World Bank.

Slover, C.H. (1991) 'The Effect of Membership Homogeneity on Group Size, Funds Mobilization, and the Engenderment of Reciprocal Obligations among Informal Financial Groups in Rural Zaire', paper presented at the seminar on 'Finance and Rural Development in West Africa', OSU/CIRAD, Ouagadougou, 21–5 October.

Social Development Consultants (1990) 'Financial Intermediation for Microenterprises in Bangladesh, Kenya, Tanzania and Zambia', draft mimeo, Helsinki: Sodecon.

Soyibo, A. (1996a) 'Financial Linkage and Development in sub-Saharan Africa: the Role of Formal Financial Institutions in Nigeria', Working Paper 88, London: Overseas Development Institute.

Soyibo, A. (1996b) 'Financial Linkage and Development in sub-Saharan Africa: the Informal Financial Sector in Nigeria', Working Paper 90, London: Overseas Development Institute.

Steel, William F. (1996) 'Demand for Finance by SMEs in West Africa: how can the Constraints be broken?' in E. Aryeetey (ed.) *Small Enterprise Credit in West Africa*, Accra: British Council/ISSER.

Steel, William and Ernest Aryeetey (1995) 'Savings Collectors and Financial Intermediation in Ghana', *Savings and Development*, 19.

Steel, William F. and Leila Webster (1991) *Small Enterprises under Adjustment in Ghana*, World Bank Technical Paper 138, Industry and Finance Series, Washington DC: World Bank.

Stein, Howard (1996) 'The Nigerian Banking Crisis and Japanese Financial Development: in Search of Lessons', paper prepared for the seminar on 'Financial Deregulation and the Banking Crisis in Nigeria', Lagos, July.

Stein, Howard and Peter Lewis (1996) 'Shifting Fortunes: the Political Economy of Financial Liberalization in Nigeria', discussion paper Series A, No. 318, Kunitachi, Tokyo: Institute of Economic Research, Hitotsubashi University.

Stiglitz, Joseph E. (1989) 'Financial Markets and Development', *Oxford Review of Economic Policy* 5, 4.

Stiglitz, Joseph E. (1994) *The Role of the State in Financial Markets*, proceedings of the World Bank Annual Conference on Development Economics, Washington DC: 1993.

Stiglitz, Joseph E. and Andrew Weiss (1981) 'Credit Rationing in Markets with Imperfect Information', *American Economic Review* 71: 393–410.

Taylor, Lance (1983) *Structuralist Macroeconomics: Applicable Models for the Third World*, New York: Basic Books.

Temi, E. and P. Hill (1994) 'Some Lessons from Informal Financial Practices in Rural Tanzania', *African Review of Money, Finance and Banking* 1, 94.

Teranishi, Juro (1994) 'Modernization of Financial Markets: an Analysis of Informal Credit Markets in Prewar Japan', *World Development* 22, 33: 315–22.

Teranishi, Juro (1996) 'Market Failures and Government Failures: a Conceptual Framework and Japan's Experience', background paper for the conference on 'Market and Government: Foe or Friends?' International Conference on the World Economy in Transition, Hitotsubashi University, Tokyo, 2–8 February.

Thomas, J.J. (1993) 'The Informal Financial Sector: How does it Operate and who are the Customers?' in S. Page (ed.) *Monetary Policy in Developing Countries*, London: Routledge.

Tseng, Wanda and Robert Corker (1991) *Financial Liberalization, Money Demand and Monetary Policy in Asian Countries*, IMF Occasional Paper 84, Washington DC: IMF.

Udry, C. (1990) 'Credit Markets in Northern Nigeria: Credit as Insurance in Rural Economy' *World Bank Economic Review* 4, 3: 251–69.

UNCTAD (1991) *Trade and Development Report 1991*, Geneva: UN.

UNCTAD (1992) *Trade and Development Report 1992*, Geneva: UN.

USAID (1989) *Informal Financial Markets: Senegal and Zaire*, final report of a study prepared for the Bureau for Africa/Office of Market Development and Investment (MDI) by Arthur Young.

U Tun Wai (1992) 'What have we learned about informal finance in three decades?', in Dale W. Adams and Delbert A. Fitchett (eds) *Informal Finance in Low-income Countries*, Boulder: Westview Press.

Van Wijnbergen, Sweder (1983) 'Interest Rate Management in LDCs', *Journal of Monetary Economics* 12, 3: 433–52.

REFERENCES

Von Pischke, J.D. (1991) *Finance at the Frontier*, Economic Development Institute, Washington DC: World Bank.

Wall, Martin (1995) 'Compiling a Set of Flow of Funds Accounts for Ghana: a Technical Note', mimeo, London: School of Oriental and African Studies.

World Bank (1989a) *World Development Report 1989: Financial Systems and Development*, New York: Oxford University Press

World Bank (1989b) *Sub-Saharan Africa: Crisis to Sustainable Growth*, Washington DC: World Bank.

World Bank (1993) *The East Asian Miracle: Economic Growth and Public Policy*, World Bank Policy Research Report, Washington DC: World Bank.

World Bank (1994a) *Adjustment in Africa: Reforms, Results and the Road Ahead*, World Bank Policy Research Report, Washington DC: World Bank.

World Bank (1994b) 'Interest Rate Deregulation', Policy Review Note, mimeo, Washington DC: World Bank

World Bank (1994c) *Ghana Financial Sector Review: Bringing Savers and Investors Together*, Report 13423-GH, Washington DC: Country Operations Division, World Bank.

World Bank (1995) 'The Nigerian Rural Financial System: Assessment and Recommendations', Report 13911-UNI, 26 January, Washington DC: Western Central Africa Department, Agriculture and Environment Division, World Bank.

Yaron, Jacob (1994) 'What Makes Rural Financial Institutions Successful?' *World Bank Research Observer* 9: 49–70.

Yotopoulos, P.A. and L. Floro (1991) 'Transaction Costs and Quantity Rationing in the Informal Credit Markets: Philippine Agriculture', in M. Roemer and C. Jones (eds) *Markets in Developing Countries*, San Fransisco: ICS Press.

319

INDEX

accounting 23, 92, 295

Adam, Christopher 38, 69, 70, 139, 141, 290

Adams, Dale W. 25, 27, 33, 34, 118, 215, 259

adaptability 8, 32, 111, 286

Adegboye, R.O. 208

adjustment, structural 1, 8, 42, 50–60 *passim*, 89, 94, 109, 110, 112, 116, 131, 141, 142, 146, 150, 278, 290; *see also* FINSAPs

ADMARC 69, 70, 73, 89, 139, 141

Africa 33, 37–8, 63, 266; Monetary Union 288; sub-Saharan 3, 10, 11, 14, 19, 27, 34–40, 44, 45, 111, 112, 114, 119, 121, 122, 126, 133; West 190, 192, 205, 226, 227, 229, 252, 304; *see also individual countries*

agriculture 39, 40, 65, 69, 90, 91, 117, 122, 198, 204, 266

aid 1, 4, 26, 52, 53, 55, 65, 73, 84, 96, 133, 139, 171, 181

Alashi, S.O. 76

Alderman, H. 214

'Anglo-Saxon' model 291–4 *passim*

Aoki, Masahiko 291, 292

arbitrage 74, 91, 215, 289

Ardener, S. 190

Argentina 7, 39

Aron, Janine 63

Arusha Declaration 93

Aryeetey, Ernest 27, 32, 33, 35, 42, 67, 68, 114, 158, 183, 192, 199, 205, 206, 246–8 *passim*, 252, 254–6

passim, 260, 261, 267–9 *passim*, 296, 303, 304

Asia 7–9 *passim*, 18, 27, 29, 30, 32, 36, 111, 112, 117, 266, 270, 282; East 6, 38, 286; South 4, 38; *see also individual countries*

Asian Development Bank 27

assets 14, 21–2, 37–8, 145, 181, 196–212; net foreign 45, 144, 150, 153, 155, 156, 160, 285; swap 70, 141

auditing 23, 95, 295

Badan Kredit Kecamatan 300

Bagachwa, M.S.D. 32, 63, 82, 114, 115, 230, 301

balance of payments 38, 53–5 *passim*, 133, 144

Balkenhol, B. 256

Bangladesh 269, 300

bankruptcy 21, 114

banks 5, 23, 25, 28, 29, 33, 36, 39–46 *passim*, 113–31, 139, 141, 144, 154–6, 159, 170, 181–90, 194–203, 217–25, 233–40, 251–64, 279–82 *passim*, 289, 291–4, 302, 304, 305; central 25, 40, 45, 132, 136, 138–44, 150–6 *passim*, 160, 167, 170, 171, 296–8 *passim*; community 74, 76, 186, 218, 224, 236, 299; development 25, 180, 182, 185, 196, 199, 202, 236–40 *passim*; *see also* DFIs; merchant 25, 64, 66, 68, 74, 75, 91, 92, 155–6, 182, 197, 203, 219, 224, 238; people's 76,

186, 199, 203, 236, 249n1; unit 65, 76, 202, 261, 298; universal 292–4; *see also under individual countries*

Basu, Priya 112

Bates, Robert 130, 271

Bauchi State Co-operative Finance Agency 79

Bell, C. 24, 29, 255, 256

Benin 3, 205

Biggs, Tyler S. 18, 29, 30, 262, 296–7, 306

Binswanger, Hans 22

Blommestein, Hans J. 294, 295

Bolnick, Bruce R. 72

bonds 85–6, 142, 156, 184, 285, 289–90, 293

Boomgard, J. 267, 269

borrowers 21–2, 26, 27, 116, 199–200, 207, 208, 215–33 *passim*, 245–9, 262–3, 281, 282, 299–300; first-time 218, 227

borrowing 7, 126, 132, 182–3; abroad 132, 136, 139, 141, 142, 157, 170–1; interbank 41

Botswana 117–18

bottlenecks 13, 23, 117

Bottomley, Anthony 25

Bouman, F.J.A. 190, 191

Brekk, O.P. 43, 46

Britain 294

Buechler, S. 301, 303

building societies 64, 68

Burgess, R. 133

Calgagovski, Jorge 4

Camen, Ulrich 288

Cameroon 3, 191

capital 6, 9, 66, 87, 130, 267, 269–71 *passim*, 289; adequacy 76, 77, 87, 92, 116, 182, 259, 285, 297; flight 7, 37–9 *passim*, 48n26, 63, 157, 284; formation 63, 271, 294; market 19, 22, 41, 66, 74, 81, 90, 93, 96, 157, 289–91 *passim*, 294

Caprio, Gerard 5, 9, 23, 112, 118, 123, 286

Cavallo, Domingo 9, 289

Chamley, Christophe 44, 84, 90, 119

Chang, Kevin 38–9

Chile 7

Chipeta, C. 32, 72, 73, 106, 114, 125, 160, 204, 209, 211, 223, 232

Cho, Yoon Je 6–8 *passim*

Christen, R.P. 300, 301, 303

Christensen, Garry 27–8

Claessens, S. 38

clientelism 90, 112

cocoa 53, 170, 185

Cole, David C. 8–9

collateral 22, 24, 27, 30, 42, 77, 130, 217, 220, 221, 228, 231–2, 258, 261, 263, 272, 282, 295, 300

Collier, Paul 4, 8, 9, 38, 43, 82, 110, 291

comparative advantage 12, 13, 25, 27, 28, 34, 68, 79, 215, 273, 280, 287, 302, 306

competition 1, 8, 9, 25, 29, 34, 46, 64, 68, 69, 74, 75, 82, 89, 90, 95, 113, 121, 125, 182, 194–6, 256, 262, 268, 272, 283, 290

concentration 113–14, 217

consumption 4, 34, 39, 40, 46n8, 56, 113, 204, 283

control 6, 8–9, 19, 24, 43, 45, 84, 89, 90, 92–3

co-operatives 79, 83, 94, 115, 116, 225, 255; African Confederation of (ASSOSCA) 193; MUSCCO 69, 72, 73; savings and credit (SACCOs) 25, 69, 73, 183, 193–4, 203–5, 226, 241–2, 251, 253, 262, 264, 303

Corbo, Vittorio 7

Corker, Robert 7

corruption 7, 8, 45, 116

costs 8, 13, 14, 21, 29, 89, 121, 124, 125, 253, 256, 281; opportunity 25, 29, 210, 244–5; transaction 12–15, 18–20, 24–8 *passim*, 33, 37, 39, 68, 78, 79, 117, 121, 122, 127, 180, 201, 215, 233–45, 253, 272, 281, 282, 299–303 *passim*

Côte d'Ivoire 3, 44

Cottani, Joaquin 9, 289

Courakis, Antony 121

credit 5, 6, 26–36 *passim*, 42–6, 65, 72–3, 78, 89–96 *passim*, 102, 103, 106–10 *passim*, 113, 117, 126, 197–203, 254–9, 263–74, 278, 282–3, 304–6; ceilings 45, 84, 90, 94, 122; controls 1, 9, 19, 40, 43, 45, 84, 91; 'crunch' 122, 130, 279; gaps 13, 263–74, 277, 282–3, 287; 'layering' 30, 32, 282, 305; rationing 6, 8, 20, 21, 122–3, 133, 246, 259; subsidized 24, 43; unions 25, 28, 67, 72–3, 80, 82, 83, 181, 183, 193–4, 211–12, 226, 228–30 *passim*, 242, 243, 251–3 *passim*, 257, 260–5 *passim*, 303, 304
creditworthiness 10, 21, 115, 220–1, 228, 284, 301
Crotty, James 294
crowding out 11, 33, 126, 138, 180, 279, 285
Cumby, Robert 38–9

Deaton, Angus 20, 39
debentures 293
debt 53, 55, 114, 117, 118, 121, 131, 132, 136–7, 139–43 *passim*, 161, 167, 219, 301; provision for 239–40; rescheduling 53, 55, 139; service 1–2, 53, 55, 56, 59, 60, 142, 167
deepening, financial 5, 7, 12, 64, 101–12, 184, 278, 288–94
default 13, 21, 22, 65, 115–18 *passim*, 121, 180, 215, 223–5, 229–34 *passim*, 239–40, 246–9, 296, 300, 305
deficit financing 132–44, 152, 153, 156, 167, 170–2
deficits, balance of payments 53; budget 43, 56, 58, 82, 122, 133–44, 152, 155, 167, 171, 285
de Juan, Aristobuo 114, 116
delinquency 13, 81, 115, 223, 225, 229, 230, 232
demand, for credit 10, 20, 27, 29, 33, 36, 42, 67–8, 73, 83, 118, 125–7 *passim*, 130, 154, 210, 215, 254, 257, 266–8, 279

De Melo, Jaime 7
de Melo, Martha 43–4
demonetization 37–9 *passim*, 63
density, bank 64, 69, 74
deposit mobilization 14, 27, 44, 68, 181–96, 244, 250–4, 272, 280, 287, 302–4 *passim*, 306
deregulation 7–9 *passim*, 12, 34, 74, 89–92 *passim*, 95, 96, 109, 111, 115, 285
devaluation 7, 38, 53, 122, 142, 146, 150, 153, 155
Development of Malawian Traders Trust (DEMATT) 73
developmental-financial institutions (DFIs) 33–4, 40, 64–5, 68–70, 74, 75, 80–1, 115–18 *passim*, 121, 139, 173n15, 182, 289
Diaz-Alejandro, Carlos 7
discount facility 41, 95, 144; houses 64, 66, 74, 88, 182, 257
dissaving 1, 58, 171
divestiture 89, 117, 141, 290
dollarization 37, 38
Dondo, C. Aleke 266
Dornbusch, Rudiger 9
drought 56, 58, 171
dualism 11, 18–25, 27, 29
Duesenburry, James S. 8–9
Duggleby, Tamara 299–300

Easterly, W. 285
Eastern Europe 291
Edwards, Jeremy 292
employment 265; self- 73, 280
enforcement, contract 14, 20–2 *passim*, 30, 44, 73, 116, 215, 217, 223–5, 229–33, 237–9, 243, 246–7, 281, 287, 295, 302
environment, policy 14, 84–95, 284, 290
Eriksson, Gun 223
esusu collectors 78, 79, 192–3, 207, 227–8, 251, 255
European Union 70
exchange rates 19, 37, 53–5 *passim*, 93, 126, 133, 144, 146, 150, 153, 284, 285

expenditure, government 44, 56, 57, 133, 136, 138, 139, 141, 142
exports 53, 198
external factors 23, 116–17, 122, 126, 131, 285; finance 1, 22, 26, 58, 132, 136, 141, 142, 277

FAO 78
Faruqee, Rashid 56
fees 202, 207, 253
finance houses 76–7, 254, 257, 304
Financial Sector Adjustment Projects (FINSAPs) 1, 65, 84, 126–7
Fischer, Klaus 292
Fisseha, Yacob 266
Fitchett, Delbert A. 27, 34, 215
Flammang, R.A. 192
flexibility 8, 32, 34, 68, 111, 286
Floro, L. 30, 34, 190, 226, 229, 305
flows, financial 11, 13, 14, 30–2, 35, 131–72, 278, 279, 283, 288, 306
foreclosure 224, 232, 237
foreign exchange 38, 45, 53, 74, 90–1, 109, 117, 144, 218; auctions 74, 84, 90
formal system 11, 14, 18, 25–9, 32, 33, 36, 40–1, 101–80, 183–90, 194–203, 216–25, 233–40, 250–63, 279, 280, 284, 296; see also under individual countries
fragmentation 11–12, 14, 18–49, 83, 113, 180–214, 263, 277, 278, 295, 302
fraud 116
Frischtak, Claudio 33
Fry, Maxwell J. 6, 119, 121
fungibility 26, 214, 300

Galbis, Vincente 5
Gambia 2, 192
gaps, credit 13, 263–74, 277, 282–3, 287; financial 13, 14, 130–1
Germany 131, 291, 293–4
Germidis, Dimitri 26, 27, 35, 41
Gerschenkron, A. 131
Gertler, Mark 5, 10, 21–2, 113, 265
Ghana 13, 38, 42–4 passim, 50–2, 64–8, 84–9, 96, 103–7, 111–15,

119, 120, 124–9, 144, 161–2, 182, 183, 251–2, 255, 257–8, 260–2, 268–72, 279, 284, 296, 298, 299, 303–5; aid to 52, 53, 65; banks 64–5, 114–15, 119, 124–6, 195, 196, 203, 218–25 passim, 298; deficit financing 133–4, 136–8; deposit mobilization 185–6, 191–4; devaluation 53; ERP 58, 84; financial deepening 103–6; financial structure 64–8; formal system 64–6; informal sector 67–8; interest rates 216–17; intermediation 146–52, 161–2, 164, 167–8, 170; law 296; lending 197–212, 218–45 passim; NBFIs 65–6, 257–8, 296, 298; private sector 157–9, 167, 168; savings/investment 2, 50–2, 56, 58, 59, 61, 65, 67, 68, 150, 157–9, 161, 162, 164, 167–8, 170, 185–6, 191–4 passim, 254; stock exchange 66, 88; transaction costs 234–43 passim
Ghate, P.B. 18, 24, 26, 27, 29, 30, 34, 210
Giovannini, Alberto 43–4
Global Coalition for Africa 4
Gnansounou, S. 192, 205
Gockel, F. 158, 183, 192, 205, 255
Goldsmith, Raymond W. 5, 10, 265
Goldstein, Don 294
Grameen Bank 76, 300, 301
grants 56, 57, 133, 139, 141, 161, 167, 170, 171
Grilli, E.R. 53
growth, economic 1, 4–6 passim, 19, 50–2, 63, 126, 133, 284, 286
guarantees, credit 24, 66, 82, 115, 305
Gueye, E.H. 256
Gulf crisis 142
Gunning, Jan W. 38, 43, 82
Gurley, J.G. 10, 265

Hamid, Javed 291, 293, 294
Harris, Laurence 294
Hettige, Hemamala 4–5
Hoff, Karla 21, 201
Honohan, Patrick 44, 84, 90, 118, 119

Hyuha, M. 35, 261

IFC 66
illiteracy 216, 234
imports 53, 55, 121
incentives 7, 14, 21, 91, 115, 123, 125, 186, 190, 268, 283, 287, 288, 298, 299, 305, 306
income 33, 39, 50, 52, 62, 63, 113, 125, 185, 214, 216, 234, 269
INDEBANK 68–70 passim, 90
INDEFUND 68, 70
India 4, 26, 30, 255
indigenization 75, 78
Indonesia 4, 30, 105, 106, 300
industry 130, 266
inflation 7, 9, 37, 38, 43, 81, 82, 84, 89–91 passim, 94, 102, 112, 132, 133, 136, 175n36, 183, 284; tax 132
informal sector 10, 16n11, 18, 20, 22, 24–9, 32–6, 40–2, 126, 157–60, 180–3, 190–4, 203–12, 216–17, 225–33, 240–5, 250–63, 279–87 passim, 296–8, 304–5; see also under individual countries
information 5, 6, 12, 14, 15, 20–5 passim, 29, 30, 44, 83, 112, 122–3, 214–16 passim, 219, 221, 225–8, 233, 234, 278–83 passim, 287, 293, 295, 301, 303, 306
infrastructure 7, 9, 12, 14, 22, 23, 27, 84, 111, 112, 184, 278, 279, 288, 295
innovation 6, 23, 195, 284, 297, 301–2
insider lending 299; trading 290
insolvency 7–9 passim, 21, 65, 74, 82, 115, 117, 284
instability 7, 9, 63, 93, 96, 112, 131, 133, 150, 284–5
institutions 5, 9–12 passim, 15, 20, 22, 24–6, 32–4, 40–2, 44, 87, 90, 96, 111, 112, 116, 250–4, 279–82, 285–94 passim, 303; semi-formal 79, 181, 254, 257–9, 273, 275, 283, 287, 297–9, 302–4 passim
insurance 21, 22, 75, 214; companies

40, 64, 66, 68, 70, 74, 77, 78, 81, 93, 139, 141, 154, 171, 172, 289
integration 10–15 passim, 18, 25, 28, 34–6, 283–307
interest rates 6–9 passim, 11, 16n8, 19–26 passim, 35–6, 42–6 passim, 79, 83–96 passim, 102, 106, 110–12, 122–8 passim, 133, 200–2, 205–12 passim, 216–17, 244, 254, 256, 260–4, 271–3 passim, 283, 284, 286, 301; controls 1, 7, 19–21 passim, 43, 45, 84, 92, 93, 122; negative 6, 20, 87
intermediation 1, 5, 6, 8, 10–14 passim, 18, 19, 22, 27–34, 68, 79, 82, 101–13, 125, 130, 132, 144–56, 253–4, 280, 282, 284
International Monetary Fund (IMF) 94
intervention, government 6–9 passim, 19, 43, 45, 82, 112, 122
investment 1–6 passim, 8, 13, 16n2, 19–21, 26, 29, 56–60 passim, 66, 71, 121, 124, 125, 130, 131, 154, 157, 282–5 passim, 289, 292–3; foreign 53
IPC 158
Islam, Roumeen 138

Japan 114, 130, 131, 291–4 passim
Johnston, B. 43, 46
Jones, Christine 24, 34, 214, 304

Kenya 2, 44, 66, 77, 105, 106, 191, 259, 288, 297
Kessides, Cristine 5
Khatkhate, Deena 6–8 passim
Killick, T. 285
Kimei, C.S. 81
King, Robert 5, 101
Kitchen, Richard L. 119
Korea 7, 24, 26, 30, 35, 36, 130, 289, 294

land tenure 22, 295
landlords 25, 41, 72, 82, 83, 229, 262, 265
Latin America 7, 9, 37–9 passim, 44, 91, 96, 266; see also individual countries

leasing companies 64, 80, 257, 306
legal system 12, 22, 90, 112, 217, 224, 232, 278, 281, 285, 295
Lelart, M. 192, 205
Levine, Ross 5, 101, 285
Levitsky, J. 300
Levy, Brian 33, 266, 267
Lewis, Peter 74, 91–3 *passim*, 142
liabilities 14, 144, 145, 181–96, 280
liberalization 1, 6–13 *passim*, 19, 24–5, 35–6, 44, 58, 67, 79, 84, 93, 96, 104, 106, 109, 111, 121, 124–7 *passim*, 154, 253–61, 277–85 *passim*
Liedholm, Carl 265–7 *passim*, 269, 270
linkages 10–15 *passim*, 19, 28–36 *passim*, 68, 73–4, 83, 126, 250–63, 273, 277, 282, 287–8, 298, 302–6
liquidity 26, 28, 33, 35, 37, 39, 45, 65, 72, 76, 89, 92, 95, 109, 118–30, 144, 279, 288
Little, I.M.D. 268
loans/lending 21, 22, 26, 28–30, 72, 83, 90, 109, 113–15 *passim*, 123, 124, 127–30, 182–3, 197–249, 259–62, 268–73, 280, 281, 300–2; foreign 141, 171; interbank 145; 'low lending trap' 125–6, 279; non–performing 7, 8, 33, 40, 65, 75, 76, 81–90, 94–6 *passim*, 109, 114–22 *passim*, 145, 279; recovery/repayment 26, 33, 35, 73, 76, 79, 114–17 *passim*, 123, 206–8, 218, 223–5, 229–34, 246–9, 272, 281
Loans and Advances Realization Trust (LART) 95

McKinnon, Ronald 1, 6, 7, 19, 35
Mcpherson, Michael 266
Maizels, Alfred 53
Malawi 13, 43, 50, 85, 87, 89–90, 96, 111–15 *passim*, 119–21, 124–6, 144, 163, 165, 169–72, 182, 184, 198, 255, 260, 262, 271, 279; aid to 52, 73, 171; banks 68–9, 90, 115, 119–21, 124–6, 154, 195–7, 202, 218–24 *passim*; deficit financing 134, 139–41, 170–1; deposit mobilization 186, 191, 192, 195; financial deepening 104, 106–9; financial structure 68–74; formal system 68–72; informal sector 72–4; interest rates 216; intermediation 147, 149, 153–5, 165; lending 197–212, 218–45 *passim*; NBFIs 70–2; private sector 159–60, 169, 171; savings/investment 2, 51–2, 56, 58, 59, 61, 72, 159–60, 186, 191, 192; transaction costs 235, 240–2 *passim*
Malawi Development Corporation (MDC) 69, 70, 89, 139, 141
Malaysia 7, 26, 30, 105, 106
Mans, Darius 63, 94
manufacturing 130, 198–200 *passim*, 266
marketing 198; boards 82, 95, 115, 116
markets 6–9, 11–14 *passim*, 18, 20–5, 29–34 *passim*, 41, 45, 71, 81–2, 93, 96, 111, 118, 125, 131, 144, 150, 214, 231, 273, 282, 285–95 *passim*; failure 6–8 *passim*, 13, 16n5, 20, 21, 131, 278, 289; interbank 46, 130, 144, 145, 288; kerb 35–6, 47n20, 262, 297; parallel 11, 24, 38, 67, 146, 150, 153, 155, 278, 280, 286; stock 41, 66, 294; *see also* capital
Marx, K.T. 34
maturities 5, 11, 26, 41, 90, 91, 105, 106, 112–14 *passim*, 130, 180, 184, 185, 196–7, 202–3, 208, 212, 260, 264, 272, 273, 280, 287, 289, 290, 293
Mayer, Colin 8, 9, 131, 291
Mead, Donald 265, 267
mergers 290, 294
Mexico 39, 291
Meyer, Richard 32, 33, 118
micro-enterprises 26, 32, 130, 199, 200, 216, 265–73 *passim*, 283, 300, 301
Middle East 38
Miracle, M.P. 42, 190
'missing middle' 283, 295
Mkandawire, M. 32, 72, 106, 114, 125, 160, 204, 209, 211, 223, 232

monetary base 145–8, 150, 153, 155, 285
monetization 37, 38, 136, 138
money creation 132, 136, 285; multiplier 126, 145, 150, 151, 153; supply 45, 46, 82, 122, 126, 144, 146, 150, 153, 155, 285
moneylenders 25, 26, 41–2, 67, 72, 78, 79, 82, 183, 203, 205, 208–11, 216, 217, 226–31, 241–5 passim, 255, 256, 261–4 passim, 268, 270, 283, 297, 305
monitoring 21, 22, 29, 35, 44, 73, 141, 180, 215, 217, 221–2, 228–9, 233, 236–7, 242–3, 281, 291–4 passim, 302
monopoly profits 25, 210–11, 244, 272
Montiel, Peter 5–6, 25–7 passim, 43, 146, 286
moral hazard 8, 21, 44, 91, 115, 123, 125, 203, 215, 217, 226, 228, 231, 237, 264, 281, 284, 286; suasion 231
mortgage institutions 77
Mudzi Fund 69, 72, 73
Mwega, F.M. 285

Naho, A. 63
Nash equilibrium 247, 248
nationalization, bank 40, 79, 80
Naude, D. 38
Neal, Craig R. 103
NERFUND 74, 75
NGOs (non-governmental organizations) 25, 211, 220, 256, 297, 302–5 passim
Nigeria 13, 38, 42–4 passim, 51–2, 56, 86, 88, 90–3, 96, 108, 111–17 passim, 146, 166, 182, 251, 184, 255, 257, 259, 262, 278, 281, 297, 299; banks 74–5, 91, 109, 115–17, 195–7 passim, 203, 218–25 passim; debt 53, 56, 59–60, 142–3; deficit financing 135, 142–4; deposit mobilization 186, 188–92 passim, 194–5; FDI 53; financial deepening 105, 109–10; financial structure 74–9; formal system 74–8; informal sector 78–9; interest rates 216–17; intermediation 148, 149, 155–6, 166; lending 197–212, 218–45 passim; NBFIs 76–7, 257; savings/investment 2, 51–2, 58–62, 77–9 passim, 110, 156, 186–94 passim, 254; stock exchange 78; transaction costs 235–43 passim
Nigerian Deposit Insurance Corporation (NDIC) 76, 92
Nissanke, Machiko 30, 39, 63, 112, 125, 130, 180, 185, 286
non-bank financial institutions 25, 40–1, 45, 64, 88, 139, 141, 157, 159–60, 171, 283, 296, 297, 305; see also under individual countries
Nwandike, Comfort I. 195

O'Connell, Stephen A. 38
Ohio State University 118
oil 52, 53, 56, 59, 142, 155
open market operations 45–6, 66, 89, 90, 93, 95, 144, 150
Organization for Economic Cooperation and Development (OECD) 27, 146
Otero, Maria 300
overdraft facilities 79, 113, 115, 127, 131, 136, 138, 144, 161, 167, 170, 270, 289, 305
overhang, monetary 110, 118, 173n16
ownership 45, 48n32, 33, 69, 75, 79, 80, 82, 113

parastatals 5, 43, 58, 80, 82, 89, 93–6 passim, 115, 136, 138, 139, 141, 144, 161, 167, 170–2 passim, 200, 265, 278; Reform Commission 95
Park, Young Chul 8
Parker, Joan 266
Patrick, Hugh 5, 291, 292
pawnbrokers 24, 25
Paxson, C. 214
penalties 210–11, 215, 232, 246, 248
pension schemes/funds 41, 74, 77, 78, 93, 289
Philippines 24, 30, 239, 240, 305
political factors 96, 97n2, 114, 116, 117, 141, 171

Popiel, P.A. 217, 240, 299
portfolios, bank 1, 8, 14, 21, 23, 24, 33, 34, 82, 85, 95, 96, 106, 112–30, 180–215, 279, 280, 285, 287
premium, parallel market 146, 150, 153, 155; risk 14, 20–2 *passim*, 25, 122, 210
Press Holdings Corporation 69, 70, 89, 141
prices 8, 11, 19, 53, 116, 119, 142, 185, 233, 259, 261–2, 290, 294
principal–agent relations 14, 245–9
private sector 10, 44, 72, 81, 94, 103, 106, 109, 110, 121–7 *passim*, 130, 141, 152–61 *passim*, 183, 184, 196–8 *passim*, 265, 278, 279, 285
privatization 45, 75, 78, 93, 141, 152, 290
property 221, 261, 272, 295
provident funds 40, 41
public sector 126, 132–44, 161, 197, 278, 279, 290
pyramid schemes 92, 259, 297

questionnaires 13, 15–16

real sector 9–10, 13, 18, 22, 32, 280, 282, 284, 302, 306
recapitalization 45, 65, 86, 89, 111, 117, 138, 182
record keeping 233, 275, 295
rediscount 45, 144
references 219, 226, 295
reform 1, 5, 7–10 *passim*, 13, 14, 41, 44–6, 50, 58, 84–96, 110–12, 131–60 *passim*, 184–90, 256, 277–86 *passim*; pace 91, 93, 111, 278; sequencing 8, 9, 46, 91, 93, 96, 111, 278, 284; timing 8, 9, 91, 93
registration 297
regulation 1, 8, 16n6, 23, 24, 44, 67, 74, 86, 90, 91, 95, 96, 111, 112, 116, 258–9, 266–7, 281, 284–6 *passim*, 290, 294, 296–9; self- 298
remittances 38, 71
rent-seeking 45, 92, 93
repatriation 58

repression, financial 6, 9, 11, 19–20, 23–5, 38, 42–6, 46n3,4, 67, 84, 89, 119, 122, 124, 125, 182, 278, 293
reputation 21, 22, 24, 246, 291
reserves, bank 27–8, 36, 43, 44, 45, 65, 77, 92–4 *passim*, 109, 119, 121, 126, 127, 150, 174n24, 259, 285, 297; international 53, 54, 144
restructuring 1, 10–12, 41, 44–5, 85, 86, 89, 94–6 *passim*, 104, 106, 110, 111, 115, 195, 217, 218, 294, 299
retained earnings 130, 131, 271, 289
revenue 43–4, 53, 56, 57, 133, 139, 142, 146, 160, 161, 167, 170, 171
Reynoso, Alejandro 9
Rhyne, Elizabeth 300
risk 5, 11, 13–15, 20–6, 30–5 *passim*, 44, 68, 75, 77, 79, 82, 83, 91, 112–17, 121–4 *passim*, 127, 130, 197, 210, 214–49, 278, 281, 287, 293, 299–303 *passim*, 306; management 229–45, 279, 287, 290
Roe, Alan R. 20, 45, 117–18
Roemer, Michael 24, 34, 304
Rose, Andrew 5, 10, 21–2, 113, 265
Rosenzweig, Mark 22
round-tripping 92
Russia 291

Saito, K.A. 233, 234, 239, 240, 300
savings 1–6 *passim*, 8, 10, 13, 14, 16n1, 19, 20, 26, 28, 31, 33, 34, 37–42, 44, 56, 58–63 *passim*, 68, 101–13, 117, 118, 122, 125, 131, 157–60, 181–94, 253, 278–80 *passim*, 282, 284, 286; *see also under individual countries*; and credit associations (SCAs) 28, 180, 183, 190–1, 203–6, 216, 226, 229, 241, 242, 260, 261, 264, 297, 304, accumulating (ASCRAs) 190; revolving (ROSCAs) 20, 24, 25, 28, 39, 42, 67, 82, 83, 190, 204–6, 216, 226, 229, 244, 251, 252, 297; and loan companies 67, 254, 257–8, 293, 304; collectors 192–3, 206–8, 251–2, 280, 304 *see also esusu; susu*
Schmidt-Hebbel, Klaus 133, 146

screening 21, 29, 35, 180, 215,
217–21, 226–8, 230, 234–6, 238,
241–2, 281, 291, 301, 302
'second' economy 63
securities, government 24, 41, 46, 65,
71, 77, 81, 93, 119, 121–7 *passim*,
132, 139, 141, 142, 144 156, 157,
160, 161, 171, 172, 285, 288–90,
293; market 22, 291
segmentation 11, 12, 18–49, 68, 73,
203–12, 214, 261, 277, 279, 283
Seibel, Hans Dieter 25, 33, 34
seigniorage 39, 44, 48n35, 146, 150,
153, 155, 177n53
selection, adverse 8, 21, 44, 91, 115,
123, 125, 203, 215, 217, 226, 231,
246, 263, 264, 281, 293, 301
Senegal 2, 192, 256
services, financial 5, 10, 13, 14, 32,
40, 70–1, 113, 273
'shallowing', financial 67, 84, 103
Shaw, Edward S. 6, 7, 10, 19, 35,
265
Shipton, Parker 192
short-termism 113–14, 294
Singh, Ajit 291, 293, 294
Slover, C.H. 205
small and medium-sized enterprises
(SMEs) 23, 32, 33, 36, 68, 72, 77,
130, 202, 203, 216, 234–5, 240,
263, 266–71 *passim*, 283
Smallholder Agricultural Credit
Administration (SACA) 72–3
Social Security and National Insurance
Trust (SSNIT) 64–6 *passim*, 138,
152, 159, 161, 167, 177n55
social welfare schemes 72
SODECON 191
South Africa 288
Soviet Union, former 291
Sowa, Nii K. 45
Soyibo, A. 76–8 *passim*, 114, 257
specialization 11, 14, 15, 18, 20, 25,
27–35 *passim*, 40, 79, 82, 113, 117,
180–214, 263–72, 277, 278, 281,
282, 287, 289, 299
speculation 7, 92, 294
Spencer, Michael G. 294, 295

Sri Lanka 7
stability 9, 111–12, 284, 286
stabilization 7, 8, 42, 45, 84, 126,
136, 285
Steel, William F. 32, 33, 68, 206,
252, 265, 267, 268, 304
Stein, Howard 74, 91–3 *passim*, 142,
291–3 *passim*
Stern, N. 133
Stiglitz, Joseph E. 6, 21, 201, 245
stock exchanges 66, 77, 78, 88
subcontracting 30, 32, 270, 306
subsidies 43, 94, 138
Sudan 38
supervision 1, 8, 23, 74, 82, 86, 87,
90–2 *passim*, 95, 96, 111, 112, 116,
218, 222, 281, 284–6 *passim*, 290,
296, 297, 299, 301
susu collectors 25, 39, 42, 67, 68,
192–3, 205–8, 228, 230, 241–4
passim, 251–2, 254, 255, 257–8,
262, 264, 268, 296, 298, 303–5
passim; companies 67, 254, 257,
299; GASCCS 67, 251–2, 254,
298, 304; groups 191, 251

Taiwan 29, 30, 262, 289, 297, 306
take-overs 290, 294
Tanzania 13, 38, 42, 43, 50, 86, 88,
93–6, 108, 112, 113, 115, 146,
174n31, 182, 183, 251, 255, 262,
263; aid to 4, 52, 55; banks 79–80,
94, 95, 110, 115, 195–7 *passim*,
202–3, 220–5 *passim*; debt 55;
deficit financing 135; deposit
mobilization 186, 187, 191–3
passim, 195; ERP 91; financial
deepening 105, 110; financial
structure 79–83; formal system
79–82; informal sector 82–3;
intermediation 148, 149; lending
197–212, 218–45 *passim*; NBFIs 80;
PTFSR 301; savings/investment 2,
51–2, 56, 58, 60–3, 80–3 *passim*,
110, 186, 187, 191; transaction costs
241–3 *passim*
taxation 41, 44, 157, 160, 161, 167,
170, 266–7, 290, 305

Taylor, Lance 35
tea 71, 171
technology 287, 288, 299–302
Teranishi, Juro 23, 131, 293
terms of trade 53–5 *passim*, 122
Thailand 26, 30
thrift institutions 81
tobacco 71, 89, 119, 125, 153, 198
tontines 192, 205, 256
traders 25, 41, 42, 67, 72, 78, 82, 83,
  216, 229, 255, 262, 264, 265, 280
treasury bills 41, 46, 66, 71, 77, 81,
  88, 90, 93–5 *passim*, 124, 127, 139,
  140, 142, 152, 154–6 *passim*, 161,
  171, 172, 184, 196, 288; auctions
  93, 94, 127
Tseng, Wanda 7

U Tun Wai 27, 46n1
Udry, C. 42, 78, 226, 228–31, 246–8
  passim
Uganda 2, 38
uncertainty 63, 217–33, 279, 284, 293
UNCTAD 118, 125, 286
under-invoicing 39
United States 118, 294; USAID 192
Uruguay 7

Van Wijnbergen, Sweder 35
Villanueva, D.P. 233, 234, 239, 240,
  300
visits, to sites 221-2, 229, 236
von Pischke, J.D. 11, 33, 190

Webster, Leila 33, 267
Weiss, Andrew 6, 245
Wetzel, Deborah L. 138
women 73, 158; market 191, 192, 205,
  208, 252, 257-8, 275n5, 280
Women's World Banking 302
World Bank 4-9 *passim*, 33, 50, 52, 58,
  63, 84, 110-11, 114, 144, 146, 150,
  197, 219, 224, 225, 236-8 *passim*,
  285

Yang, M.C. 53
Yaron, Jacob 300
Yotopoulos, P.A. 30, 34, 190, 226,
  229, 305

Zaire 64, 103, 205
Zambia 3, 38, 44, 191
Zanzibar 80
Zimbabwe 2, 48n33, 66, 105, 117,
  288